FROM ANGLO-SAXON TO
EARLY MIDDLE ENGLISH

E. G. Stanley

From Anglo-Saxon to Early Middle English

STUDIES PRESENTED TO

E. G. STANLEY

Edited by

Malcolm Godden, Douglas Gray,
and Terry Hoad

CLARENDON PRESS · OXFORD

1994

Oxford University Press, Walton Street, Oxford OX2 6DP

Oxford New York Toronto
Delhi Bombay Calcutta Madras Karachi
Kuala Lumpur Singapore Hong Kong Tokyo
Nairobi Dar es Salaam Cape Town
Melbourne Auckland Madrid

and associated companies in
Berlin Ibadan

Oxford is a trade mark of Oxford University Press

Published in the United States
by Oxford University Press Inc., New York

British Library Cataloguing in Publication Data
Data available

Library of Congress Cataloging in Publication Data
From Anglo-Saxon to early middle English: studies presented to E. G. Stanley / edited by Douglas Gray, Malcolm Godden, and Terry Hoad.
Includes bibliographical references and index.
1. English philology—Middle English, 1100–1500. 2. English philology—Old English, ca. 450–1100. I. Gray, Douglas. II. Godden, Malcolm. III. Hoad, T. F. IV. Stanley, Eric Gerald.
PE26.S73F76 1994 429—dc20 93–42012
ISBN 0–19–811776–0

1 3 5 7 9 10 8 6 4 2

Typeset by Selwood Systems, Midsomer Norton
Printed in Great Britain
on acid-free paper by
Biddles Ltd.,
Guildford and King's Lynn

CONTENTS

PREFATORY NOTE

Eric Stanley was educated at University College, Oxford, and subsequently awarded a Ph.D at Birmingham University. He was lecturer in English at Birmingham from 1951 to 1962 and then successively Reader and Professor of English in the University of London at Queen Mary College from 1962 to 1975. He was lured to Yale to become Professor of English in 1975, and lured back again to Oxford in 1977, when he took up the Rawlinson and Bosworth Chair of Anglo-Saxon, which he held until his retirement in 1991. His distinguished record as an Anglo-Saxon philologist and textual scholar, beginning with an article on 'The Chronology of *r*-metathesis in Old English' in 1952 and 'A note on Genesis B, 328' in 1954, has been sustained for some forty years with the same unflagging enthusiasm and sharpness; his 1956 article on 'Old English poetic diction and the interpretation of *The Wanderer, The Seafarer,* and *The Penitent's Prayer*', the collection of critical essays which he commissioned and edited as *Continuations and Beginnings* in 1966, and his study of nineteenth- and early twentieth-century scholarship on Anglo-Saxon, *The Search for Anglo-Saxon Paganism* (1975), have been particular landmarks. In recent years his scholarship and wisdom have been especially devoted to the progress of the Old English Dictionary in Toronto. But Anglo-Saxon has always been just one of his accomplishments. His publications in Middle English range from his magisterial edition of *The Owl and the Nightingale* in 1960 and his seminal article on 'Laȝamon's antiquarian sentiments' in 1969 to 'Directions for making many kinds of laces' (1974). As a reviewer he is indefatigable: the total number had risen to well over two hundred reviews by 1992 and the stream has continued unabated. His name is also closely associated with the quarterly periodical *Notes and Queries,* which he has co-edited for the last thirty years, encouraging the work of younger scholars and trimming the long-windedness of older ones. As a Fellow of the British Academy, an adviser to the University Grants Committee in Britain, and an energetic external examiner he has played a major role in fostering university scholarship in all fields of English, and his generosity with advice and help to colleagues and students has been marked. In Oxford especially his sympathetic concern for graduate students and his devotion to Pembroke College, where he served as librarian and took delight in teaching undergraduates, has made him a familiar and influential figure.

His interests and expertise range very widely and this collection of essays, concentrating on the late Old Engish and early Middle English periods, bears witness to just one of the areas to which he has contributed: the continuity of early English language and literature across the chronological divide of the eleventh century. It is the work of only a small number of his many academic friends. We would like to dedicate it to him on behalf of all his colleagues and friends, in honour of a most distinguished career.

ABBREVIATIONS

The following abbreviations are used throughout this volume.

ASE	*Anglo-Saxon England*
EETS	Early English Text Society
os	Ordinary Series
ss	Supplementary Series

Did Grendel's Mother Sit on Beowulf?

FRED C. ROBINSON

Admirers of Professor Stanley's learned and witty textual studies of Old English prose and verse will recognize in my title an echo of 'Did Beowulf Commit "Feaxfang" against Grendel's Mother?' – the title of one of his masterly analyses of a disputed reading in Old English.[1] My respectfully imitative title does not, alas, promise in the text of the article the range of learning and depth of insight that distinguish the work of the man we salute in this volume.

The passage that Professor Stanley dealt with in his 1976 article is the same one that this study addresses, only I am concerned with a word which occurs eight lines after the commission of *feaxfang*:

Gefeng þa be *f*eax*e* —nalas for fæhðe mearn—
Guð-Geata leod Grendles modor;
brægd þa beadwe heard, þa he gebolgen wæs,
feorhgeniðlan, þæt heo on flet gebeah.
Heo him eft hraþe *a*ndlean forgeald
grimmum grapum ond him togeanes feng;
oferwearp þa werigmod wigena strengest,
feþecempa, þæt he on fylle wearð.
Ofsæt þa þone selegyst, ond hyre sea*x* geteah
brad [ond] brunecg; wolde hire bearn wrecan,
angan eaferan.[2]

(1537–47)

The man of the War-Geats then seized Grendel's mother by the hair; he did not shrink from the conflict. Enraged as he was, the man brave in battle flung then the deadly foe so that she fell to the ground. She swiftly gave him requital with her grim claws and clutched against him; weary in spirit, the strongest of warriors, of fighters, stumbled then so that he started to fall. She sat down on the hall-guest then and drew her knife—large and with gleaming blade; she wanted to avenge her son, her only child.

My translation gives the sense of the passage as the glossaries of our editions

[1] *Notes and Queries*, 221 (1976), 339–40.

[2] Quoted from *Beowulf and the Fight at Finnsburg*, ed. Fr. Klaeber, third edition with first and second supplements (Boston, 1950), except that I have not reproduced Klaeber's macrons, and in deference to our jubilarian I have introduced the emendation he recommended in 'Did Beowulf Commit "Feaxfeng" against Grendel's Mother?'.

direct us to read it. And those who have taught *Beowulf* will remember the titters and smiles that invariably greet the half-line 'Ofsæt þa þone selegyst.' The dignity which elsewhere prevails in the poet's description of Beowulf's hand-to-hand encounters suddenly falters here as we are told that the ugly female with whom Beowulf is grappling takes a seat on the hero before drawing her knife to dispatch him. The glossaries and commentators leave no doubt that this is what she does: they define *ofsittan* (which occurs only here in *Beowulf*) as 'sit upon' (Klaeber, Chambers, Wyatt), 'sit on' (Wrenn–Bolton), 'über einem sitzen' (Holder), 'über jemand sitzen' (Schücking, Heyne), 'sich auf etwas setzen' (von Schaubert).[3] And Hoops translates the half-line 'Sie sass da auf dem Saalgast'.[4]

Like the students in our classes, the translators of the poem, however, are often uncomfortable with the meaning which the glossaries stipulate for *ofsittan.* To avoid the comic indignity of Beowulf's being sat upon, they fudge the verb's meaning in artful ways, accepting the glossaries' basic sense but trying to make the scene a little less ridiculous: 'she knelt upon him' (Charles W. Kennedy), 'she bestrode her hall-guest' (Edwin Morgan), 'and bestriding her guest' (Bernard F. Huppé), 'she straddled her hall-guest' (Marijane Osborn), 'she then straddled her hall-guest' (S. B. Greenfield), 'on the hall-guest she hurled herself' (Francis B. Gummere), 'she dropped on her hall-guest' (Kevin Crossley-Holland), 'she threw herself then on her hall-visitant' (Clark Hall–Wrenn), 'then she threw herself on her visitor' (David Wright), 'and over that guest in her chamber she croucheth' (Archibald Strong), and 'the demon pounced on the intruder' (Constance Hieatt).[5] There is no hint in the dictionaries of Old English that *ofsittan* can mean 'kneel', 'bestride', 'straddle', 'hurl', 'drop', 'crouch', 'throw', or 'pounce', but all these words put the ogress on top of Beowulf without the translators' having to say that she sat on him.

Considering how arduously translators have struggled to blur the meaning of *ofsittan* which the glossaries (and the dictionaries) dictate,[6] it is surprising

[3] The editions cited are those by R. W. Chambers [a revision of Wyatt] (Cambridge, 1933), Moritz Heyne (Paderborn, 1898), Alfred Holder (Freiburg i. B., 1899), C. L. Wrenn revised by W. F. Bolton (New York, 1973), Levin L. Schücking [revision of Heyne] (Paderborn, 1910), and A. J. Wyatt (Cambridge, 1898).

[4] Johannes Hoops, *Kommentar zum Beowulf* (Heidelberg, 1932), 178.

[5] The translations cited are those by John R. Clark Hall revised by C. L. Wrenn (London, 1950), Kevin Crossley-Holland (New York, 1968), Stanley B. Greenfield (Carbondale, Ill., 1982), Francis B. Gummere (New York, 1920), Constance B. Hieatt (New York, 1967), Charles W. Kennedy (New York, 1940), Edwin Morgan (Aldington, Kent, 1952), Marijane Osborne (Berkeley, Calif., 1983), Archibald Strong (London, 1925), David Wright (Harmondsworth, Middlesex, 1957).

[6] A few translators accept the proposed meaning 'to sit on': G. N. Garmonsway and J. Simpson (New York, 1971) say, 'She then seated herself on the guest in her hall'; R. K. Gordon

that no one, apparently, has thought to question the evidence for *ofsittan* meaning 'sit upon'. Since they recognize in *-sittan* the modern English word *sit*, they seem to concede without further scrutiny that *ofsittan* must mean 'sit upon'. But when we examine the thirty-six occurrences of *ofsittan* in the corpus of Old English writings, we discover that the evidence points in a very different direction.

While the central meaning of the simplex *sittan* is indeed 'sit', the derivatives of this verb have quite diverse meanings. Consider, for example, *forsittan* 'neglect, delay, obstruct', *asittan* 'apprehend, fear, dwell together, run aground', *besittan* 'surround, besiege, hold council, occupy, possess', *ætsittan* 'remain, stray', *eftsittan* Lat. '*residere*' (in Ælfric's *Glossary*),[7] *tosittan* 'to be separated', *undersittan* Lat. *subsidere* (in Ælfric's *Glossary*),[8] and *ymbsittan* 'surround, reflect upon'. We are apt to forget that in Germanic languages when verbal roots are combined with prefixes they can acquire meanings which are quite remote from that of the verbal simplex. A student translating modern German would be ill-advised to attempt to guess the meaning of the common verb *besitzen* by identifying the root *-sitzen* 'sit' and trying from that datum to deduce its meaning. And students of Latin would be similarly stymied if they tried to determine the meanings of that large range of derivatives based on the root *sedere* 'sit' (whence English has borrowed, among many others, *obsess, preside, possess, subside,* and *supersede*) by working from the meaning 'sit'.

A Microfiche Concordance to Old English by Antonette DiPaolo Healey and Richard L. Venezky (Toronto, 1980) tells us that *ofsittan* occurs thirty-six times in the Old English corpus. An investigation of these occurrences reveals a considerable range of senses. One of the more commonly documented meanings is 'beset, besiege' translating Latin *obsideo*:

Forðon ymbsealdon me hundas monige; geþeaht awergdra *ofsæt* me.[9]

Therefore many dogs surrounded me; a band of evil ones beset me.

Me ymbhringdon swiðe mænige calfru, þæt synt lytle and niwe fynd; and þa fættan fearas me *ofsæton*, þæt synd strengran fynd.[10]

(New York, 1954) says, 'then she sat on the visitor to her hall'; G. Roberts (n.p., 1984) says, 'she then sat upon her hall-guest'.

[7] *Ælfrics Grammatik und Glossar*, ed. J. Zupitza (Berlin, 1880), repr. with a preface by H. Gneuss (Berlin, 1966), 157.

[8] Ibid.

[9] *Der altenglische Junius-Psalter*, ed. E. Brenner, Anglistische Forschungen, 23 (Heidelberg, 1908), 24. Here and in subsequent quotations abbreviations have been silently expanded and punctuation added or modernized.

[10] *Libri psalmorum versio antiqua cum paraphrasi Anglo-Saxonica*, ed. B. Thorpe (Oxford, 1835), 46.

A great many calves (that is, small, inexperienced enemies) surrounded me; and the fat bulls (that is, stronger enemies) beset me.

Ofsittan also means 'oppress' in various senses. In several documentations it refers to someone oppressing a nation with tyranny:

Gif he þonne mid his riccetere hi *ofsit*, þonne bið he *tyrannus*...[11]

If he oppress them with his tyranny, then he is a tyrant...

Þæt is cyninges rihtwisnyss þæt he mid riccetere ne *ofsitte* ne earmne ne eadigne, ac ælcum deme riht.[12]

It is right for the king that he oppress neither the poor nor the rich with tyranny, but that he grant justice to both.

In a translation of Deuteronomy 28: 33 *ofsittan* renders a form of Latin *opprimere* 'oppress':

Ete elðeodig folc ðine tilunga, and ðe mid bysmore *ofsittan* ealle ðine dagas...[13]

May a foreign people eat your substance, and may they oppress you shamefully all of your days.

Several occurrences suggest a sense somewhere between 'oppress' and 'occupy':

Seo menigu getacnað ure unlustas and leahtras þe us hremað, and ure heortan *ofsittað*, þæt we ne magon us swa geornlice gebiddan, swa we behofedon.[14]

The multitude signifies our evil desires and vices, which encumber us and oppress our hearts so that we cannot pray as fervently as we need to.

Ic wat þeah þæt þu wilt cweðan þæt wrænnes ond ungemetfæstnes hi *ofsitte*.[15]

I know that you will say that lust and intemperance occupy them.

At times *ofsittan* means 'to press down, to cause to be impacted':

Eft þus þu scealt þa yfelan *ofsetenan* wætan utadon þurh spatl and hræcean...[16]

Again, in this way you must remove the noxious, impacted fluid through spittle and clearing the throat...

In several occurrences *ofsittan* means 'possess' in the sense of demonic possession:

[11] *Ælfrics Grammatik und Glossar*, 294.

[12] *Old English Homilies*, ed. R. Morris, EETS OS 34 (London, 1868), 302. Cf. *Early English Homilies*, ed. R. D.-N. Warner, EETS OS 152 (London, 1917), 14.

[13] *The Old English Version of the Heptateuch*, ed. S. J. Crawford, EETS OS 160 (London, 1921), 361.

[14] *The Homilies of the Anglo-Saxon Church*, ed. B. Thorpe (London, 1844), i. 156.

[15] *King Alfred's Old English Version of Boethius*, ed. W. J. Sedgefield (Oxford, 1899), 109.

[16] *Leechdoms, Wortcunning and Starcraft of Early England*, ed. T. O. Cockayne, Rolls Series 35, vol. 2 (London, 1865), 25.

He . . . sona ut adraf ðone ealdan feond of þam *ofsetenan* men.[17]

He . . . immediately drove out the old devil from the possessed man.

De puero a diabolo obsessa: Sum cild wæs þæt se unrihtwisa deofol *ofsæt*.[18]

Concerning a boy possessed by the devil: There was a child whom the evil devil possessed.

The context and at times the Latin words being translated indicate fairly precisely the meanings of *ofsittan* in its various occurrences cited here, and it has never occurred to anyone to suggest that the fat bulls and the band of evil ones in the Psalter passages quoted were sitting on the speaker or that the unrighteous king was sitting on his subjects or that a person suffering from demonic possession has someone sitting on top of him. Indeed, other than the *Beowulf* verse with which we are concerned, there is only one passage out of the thirty-six documentations which anyone has tried to read while ascribing the sense 'sit on' to *ofsittan*. The Bosworth–Toller *Dictionary* s.v. *of-sittan* translates the verb 'to sit on, to press down by sitting' in the following passage:

Nu sceal se ðe wile sittan æt Godes gereorde ðæt gærs *ofsittan*, ðæt is, ðæt he sceal þa flæsclican lustas gewyldan.[19]

But when we compare this quotation with the source from which it was taken, we discover that the lexicographer has abridged the passage so drastically that its sense has been distorted. This is the full sentence as it appears in Ælfric's sermon:

Nu sceal gehwa, seðe wile sittan æt Godes gereorde and brucan þære gastlican lare oftredan þæt gærs and *ofsittan*, þæt is þæt he sceal þa flæsclican lustas gewyldan, and his lichaman to Godes þeowdome symle gebigan.[20]

Now anyone who wishes to sit at God's feast and partake of the spiritual instruction

[17] *Bischof Wærferths von Worcester Übersetzung der Dialoge Gregors des Grossen*, ed. H. Hecht, Bibliothek der angelsächsischen Prosa, 5 (Leipzig, 1900), 135. Cf. p. 223: 'Soðlice to urum Alysende sylfum wæs gecweden fram þam deofla heape, þe þone wedenseocan man ofseten hæfde: "gif þu us ut adrife of þysum men, sænd us in þysra swyna heap."' ('Verily it was said to our Redeemer himself by the band of demons who had possessed the insane man, "If you drive us out of this man, send us into this herd of swine."')

[18] *The Old English Life of Machutus*, ed. D. Yerkes (Toronto, 1984), 77.

[19] J. Bosworth, *An Anglo-Saxon Dictionary*, ed. and enlarged by T. N. Toller (London, 1898), s.v. *ofsittan*.

[20] *The Homilies of the Anglo-Saxon Church*, i. 188. (Thorpe translates 'oftredan þæt gærs and ofsittan' as 'tread and press down the grass'.) In another passage where the pressing down of grass is allegorized as referring to subduing fleshly desires (' . . . us is beboden ðurh ealdan æ ofsittan and fortredan ða gewilnigendlican lustas . . . ') *ofsittan* is correctly defined by Toller as 'to repress, check', see *An Anglo-Saxon Dictionary: Supplement* by T. N. Toller (London, 1921), s.v. *ofsittan*.

must trample and press down the grass; that is, that he must subdue the fleshly desires and subject his body always to God's service.

'Press down the grass' is Thorpe's rendering of 'þæt gærs ... ofsittan' in his edition; Bosworth apparently departed from this sense in order to provide some supporting evidence for the meaning 'to sit upon, press down by sitting', a sense which is otherwise supported only by the *Beowulf* verse.

The passage containing *ofsittan* that is most similar to the passage in *Beowulf* is this sentence from Ælfric's sermon on the twenty-second Sunday after Pentecost, in which he is explaining the Old Testament injunction to 'love thy friend, hate thy foe':

þus wæs alyfed þam ealdum mannum þæt hi moston Godes wiðerwinnan and heora agene fynd mid stranglicere mihte *ofsittan* and mid wæpne acwellan.[21]

Thus it was permitted to these ancient peoples that they might with strong power set upon the adversaries of God and their own enemies and kill [them] with a weapon.

Here, as in *Beowulf* 1545–6, an assailant is described as first closing in on his enemy and then wielding his weapon. We are not to imagine that the Old Testament specifies that a person is permitted to sit upon his enemy before killing him.

Having surveyed the meanings attested for *ofsittan* and determined that there is no support for the sense 'to sit upon',[22] we must consider which of the known senses of the word best serves the passage in *Beowulf.* Some senses seem manifestly inappropriate. 'Possess', either in the sense of ownership or of demonic possession would make little sense in *Beowulf* 1545, and the same seems true of 'occupy'. 'Repress' (as in 'repress wilful desires'—'ofsittan ... ða gewilnigendlican lustas'[23]) is inappropriate, as is the sense 'besiege', with its implication of 'surround'. But a slight narrowing of 'besiege' to 'beset, close in on, set upon' would suit the passage well, and it is the sense which seems to fit the passage just quoted, which was said to be most like the *Beowulf* passage. However, the central meaning of *ofsittan*, 'press down', might also seem appropriate, especially with the slight modification 'force down': 'she forced the hall-guest down and drew her sword'. But the example of the passage from Ælfric describing people attacking their adversaries persuades me to suggest:

[21] *The Homilies of the Anglo-Saxon Church*, i. 522.

[22] It may be added that cognates of *ofsittan* are preserved in Old Saxon and Old Frisian, and in neither of these languages is there any support for interpreting the verb as meaning 'to sit upon'. Old Saxon *ofsittan* means 'possess' ('besitzen'); Old Frisian *ofsitta* 'dismount' ('absitzen, absteigen'). See, respectively, Edward H. Sehrt, *Vollständiges Wörterbuch zum Heliand*, 2nd ed. (Göttingen, 1968), and Karl von Richtofen, *Altfriesisches Wörterbuch* (Göttingen, 1840).

[23] *The Homilies of the Anglo-Saxon Church*, vol. 2, p. 398.

Ofsæt þa þone selegyst, ond hyre sea*x* geteah
brad [ond] brunecg

She set upon the hall-guest then and drew her large knife with gleaming blade.

But making subtle distinctions as to which of the attested and suitable meanings for the word is best to render the passage in modern English is less a matter of textual criticism than of the translator's art. The important point is that the long-accepted sense 'sit upon' for *ofsittan* is without evidentiary support, and the supposed breach of dignity in the poet's conception of the hero's encounter with Grendel's dam is a lexical illusion handed down from editor to editor and lexicographer to lexicographer over the years. To point this out is a modest textual gain, perhaps, but it is a useful reminder that many of the textual judgements which have become established in the past might well be due for reassessment in light of the evidence which has been placed at our disposal by the Healey–Venezky *Concordance*, a scholarly tool the importance of which can hardly be overemphasized.[24]

[24] In addition to helping us identify assumed but unsubstantiated meanings of words in Old English texts, the *Microfiche Concordance* can serve to vindicate established readings which come under frivolous attack. In the *Old English Newsletter* vol. 17, no. 2 (Spring, 1984), A-45, Ronald E. Buckalew singled out Bruce Mitchell and me as perpetrators of a 'mistranslation' in our *Guide to Old English*, 3rd ed. (Oxford, 1984), p. 195, when we stated that Ælfric's 'he cuðe be dæle Læden understandan' in the Preface to *Genesis* means that Ælfric's erstwhile teacher could understand Latin 'in part'. Now 'in part, partially' is the meaning that has been universally assumed for *be dæle*. Toller, *Supplement* s.v. *dæl* renders it 'somewhat, in some measure', noting that the phrase translates Latin *aliquid*. J. R. Clark Hall's *Concise Anglo-Saxon Dictionary*, 4th ed. with a supplement by H. D. Meritt (Cambridge, 1960) renders it 'in part, partly'. The *Dictionary of Old English* by Angus Cameron et al. (Toronto, n.d.) s.v. *dæl* D.3 renders it 'in part, to some extent'. But according to the critique in the *Old English Newsletter* 'the true meaning' of *be dæle* is 'by part of speech,' for 'what Ælfric means is that his teacher could parse the Latin appropriately . . .' On seeing this assertion that the standard way of reading *be dæle* 'is a heretofore unrecognized error,' one turns of course immediately to the Healey–Venezky *Concordance* to discover how frequently *be dæle* in Old English has the sense 'by part of speech.' What one finds is that although *be dæle* (and slightly less frequently *be sumum dæle*) can be seen to occur very commonly both in Ælfric and in Old English at large, never once does the phrase have the meaning 'by part of speech.' Our critic's 'true meaning' of *be dæle* turns out to be nothing more than an arbitrary assertion with no evidentiary basis whatever. The fact that we do find in the concordance such statements as the observation that from an English translation one can understand 'be suman dæle hwæt þæt Leden cwede' suggests strongly that *be dæle* in Ælfric's Preface means exactly what it means everywhere else—'in part, to some extent'. And this makes the best sense in the context of the Preface, where Ælfric is concerned with priests who are only partially learned, not with methods of construing Latin. The totally unsubstantiated assertion that in this one occurrence out of a multitude of *be dæle*'s in Old English the phrase has the unique meaning 'by part of speech' has, then, nothing to recommend it at all.

An Alfredian Legacy? On the Fortunes and Fate of some Items of Boethian Vocabulary in Old English

JANET BATELY

In a pioneering study of Latin abstract nouns employed in Boethius' *De Consolatione Philosophiae* and their vernacular counterparts in the translations of that work by King Alfred in the ninth century and by Chaucer in the fourteenth, Olga Fischer compared and contrasted the ways in which these two English writers rendered Boethius' philosophical terminology.[1] Among her conclusions were (1) that the lexical resources of Old English were as adequate as, if not more adequate than, those of Middle English to render 'the often difficult and, in many instances, new philosophical concepts',[2] (2) that whereas Chaucer borrowed words freely from Latin and French, Alfred very frequently took advantage of his own language's capacity for compounding and loan-translation to supplement semantic borrowing,[3] and (3) that in a significant number of cases the king himself was responsible for these coinages.[4] When I began work on this paper my aim was to use Dr Fischer's study as the starting point for an exploration of the extent to which Alfred's terminology became accepted as part of the Old English lexis and an examination of the ways in which certain lexical 'gaps' left by Alfred in his renderings of philosophical terms were filled in later Old English. However, over the last few years a number of new research aids have been produced,[5] providing information that was not available when Dr Fischer was writing; as a result, a reassessment of certain of her findings has proved necessary. The present study is therefore a highly selective and limited one,

[1] O. Fischer, 'A Comparative Study of Philosophical Terms in the Alfredian and Chaucerian Boethius', *Neophil*, 63 (1979), 622–39.

[2] Ibid. 623.

[3] Ibid. 634–6.

[4] Ibid. 635–6.

[5] Apart from glossaries to individual texts, these include the Toronto microfiche concordance and dictionary (fasc. B, C, and D), to which will shortly be added an Old English Thesaurus. I am indebted to Prof. Jane Roberts for allowing me to consult parts of the latter in draft. I should also like to acknowledge the invaluable help of Dr Julie Coleman and Dr Bill Griffiths.

closing with a discussion of the representation in late Old English of two of the more distinctive terms used by Boethius in his *De Consolatione* (CPh), 'predestination' and 'providence', but starting still from Dr Fischer's lists, with a scrutiny of some of her assumptions and conclusions.[6]

1. Dr Fischer's lists

1.1. Words 'first used by Alfred'

In her lists of equivalences, grouped under the headings *Lehnübersetzung, Lehnübertragung,* and *Lehnschöpfung,*[7] Dr Fischer includes a substantial body of OE words 'first found in the Boethius'. I shall be discussing in detail later three of these equations—**praedestinatio**: *foretiohhung,* **providentia**: *foresceawung,* and **providentia**: *foreþanc.* Of the remainder, as the following discussion will show, a significant number are found in Werferth's translation of Gregory's *Dialogues* (GD),[8] the Old English Martyrology (Mart)[9] and Alfred's own translation of Gregory's *Pastoral Care* (CP),[10] all of which were arguably composed before the Boethius (Bo and Bo met),[11] as well as in

[6] Dr Fischer has as one of the criteria for inclusion in her study the presence of the words in two dictionaries of philosophical terminology consulted by her (see 'A Comparative Study', 624). However, a number of the Latin terms cited might equally well be described as religious, some (e.g. **velocitas**) belong to neither philosophical nor religious registers, while the majority are polysemous. I follow Dr Fischer in considering only nominal representations of Latin nouns along with a handful of adjectival representations of adjectives.

[7] For the terminology see H. Gneuss, *Lehnbildungen und Lehnbedeutungen im Altenglischen* (Berlin, 1955) and Fischer, 'A Comparative Study', 634–6.

[8] *Bischof Wærferths von Worcester Übersetzung der Dialoge Gregors des Grossen,* ed. H. Hecht, Bibliothek der angelsächsischen Prosa, 5 (Leipzig, 1900–7, repr. Darmstadt, 1965). Short titles and abbreviations in this paper normally follow the format originally suggested by Angus Cameron and adopted for the Toronto microfiche concordance: see A. diP. Healey and R. L. Venezky, *A Microfiche Concordance to Old English: The List of Texts and Index of Editions* (Toronto, 1980, repr. with revisions, 1985).

[9] *An Old English Martyrology,* ed. G. Herzfeld, EETS OS 116 (1900, repr. 1973) and *Das altenglische Martyrologium,* ed. G. Kotzor, Bayerische Akademie der Wissenschaften, Phil.-Hist. Klasse, Neue Forschung 88 (Munich, 1981). Since Kotzor's important edition is less widely available than Herzfeld's, references are normally to the latter.

[10] *King Alfred's West-Saxon Version of Gregory's 'Pastoral Care',* ed. H. Sweet, EETS 45 and 50 (1871–2), repr. with corrections and additions by N. R. Ker, 1958. For a valuable, though necessarily partial, glossary based on a fire-damaged copy of this text see I. Carlson, *The Pastoral Care edited from British Library MS Cotton Otho B.ii,* part 1, Stockholm Studies in English, 34 (Stockholm, 1975) and part 2, completed by L.-G. Hallander together with M. Löfvenberg and A. Rynell, *Stockholm Studies in English,* 48 (Stockholm, 1978).

[11] *King Alfred's Old English Version of Boethius De Consolatione Philosophiae,* ed. W. J. Sedgefield (Oxford, 1899), cited according to page and line of prose and meter number and line of verse. References to the Latin text (CPh) are taken from *Boethius: The Theological Tractates; The Consolation of Philosophy,* ed. and trans. H. F. Stewart, E. K. Rand, rev. S. J. Tester (Loeb, 1918, new edn. 1973, repr. 1978).

Alfred's *Soliloquies* (Solil)[12] and prose rendering of the psalms (Ps),[13] and in a handful of other works which were most probably in circulation in Alfred's time—notably the gloss to the Vespasian Psalter and Hymns (PsGlA and PsCaA)[14] and the OE translations of Bede (Be)[15] and Orosius (Or),[16] while in a handful of cases the OE word cited is not in fact a rendering of the Latin term given as its equivalent and thus has no place in the lists.[17]

1.1.1. *Lehnübersetzung*

In addition to **praedestinatio**: *foretiohhung* and **providentia**: *foresceawung*, the pairs of equivalents with an OE element marked by Dr Fischer as first used by Alfred in Bo are **divinitas**: *godcundnes*, **firmitudo**: *fæstnes*, **infortunium**: *unsælþ*, **inpatientia**: *ungeþyld*, **mutatio** (*recte* **mutabilitas**): *wandlung*, **rogatio**: *acsung*, **simplicitas**: *anfealdnes*, **unitas**: *annes*, **velocitas**: *hwætnes*, **indivisus**: *untodæled (recte untodælendlic)*, **infinitus**: *ungeendod*, and **mortalis**: *deadlic*.[18]

Of these pairs three—**divinitas**: *godcundnes*, **inpatientia**: *ungeþyld*, and **mortalis**: *deadlic* (var. *deaðlic*)[19]—are found in GD,[20] with the second two employed also in CP,[21] along with *ungeendod* and the equivalence **simplicitas**: *anfealdnes*.[22] Shared with Be are the equations **divinitas**: *godcundnes*,

[12] *King Alfred's Version of St Augustine's Soliloquies*, ed. T. A. Carnicelli (Cambridge, Mass., 1969).

[13] *Libri Psalmorum Versio Antiqua Latina cum Paraphrasi Anglo-Saxonica*, ed. B. Thorpe (Oxford, 1835). Latin equivalents are taken from the Roman Psalter.

[14] *The Vespasian Psalter*, ed. S. M. Kuhn (Ann Arbor, Mich., 1965).

[15] *The Old English Version of Bede's Ecclesiastical History of the English People*, ed. T. Miller, EETS os 95, 96, 110, 111 (London, 1890–8, repr. 1959–63). For Latin–OE equivalents in Be see the invaluable study by G. G. Waite, 'The Vocabulary of the OE Version of Bede's Historia ecclesiastica' (Ph.D. dissertation, Toronto Univ., 1984).

[16] *The Old English Orosius*, ed. J. Bately, EETS ss 6 (1980). For the problems of dating 'early' texts see *eadem*, 'Old English Prose before and during the Reign of Alfred', *ASE* 17 (1988), 93–138. For the problems of deciding 'whether a paraphrase in the O.E. text is a translation or not' see Fischer, 'A Comparative Study', 624.

[17] I am not concerned here with the important stylistic differences discussed by Dr Fischer, 'A Comparative Study', 625–6, and the evidence she provides to show that Chaucer follows Boethius in using a high proportion of nominals whereas Alfred's style 'tends to be much more verbal'. See Fischer, 625, and K. Otten, *König Alfreds Boethius* (Tübingen, 1964), 217.

[18] Fischer, 'A Comparative Study', 635. I follow Dr Fischer in generally adopting normalized eOE spellings, for which see J. R. Clark Hall, *A Concise Anglo-Saxon Dictionary*, 4th edn., with a supplement by H. D. Meritt (Cambridge, 1960).

[19] See e.g. Bo 85.20, 25.6, 13.13, and 52.16.

[20] See e.g. GD 136.5–6, 274.16–17, and 337.2.

[21] See e.g. CP 220.11 and 159.5. The word *deadlic* is also used in Solil 49.1; for the use of *godcundnes* in the phrase 'on ðære sceawunge ðære godcundnesse', where the equivalent Latin has *contemplando*, see CP 101.13–14.

[22] See e.g. Bo 44.18 and 100.11, CP 407.30 (corresponding to 'sine transitu' in the Latin text), and CP 237.16.

infinitus: *ungeendod*, **mortalis**: *deadlic, deaðlic*,[23] and **unitas**: *annes*.[24] Other pairs are not found in known early texts apart from Bo, but have as their OE components words which do occur in these texts, where they render Latin terms of very similar meaning to those given by Dr Fischer. So **velocitas**: *hwætnes* is paralleled by GD **celeritas**: *hwætnes*,[25] while **rogatio**: *acsung* and **infortunium**: *unsælð* (var. *ungesælþ*) may be compared with **quaestio**: *acsung*[26] and **inquisitio**: *acsung* in GD[27] and **infelicitas**: *unsælþ* in Ps.[28] The word *fæstnes* is found also in Or.[29] At the same time the early texts also provide possible OE alternatives for the Latin elements in the equations.[30] In GD *frignung* is linked with *acsung* and *socn* as a translation of **quaestio**;[31] in Be *frignes* is used for **interrogatio** and—along with *socn*—**quaestio**;[32] in Be and PsA **infelicitas** is translated by *ungesælignes*,[33] while in Bo itself there are alternative renderings for **infortunium** and **infinitus**—namely *heardsælþ* and *endeleas, ungeendodlic*.[34] Also used to render 'misfortune' in these texts are the words *heardsælnes* and *ungelimp*, the latter either alone or in collocation with *un(ge)sælþ*.[35] Alternative nominal translations likewise existed for other words in Dr Fischer's list: for **velocitas** the king

[23] See e.g. Be 134.9, 308.35, and 78.20, beside *deadlic*: **mortuus** 360.7. In addition, the OE word *godcundnes* occurs in Mart 50.6; for *deadlic, deaðlic* see e.g. Or 67.13, Mart 108.12 and 190.18, and PsGlA 78.2. Be and GD also have the noun *deaðlicnes* for **mortalitas**, a word not used in CPh.

[24] See e.g. Be 62.15. As Dr Fischer points out ('A Comparative Study', 627), Bo *annes* never actually occurs as a direct translation of CPh **unitas**. Cf e.g. Bo 90.21 'sio annes 7 sio goodnes', where CPh III, pr. 11.24 has 'unum atque bonum', and Bo 90.15–16 'forðæm is þæt fulle good þæt eall ætgædre is untodæled', corresponding to CPh III, pr. 11.20–1 'nonne haec ut bona sint, unitatis fieri adeptione contingit'. For *annes* in conjunction with *þrines* see Solil 86.8.

[25] Bo 54.24, GD 299.15 (var. *hrædnes*).

[26] See e.g. Bo 12.30, GD 323.23.

[27] GD 7.5; cf. CP 155.5 'fandunge 7 ascunge', Latin text 'percunctationibus', and CP 155.1 'scearplicu 7 smealicu fandung ðæs modes', Latin text 'acutis inquisitionibus', also Bo 127.6 *acsung*, possibly inspired by CPh IV.6.6 *quaesitu*. See also Solil 82.1 *acsung* and (in a passage of paraphrase) Bo 148.9 *geascung* (MS B; MS C 'geæscum').

[28] Bo 21.17, Ps 13.7. cf. Bo 78.11 and CP 407.30 **felicitas**: *gesælþ*, also Bo 120.31 *unsælþ* (beside CPh IV.4.85 'infelicissimam'), CP 455.10 *ungesælþ* (= **tristitia**).

[29] Or 43.25, Bo 72.16.

[30] Some of these terms may have been associated with non-West Saxon dialects (see e.g. F. Wenisch, *Spezifisch anglisches Wortgut in den nordhumbrischen Interlineargbossierungen des Lukasevangeliums* (Heidelberg, 1979) and below, p. 21. However, this does not mean that Alfred, lacking a term of his own, might not, on occasion, have adopted that of his helpers.

[31] See GD 323.23 'þære frignunge (MS O frægninge) 7 acsunge' and 137.29 'socn 7 frignung' (MS O 'acsuncge 7 frininge', MS H 'axung').

[32] Be 64.3 and 434.13; cf. **quaestio**: *geflit* Be 26.22.

[33] See Be 142.26 and PsGlA 13.7.

[34] Bo 117.24, 104.15, 44.21; cf. Or 89.27.

[35] Or 58.10, Bo 125.18–19; cf. Ps 40.11 'fægnað mines ungelimpes' corresponding to Psalter 'gaudebit . . . super me'.

might have used not *hwætnes* but—as in CP—*hwætscipe*,[36] or—as in GD—*hrædnes*[37] or indeed (variants he uses elsewhere in Bo) *swiftnes, swifto*, or *hrædfernes*;[38] instead of *annes* for **unitas** and the hapax legomenon *wandlung*[39] for **mutabilitas** he might have used in some contexts[40]—again as in CP—*anmodnes*,[41] *hwurfulnes*, and either *wending* or—as elsewhere in Bo—*hwearfung*.[42] Lastly, for **simplicitas**[43] he employs not only *anfealdnes* but also—as in CP, GD, and Be—*bilewitnes*,[44] sometimes using the two words in collocation[45] and thus clearly demonstrating that far from needing to coin a word to translate Boethius' Latin, he had more than one appropriate term already available to him. Only the adjectival pair **indivisus**: *untodælendlic*[46] is unparalleled in known early texts, and even here there were alternatives in existence, with Be employing *untodæled* to translate **individuus** and Bo itself using both *untodæled* and *untodæledlic* in comparable contexts.[47]

[36] CP 149.13; cf. Or 30.10 *hwætscipe* 'bravery, courage'.

[37] See e.g. GD 221.23 and above, n. 25. GD also uses *hrædnes* to translate Latin **celeritas** and **festinatio** (see e.g. GD 123.13 and 195.28); cf. Be 50.3, rendering Latin 'in brevi'.

[38] Bo 125.32, Bo met 28.3 (CPh IV, met. 5.5 'celeres') and Bo 72.17 (CPh **celeritas**); cf. Ps 32.15 *swiftnes* in an expansion of the Psalter text.

[39] Bo 15.27. Dr Fischer ('A Comparative Study', 635) is wrong in giving the corresponding Latin (CPh II, pr. 1.31) as **mutatio** (for which see below, p. 14).

[40] The study of equivalences, here as elsewhere, is greatly complicated by polysemy: see the definition of **unitas** in Charlton T. Lewis and Charles Short, *A Latin Dictionary* (Oxford, 1879, repr. 1958), 'The state of being one, oneness, unity, sameness, uniformity, unity of sentiment, agreement, concord'. Clark Hall's OE dictionary gives as the meanings of *annes* 'oneness, unity; agreement, covenant; solitude' and of *anmodnes* 'unity, unanimity; steadfastness, resolution'. For the meanings of Latin terms see also *Novum Glossarium Mediae Latinitatis*, ed. Franz Blatt, Yves Lefevre, *et al.* (Hafnae, Munksgaard, 1957–) and *A Dictionary of Medieval Latin from British Sources*, ed. R. A. Latham and D. R. Howlett (London, 1975–).

[41] e.g. CP 95.5; cf. GD 329.17 **unanimitas**: *anmodnes* and Solil 53.5 **concordia**: *anmodnes.*

[42] See e.g. CP 308.1 and 306.17, Bo 18.31, also below, p. 14 and (for Bo *wending*) n. 76. Cf. Solil 53.2 *onhwærfednes* 'change'.

[43] For **simplicitas** Lewis and Short's definitions include 'simpleness, simplicity, plainness, frankness, openness, artlessness, innocence, honesty, candour, directness, ingenuousness, naturalness'.

[44] See e.g. CP 291.8, GD 209.4, Be 62.1, beside Be 114.6–7 *hluttornes*; cf. also Or 22.18 *bilewitnes.*

[45] Cf. Bo 128.8 'his anfaldnesse 7 bilewitnesse', CPh IV, pr. 6.25 'suae simplicitatis'; CP 239.1–2 'sio bilewitnes 7 sio anfealdnes', Latin text 'simplicitate'. The Microfiche Concordance records the collocation only from these two texts.

[46] See CPh III, pr. 9.10–11 'Quod enim simplex est indivisumque natura', Bo 74.30 'God is anfeald 7 untodælendlic'.

[47] Be 456.29, Bo 76.9, 89.1; cf. Solil 53.2 *todælennes. Pace* Dr Fischer ('A Comparative Study', 635) *untodæled* is never used in Bo for **indivisus**, generally occurring in paraphrases of Latin passages with the word *unum*, though interestingly twice collocated with *anfeald*: see e.g. Bo 76.12 'þeah nu God anfeald sie 7 untodæled', CPh III, pr. 9.45–6 'Hoc igitur quod est unum simplexque natura.' Lewis and Short give the meanings 'not divided, indivisible, inseparable, not separated' for **individuus** and 'undivided, common' for **indivisus**.

1.1.2. *Lehnübertragung*

Apart from **providentia:** *foreþanc,* pairs listed by Dr Fischer under this heading are **claritudo:** *hliseadignes:* **constantia:** *fæstrædnes;* **dignitas:** *arweorþnes;* **intemperantia:** *ungemetfæstnes;* **medicina:** *læcecræft;* **musica:** *dreamcræft;* **mutatio:** *hwurfulnes;* **necessitas:** *niedþearf;* **perfidia:** *untreow;* **perturbatio:** *gedrefednes.*[48]

Evidence exists today of the use of only three of these pairs in works securely datable to the period before about 900 other than Bo. So *niedþearf* is found for **necessitas** also in CP, Be, and GD;[49] *dreamcræft* is used for **musica** in Mart,[50] while **perturbatio:** *gedrefednes* occurs in CP.[51] However, for almost all the other pairs, either the OE element in the equation is recorded as rendering Latin words of similar meaning, or alternative OE equivalents were in current use for the terms used by Boethius. (Even for **musica, necessitas, perturbatio** we find the alternatives (i) *myrgnes* in the Corpus Glossary,[52] (ii) *niedþearfnes* in PsA, Be, and GD,[53] *þearf* in CP,[54] *nied*[55] in CP, Be, and GD,[56] and (iii) *gedrefnes* in Bo meters, Solil, and Be,[57] while Ps uses *gedrefednes* for **conturbatio.**)[58] So, for instance, the rendering of the Latin word **claritudo** by *hliseadignes* is certainly unique to a single passage in Bo.[59] However, **claritudo** occurs nine times in CPh and for two of the remaining eight occurrences[60] Alfred uses *foremærnes,* another word recorded only from Bo,[61] where it also translates **claritas,**[62] and, along with

[48] Fischer, 'A Comparative Study', 635–6.

[49] See e.g. Bo 144.17, CP 75.5, Be 318.21, GD 192.20, Ps 24.15; cf. Or 118.28 *niedþearf.* None of the instances in Bo are in fact direct translations of **necessitas** in CPh.

[50] Bo 38.7, Mart 212.30.

[51] See e.g. Bo 13.8, CP 225.2.

[52] CorpGl 2 (Hessels) 11.368.

[53] PsGlA 106.5(6), Be 100.5–6, GD 113.4; see also Mart 68.11 and cf. GD 152.2 **necessaria:** 'nydþearfnessum' (var. 'neadþearfum').

[54] e.g. CP 281.12. *þearf,* 'necessity', is found also in Bo, GD, and Be.

[55] I include here the variants *nead, neod.*

[56] CP 81.7, Be 130.33, and GD 157.27 (var. *neadung*). The OE word occurs also in Solil 53.3, Or 94.8, and, adverbially, in Bo 94.15; cf. GD 15.27 'mid nyde' (var. *neadlunga*) rendering 'inuitum'.

[57] Bo met 5. 40, Be 112.1; also (under the influence of Latin *perturbavit*) Solil 70.30.

[58] Ps 30.22; similarly PsGlA 30.22(21). The OE word occurs also in GD.

[59] Bo 75.28.

[60] Five instances occur in passages rewritten by Alfred; in four of these the adjectives *foremære* and *mære* appear, along with *hliseadig.*

[61] Bo 56.10 and 76.4 (= **claritudo**), also Bo 77.14, referring back to the passage on p. 76. The related adjective *foremære* occurs more widely; cf. e.g. GD 317.25 **inlustris:** *foremæra,* and 307.1–2 'swiðe ænlic wer 7 foremære' ('quidem spectabilis uir'), also Ps 15.6 **praeclara:** *foremære.* For *foremærlic* see below, n. 66.

[62] Bo 87.14; see also Bo 86.24.

mærð—likewise used for **claritudo** in Bo[63]—**celebritas.**[64] On one of these occasions it is coupled with *hlisa,* in the collocation *good hlisa 7 foremærnes.*[65] The reason for Alfred's choice of *hliseadignes* at Bo 75.28 is apparently the use immediately beforehand in the same section of text of the adjective *hliseadig,* which in its turn is there employed as a variation on *foremærlic* and *mærlicost.*[66] Other alternatives might have been *bierhto* and *mærsung,* found in CP and Be for **claritas** and **celebratio** respectively.[67] At the same time, **medicina** is translated not only by *læcecræft* but also (in the sense 'remedy') by *læcedom.*[68] The former term occurs also in GD, for Latin *medicinae ars,*[69] the latter for **medicamentum** in CP and Be and for **medicina** in CP, while Mart has the collocation *læcedomes cræft.*[70] Another possible term—found in GD in collocation with *gehælednes* for **curatio**—is *lacnung.*[71] As for the equation **intemperantia:** *ungemetfæstnes,*[72] this has to be seen in the context of the positive *gemetfæstnes:* **moderamen** in Be,[73] which in its turn belongs to a group of words containing also *metgung, gemetgung,* and *ungemetgung,* all occurring in texts of the period.[74] The instance of *hwurfulnes* for **mutatio** ('a changing, change, alteration, mutation, etc.')[75] has to be seen in the context of the use of *wending,* 'changing', in Ps and of *onwendednes* for **commutatio** and **inmutatio** in PsGlA[76] on the one hand, and on the other the equating of **mutabilitas** ('changeableness', 'mutability') with *hwurfulnes* in CP,[77] and with *wandlung* and *hwearfung* in Bo itself,[78] while for **perfidia:** *untreow*[79] GD, Be, and the Corpus, Épinal, and Erfurt glossaries

[63] See e.g. Bo 54.6.

[64] Bo 56.24 and 74.24. Lewis and Short define **claritudo** as 'clearness, brightness; renown, celebrity, splendour, fame, reputation' and give as **celebritas,** sense II B 'fame, renown, celebrity'.

[65] Bo 56.9–10. Cf. CP 339. 25 'for ðæm godan hlisan', Latin text 'de boni specie'.

[66] See Bo 75. 21 'weorþlicosð 7 mærlicost', 75.24 'weorðlic 7 foremærlic'; and cf. (in this same passage) 75.19 *unmærlic.*

[67] e.g. CP 387.15 and Be 120.27; cf. Bo's use of *bierhto* 'brightness'. Lewis and Short define **claritas** as 'clearness, brightness, splendour; distinctness, perspicuity; celebrity, renown, reputation, splendour, high estimation'. cf. **celebratio:** *weorþung* Be 418.14 etc.

[68] See e.g. Bo 38.8 and 127.24; for **remedia:** *læcecræft* and **remedia:** *læcedom* see Bo 51.1 and 50.21, and cf. Solil 79.27 *læcedom.*

[69] See e.g. GD 344.6.

[70] See e.g. CP 153.4, Be 78.26 (= **medicamentum**); CP 397.16 (= **medicina**); Mart (ed. Kotzor) 82.8.

[71] GD 247.11. The word *lacnung* is also found in medical texts for which an early date is sometimes assumed.

[72] Bo 109.9.

[73] Be 158.13.

[74] See e.g. Be 164.16; CP 145.25; Bo 62.26; CP 141.8.

[75] Bo 47.19.

[76] Ps 9.26 ('non movebor'), PsGlA 54.19(20) and 76.9(11); cf. Bo met 7.41 *wending.*

[77] CP 308.1 and 10.

[78] See above, p. 12 and see also *onhwerfednes,* Solil 53.2.

[79] Bo 16.5; see also Bo met 2.13.

provide (*ge*)*treowleasnes*.[80] We may compare the use of *untreowþ*, 'perfidy', in Or and *ungetreownes* for **infidelitas** in CP and GD.[81] Again, to match Bo *fæstrædnes*[82] CP has *unfæstrædnes*, along with *unbieldo*, for *inconstantia*;[83] however, in Be the words chosen to render **constantia** are *anrædnes* and *bieldo*.[84]

Lastly, in the case of **dignitas**: *arweorþnes* Dr Fischer has made a false equation. The two instances of *arweorþnes* in Bo occur in a section which has been considerably reworked by Alfred but in neither case does the equivalent Latin have the word **dignitas**. Both instances relate to passages referring to 'blessings' and things bringing joy.[85] In those places where **dignitas**, or its plural **dignitates**,[86] has been translated in Bo, then the most usual renderings are with *anwald*[87] and *weorþscipe*.[88] On one single occasion it is translated by *medemnes*.[89] We may compare CP with *medemnes* for **dignitas**,[90] Or with *weorþmynd*,[91] and Be with *weorþnes*,[92] while perhaps also to be included here as covering some of the meanings of **dignitas** is CP *geþyncþo*.[93]

1.1.3. *Lehnschöpfung*

affluentia: *ofergemet;* **facultas**: *andgites mæþ;* **intellectus**: *gearowita;* **tactus**: *gefrednes;* **vitium**: *unþeaw*.[94]

[80] See e.g. GD 162.20, Be 104.9 and 250.30–252.1; *Old English Glosses in the Épinal–Erfurt Glossary*, ed. J. D. Pheifer (Oxford, 1974), 39.726.

[81] Or 79.19–20, CP 447.6, GD 160.5.

[82] Bo 15.27 (MS C "un' fæstrædnesse', with the letters *un* inserted above the line); cf. Bo. 20.20–1 'auht fæstrædlices', CPh II, pr. 3.46 'ullam constantiam'.

[83] See e.g. CP 308.5.

[84] Be 36.32–3.

[85] Compare Bo 20.1–5 with CPh II, pr. 3.14–15 and Bo 20. 13–15 with CPh II, pr. 3.41–3; cf. GD 196.15, 254.13–14, Be 78.32, 264.12, and also CP 133.15, where *arweorþnes* renders **veneratio** and **reverentia**.

[86] Lewis and Short 'A being worthy, worth, worthiness, merit, desert, dignity, greatness, grandeur, authority, rank, official dignity, office, value, excellence', etc., with related words given as **honos (honor), honestas, laus, existimatio, gloria, fama, nomen.**

[87] See e.g. Bo 38.33 and cf. **honor**: *anweald* CP 115.17. For *miht* as a possible alternative see below, p. 23. For the spelling *anwald* (Clark Hall *onweald*), see E. G. Stanley, 'Spellings of the *Waldend* Group', *Studies in Language, Literature, and Culture of the Middle Ages and Later*, ed. E. B. Atwood and A. A. Hill (Austin, Tex. 1969), 38–69.

[88] See e.g. Bo. 17.7, beside **honor**: *weorþscipe* Bo 75.23, Ps 48.20, Solil 54.13, etc., **gloria**: *weorþscipe* Ps 7.5, CP 317.23, and **gloria**: *weorþmynd* CP 389.17–18. Cf. e.g. Bo 39.8 where *anweald* renders **potentia** and *weorþscipe* **dignitas**, and see Bo *weorþmynd*, 'honour, dignity', 30.20 etc.

[89] Bo 32.11.

[90] CP 85.22.

[91] Or 145.18.

[92] See e.g. Be 194.5.

[93] See e.g. CP 411.25 and see below, p. 23.

[94] Fischer, 'A Comparative Study', 636.

The pairs in Dr Fischer's third group again repay close scrutiny.

(i) **affluentia:** *ofergemet*

Dr Fischer's equation depends on three assumptions. First that the term **affluentia**, CPh II, pr. 5.43, is used in its secondary sense of 'extravagance', second that what is printed in Sedgefield's text as the phrase *ofer gemet* is in fact a compound noun, and third that this noun is intended as a direct translation of **affluentia**. Certainly, **affluentia** is sometimes found in Latin texts with the meaning 'extravagance'; however, in the *De Consolatione* it appears to be used in the sense 'abundance', and is so translated by Tester,[95] the concept of superfluity being expressed through the adjective *superfluus* in a subsequent sentence:

Terrarum quidem fructus animantium procul dubio debentur alimentis. Sed si, quod naturae satis est, replere indigentiam velis, nihil est quod fortunae affluentiam petas. Paucis enim minimisque natura contenta est, cuius satietatem si superfluis urgere velis, aut iniucundum quod infuderis fiet aut noxium. (CPh II, pr. 5.40–6)

The fruits of the earth are surely intended for the sustenance of living things. But if you want to satisfy your needs, which is enough for nature, there is no need to ask fortune for abundance. For nature is content with few things and small: if you want to overlay that satisfaction with superfluity, then what you add will be either unpleasant or positively harmful.

In Bo, the equivalent section elaborates on the two themes of abundance and superfluity and (according to the word-division of Sedgefield's text) twice uses the phrase *ofer gemet*:

Hwilc fremu is þe þæt þæt þu wilnige þissa andweardena gesælþa ofer gemet, þonne hie naþer ne magon ne þin gehelpan, ne heora selfra? (Bo 30.10–12)

What profit is there for you that you should desire these present happinesses to excess, when they may help neither you nor themselves?

and

Gif ðu heore mare selest, oþer twega oððe hit þe derað, oððe hit ðe þeah unwynsum bið, oððe ungetæse, oððe frecenlic, eall þæt þu nu ofer gemet dest. (Bo 30.14–16)

If you produce more of them, either it will harm you or it will nevertheless be unpleasant for you, or inconvenient, or dangerous, all that you now do to excess.

[95] Loeb edition, op. cit.; cf. the Penguin Classics edition (Harmondsworth, 1969), where V. E. Watts's freer translation uses the word 'excess'. A second example of the Latin word, CPh II, pr. 2.13 (translated 'affluence' by Tester and Watts), is in a passage rewritten by Alfred (Bo 17.11–14) and without exact equivalent. However, it may have influenced the king's choice of the word *woruldar* at line 13.

In the second passage *ofer gemet* is unambiguously a phrase and clearly inspired by CPh *superfluus*. In the first passage either compound noun or phrase is grammatically possible.[96] However, although the Toronto concordance records a substantial number of instances of the phrasal construction, the only examples of *ofer* + *gemet* that could possibly be construed as constituting compound nouns are confined to this and a couple of no less disputable instances in CP and Solil.[97] In all three cases the phrasal interpretation is arguably the more appropriate one. At the same time, it can plausibly be argued that in the first passage quoted above Alfred is modifying and rewriting Boethius' statement about abundance in the light of his subsequent reference to superfluity.

The equation **affluentia**: *ofergemet* must therefore be treated with some caution. However, just as the term **affluentia** ('a flowing to; affluence, abundance, copiousness, fullness, profusion; immoderate pomp or splendour in the management of one's household, extravagance') is capable of more than one interpretation, so there was more than one suitable rendering of it in existence at the time when Alfred was writing. Thus, for instance, for 'abundance, fullness, copiousness' (meanings also of Latin **abundantia**, **plenitudo**, and **ubertas**) we find *gefyllednes* (GD),[98] *fylnes* (PsGlA),[99] *genyht* (Ps, Solil, and CP),[100] *genyhtsumnes* (CP, GD, Be),[101] and also *oferfyll*[102] and *oferfylnes* (GD),[103] though these two last appear rather to be used in the sense of **satietas** or of **superfluitas**, the latter a word rendered in Bo by *ofering* and in Be by *oferflownes*.[104]

(ii) **facultas**: [*andgites*] *mæþ*

The word **facultas** ('capability, possibility, power, means, opportunity, skill, ability to do anything easily, a sufficient or great number, abundance, plenty, supply, stock, store, pl. goods, riches, property') occurs twice in CPh:

Omne enim quod cognoscitur non secundum sui vim sed secundum cognoscentium potius comprehenditur facultatem. (CPh V, pr. 4.75–7)

[96] For use of either acc. or dat. with the verb *wilnian* see J. E. Wülfing, *Die Syntax in den Werken Alfreds des Grossen*, 2 vols. (Bonn, 1894, 1901), i. 11 and 115.

[97] CP 313.14 'for giefernesse ofergemet' ('per immoderatum usum'); Solil 58.13 'loca nu þæt þu ofer gemeð ne wilnige'.

[98] See e.g. GD 120.25.

[99] See e.g. PsGlA 23.1.

[100] See e.g. Ps 35.8, Solil 53.5, CP 183.1; cf. Bo 76.4 (= **sufficientia**).

[101] See e.g. CP 325.12, GD 98.16, GD 251.5, Be 194.8 and (= **copia**) 48.26; cf. **affluentia**: *menige* CP 113.19.

[102] GD 339.8.

[103] GD 339.3; cf. Bo 70.5 *oferfyll*, 'superfluity, excess'.

[104] Bo 31.23, Be 78.8. The word *ofering* is not recorded outside Bo, where it occurs twice.

For everything which is known is grasped not according to its own power but rather according to the capability of those who know it.

and

Videsne igitur ut in cognoscendo cuncta sua potius facultate quam eorum quae cognoscuntur utantur? (CPh V, pr. 4.115–17)

Do you therefore see that in knowing, all these use their own capability rather than that of those things which are known?

The first of these passages corresponds to Bo 145.5–7:

Hu ne wast þu þæt manig þing ne bið no ongiten swa swa hit bið, ac swa swa þæs andgites mæð bið þe þæræfter spyreð?

Do you not know that many a thing is not perceived as it is but according to the capacity of the intellect that is investigating it?

The second has no precise equivalent in the final, greatly modified, section of Bo. However, the OE word *mæþ* appears with the meaning 'measure, ability, capacity', both on its own elsewhere in Bo, Solil, and CP[105] and (in Bo and Solil) in the collocation *þæs andgietes mæþ*,[106] while in Be another area of meaning covered by **facultas** is recognized by the translation *sped*.[107]

(iii) **intellectus:** *gearowita*

The word *gearowita* is recorded in the Toronto microfiche concordance only from Bo, where it occurs three times, twice in a passage where Alfred is reworking a section of CPh dealing with different levels of knowledge and intelligence,[108] and once rendering the single instance of **intellectus** in CPh.[109] However, translations of **intellectus** ('a perceiving, discerning, perception, discernment, understanding, comprehension, knowledge, intellect, meaning, sense, signification of a word', etc.) in early OE are not confined to Bo, the terms selected including also 'þæt inre gewitt' (Solil),[110] *ingeþanc* (Solil),[111] and *andgiet* (Be).[112] *Andgiet* is a word of common occurrence in Bo, where it renders a number of Latin terms, including **intellegentia** ('the power of discerning or understanding, discernment, understanding, intelligence,

[105] e.g. Bo 147.13, Solil 69.20, CP 101.11.

[106] e.g. Bo 145.7, Solil 70.3.

[107] Be 230.28. Other early OE words for 'riches, prosperity' include *æht*.

[108] Bo 146.21 and 23.

[109] Bo 130.30, CPh IV, pr. 6.79. cf. GD 331.15 'ungeare witolnesse' and OccGl 28 (Nap) 108 'sagaci: gearwitelum'.

[110] Solil 59.11.

[111] Solil 59.13.

[112] Be 84.28.

knowledge, perception, art, skill', etc.).[113] *Gewitt* is also found on a number of occasions both here and in other texts of the period.[114]

(iv) **tactus**: *gefrednes*

Since **tactus** includes amongst its meanings not only 'touch' but also 'feeling', 'sense of feeling', *gefrednes* is an acceptable translation for it. Of the two instances of the word in CPh the first (I, pr. 5.44) is without equivalent in Bo. The second,

Nam ut hoc brevi liqueat exemplo, eandem corporis rotunditatem aliter visus aliter tactus agnoscit (CPh V, pr. 4.77–9)

For—that this may become clear by a brief example—the same roundness of a body sight recognizes in one way and touch in another

corresponds to

Hwæt, þu wast þæt gesihð 7 gehernes 7 gefrednes ongitað þone lichoman þæs monnes, 7 þeah ne ongitað hi hine no gelicne; þa earan ongitað þæt hi geherað, 7 ne ongitað hi þeah þone lichoman eallunga swylcne swylce he bið; sio gefrednes hine mæg gegrapian 7 gefredan þæt hit lichoma bið, ac hio ne mæg gefredan hwæðer he bið þe blæc þe hwit, ðe fæger ðe unfæger. (Bo 145.18–24)

Now, you know that sight and hearing and touch perceive the body of the man and yet they do not perceive it as like; the ears perceive that they hear and yet they do not perceive the body entirely such as it is; the touch may handle it and feel that it is body, but it may not feel whether it is black or white, fair or unfair.

However, once again there are words for **tactus** 'touch' recorded from early OE other than this hapax legomenon.[115] So Be has *hrinenes* and *gehrinenes*,[116] Solil *hrinung*,[117] GD[118] and Solil *hrine*.[119]

[113] See e.g. Bo 146.27–8 'þæs hehstan andgites' and 145.32 'gewis andgit'. See also Bo 146.18–26, where *andgiet* and *gearowita* are both used, along with *gesceadwisnes*. For GD *ongietenes* = **cognitio**, see below, n. 218.

[114] For **sensus**: *gewitt* see further below, p. 27. Other possible renderings include *wisdom* and poetic words such as *hygecræft* and *modcræft*.

[115] The related verb *gefredan* is found in a range of texts, from Bo, CP, Solil, and GD to Ælfric's homilies and LibSc.

[116] See e.g. Be 396.11 and 322.25.

[117] Solil 59.6.

[118] GD (MSS CO) 87.24 (MS H *æthrine*); Latin text *contactus*, London, Lambeth Palace Library MS 204 *tactus* changed to *contactus*. See further below, p. 24 and n. 228.

[119] Solil 51.12. Cf. the verb forms *onhrinan* and *gehrinan* in prose and verse versions of CPh IV, met. 6, Bo 135.26 and 28 and Bo met 29.10.

(v) **vitium**: *unþeaw*

Translation of **vitium** by *unþeaw* is certainly 'Alfredian', being attested not only in Bo but also in CP.[120] However, OE vocabulary is rich in words for 'wickedness' of all kinds and a whole range of these are recorded in early texts. So in CP, for example, Alfred renders **vitium** ('fault, defect, blemish, imperfection, moral fault, failing, error, offence, crime, vice', etc.) not only by *unþeaw* but also by *unwrenc* and *uncyst*,[121] the latter a translation shared with GD and Be.[122] Common to both CP and Bo is the pair **vitium**: *yfel*,[123] while in Bo meters *unþeaw* is used in collocation with *leahtor*,[124] a word (frequent in the poetry) that also occurs for **vitium** in Be and GD[125] and for **crimen** ('crime, fault, offence', etc.) in CP and Be.[126] In Ps *uncyst* translates Latin **delictum** ('fault, offence, crime, transgression, wrong'), which in its turn appears as *misdæd* in CP and *scyld* in Be and PsGlA.[127] A common alternative for *scyld* is *gylt*.[128]

From this brief survey it emerges that of the OE words included in Dr Fischer's lists as 'first found in the Boethius' and forming genuine pairs with their claimed 'Latin equivalents', a very high proportion occur also in other surviving 'early' texts, at least some of which arguably pre-date Alfred's translation. Moreover, for a significantly large number of the Latin terms cited at least one other possible translation was available. What then of the fate of these words, both Alfredian and non-Alfredian, in the later OE period?

1.1.4. *The evidence of the later OE period*

Consultation of the Toronto microfiche concordance reveals that very few of the words discussed in the first section are recorded only from texts known to have been composed by the end of the first decade of the tenth century and so might be presumed not to have survived into the later part of the OE period. Of these, eight words are restricted to the Boethius,

[120] See e.g. Bo 109.7 and CP 63.19, and cf. **nequitia**: *unþeaw* Bo 61.8 beside **nequitia**: *uncyst* CP 273.2, **nequitia**: *yfelnes* Be 80.33.

[121] CP 215.19 and 67.1.

[122] See e.g. GD 22.28 ('uncysta', var. 'unþeawa'), GD 95.16 (MS H 'leahtra'), Be 72.26.

[123] CP 401.25, Bo 109.14.

[124] Bo met 22.25–6 and 29–30, corresponding to Bo 95.8 and 10 *unþeaw*.

[125] Be 190.25, GD 326.30; see also n. 123.

[126] CP 401.25 'yfel . . . leahtrum'; Latin text 'vitium . . . criminibus', Be 458.28.

[127] Ps 18.11, CP 413.26, Be 82.11, PsGlA 18.12(13).

[128] For this and other alternatives see G. Büchner, *Vier Altenglische Bezeichnungen für Vergehen und Verbrechen (Firen, Gylt, Man, Scyld)*, Inaugural Dissertation (Berlin, 1968), also J. M. Bately, 'Lexical Evidence for the Authorship of the Prose Psalms in the Paris Psalter', *ASE* 10 (1982), 69–95 at 93. For distribution patterns see H. Gneuss, 'The Origin of Standard Old English and Æthelwold's School at Winchester', *ASE* 1 (1972), 63–83.

namely *foremærnes, gefrednes, gearowita, hliseadignes,*[129] *hrædfernes, ofering, wandlung,* and (in the verse meters) *swifto.* One other (*hwurfulnes*) has not been found outside the works of Alfred,[130] while recorded only from Alfred and Genesis B is the noun *untreow.*[131] A few others can be added if we include words restricted to demonstrably early texts other than the works of Alfred or a combination of the two, namely:

dreamcræft; frignes; frignung;[132] heardsælnes; heardsælþ; hrine; hrinenes; gehrinenes; hwætscipe; myrgnes.

Of the remaining words discussed in sections 1. 1. 1–3 a few are confined to a mixture of early works and texts preserved in post-ninth century manuscripts whose date of composition is uncertain:[133]

bierhto;[134] gedrefnes;[135] fæstrædnes;[136] fyllnes;[137] hrinung;[138] hwearfung;[139] medemnes;[140] genyht;[141] oferflownes;[142] oferfyllnes;[143] onwendednes;[144] treowleasnes;[145] getreowleasnes;[146] ungemetfæstnes;[147] ungesælignes;[148] unsælþ;[149] untodælendlic;[150] ungetreownes;[151] weorþnes.[152]

However, the majority are recorded both from early works and from demon-

[129] For the related adjectives *foremære, hliseadig, gearowitol,* the noun *ungearuwitolnes,* and the verb *gefredan,* see above, pp. 13, 14, and nn. 109 and 115.

[130] See above, pp. 12, 13, and 14.

[131] See GenA, B 773 and cf. OSaxon *untrewa.*

[132] For suggestions that the related verb *frignan* is typical of Anglian dialects see e.g. R. Jordan, *Eigentümlichkeiten des anglischen Wortschatzes* (Heidelberg, 1906), 95.

[133] Specimen references only are given in this and subsequent sections. In a handful of instances, where printed texts were unavailable, they have been taken directly from the Toronto concordance.

[134] HomS 1(VercHom 5) 171, LS 10 (Guth) 20.112.

[135] AldV 13.1 (Nap) 2420, MonCa 3 (Korhammer) 10.18.

[136] HomU 9 (VercHom 4) 357. The corresponding adjective, *fæstræd,* however, is used by a number of writers including Ælfric and Wulfstan.

[137] DurRitGl (Thomp-Lind) 9.11.

[138] DurRitGl 9(Skt) 43.

[139] Prog 3.1 (Forst) 14.

[140] HomS 1 (VercHom 5) 1.

[141] HomU 34 (Nap 42) 128.

[142] ChrodR 1 4.0.

[143] OccGl 89.1 (Schlutter) 3.

[144] HomS 4 (VercHom 9) 119.

[145] HomU 37 (Nap 46) 32.

[146] Conf 9.4 (Logeman) 5.

[147] ChrodR 1 30.37.

[148] HomU 18 (BlHom 1) 2.

[149] HomS 19 (Schaefer) 62.

[150] LawIudDei VIII 2.

[151] HomS 36 (Willard) 26.

[152] LibSc 44.11.

strably late texts such as the works of Ælfric, Wulfstan, and Byrhtferth and the later continuations of the Anglo-Saxon Chronicle:[153]

andgiet;[154] anfealdnes;[155] anmodnes;[156] annes;[157] anrædnes;[158] anwald;[159] arweorþnes;[160] ascung;[161] bilewitnes;[162] deadlic;[163] deaþlic;[164] gedrefednes;[165] endeleas;[166] fæstnes;[167] gefyllednes;[168] godcundnes;[169] gylt;[170] hrædnes;[171] hwætnes;[172] lacnung;[173] læcecræft;[174] læcedom;[175] leahtor;[176] mærsung;[177] mærþ;[178] mæþ;[179] misdæd;[180] nied;[181] niedþearf;[182] niedþearfnes;[183] genyhtsumnes;[184] oferfyll;[185] scyld;[186] socn;[187] sped;[188] swiftnes;[189] þearf;[190] geþyncþo;[191] uncyst;[192] ungeendod;[193] ungeendodlic;[194] ungelimp;[195]

[153] Since it is occurrence not sense that is relevant to the arguments at this point, no attempt is made in the following sections to consider the range of meanings with which words cited are used.

[154] ÆHom 29.100, WHom 9.23, ByrM 1 (Crawford) 182.34.

[155] ÆCHom II, 21.184.130, WHom 9.129.

[156] ÆCHom I, 25.360.7.

[157] ÆHom 1.166, WHom 10c.142, ByrM 1 (Crawford) 198.15.

[158] ÆHom 9.141, WHom 9.40.

[159] ÆHom 21.369 (for Latin *potestas*).

[160] ÆHom 6.5, WCan 1.1.1 (Fowler) 26.

[161] ÆGram 116.9.

[162] ÆHom 16.226, WHom 9.43.

[163] ÆGram 54.10.

[164] ÆCHom I, 15. 222.10.

[165] ÆHom 5.184.

[166] ÆHom 6.158, WHom 7.76.

[167] ÆGram 41.3 (= **munimen**).

[168] ÆCHom II, 7.63.82, ByrM 1 (Crawford) 64.26.

[169] ÆHom 1.3, WHom 6.163, ByrM 1 (Crawford) 142.13.

[170] ÆCHom I, 33.498.20, ByrM 1 (Crawford) 124.22. See Gneuss, 'The Origin', 76.

[171] ÆCHom II, 11.103.394.

[172] ByrM 1 (Crawford) 116.17.

[173] ÆLS (Apollinaris) 41.

[174] ÆHom 13.3.

[175] ÆHom 1.216.

[176] ÆHom 2.102. See Gneuss, 'The Origin', 76.

[177] ÆCHom II, 17.165.154.

[178] ÆHom 1.360, WHom 7.152.

[179] ÆHom 6.216, WHom 6.149.

[180] ÆHom 6.261, WHom 3.29.

[181] ÆHom 1.218, ByrM 1 (Crawford) 38.14.

[182] ÆLS (Christmas) 47, WPol 2.1.2 (Jost) 115.

[183] ÆCHom II, 10.90.312.

[184] ÆHom 11.567.

[185] ÆHom 16.77, WHom 14.27.

[186] ÆHom 15.131. See Gneuss, 'The Origin', 76.

[187] ÆCHom II, 39.1.292.146 ('idol, altar')

[188] ÆHom 15.121.

[189] ÆHomM 1 (Bel 9) 188, ByrM 1 (Crawford) 74.4.

[190] ÆHom 19.117, WHom 7.166.

[191] ÆHom 19.14, WPol 2.1.2 (Jost) 36.

[192] ÆHom 30.53.

[193] ÆHom 21.21.

[194] WCan 1.2 (Torkar) 18.

[195] ÆCHom II, 35.263.89, WHom 20.2.105.

ungesælþ;[196] ungeþyld;[197] untodæled;[198] untodæledlic;[199] untreowþ;[200] unþeaw;[201] unwrenc;[202] wending;[203] weorþmynd;[204] weorþscipe;[205] yfel.[206]

At the same time it is clear that by the second part of the tenth century at latest the range of choices was greater than that indicated by the evidence of the handful of known early works that have survived. Even a cursory examination of late texts and of those undatable texts that are preserved in manuscripts of the tenth century and after reveals a number of further alternatives not attested in texts of known early composition. Instances that I have noted include the following:[207]

affluentia/abundantia: genyhtsumung, oferflowendnes[208]
claritudo/celebritas/claritas: beorht, beorhtnes[209]
constantia: geornfulnes, stedefæstnes[210]
dignitas/honestas: gemedemnes, miht, geþungennes[211]
facultas: acumendlicnes[212]
firmitudo/firmitas: trumnes, trymnes[213]
indivisus: untodællic[214]
infinitus/infinitivum: endeleaslic, ungeendigendlic[215]
infortunium: ungewyrd[216]
inpatientia: unþolemodnes[217]

[196] ÆCHom I, 28.408.22, ChronD (Plummer) 1011.
[197] ÆCHom II, 37.314.124.
[198] WHom 7.32, ByrM 1 (Crawford) 198.15
[199] ÆHom 6.247.
[200] ChronE (Plummer) 1086.145.
[201] ÆHom 10.39, WHom 8c.173, ByrM 1 (Crawford) 96.9. See Gneuss, 'The Origin', 80.
[202] ÆHom 18.324, WHom 4.58.
[203] ÆHex 46.
[204] ÆHom 30.41, WHom 12.82.
[205] ÆHom 23.56, WCan 1.1.2 (Fowler) 68, ByrM 1 (Crawford) 170.4.
[206] ÆHom 1.184, WHom 4.62.
[207] A number of these are glosses and therefore must be treated with some caution; see e.g. entries with *clipa* alongside *medecina*, glossing **cataplasma**.
[208] PsGlD (Roeder) 77.25, AntGl 4 (Kindschi) 837.
[209] HomS 1 (VercHom 5) 192, PsCaD (Roeder) 5.19, BoGl (Hale) P.9.54, BoGl P.2.29, ArPrGl 1 (Holt-Campb) 32.14.
[210] ArPrGl 1 (Holt-Campb) 43.13, DurRitGl 1 (Thomp-Lind) 50.13.
[211] DurRitGlCom (Thomp-Lind) 192.19, AldV 1 (Goossens) 1582, HlGl (Oliphant) 3353; cf. *þungennes* BenRW 60.12.
[212] AldV 1 (Goossens) 3285.
[213] LibSc 209.5, ÆHom 5 (MS H) 109, ProgGl 1 (Först) 143; HlGl (Oliphant) 2023 (= **confirmatio**). Cf. CP 247.7 *trumnes* (= **salus**).
[214] AldV 1 (Goossens) 1077.
[215] ÆLS (Auguries) 154, ÆGram (= **infinitivum**) 113.18.
[216] BoGl P.5. 58. Cf. *unsæl*, 'unhappiness' HomU 37 (Nap 46) 121.
[217] ConfGl (Först) 17; cf. ÆLS (Memory of Saints) 334 'Seo feorðe miht is patientia. ðæt is geðyld 7 þolmodnys gecwæden.'

intellectus/intellegentia: ongietnes, understanding[218]
mortalis: beheafodlic, deadbære[219]
musica: sangcræft, soncræft, swinsungcræft[220]
mutabilitas: onwendedlicnes[221]
mutatio/commutatio/inmutatio: awendednes, awending, wandung;[222]
necessitas: neadclamm, neadneod, nearones, niedbehefe, niedbehef(ed)nes, niednes, þearfnes[223]
perfidia: untreowleast, ungetreowþ[224]
perturbatio/conturbatio: drefednes, drefing, styrenes[225]
rogatio/interrogatio/sciscitatio: æsce, befrignung, frasung, smeagung[226]
superfluitas: oferflewednes, oferflowedlicnes, oferflowendnes[227]
tactus: æthrine, grapung, hrepung, gehrine[228]
velocitas: hræding, hrædlicnes, gehwætnes[229]
vitium: wierdnes.[230]

This list does not pretend to be complete: there are many other possible candidates, including poetic compounds, which I have omitted, and doubtless a number which I have overlooked.[231] However, it contains ample material to demonstrate the wealth of choice available to writers of the late Old English period in addition to that provided by King Alfred and his contemporaries.

[218] MkGl (Ru) 12.33, ArPrGl 1 (Holt-Campb) 42.18; cf. GD 256.9 and 139.16 (with *ongietenes* for **cognitio**).

[219] AldV 13.1 (Nap) 4042; AldV 13.1 (Nap) 1872 (usually however = **mortiferus**).

[220] Ald V 1 (Goossens) 3018, AldV 7.1 (Nap) 408, ClGl 1 (Stryker) 295.79.

[221] BoGl (Hale) P.8.36 ('on wendedlicnysse').

[222] PsGlG (Rosier) 76.11, LibScEcc 26.18, ChrodR 1 50.53; cf. ÆCHom II, 12.1.117.272.

[223] PsGlH (Campbell) 106.28, ChrodR 1 50.28, PsGlI (Lindelöf) 106.6, MkGl (Ru) 2.25, LS 8 (Eust) 9, LS 23 (MaryofEgypt) 2.150, BoGl (Hale) P.6.42, PsGlG (Rosier) 30.8, BenRGl 42.6.

[224] HomU 54 (Priebsch) 77, ÆCHom 1, 17 (App) 185.6, ÆHom 14.144, WHom 20.1.64.

[225] PsGlK (Sisam) 30.21, LibSc 28.23, AntGl 2 (Kindschi) 154, DurRitGl 1 (Thomp-Lind) 59.3; cf. *drefnes* HomM 14.2 (Healey) 134.

[226] BenR 56, AldV 1 (Goossens) 2267, AldV 13.1 (Nap) 2309, DurRit Gl 3 (Skeat) 75.

[227] RegCGl 5.61, BenRGl 61.1, ÆCHom II, 12.2.124.494.

[228] AntGl 4. (Kindschi) 971, ArPrGl 1 (Holt-Campb) 38.16, ÆHomM 1 (Bel 9) 255, ÆHom 17.82, AntGl 4 (Kindschi) 971, Alex 800. For GD MS H *æthrine* see D. Yerkes, *The Two Versions of Wærferth's Translation of Gregory's Dialogues: An Old English Thesaurus* (Univ. of Toronto, 1979) item 1461 and above, p. 20.

[229] ÆLS (Mark) 43, WHom 7.50 and 20.3.170, LS 10 (Guth) 105.27, ByrM 1 (Crawford) 118.29.

[230] DurRitGl 1 (Thomp-Lind) 16.13.

[231] A complete study not only must await the publication of the OE Thesaurus but must take into account contexts and non-substantival alternative renderings. Mine has deliberately been centred on texts with identified Latin sources.

1.2 Linguistic gaps

Dr Fischer also identifies a number of Latin abstract nouns used in CPh for which there are no nominal equivalents in Bo. For some of these she supposes that 'a nominal translation must have been possible'[232]—as, for instance, **perfectio**, rendered by *gefremednes* in the Life of St Chad.[233] For others she assumes a 'linguistic gap' in Old English, which is filled by paraphrase or by the use of 'vague' equivalents—as, for instance, **causa**, rendered by *dæl*, and **ratio**, rendered by *spell*.[234] Once again, however, a significant number of the words in Dr Fischer's list are to be found with what might be called reasonably close rendering of one or more of their senses in other OE texts, both early and late, and sometimes indeed in Bo itself. Even the potentially "fillable" 'linguistic gap' that she cites is in fact filled in Bo by a word which is found also in CP and a range of other texts, namely *fulfremednes*.[235] In other instances the semantic richness of the Latin words in her list is such that it would be unreasonable to expect any single vernacular term to cover more than a small portion of their meaning. So, for instance, Lewis and Short include among their definitions of **causa** renderings as various as 'cause, reason, inducement, occasion, opportunity, just cause, faction, pretext, condition, state, relation of friendship, apology, excuse, employment, lawsuit'. For **condicio** they suggest amongst other meanings 'agreement, stipulation, condition, proposition, terms, demand, situation, circumstances, nature, mode, manner, matter, subject, amour'. At the same time there exist a number of other Latin words which share at least part of the meaning of the words in Dr Fischer's list. In all these cases a range of OE words emerges as available to the OE translator. So, for instance, translating **casus** ('a falling, fall, overthrow, error, accident, occurrence, event, chance, mischance, misfortune, opportunity, calamity, grammatical case', etc.) beside the paraphrase 'weas gebyrian' noted by Dr Fischer,[236] we find *fiell* in Be, and *gelimp* in a range of glosses, along with terms such as *ungelimp* and *unwyrd*.[237] The semantic richness of the Latin

[232] Fischer, 'A Comparative Study', 627.

[233] LS 3 (Chad) 54. *Gefremednes*, however, is normally used to render the Latin terms **effectus, perpetratio**, etc.: see e.g. GD 318.15, GD 334.14, Be 32.7.

[234] Fischer, 'A Comparative Study', 628–30.

[235] Bo 84.9–10, 'God is full ælcere fullfremednesse 7 ælces godes 7 ælcere gesælðe' (CPh III, pr. 10.41–2 'boni summi summum deum diximus esse plenissimum'); see also GD 98.4–5, Be 412.19, Mart 130.24, CP 467.21–2, ÆHom 18.120, LibSc 107.8, etc. Cf. *unfulfremednes* PsGlA 138.14(16), CP 467.13, ÆCHom I, 35.530.11; *ungefreming* PsGlK (Sisam) 138.16; *unfulfremming* (= **inperfectum**) PsGlI (Lindelöf) 138.16; and cf. **consummatio**: *geyfyllnes, gefyllednes, gefylling*.

[236] Fischer, 'A Comparative Study', 624. This usage may have been obsolescent: *weas* is otherwise recorded only from ClGl 1 (Stryker) 189.85 and CollGl 12 (Holthausen) 54. See further *Pastoral Care*, ed. Carlson, part 2, p. 91, note to CP 199.22 *weas*, var. *gewealdes*.

[237] See further below, p. 26.

words in question and the number of different spheres of reference involved, each demanding separate investigation, rule out a full discussion of all the possible renderings here or their adequacy. However, as an encouragement to those who might be persuaded to take on such detailed investigations and by way of answer to Dr Fischer's claim of 'genuine linguistic gaps' I list below a selection of the OE nouns that I have found employed as translations for the Latin words in her list, some of them used already in early OE, others first recorded in the later period:[238]

affectus: hyldo, lufu, tosetednes, willa, gewilnung[239]
casus: belimp, gebigednes, casus, fær, fiell, gegang, hryre, gelimp, mislimp, misgelimp, nied, unbelimp, ungelimp, untima, ungetima
causa: inca, intinga, inþing, nied, racu, spræc, þing, wise[240]
conclusio: beclysung, betynung, loc
condicio: arædnes, gecwide, gecynd, dihtnung, ræden, gesceaft, gesceap, wyrd, gewyrd
confusio: bysmer, gedrefednes, gedrefnes, forscendung, forwandung, gemang, gemeng, gemengednes, gemengnes, gemengung, scamu, scamung, scand, scandlicnes, gescendnes, gescendþ[241]
conscientia: ingehygd, ingeþanc, ingeþoht, ingewitnes, gewitnes, gewitscipe, gewitt
disputatio: cneatung, geflit, smeagung, spræc, talu
habitus: gebære, had, onlicnes, gesceap; *beside* gierela, gegierela, hrægl, reaf, ryft, scrud[242]
impunitas: unwitnung
ingenium: andgiet, cræft, gleawnes, ingehygd, ingeþanc, orþanc, orþancscipe, searocræft
intentio: atyhting, geornfulnes, georngewilnung, giemen, ingehygd, onbryrdnes, ontyhting, gerad, tyhting, willa, gewilnung
iustitia: rihtwisnes, soþfæstnes[243]
propositum/propositio: foresetednes, foresetnes, racu

[238] This list would be considerably longer if it were to include not only direct translations but also OE equivalents of individual meanings of the Latin terms—as e.g. *ende* and *geendung* for **conclusio**; *wise* for **conditio**. For caveats see above, p. 25. For details of distribution see the Toronto microfiche concordance.

[239] Cf. CorpGl 2 (Hessels) 1.371 'affectui megsibbe vel dilectione'.

[240] I have omitted from this list paraphrases such as Ps 3.6 'butan gewyrhton' ('sine causa'). For *intinga* see *The Life of St Chad*, ed. R. Vleeskruyer (Amsterdam, 1953), 30–1.

[241] Cf. *hosp* PsGlI (Lindelöf) 43.16.

[242] Cf. *munchad* (var. *munucreaf*) GD 27.17; *woruldhad*: **habitus secularis** Be 332.1, beside *haligryft*: **sanctimonialis** Be 318.8.

[243] Wenisch, *Spezifisch anglisches Wortgut*, 227–8, suggests that the sense 'justice' is restricted to Anglian texts.

qualitas: andefn, hwilcnes, gehwilcnes, gelicnes[244]
ratio:[245] racu, gerad, riht, geriht, rihtnes, rihtwisnes, gescead, sceadwisnes, gesceadwisnes, wisdom,
sensus: andgiet, endebyrdnes, felnes, gefelnes, gehygd, sefa, þoht, gewitt
status: anrædnes, fæstrædnes, had, ontimber, staþol, staþolfæstnes, steall, gesteall, stede, geþyncþo, wunung
substantia: æht, bisen, edwist, feoh, genyhtsumnes, sped, standnis, streon, gestreon, þing.[246]

2. Providentia and Praedestinatio

In Bo, as Dr Fischer points out, the Latin term **providentia** is translated both by *foresceawung* ('*Lehnübersetzung*') and *foreþanc* ('*Lehnübertragung*'), while **praedestinatio** is rendered by *foreteohhung* ('*Lehnübersetzung*'). All three, she claims, are first found in Alfred's Boethius.[247] In fact, as with the bulk of the other 'philosophical' terms used by Alfred, the first two of these words apparently already had some currency in early OE at the time when Alfred was writing. However, before their distribution patterns and history are examined, it is necessary first to consider the contexts in which the various terms are employed in Bo itself.[248]

2.1. **Providentia** ('foresight, foreknowledge; providence; Providence')

In CPh Boethius from time to time employs the term **providentia** in contexts where the translation 'Providence', or 'the deity', might seem appropriate, and indeed in his version Alfred on occasion renders the word by *scieppend* or by *God*.[249] In other contexts one or other of the meanings 'foresight' and 'foreknowledge' (or 'forethought') is indicated. So in a key passage on **providentia** and **fatum** (IV, pr. 6.22–42) Boethius describes providence as the divine reason itself (the manner in which all things behave, 'contemplated in the utter purity of the divine intelligence'), established in the highest ruler of all things, 'the reason which disposes all things that

[244] Cf. *missenlicnes* (for 'dispar qualitas') GD 315.24.

[245] Cf. Fischer, 'A Comparative Study', 628, *ratio*, 'some meanings of'.

[246] Cf. *landar* BenRGl 2.26. Also in Dr Fischer's lists are the words **inlatum**, **musae**, and **res**. Amongst translations of **res** see *þing* GD 16.19 and *wise* Be 80.33. **Musa** is once glossed *landælf* (see ClGl 3 (Quinn) 1451 'Ruricolas musas: landælfe'); cf. *Oreades; wuduælfenne* ClGl 1 (Stryker) 4640.

[247] Fischer, 'A Comparative Study', 635.

[248] Since this paper is concerned with terminology, no attempt is made here to consider Alfred's handling of Boethian concepts. For important discussions of the latter see e.g., Otten, *König Alfreds Boethius*, F. A. Payne, *King Alfred and Boethius* (Madison, Wis. and London, 1968), L. Helbig, *Altenglische Schlusselbegriffe in den Augustinus- und Boethius-Bearbeitungen Alfreds des Grossen* (dissertation, Frankfurt, 1960).

[249] See e.g. Bo 93.20, CPh III, pr. 11.98, and Bo 128.18, CPh IV, pr. 6.35.

exist', and also as the unfolding of temporal order united in the foresight of the divine mind. In another place (V, pr. 2.27–9) Philosophia is made to refer to 'that regard (*intuitus*) of providence which looks forth on all things from eternity' and 'sees'.

The OE compound *foresceawung*, reflecting the 'sight' element of *providentia*, is found only four times in Bo. Two of the occurrences are collocated with the adjective *godcund* and are without equivalent in CPh.[250] The others are both used in the collocation 'Godes foresceawung' to render CPh **providentia**, on the first occasion standing alone: 'sio anfealde foresceawung Godes' (Bo 127.18–19): 'providentiae simplicitate' (CPh IV.6.11); on the second occasion coupled with the alternative rendering *foreþanc*: 'Godes foreþonc 7 his foresceawung' (Bo 128.10–11): 'prouidentia' (CPh IV, pr. 6.28). It is in fact *foreþanc* that is used in the majority of contexts where Alfred is rendering Latin **providentia** in either direct translation or passages of paraphrase, the word occurring eleven times in all, usually in collocation with either *Godes* or *godcund*.[251] However, as a result of rewriting, a significant number of references to 'providence' in CPh have been replaced by references to 'predestination'.

2.2. **Praedestinatio** ('predestination')

In the *De Consolatione* the term **praedestinatio** ('a determining beforehand, predestination') occurs only once, with a single instance of the verb form *praedestinata*. Its Alfredian counterpart, *foreteohhung*, in contrast, is found no fewer than eleven times, usually in one or other of the collocations 'seo godcunde foreteohhung' and 'Godes foreteohhung', paralleling the collocations in which Alfred uses the words *foresceawung* and *foreþanc*.[252] The one exception, 'þære foreteohunga Godes', occurs in the list of chapter headings, which may well not have been compiled by Alfred himself.[253]

So, beside

Forðæm se ðe ymb þæt acsian wile, he sceal ærest witan hwæt sie sio anfealde foresceawung Godes, 7 hwæt wyrd sie, 7 hwæt weas gebergie, 7 hwæt sie godcund andgit 7 godcund foretiohhung, 7 hwæt monna freodom sie. (Bo 127.17–21)

For he who may wish to enquire into it must first know what the single providence of God is, and what Fate is, and what happens by chance, and what divine intelligence

[250] Bo 136.7 and 146.31.

[251] See e.g. Bo 129.2 and 128.20.

[252] See e.g. Bo 143.18 and 142.25.

[253] Bo 6.23–4, relating to ch. xxxix. For a discussion of the authorship of chapter headings in late 9th-cent. texts see D. Whitelock, 'The List of Chapter-Headings in the Old English Bede', *Old English Studies in Honor of John C. Pope*, ed. R. B. Burlin and E. B. Irving, Jr. (Toronto, 1974), 263–84.

and divine predestination are, and what the freedom of men is.

for

In hac enim de providentiae simplicitate, de fati serie, de repentinis casibus, de cognitione ac praedestinatione divina, de arbitrii libertate quaeri solet. (CPh IV, pr. 6.11–13)

For under this head enquiry is made concerning the singleness of providence, the course of fate, the suddenness of chance, the knowledge and predestination of God, and the freedom of the will.

we find passages such as

Swiðe riht is þin lar; ac ic wolde þe nu myndgian þære mænigfealdan lare þe þu me ær gehete be þære Godes foretiohhunge. Ac ic wolde ærest witan æt þe hwæðer þæt auht sie þæt we oft geherað ðæt men cweðað be sumum þingum þæt hit scyle weas gebyrian. (Bo 139.20–4)

Your teaching is very true; but I would now remind you of the manifold doctrine you previously promised me concerning the predetermination of God. But I would like first to know from you whether there is anything in what we often hear that men say about certain things, that it must happen by chance.

corresponding to CPh V, pr. 1.2–7:

'Recta quidem', inquam, 'exhortatio tuaque prorsus auctoritate dignissima, sed quod tu dudum de providentia quaestionem pluribus aliis implicitam esse dixisti, re experior. Quaero enim an esse aliquid omnino et quidnam esse casum arbitrere.'

Your exhortation is right indeed and very worthy of your authority, but what you said just now about providence, that it was a question involving many others, I know from experience. For I want to know whether you think chance is anything at all, and if so, what?

while Bo 142.24–8:

Hwæt is sio micle unrotnes? ða cwæð ic: Hit is ym ða Godes foretiohhunge; forðæm we geherað hwilum secgan þæt hit scyle eall swa geweorðan swa swa God æt fruman getiohhad hæfde, þæt hit ne mæge nan mon onwendan.

What is this great sorrow? Then I said, 'It is about God's predetermination; for we hear it sometimes said that it must all happen just as God had appointed at the beginning, so that no man may change it.'

appears to have been inspired by CPh V, pr. 3.95–100:

cum ex providentia rerum omnis ordo ducatur nihilque consiliis liceat humanis, fit ut vitia quoque nostra ad bonorum omnium referantur auctorem. Igitur nec sperandi aliquid nec deprecandi ulla ratio est. Quid enim vel speret quisque vel etiam deprecetur, quando optanda omnia series indeflexa conectit?

since the whole ordering of things proceeds from providence and nothing is really possible to human intentions, it follows that even our vices are to be referred to the author of all things good. And therefore there is no sense in hoping for anything or in praying that anything may be averted; for what even should any man hope for or pray to be averted when an inflexible course links all that can be desired?

We may compare two other passages, which have no exact equivalent in the Latin:

Ic þonne secge, swa swa ealle cristene men secgað, þæt sio godcunde foretiohhung his walde, næs sio wyrd. (Bo 131.10–12)

I then say, just as all Christian men say, that the divine predetermination rules it, not Fate.

and

Wit sædon ær þæt sio godcunde foretiohhung ælc god worhte 7 nan yfel, ne nan ne tiohhode to wyrcanne, ne næfre ne worhte. (Bo 143.18–20)

We said earlier that the divine predetermination made every good and no evil, and it did not determine to make any, nor did it ever do so.

Dr Fischer is correct in her claim that the term *foretiohhung* is first found in the Boethius. In fact, although the related verb **(ge)teohhian** is of not infrequent occurrence in OE[254] and two instances of an (Anglian?) *foreteon* are recorded, along with a single instance of the noun *geteohhung*,[255] the Toronto microfiche concordance cites *foreteohhung* only from Bo, and it is possible that in the process of thinking through, and in many respects rewriting, Boethius Alfred coined the term to suit his own special needs. However, there was an alternative word of similar meaning, *forestihtung*, which is found in a range of OE texts from GD and Be to LibSc and the

[254] It occurs, for instance, in GD, Be, Bo, Ps, CP, Solil, and Æ. Cf. *geteon* and *foreteon*, which are described as 'probably Anglian' by Jordan, *Eigentümlichkeiten*, 65–6.

[255] Be 138.31, PPs 72.12, HomS 22 (CenDom 1) 69. Cf. HlGl (Oliphant) 3114 *foreteohþad*.

works of Ælfric[256] and which might be supposed to have been known to him.[257] The corresponding verb, *forestihtian*, occurs frequently for **praedestinare**, again in texts from GD to Ælfric.[258]

In contrast to *foreteohhung*, the word *foresceawung* is recorded from a range of texts current at the time when Alfred was translating Boethius, being used also in CP and Be.[259] It occurs also in a number of later works, including those of Ælfric and Byrhtferth, and is found as a translation for **providentia** in glosses.[260] *Foreþanc* is likewise not confined to Bo, though here the only other recorded instances are in Alfred's CP, in a couple of glosses, and in verse.[261]

Alfred, then, may well have innovated in using *foreteohhung* for Boethius' **praedestinatio** and and possibly also *foreþanc* for **providentia**. However, for both of these Latin terms there were rivals already established in the language, namely *forestihtung* and *foresceawung*, while at around the same period the author of the Old English Bede was likewise drawing on native resources to create the word *foreseonnes* as a translation for (*divina*) **provisio**.[262] Interestingly, of all these terms only *foresceawung* seems to have become well established – surviving indeed into the Middle English period.[263] *Forestihtung* certainly spans the early and late Old English periods. However, there is no instance of it recorded in the Middle English Dictionary. *Foreþanc*, as we have seen, is of very limited occurence, while no examples of *foreteohhung* other than those used by Alfred are recorded in the Toronto microfiche.

King Alfred's role in the restoration of learning in the late ninth century was considerable, and his rendering of Boethius' *De Consolatione Philosophiae* continued to be read long after his death.[264] However, as the above survey shows, the contribution of this particular work[265] to Old English vocabulary in respect of the groups of concepts categorized by Dr Fischer as

[256] See e.g. GD 54.19, Be 372.27, ÆHom 11.472, LibScSen (Rhodes) 6.6, AldV 31.1 (Nap) 1489.

[257] For Alfred's use of (*ge*) *teohhian* where the author of the OE Orosius has *gestihtian* see J. M. Bately, 'King Alfred and the OE Translation of Orosius', *Anglia*, 88 (1970), 433–60 at 446–7 and 456–7; cf. also 'Godes gestihtunge' Or 37.4 etc.

[258] See e.g. GD 54.17, LS 13 (Machutus) 1.5; BoGl P.3.8, AldV 1 (Goossens) 855, ÆCHom II, 25.209.107.

[259] See e.g. Be 292.4, GD 214.4, CP 169.6.

[260] See e.g. ÆCHom II, 36.1.269.53, ByrM 1 (Crawford) 82.27; SedGl 3 (Meritt) 19.

[261] See e.g. AldV 7.1 (Nap) 344, AldV 9 (Nap) 355, Beo 1060, El 356, Az 19.

[262] See e.g. Be 284.8.

[263] See e.g. Cursor Mundi 5745.

[264] B. S. Donaghey, 'Nicholas Trevet's Use of King Alfred's Translation of Boethius, and the Dating of his Commentary', *The Medieval Boethius: Studies in the Vernacular Translations of De Consolatione Philosophiae*, ed. A. J. Minnis (Cambridge, 1987), 1–31.

[265] As this study has shown, a number of the words discussed above occurred in CP, probably Alfred's first translation.

'philosophical' appears to have been surprisingly slight. A range of vernacular terms for these concepts was already in circulation by the end of the ninth century and some of these outlived Alfred's own apparently original creations. Not the least significant conclusions to be drawn from this study[266] are, first, that at the time when the king was writing of a serious decline in learning south of the Humber, he himself was part of a group possessed of a vocabulary capable of expressing a wide range of abstract and learned concepts, and, second, that the effects of the intellectual vigour fostered by the king at the end of the ninth century were to continue into the tenth.

[266] A further study, this time of words for 'philosopher', 'philosophy', etc., is in progress.

Some Reflections on the Metre of Christ III

JANE ROBERTS

> It is a feature of the work of Anglo-Saxon metrists that their various findings cannot be reconciled.
>
> E. G. Stanley[1]

Some time ago Eric Stanley drew together all the A3 verses of *Beowulf*, thus providing a valuable tool for the understanding of the poem's metre. In this article I should like to begin by using his tool in an investigation of the comparable verses of a much shorter poem, *Christ III*. Like Stanley's, my corpus depends upon a conservative estimate, more conservative than Alan Bliss's would have been,[2] and certainly far smaller than a selection made according to the criteria put forward more recently by Kendall.[3] There is a virtue in holding to old conventions, if the resulting data allow interesting comparisons to be drawn. Although *Christ III* is approximately a quarter the length of *Beowulf*, it yields some 100 comparable verses, rather more than might be expected by comparison with their distribution in the longer poem. The meat of this paper lies, therefore, in the presentation of the A3 half-lines of *Christ III* (Table 1), and I hope Eric Stanley will approve of the use made of his methodology. Discussion of certain interesting features thrown up by the analysis of A3 half-lines leads into examination of anacrusis in *Christ III*, a topic that has drawn some attention within the context of the examination of Old English hypermetric verses.[4] By drawing together

[1] E. G. Stanley, 'Some Observations on the A3 lines in *Beowulf*', *Old English Studies in Honour of John C. Pope*, ed. R. B. Burlin and E. B. Irving, Jr. (Toronto, 1974), 139–64, at 139.

[2] See ibid. 139–40.

[3] C. B. Kendall, 'The Metrical Grammar of *Beowulf*: Displacement', *Speculum*, 58 (1983), 1–30: esp. p. 8; *idem*, *The Metrical Grammar of 'Beowulf'*, Cambridge Studies in Anglo-Saxon England, 5 (Cambridge, 1991). Contrast the stance taken up by S. Cosmos, 'Kuhn's Law and the Unstressed Verbs in *Beowulf*', *Texas Studies in Literature and Language*, 18 (1976–7), 325, who argues that 'the *Beowulf* poet's use of language is better described in terms of the utterance dimension than in terms of grammatical classes'.

[4] E. Clemons Kyte, 'On the Composition of Hypermetric Verses in Old English', *Modern Philology*, 71 (1973–4), 160–5; see also R. Willard and E. D. Clemons, 'Bliss's Light Verses in the *Beowulf*', *Journal of English and Germanic Philology*, 66 (1967), 230–44.

the examples of anacrusis to be found in *Christ III* and placing them in a wider context within the poem I wish to illustrate some of the poem's more unusual features.

In my examination of the poem's A3 verses I have chosen to address the same questions put by Stanley.[5] I therefore follow his lay-out in presenting my smaller corpus. There are accordingly two main divisions: B, verses where the stress falls on a verb, and A, those where it does not; and within these divisions an order similar to Stanley's is observed. In each of divisions A and B the verses are presented according to their openings. First come connectives and then pronouns, except for those subject pronouns which immediately precede their verb. These are to be found arrayed under those verses whose onset otherwise begins with a verb. Where Stanley indicates the metrical weight of the stressed part of each verse and the presence of any unstressed prefix before the stressed form, I append a categorization that makes clear the number of unstressed lead-in syllables, information of use in drawing comparisons.[6] It should be noted that *Christ III* contains five verses that end either in a stressed monosyllable or with a short open syllable.[7] I have not excluded these verses as anomalous, and they can be recognized easily in Table 1, either through the identification of verse endings or through the appended metrical categorization. As well, I have included a half-line that ends in two monosyllables,[8] because, although such verses are unparalleled in *Beowulf*, they are to be found elsewhere.[9] Brief notes follow as to possibilities of cross or transverse alliteration.[10] Each verse is cited in the form found in the Anglo-Saxon Poetic Records text,[11] and is preceded and followed by brackets within which are to be found any marks of punctuation used in that edition.

[5] Stanley, 'Some Observations', 140–1.

[6] Here the metrical notation developed by A. J. Bliss, *The Metre of 'Beowulf'* (Oxford 1958, 2nd edn. 1967), is used. Thus, A3 is represented by a1x, where x indicates the number of syllables before the stress; where 2 follows a, secondary stress may be present.

[7] They are: *þurh ealle list* 1318a, *Hwæt, ic þec mon* 1379a, *þæt ic þurh þa* 1430a, *Ic onfeng þin sar* 1460a, and *þæt ic þe for lufan* 1470a. These are represented by e1x.

[8] It is: *ðonne eall þreo* 964a. Any verse categorized a2 normally ends with a compound: compare P. J. Lucas, 'Some Aspects of the Interaction between Verse Grammar and Metre in Old English Poetry', *Studia Neophilologica*, 59 (1987), 161–2 and n. 107.

[9] Compare e.g. *Exodus* 63a *Heht þa ymb twa niht*, *Soul and Body II* 82a *Þonne þu for unc bu*, and see further J. Roberts, 'A Metrical Examination of the Poems *Guthlac A* and *Guthlac B*', *Proceedings of the Royal Irish Academy*, 71. C (1971), 116 and n. 117.

[10] The abbreviations used in Stanley, 'Some Observations', are: allit. = alliteration, with the various types cr. = crossed, d. = double and tr. = transverse: ? or even ?? indicates doubt; n.p. = new paragraph. I also follow his presentation of editorial punctuation to either side of the verses, because this makes clear their typically clause-initial nature. Note also hyp. for hypermetric.

[11] G. P. Krapp and E. Van K. Dobbie, *The Exeter Book*, Anglo-Saxon Poetic Records, 3 (New York, 1936). Other verse citations are also to the ASPR texts.

TABLE I *List of A3 Lines in* Christ III

A. The stress falls on a noun, adjective, adverb, numeral, or 'heavy' pronoun:

The first element is (or contains) a connective (other than a negative or relative pronoun)

ac

(,) ac fore þam mæstan ( ) 963a / x [aɪd]

for hwon

(.) For hwon ahenge þu mec hefgor ( ) 1487a / x [aɪg]

for þon

(.) Forþon nis ænig wundor ( ) 1015a / x [aɪe]
(;) forþon þær to teonum ( ) 1214a / x [aɪd]

nu

(. n.p.) Nu we sceolon georne ( ) 1327a / x [aɪd][12]

ond

(,) ond on þone eadgan ( ) 1122a / x [aɪd]
(,) ond ymb his heafod ( ) 1125a / x [aɪc]
(;) ond be hyra weorcum ( ) 1289a / x [aɪd]
(;) ond þa þe on sare ( ) 1355a / x [aɪd]
( ) ond þe on þam eallum ( ) 1400a / x [aɪd]
(,) ond þe mine deaðe ( ) 1462a / x [aɪd]

swa

(?) Swa þam bið grorne ( ) 1204a / x [aɪc]

þa

(,) þa hyra scyppend ( ) 1131a / x [aɪc]
( ) þa þe heo ær fæste ( ) 1157a / x [aɪd] tr. allit. *h*eo??
(.) Þa ic ðe swa scienne ( ) 1386a / x [aɪd]
(,) ða ic þe on þa fægran ( ) 1389a / x [aɪe ~ dɪe][13]
(,) ða þu of þan gefean ( ) 1403a x / x [aɪe ~ eɪe][14]
(.) Þa ðu þæs ealles ( ) 1497a / x [aɪc] tr. allit. *Þ*a or *ð*u??

þær

(,) þær hy hit to gode ( ) 1106a / x [aɪd]
(,) þær bið on eadgum ( ) 1234a / x [aɪc]

[12] This verse opens a new fitt. Compare the opening of the poem, *Đonne mid fere* 867, and *Næs me for mode* 1428.

[13] With decontraction this verse could be scanned as a Sievers C type, i.e. Bliss d type.

[14] Line 1403a is among those verses examined by A. Crandell Amos, *Linguistic Means of Determining the Dates of Old English Literary Texts* (Cambridge, Mass., 1980), 58.

(.) Þær he fore englum ( ) 1336a / x [aɪd] cr. allit. *f*ore?? tr. ~ *þ*ær??
(,) þær þu hit wolde sylfa ( ) 1494a / x [aɪe] tr. allit. *h*it??
(.) Đær sceolan þeofas ( ) 1609a / x [aɪc]
(,) þær is seo dyre ( ) 1650a / x [aɪc]

þæt
( ) þæt hy fore leodum ( ) 1238a / x [aɪd]
(,) þæt hy þurh miltse ( ) 1254a / x [aɪc]
(,) þæt he mæge fore eagum ( ) 1323a / x [aɪc]
(,) þæt ic þurh þa ( ) 1430a / x [eɪc] d. allit. *þ*æt or *þ*urh??
( ) þæt þu moste gesælig ( ) 1460b x / x [aɪe][15] cr. allit. *þ*æt or *þ*u??

þonne
(. n.p.) Đonne mid fere ( ) 867a / x [aɪc][16]
(.) Þonne weorþeð sunne ( ) 934a / x [aɪd] tr. allit. *w*eorþeð??
(.) Þonne bið untweo ( ) 960a /' \ [a2c]
(,) ðonne eall þreo ( ) 964a / \ [a2c]
( ) þonne hit ænig on mode ( ) 989a / x [aɪf] tr. allit. *þ*onne??
(.) Đonne beoð bealde ( ) 1076a / x [aɪc] d. allit. *b*eoð??
(,) ðonne sio reade ( ) 1101a / x [aɪc]
(.) Đonne bið þridde ( ) 1247a / x [aɪc] tr. allit. *b*ið??
(.) Đonne hi þy geornor ( ) 1255a / x [aɪd] tr. allit. *Đ*onne or *þ*y??
(. n.p.) Đonne bið þam oþrum ( ) 1262a / x [aɪd]
(.) Þonne is him oþer ( ) 1272a / x [aɪd]
(.) Đonne bið þæt þridde ( ) 1284a / x [aɪd]
(." n.p.) Đonne þær ofer ealle ( ) 1515a / x [aɪe]
(. n.p.) Þonne þa gecorenan ( ) 1634a x /‿x x [aɪd]

The first element is a negative

nales
(,) nales fore lytlum (,) 962a / x [aɪd]

The first element is a pronoun

Relative or demonstrative pronouns
( ) þæs þe he on foldan ( ) 1033a / x [aɪd]
(.) Þæt þeah to teonum ( ) 1090a / x [aɪc]
( ) þæt ær ðam halgan ( ) 1135a / x [aɪc]
( ) þa þe heo ær fæste ( ) 1157a / x [aɪd] tr. allit. *h*eo??
( ) þæt ic þe for lufan ( ) 1470a /‿x [eɪd]

[15] All verses in Table 1, apart from this, are a-verses. This half-line is discussed below.

[16] This is the opening of the poem. In the manuscript the first line of script is filled with capitals, except for the last letters *fold*, which begin the next verse.

( ) þam þe him on gæstum ( ) 1590a / x [a1d] tr. allit. *h*im??
(.) Ðæt is se eþel ( ) 1639a / x [a1c]

'Heavier' (object) pronoun

(.) Eall þis magon him sylfe ( ) 1115a / x [a1e] tr. allit. *þ*is??
(,) eall æfter ryhte ( ) 1220a / x [a1c]
(,) hwæt him se waldend ( ) 1601a / x [a1c] tr. allit. *s*e??

Personal pronouns (other than subject personal pronouns immediately preceding their verb)

—[17]

The first element is an interjection

(: ") Hwæt, ic þec mon ( ) 1379a / [e1c] tr. allit. *H*wæt??

The first element is a verb (*or a verb preceded by a negative or a subject personal pronoun*)

(,) geseoð him to bealwe ( ) 1105a / x [a1d] cr. allit. *h*im??
(.) Geseoð hi þa betran ( ) 1291a / x [a1d]
(.) Wære him þonne betre ( ) 1301a / x [a1e] cr. allit. *h*im??
(,) hateð hy gesunde ( ) 1341a x / x [a1c]
(." n.p.) Onginneð þonne to þam yflum ( ) 1362a / x [a1g] d. allit. *O*n-??
(.) Bið þær seo miccle ( ) 1370a / x [a1c]
(.) Geseoð nu þa feorhdolg ( ) 1454a / \ [a2d]
(?) Wurde þu þæs gewitleas ( ) 1472a / x \ [a2e] cr. allit. *þ*u or *þ*æs??
(: ") Farað nu, awyrgde(,) 1519a x / x [a1d] [d. ~ *W*urde??

With initial negative

(.) Ne bið him to are ( ) 1083a / x [a1d]
(;) ne bið him hyre yrmðu ( ) 1292a / x [a1e]
(.) Ne þurfon hi þonne to meotude ( ) 1365a / x x [a1g]
(. n.p.) Næs me for mode (,) 1428a / x [a1c][18] d. allit. *m*e??
(.) Ne bið þær ængum godum ( ) 1575a / x [a1e]

Verb preceded by subject personal pronoun

(. n.p.) He bið þam godum ( ) 910a / x [a1c]
(.) He bið þam yflum ( ) 918a / x [a1c]
(!) Ic onfeng þin sar ( ) 1460a / [e1d] cr. allit. *þ*in??

Verb precedes main clause occupying only part of half-line

—

[17] It is curious that none of these verses begins in this way: Stanley 'Some Observations', 152, cites 11 verses from *Beowulf*, e.g. *Ic þē þā fǣhðe* 1380. When some other element opens the clause, the subject pronoun may be separated from its verb: e.g. lines 1106, 1238, 1254, 1255, 1336, 1386, 1389, 1403, 1430, 1470, 1497.

[18] This verse opens a new fitt; compare n. 12.

The first element is a preposition at the head of a noun phrase[19]

( ) mid þy mæstan ( ) 1008a _/_ x [a1b] tr. allit. *þy*??
( ) of þam eðle ( ) 1075a _/_ x [a1b] cr. allit. *þam* d. allit. *of*??
(,) mid þy weorðe (,) 1097a _/_ x [a1b] cr. allit. *þy*??
( ) of hyra æþelum ( ) 1184a _/_x x [a1c] d. allit. *of*??
( ) mid hu micle elne ( ) 1317a _/_ x [a1d]
( ) þurh ealle list ( ) 1318a _/_ [e1c]
( ) ymb min heafod ( ) 1444a _/_ x [a1b]
( ) of minre sidan ( ) 1448a _/_ x [a1c]
( ) on minum folmum ( ) 1455a _/_ x [a1c] cr. allit. *on*??
( ) on minre sidan ( ) 1458a _/_ x [a1c]
( ) of þam æhtum ( ) 1501a _/_ x [a1b] d. allit. *of*??

The first element in the noun phrase is eall

( ) eallum þam gesælgum ( ) 1651a x _/_ x [a1d]

B. The stress falls on a verb:

THE STRESSED VERB IS AN INFINITIVE OR A PAST PARTICIPLE

Without preceding finite verb

—[20]

With preceding finite verb

The first element is a connective

swa

(.) Swa sceal gewrixled ( ) 1260a x _/_ x [a1c]

þa

(.) Ða mec ongon hreowan ( ) 1414a _/_ x [a1d] cr. allit. *Ða* or *mec*??
(.) Ða ic wæs ahongen ( ) 1446a x _/_ x [a1d]

þæt

( ) þæt ðu mostes wealdan ( ) 1388a _/_ x [a1d]
(,) ðæt sceolon fyllan ( ) 1605a _/_ x [a1c]

þonne

(. n.p.) Ðonne biþ geyced ( ) 1039a x _/_ x [a1c]
(.) Ðonne beoð gesomnad ( ) 1221a _/_ x [a1d] cr. allit. *Ðonne*??

[19] This entry does not occur in Stanley ('Some Observations'), who places two examples of *Æfter þæm wordum* (1492, 1669), both sentence-initial and following immediately after the end of a speech, under his first heading in Group A.

[20] It might be possible to place here ( ) *to geseonne* (,) 919a x _/_ x [dib ~ aib], without assumed decontraction (compare Amos, *Linguistic Means*, 58).

The first element is a pronoun

(. n.p.) Þæt we magon eahtan ( ) 1549a _/_ x [aɪd]

The first element is a finite verb

(,) hateð arisan ( ) 1024a x _/_ x [aɪc]

(,) hateð him gewitan ( ) 1227a x _/_ x [aɪd] tr. allit. *h*ateð??

(!" n.p.) Ne magon hi þonne gehynan ( ) 1524a x _/_ x [aɪg] d. allit. *h*i??

THE STRESS FALLS ON A FINITE VERB

The first element is a connective (*other than a negative or a relative pronoun*)

forþon

(,) forþon þe he wolde ( ) 1202a _/_ x [aɪd]

ond

(,) ond þu meahte ( ) 1431a _/_ x [aɪb]

swylce

(.) Swylce hi me geblendon ( ) 1437a x _/_ x [aɪe]

þa

(,) ða þe her forhogdun ( ) 1633a x _/_ x [aɪd]

þæt

(,)þæt he hy generede ( ) 1257a x _/̮_xx [aɪd]

(,) þæt he ne forleose ( ) 1585a x _/_ x [aɪd] cr. allit. *þ*æt??

þonne

(,) þonne ge hyra hulpon ( ) 1353a _/_ x [aɪe] d. allit. *h*yra??

The first element is a pronoun

Relative pronoun

(,) se þe nu ne giemeð ( ) 1552a _/_ x [aɪd] tr. allit. *se??*

'Heavier' subject pronoun

( ) hwa hine gesette ( ) 1164a x _/_ x [aɪd]

The first element is a preposition followed by a (*relative*) *pronoun*

(.) Of þam him aweaxeð ( ) 1252a x _/_ x [aɪd]

The last few years have seen a flurry of new metrical investigations of *Beowulf*, adding ever to one's sense of alarm as the hope for significant comparative work between texts continually slips further and further into the distant future. The notion that a metrical grammar underpins each poet's work, interdependent with and complementary to a typology of metrical patterns, has gained prominence, especially now with the publication of Kendall's monograph.[21] The mainspring of Kendall's system is, he tells us, based in his elucidation of Kuhn's *Satzpartikelgesetz*, in which his interpretation of the A3 verses of *Beowulf* plays a central role. Kendall claims that 'A significant and largely unnoticed feature of this type is that it is exclusively clause-initial'.[22] This, he points out in a footnote, is something that Pope comes close to seeing.[23] It is a possibility seen also by Eric Stanley in his investigation of the A3 lines of *Beowulf*: 'I found that, like Willard and Clemons, I was inclined to the view that A3 lines commonly begin the sentence, that being a corollary of Kuhn's *Satzpartikelgesetz* and his *Satzspitzengesetz*.'[24] But Stanley draws back from the generalization that A3 verses are by nature sentence-initial, observing that they also frequently begin relative clauses and doubting if anything can be added 'to Professor Pope's cautious statement "that type A3 is employed very frequently as a light introduction to the weighty verses that follow"'.[25] Stanley does not therefore have any need to single out for further discussion those clause openings in *Beowulf* headed by the connective *æfter*:

(!' n.p.) Æfter þǣm wordum ( ) 1492

(.' n.p.) Æfter ðām wordum ( ) 2669

These verses have, within the newer approaches of 'metrical grammar', lent themselves to interpretation as incorporating a resumptive use of the demonstrative, by way of explanation of their offence, through lack of a sentence particle in the initial dip, against Kuhn's second law.[26] Because Stanley's examination of the A3 verses of *Beowulf* is a scrupulous presentation of many contributory pieces of evidence, it enables the reader to see how the verses fit into their syntactic contexts. Essentially, therefore, Stanley presents the evidence that A3 verses appear typically in the clause-initial position. Kendall does point to the occurrence of similar prepositional phrases not in clause-initial position elsewhere in Old English poetry, in *The Panther* 44 *Æfter þære stefne*, 54 *æfter þære stefne* and *Genesis A* 1043 *æfter þære synne*, arguing that the 'weakening of the relative function [of the demonstrative] may have contributed to the use of type A3 with this syn-

[21] Lucas, 'Some Aspects', 169 n. 16, regards Kendall's term metrical grammar as 'misplaced, as the grammar applies to verse not metre: the verse is metrical but the grammar is not'.

[22] Kendall, *Metrical Grammar*, 34.

[23] Ibid., n. 14.

[24] Stanley, 'Some Observations', 144.

[25] Ibid. 144–5.

[26] Such clause-initial verses accord with the observation made by Alistair Campbell, 'Verse Influences in Old English Prose', in *Philological Essays: Studies in Old and Middle English Language and Literature in Honour of Herbert Dean Meritt*, ed. J. L. Rosier (The Hague, 1970), 93–7, at 94, who notes that exceptions 'are almost all with forms of *se*'.

tactical pattern in non-initial position'.[27] At the end of my Table 1, A, eleven comparable phrases are listed, opening variously with *mid*, *of*, *on*, *þurh* and *ymb*, and these are followed by a dative noun phrase which has the adjective *eall* in the predeterminer position:

( ) eallum þam gesælgum ( ) 1651.

One inference to be drawn is that *Christ III* yields good evidence of similar structures with prepositions other than *æfter*; another is that non-initial A3 verses may be a good indicator of different traditions within the wider corpus of Old English poetry. Differing practice is certainly to be seen in the two poems that directly follow *Christ III* in the Exeter Book. *Guthlac A*, a poem in which the pattern a1 (Sievers A3) is relatively frequent and in which there are four examples of the pattern e1 (Sievers A3 with exceptional stressed open short syllable or Sievers B3),[28] has four instances of non-initial prepositional noun phrases;[29] *Guthlac B*, where the A3 type is considerably less frequent, has none.[30] Both Guthlac poems have verses in which the adjective *eal* stands in the predeterminer position.[31] It is worth note that a short initial dip in these verses may tend to correlate with the lack of a sentence particle. At any rate this curious group of A3 verses contradicts Bliss's generalization on the A3 type in *Beowulf*: 'what the verse lacks in stress it makes up in length.'[32] The generalization may prove less appropriate to a wider range of Old English poetry.

The half-lines presented in Table 1 are not all, however, lacking in length of introductory dip. Whereas in *Beowulf* and the Guthlac poems six introductory syllables constitute the largest introductory dips in such verses, seven syllables are found in four *Christ III* verses:

Onginneð þonne to þam yflum 1362a

Ne þurfon hi þonne to meotude 1365a

For hwon ahenge þu mec hefgor 1487a

Ne magon hi þonne gehynan 1524a

For the second of these there is no alternative scansion which would make

[27] Kendall, *Metrical Grammar*, 82.

[28] *Guthlac A: ge her ateoð* 301a, *No hy hine to deaðe* (MS *deað*) 549a, *Woldun hy geteon* 574a and *þæs þe ge him to dare* 700a. Compare the *Christ III* verses cited in n. 7.

[29] *Guthlac A: to þisse worulde* 47a, *ofer þa niþas* 49a, *from þisum earde* 256a, *on þære socne* 716a.

[30] A possible example, *Guthlac B* 1018a *on þisse nyhstan*, is to be read d1c (Sievers C) with decontraction. For *Guthlac B* 892a *ealra þara wundra* see the next n.

[31] *Guthlac A: ealra þara bisena* 528a, *ealra þara giefena* 606a; *Guthlac B: ealra þara wundra* 892a.

[32] Bliss, *Metre of 'Beowulf'*, 62.

possible the treatment of all as a1g (Sievers A3), and their absence from his hypermetric tables indicates that Bliss must have read them in this way.[33] Were it not for the evidence of 1365a, the others might be categorized as extended. In the case of 1487a triple alliteration might even be argued, with stress given also to *hwon*—such alliteration would not be excessive in a Middle English poem.[34] Yet, the recognition of stress additional to that on the penultimate syllable, except for 1362a, brings problems in respect of Kuhn's law of sentence particles. Here indeed it would be convenient to regard the alliteration of the verbs in 1362a and 1487a as 'ornamental'[35] or 'extra-metrical',[36] if the evidence of 1365a did not tilt the balance towards their alliteration being accidental, except in the case of 1487a. Whereas in the other three verses the finite verbs are to be taken with a following infinitive, *ahenge* 1487a is the full lexical verb of its clause.[37] Moreover, in the case of 1487a, consideration of the verse's immediate context supports a hypermetric reading:

For hwon ahenge þu mec hefgor   on þinra honda rode
þonne iu hongade?   Hwæt, me þeos heardra þynceð!
Nu is swærra mid mec   þinra synna rod
þe ic unwillum   on beom gefæstnad,
þonne seo oþer wæs   þe ic ær gestag,
willum minum,   þa mec þin wea swiþast
æt heortan gehreaw,   þa ic þec from helle ateah,
þær þu hit wolde sylfa   siþþan gehealdan.
Ic wæs on worulde wædla   þæt ðu wurde welig in heofonum,
earm ic wæs on eðle þinum   þæt ðu wurde eadig on minum.
Þa ðu þæs ealles   ænigne þonc
þinum nergende   nysses on mode.

(1487–98)

The movement here is between lines that can—just about—be regarded as 'normal' and substantially longer lines, that is between lines that are quieter, reflective rather,[38] and lines emotively charged. The strategy is used elsewhere by this poet. No matter which syllables a modern reader chooses to stress in lines 1495–6, he will sense their difference not just because of length but also because of the antithetical joining of verses within each line and because

[33] Ibid. 160.

[34] See J. C. Pope, *The Rhythm of 'Beowulf'*, (2nd edn., New Haven, Conn. and London, 1966), 101, where this half-line is included in the summary of the hypermetric verses of *Christ III*.

[35] The point of view held by Kendall, 'Displacement': see e.g. p. 15.

[36] This is the term used by Kendall, *Metrical Grammar*: see e.g. p. 33.

[37] See Cosmos, 'Kuhn's Law', 308, for discussion of lexical and nonlexical finite verbs.

[38] Compare A. S. Cook, *The Christ of Cynewulf* (Boston, 1900), p. xlv, who complains that 'there is somewhat too much pausing for reflection'.

of end-verse decoration. Tail-rhyme holds together 1495b and the two parts of 1496, and the semantically contrasting verses of 1496 are linked by full rhyme. The effect is incantatory, and must owe something to a repetition of half-lines that are structurally alike. Such tricks are unlike anything found in *Beowulf*, the usual yardstick for Old English poetic form.[39] What is less obvious, the 'normal' half-lines, although metrically more amenable, themselves contain features that indicate that *Christ III* is very different, both from *Beowulf*, and from the Cynewulfian poems with which it is generally grouped. Where *Christ III* follows a poem that actually contains a runic Cynewulf signature, it is itself followed by *Guthlac A*, a poem that precedes a fragmentary poem once held to have lost just such a signature. Both *Christ III* and *Guthlac A* have had, undeservedly, almost more attention for their possible place within some larger authorial structure than for their own attractions. Yet Geoffrey Shepherd writes of *Christ III*: 'This is one of the most astonishing, powerful and neglected of English poems. It exhibits a mastery of the cosmic sublime rarely attempted in English and never, even by Milton, more successfully.'[40] Part of the poem's power obviously lies in the use made of hypermetric lines. Where in *The Dream of the Rood* lengthened lines reinforce the awe and terror of the cross and of the dreamer, here clusters of them place emphasis particularly on *þam worde þe se wealdend cwyð*.[41]

By comparison with such poems as *Beowulf* or *Exodus* these lines are distinctive for their lack of poetic compounds. Even the one instance of a Sievers E type, a measure that typically contains compounds, is supplied by the simple noun phrase *ænigne þonc* 1497b. Yet *Christ III* is not without compounds. Some of them, for example *tirmeahtig* 1165 or *heafodgimmum* 1330, are forms unlikely to be found in prose, and in others a small repertoire of limiting elements is effectively used over and over again, for example *firen-*, *heofon-*, *mægen-*, *man-*, *synn-*, *wom-*, *woruld-*, *wuldor-*. Far more striking than the compounds, however, is the great use made of adjectives. The apocalyptic fire that so dominates the poem's opening two divisions appears first in the phrase *wælmfyra mæst* 931, and four other compounds focus upon aspects of its advance: *Teonleg* 968, *deaðleg* 982, *fyrbaðe* 985, and *legbryne* 1001. Variation is also provided by phrases: with strong adjective (including present participle)—*cwelmende fyr* 958, *hiþende leg* 973, *widmære blæst* 975, *weallende wiga* 984; with weak adjectives—*hata leg* 932, *fyrswearta leg* 983, *swearta leg* 994; with a characterizing genitive—*fyres egsan* 974, *ældes*

[39] Contrast the effects found by Kendall, *Metrical Grammar*, 8–9, in the closing lines of *Beowulf*.

[40] G. Shepherd, 'Scriptural Poetry', in *Continuations and Beginnings*, ed. E. G. Stanley (London, 1966), 1–36, at 20.

[41] *The Dream of the Rood*, line 111.

leoma 1005, and, with adjective as well, *won fyres wælm* 965; with article—*se gifra gæst* 972, *þæt fyr* 1002, *þæt hate fyr* 1062. Even without citing the other simple nouns and adjectives used to describe the judgement fire in these two divisions of the poem, it is evident that phrases can assume greater prominence than compounds in *Christ III*.[42] The personification of the fire, implicit perhaps in the biblical-inspired description *se gifra gæst*, is brought into focus by the use of *wiga* 984. Overall these are the phrases of heightened homiletic prose, except that they are somewhat lacking in articles for that genre, and the assumption that they owe much to Latin homily is reinforced by the simile *byrneþ wæter swa weax* 988.[43]

It has often been argued that the facility to coin and manipulate compounds disappeared gradually from Old English poetry, but I would suggest that the evidence is hardly clear-cut, especially once the possibility of exercising stylistic choice is considered. It is possible that a poet choosing to move freely in and out of extended lines may well have been working in a style that itself depends less upon metaphorical compounds. There are not, after all, many poetic compounds to be found generally in hypermetric lines. It is curious that, among the longer Old English poems, *Christ III* and *Guthlac A* should stand together not only physically in their manuscript but also stylistically in their relatively restrained diction, akin rather to the prose of the Vercelli and Blickling homilies than to the intricate complexities of more generally admired poems. Sometimes an Old Saxon connection has been advanced for *Christ III* but, as Stanley has shown, it lacks the evidence of 'the *widespread* Old Saxonisms of *Genesis B*' that had allowed Sievers to argue, before proof was found, that *Genesis B* is a translation from Old Saxon.[44] Coincidentally, for Stanley *Christ III*, like *Guthlac A*, admits some four or five prosaic words.[45] At various times editors have tried to emend away three of these.[46]

[42] P. Bethel, 'Regnal and Divine Epithets in the Metrical Psalms and *Metres of Boethius*', *Parergon*, NS 9 (1991), 13, points out that in Old English verse generally 'the use of the construction of noun and characterizing adjective is far more restricted than that of *kenning* or *heiti*'.

[43] An analysis of the homiletic materials that are thought to lie behind *Christ III* is presented by F. M. Biggs, 'The Sources of *Christ III*: A Revision of Cook's Notes', *Old English Newsletter*, Subsidia 12 (1986). For the suggestion made by R. M. Trask ('*The Last Judgment* of the Exeter Book: A Critical Edition', Diss., Univ. of Illinois at Urbana-Champaign, 1972) that this simile may be adapted from PsG 96.5 *montes sicut cera fluxerunt a facie Domini* see Biggs, 'Sources of *Christ III*', 15; and for Is 4.4 behind *gæst* see p. 14.

[44] E. G. Stanley, 'The Difficulty of Establishing Borrowings between Old English and the Continental West Germanic Languages', *An Historic Tongue: Studies in English Linguistics in Memory of Barbara Strang*, ed. G. Nixon and J. Honey (London and New York, 1988), 11–12.

[45] E. G. Stanley, 'Studies in the Prosaic Vocabulary of Old English Verse', *Neuphilologische Mitteilungen*, 72 (1971), 389. (One of these, *forcuð*, should be assigned to *Christ I*.)

[46] See ibid.: *gemonian* 1100 (MS *genomian*), p. 396; *scendeð* 1548, p. 412; and *þwean* 1320, p. 415. Stanley also points out, p. 417, that *onwalg* 1420 occurs in poetry only in *Christ III*.

An infringement of Kuhn's law of sentence particles arises if the finite verb of 1490b is placed in its first dip. Two expedients are possible. Either a compound verb *onwesan* can be posited, with an unattractive 'crib' English look to it,[47] or the half-line can be added to *Christ III*'s already large group of 'heavy' verses.[48] If the latter course is pursued, structurally 1490b is comparable with such a verse as *cild geong on cribbe* 1425.[49] Proportionately, however, the number of heavy verses in *Christ III* resembles *Guthlac B* rather than *Guthlac A*, a distribution that suggests the use of such verses was due to stylistic choice. Their staccato effect is a pronounced feature of *Christ III*, and it seems likely therefore that those half-lines in which the initial verb's alliteration has sometimes been held to be accidental (or ornamental or extrametrical) should be scanned in the same way, for example:

Dyneð deop gesceaft 930a

Hlemmeð hata leg 932a

Seoþeð swearta leg 994a.[50]

Heavy verses are usually reconciled to those two-stress patterns which can have secondary stress, that is to D, E, and some A patterns, but they should be separately indexed to allow comparison among poems. If these verses are taken together with the general run of D and E types they may give an

[47] The status of *on* here is prepositional. Compare *Elene: þe us fore wæron* 637. Such compound verbs as *ætbēon* and *forebēon* seem generally to translate Latin closely, but *on* is well attested with forms of the verb 'to be' in a wide range of prose texts.

[48] Roberts, 'Metrical Examination', 113–14, notes the differing proportions of heavy verses found in the Guthlac poems. Identifiable as possibly heavy in *Christ III* are: *somod up cymeð* 875a, *Dyneð deop gesceaft* 930a, *Hlemmeð hata leg* 932a, *cyn, cearena full* 961a, *won fyres wælm* 965a, *þreo eal on an* 969b, *brecað brade gesceaft* 991a, *Seoþeð swearta leg* 994a, *gehreow ond hlud wop* 998a, *earmlic ælda gedreag* 999a, *eadig engla gedryht* 1013a, *folc anra gehwylc* 1025b, *bringan beorhtne wlite* 1058a, *berað breosta hord* 1072a, *hu tu ætsomne* 1112b, *ufan eall forbærst* 1137a, *sylf slat on tu* 1140a, *cyðde cræftes meaht* 1145a, *heofon hluttre ongeat* 1149a, *Hell eac ongeat* 1159b, *þreo tacen somod* 1235a, *grim helle fyr* 1269a, *godes bodan sægdon* 1304a, *beorht eðles wlite* 1346b, *sar ond swar gewinn* 1411a, *cildgeong on crybbe* 1425a, *hat, helle bealu* 1426a, *swat ut guton* 1448b, *wlitig, womma leas* 1464a, *on beom gefæstnad* 1490b, *sylf sigora weard* 1516a, *feoð firena bearn* 1598a, *beorht boca bibod* 1630a, *leofne lifes weard* 1642a, *freogað folces weard* 1647a, *Fæder ealra geweald* 1647b, *glæd gumena weorud* 1653a, *beorht blædes full* 1657a, *frið freondum bitweon* 1658a—39 verses, proportionately akin to *Guthlac B* rather than to *Guthlac A*. All are in line with Bliss's observation, *Metre of 'Beowulf'*, 75, that heavy verses seem not to have two unstressed syllables before the second stress.

[49] This reading, which is to be found in Thorpe and both Gollancz editions, dispenses with the otherwise uninstanced poetic adjective *cildgeong*. The proportions of heavy verses could rise with further divisions of compounds: e.g. *gesceafta scircyning* 1152a is divided into three words by Cook, *The Christ of Cynewulf*.

[50] Note that a definite article would normally be expected in 932a and 994a, but, if present, would give these verses two unstressed syllables before the second stress. Should the alliteration of the finite verb be regarded as accidental, there can be no metrical reasons for the omission of these two articles.

erroneous impression of the numbers of poetic compounds in use. Moreover, they are often somewhat cavalierly assigned to an appropriate Sievers two-stress type, as would be the case with one *Christ III* a-verse in which the poet achieves three alliterating words:

beorht boca bibod 1630a

There are only a few such a-verses in the corpus of Old English verse,[51] and this one is perhaps best read as comparable with Sievers D types, like, for example:

brecað brade gesceaft 991a

heofon hluttre ongeat 1149a

frið freondum bitweon 1658a.

These few examples of what is a marked trait of *Christ III* should be sufficient to show why *on beom gefæstnad* 1490b is best read as a heavy verse.[52] Once such a decision is taken, the emphasis given the consuetudinal *beom* is felt to contrast effectively both with the *is* (line 1489) in the initial dip that introduces the sentences in which it appears and with the *wæs* at the end of the following verse (line 1491).

As will have become evident from Table 1, the usual restriction of the Sievers A3 type to the on-verse may be broken once in *Christ III*:

Ic onfeng þin sar þæt þu moste gesælig
mines eþelrices eadig neotan.
(1460–1)

Acceptance of stress on the first syllable of *moste*, against the evidence of the alliteration, allows the verse to be drawn into the group of twelve *Christ III* hypermetric verses discussed by Clemons Kyte, who points out that these verses stand out in the inventories of hypermetric lines compiled by Pope and Bliss as an unusual proportion of single hypermetric half-lines in one

[51] Compare *Resignation* 43a *ful unfyr faca.* In the following the verbs could be taken as unstressed: *Andreas* 107a *Geþola þeoda þrea!*; *Elene* 464a *Ongit, guma ginga*; *The Phoenix* 394a *worhte wer ond wif*; *Maxims I* 132a *Woden worhte weos*; *The Riming Poem* 15a *Hæfde ic heanne had*; *Riddles* 69:1a *Wundor wearð on wege.* Note also the three stresses of *Christ III* 1162a *hloþe of ðam hatan hreþre*, a hypermetric verse. K. Stevens, 'Some Aspects of the Metre of the Old English Poem *Andreas*', *Proceedings of the Royal Irish Academy*, 81.C (1981), 7–8, discussing *Andreas* 107a, deems triple alliteration to be 'highly unlikely'.

[52] D. Donoghue, *Style in Old English Poetry* (New Haven, Conn. and London, 1987), argues (pp. 13–14) that *beom* should be stressed and that it suggests 'perhaps only momentarily, a pun' with *beam*; but he notes (p. 151) the verse as in violation of Kuhn's first law and describes (p. 210 n. 48) *beom* as 'the only unstressed auxiliary in clauses clearly dependent in *Christ III*'.

poem.[53] An alternative, hypermetric, reading is indicated here by Cook's text:

Ic onfēng þīn sār, þæt þū   mōste gesǣlig mīnes.

The removal of the possessive adjective *mines* from immediately before its headword results, however, in an unusual line break,[54] and I have therefore followed the Anglo-Saxon Poetic Records arrangement of text.[55] It is worth a moment's reflection to note how easily a comparable half-line could be produced from another of the poem's hypermetric singletons:

þæt þu meahte beorhte
uppe on roderum wesan,   rice mid englum
(1467b–68)

with possible transverse alliteration in the following line, but I have no wish here to multiply the anomalies of *Christ III*.[56] The unusual line 1460 achieves a satisfying balance without *mines*, for its atypical light ending gives to its b-verse a single focus in tune with the marked stress that falls upon the final monosyllable of its a-verse.

Clemons Kyte observes that of the twelve putatively hypermetric singletons she examines in *Christ III*, nine can be scanned as hypermetric according to the criteria for anacrusis in normal half-lines identified by Bliss.[57] Such may indeed be a safe assumption where a poem is 'metrically exact'.[58] With this poem there are enough unusual features for such a categorization of it to be questionable. Just as the introductory dips of A3 verses may tend to length, so too there may be elsewhere in *Christ III* a greater number of syllables of anacrusis than Bliss's norms would allow, unless a hypermetric scansion is assumed for 'problem' verses. I should like therefore to present for consideration two further tables: first, a description of anacrusis in the poem's normal verses; and, secondly, a summary of its hypermetric lines. It may be that at least in this poem anacrusis should be examined within the larger framework both of its A3 verses and its extended lines.

[53] Clemons Kyte, 'Hypermetric Verses', 165, reads *þæt þu moste gesælig* as hypermetric, noting that the last two words should be reversed to 'regularize alliteration' but that the verse 'might also be scanned as a light verse', given the presence of a non-alliterating auxiliary verb.

[54] With *mīnes* in line 1461a the verse becomes a second C type in which the syllabic consonant should be suppressed in scansion. Compare Amos, *Linguistic Means*, 81.

[55] Krapp and Dobbie (*The Exeter Book*, 259) observe that 'the order in the text seems natural'.

[56] It is interesting to note that Thorpe has A3 types both in 1460b and 1467b.

[57] Clemons Kyte, 'Hypermetric Verses', 164. Compare Bliss, *Metre of 'Beowulf'*, 40–3.

[58] Stanley, 'Some Observations', 161 n. 16, uses this phrase.

TABLE 2 *Anacrusis in* Christ III

The first element is prefixed:

to nouns/adjectives
tobrocene burgweallas 977a [a.1D*2]
gehreow ond hlud wop 998a [a. (1A2a): a heavy verse]
biseon mid swate 1087a [a.1A1a(1) ~ a.1A*1a(1)]
gesceafta scircyning 1152a [a.1D*3]
gecorene bi cystum 1223a [a.1A*1a(1)]
gesælgum on swegle 1659a [a.1A*1a(1)]

to infinitives
gehyran hygegeomor 890a [a.1D*2]
gemunan þa mildan 1200a [a.1A1a(1)]
geseon on him selfum 1264a [a.1A1b(1) ~ a.1A*1b(1)]
geseon on þam sawlum 1281a [a.1A1b(1) ~ a.1A*1b(1)]
geseon on þære sawle 1306a [a.1A1c ~ a.1A*1c]
geseon on ussum sawlum 1313a [a.1A1c ~ a.1A*1c]
agiefan geomormod 1406a [a.1D4]

to past participles
(wearð . . . |) birunnen under rindum 1175a [a.1A*1b]
(hafast|) ofslegen synlice 1479a [a.1D1]

to an imperative
Onfoð nu mid freondum 1344a [a.1A1c ~ a1d]

to finite verbs
toleseð liffruma 1042a [a.1D*3]
gesegon to soðe 1153a [a.1A*1a(1)]
geþolade fore þearfe 1172a [a.1A*1b]
gesihð þat fordone 1248b [a.1A1b(1) ~ a.1A*1b(1)]

The first element is proclitic:

connectives
þæt ge broþor mine 1499b [2C1b ~ b.2A1a(1)][59]
Þonne wihta gehwylce 981b [b.1A*1a(1) ~ hyp.]

relatives
þe no geendad weorþeð 1639b [c.2A1a(1) ~ hyp.]

[59] Amos, *Linguistic Means*, 81, gives 2C1b only for this verse. More recently R. D. Fulk, 'West Germanic Parasiting, Sievers' Law, and the Dating of Old English Verse', *Studies in Philology*, 86 (1989), 132 and n. 43, argues that *broþor* 1499 is accusative plural and 'so with an etymologically nonsyllabic *r*'.

prepositions
bi noman gehatne 1071b [a.1A1a(1)]
to wlite þæs huses 1139b [a.1A1a(1)]
to hleo ond to hroþer 1196a [a.1A1b(1)][60]
to widan feore 1543a [3B1a ~ a.2A1a(1)]
to wrace gesette 1601b [a.1A1a(1)]

modifying elements
þa hwitan honda 1110a [a.2A1a(1)]
hu fela þa onfundun 1178a [a.1A1b(1)]
ðæs lifes ic manige 1478a [a.1A*1a(1)]

Of the twenty-five examples of anacrusis in the first half-line, most are in verses with early juncture, which is where single syllables of anacrusis occur most frequently in *Beowulf*.[61] There are two verses in which the stressed elements are evenly divided. Of these one,

to widan feore 1543a,

can alternatively be scanned as a Sievers B type, if lengthening is not assumed in *feore* to compensate for *-h-*, and need not therefore contain anacrusis.[62] The other presents an interesting balance of phrases between the first and second half-lines

þa hwitan honda   ond þa halgan fet 1110.

Similarly, balance, as well as wordplay and tail-rhyme, may play a part in the yoking of the verses of line 1178:

hu fela þa onfundun   þa gefelan ne magun.

Here the b-verse ends with a disyllable that should normally be resolved, but the verse could be read with a short unresolved second stress, a pattern well attested as a sporadic feature of Old English verse.[63] Part of the effect of this line is the b-verse's repetition of the introductory anacrusis of the a-verse. In line 1478

ðæs lifes ic manige

[60] See Stevens, 'Metre of ... *Andreas*', 16, for two comparable half-lines in *Andreas: to hleo ond to hroðre* 111a and 567a.

[61] Bliss, *Metre of 'Beowulf'*, 40–1.

[62] Compare the 3B1C (Sievers B type) scansion advanced by Amos, *Linguistic Means*, 37, for *ond þæs to widan feore* 1343a.

[63] See H. Schabram, '*The Seasons for Fasting*, 206f. Mit einem Beitrag zur ae. Metrik', *Britannica, Festschrift fur Hermann M. Flasdieck* (Heidelberg, 1960), 220–41. See also Roberts, 'Metrical Examination', 114.

the unstressed *ic* should be seen within the light afforded by the absence of A3 verses headed by 'Personal pronouns (other than subject personal pronouns immediately preceding their verb)' among A3 half-lines (see Table 1, A). It looks as if the *Christ III* poet is less prone to begin a clause or sentence by placing subject pronouns at some distance from the verbs with which they agree than is the *Beowulf* poet.[64] The anomalous a-verse

in Hierusalem 1134

is omitted from Table 2 but should be noted as a possible further example of anacrusis. There are not any such verses in *Beowulf*, but a sufficient number of them appear in the Exeter and Vercelli Books to suggest that they are not to be dismissed as aberrant.[65]

Two of the seven b-verses in Table 2 can alternatively be viewed as hypermetric. Both are singletons:

Þonne wihta gehwylce 981b
þe no geendad weorþeð 1639b.

The first is one of those half-lines Pope identified only tentatively as hypermetric, but it is included in Bliss's index of hypermetric lines. The second is in neither list.[66] For Pope, most of the isolated extended verses he identifies can be read as normal, an effect he prefers on the whole. The striking

þæt ge broþor mine 1499b,

with the stressed portion containing what at first sounds like an admonitory vocative but is the object of its clause, might confidently, together with a second verse that also requires suppression of its syllabic consonant for a 'normal' reading, be viewed as a C type, so long as an alternative scansion, whether with anacrusis or as hypermetric, is not considered.[67] It is worth noting here that the poet may have avoided anacrusis in an evenly balanced half-line by the simple expedient of omitting a definite article from the qualifying phrase that fills 868b:

se micla dæg   meahtan dryhtnes.[68]

[64] The absence of such verses from Table 1 should be compared with Stanley, 'Some Observations', 152, where 9 of the 11 verses cited begin with the subject personal pronoun. Compare n. 17.

[65] Compare *Guthlac A* 599b *his ombiehthera* and see Roberts, 'Metrical Examination', 115 and n. 113 for further examples.

[66] Pope, *Rhythm of 'Beowulf'*, 101; Bliss, *Metre of 'Beowulf'*, 160.

[67] See above, p. 48, and n. 59.

[68] Compare Amos, *Linguistic Means*, 121, who suggests 'metrical exigencies' as an occasional reason for the omission of expected articles, noting further that 'disproportionate numbers of weak adjectives might therefore appear in late poems'.

Similarly, the lack of article at the head of *fyrswearta leg* 983b means that it is an unexceptional E type.[69]

Two further b-verses could be removed from Table 2 by the recently proposed expedient that the mid-verse *ge-* can be viewed as extra-metrical:[70]

bi noman gehatne 1071b

to wrace gesette 1601b

This theory would allow them to be treated as Sievers C type and removed from the group of verses with anacrusis, were it not for two verses with forms of the definite article similarly positioned that cannot so easily be massaged away:

to wlite þæs huses 1139b

gesihð þæt fordone 1248b

The accommodation of such verses to a Sievers C type may, within the context of the scansion of *Beowulf*, appear appropriately tidy, but within the wider context of the whole corpus it has less to recommend it. On balance, it would seem best therefore to acknowledge that anacrusis is to be found in four 'normal' b-verses in *Christ III* and to recognize that in three b-verses (981b, 1499b, and 1639b) two syllables of anacrusis could be advanced. Overall, even with the lower figure of 28 verses rather than 31 with anacrusis for *Christ III*, the proportions are similar to those recorded for *Andreas* and twice those recorded for *Beowulf*.[71]

There have appeared, both in Table 1 and in Table 2, some half-lines for which it is possible to offer either a 'normal' or a hypermetric scansion.[72] Thus, it is necessary to present as Table 3 a summary of the hypermetric verses of *Christ III*, to make plain the context within which these verses occur.[73] It may be that the unusual number of hypermetric singletons in some way complements overall a relatively high proportion of half-lines

[69] Bliss, *Metre of 'Beowulf'*, 43, points out that 'anacrusis is not to be expected in Type E'.

[70] D. Donoghue, 'On the Classification of B-Verses with Anacrusis in *Beowulf* and *Andreas*', *Notes and Queries*, 232 (1987), 1–5; *Style and Old English Poetry: The Test of the Auxiliary* (New Haven, Conn. and London, 1987), 189. See also Kendall, *Metrical Grammar*, 126. Similarly, Stevens, 'Metre of . . . *Andreas*', 23–4, recommends 'dropping the verbal prefix *ge-*' to regularize *Andreas* 493a and 499a.

[71] See Stevens, 'Metre of . . . *Andreas*', 15.

[72] This problem is seen clearly by Clemons Kyte, 'Hypermetric Verses', who identifies as hypermetric on distributional grounds those verses for which Pope prefers a 'normal' reading.

[73] Here I again use modifications to Bliss's system put forward in my 1971 paper on the metre of the Guthlac poems, p. 94. Thus, the convention adopted in Table 2 to display syllables of anacrusis is followed for two-stress hypermetric verses; for three-stress verses the symbols used for light verses are placed before a bracketed normal verse reading of the last two stresses.

with anacrusis, especially as the singletons are to a very great extent of the two-stress type.[74]

TABLE 3 *Hypermetric verses*

Group 1

Type b.1A1a

Þu þæs þonc ne wisses 1385b (allit. *þ*u or *þ*æs??)

Type c.1A1a

hatað hy upp astandan 888b

Type d.1A1a

þæt ðu wurde welig in heofonum 1495b (allit. *w*urde??)

Type f.1A1a

Mid þy ic þe wolde cwealm afyrran 1425b w. heavy verse

Type d.1A*1a

ond mec þa on þeostre alegde 1422b (allit. *þ*a??)

Hwæt, ic þæt for worulde geþolade 1423b

þæt þu wurde eadig on minum 1496b (allit. *w*urde??)

Þæs ge sceolon hearde adreogan 1513b[75] (allit. *h*won??)

Type c.1A*1b

For hwon ahenge þu mec hefgor 1487a

Type b.1D*1

Þæt mæg wites to wearninga 921a[76] w. 3B*1d ~ hyp., (allit. *Þ*æt??)

Type b.2A1a

ond þe ondgiet sealde 1380b w. 1A*1a

þær þu þolades siþþan 1409b w. 3B1b (allit. *þ*ær or *þ*u??)

Type c.2A1a

Ond eac þa ealdan wunde 1107a w. 3B1b (allit. *O*nd or *e*ac??)

Ic wæs on worulde wædla 1495a (allit. *w*æs?)

þæt hi to gyrne wiston 1304b w. heavy verse

ond hwæþre ealle mæneð 1377b w. 3B1c (allit. *h*wæþre??)

þæt þu on leohte siþþan 1463b w. 3B1a

on þinra honda rode 1487b

Hwæt, me þeos heardra þynceð 1488b[77] w. dic

[74] The singletons can be identified by the added information w. (= paired with) followed by scansion appropriate to the adjacent half-line.

[75] The accompanying half-line *to hynþum heofoncyninge* 1513a will be discussed below.

[76] P. J. Lucas, 'Some Aspects of *Genesis B* as Old English Verse', *Proceedings of the Royal Irish Academy*, 88 (1988), 168 n. 89, suggests a hypermetric scansion for 921b.

[77] The accompanying half-line *þonne iu hongade* 1488a seems to have lost at least a subject pronoun before the first stressed element. Despite the hypermetric context for this line, Lucas suggests ('Aspects of *Genesis B*', n. 89), that *Christ III* 1488b be read as a normal B type with *þyncð* for *þynceð*.

ond mid þy egsan forste 1546b

Type d.2A1a

Ne sindon him dæda dyrne 1049a w. 3B1c

þæt þu moste halig scinan 1426b w. heavy verse

þæt þu meahte beorhte uppe 1467b[78] w. d1a

Type e.2A1a

ðonne ge hy mid sibbum sohtun 1359a w. 2C1c

Type f.2A1a

gedyde ic þæt þu onsyn hæfdest 1382b (allit. *þ*æt or *þ*u??)

Type c.3E1

Þær mon mæg sorgende folc 889b (cr. allit. *f*olc??, d. allit. *m*on??)

Geaf ic ðe lifgendne gæst 1383b (cr. allit. *G*eaf??)

Type d.3E1

forðon ic þæt earfeþe wonn 1427b (d. allit. *i*c??)

Type b.3E2

Þæt bið foretacna mæst 892b w. 1A*1a(1)[79]

Group 2

Type a1a(b.1A1a)

Of lame ic þe leoþo gesette 1381a (allit. *þ*e??)

Type d2(1A1a)

mægwlite me gelicne 1383a w. 3B1d

Type e1(b.1A*1a)

wræc mid deoflum geþolian 1514b

Type a1(1A*1a)

sawlum sorge toglidene 1163a w.2C1b

Type a1(b.1A*1a)

sneome of slæpe þy fæstan 889a (cr. allit. *f*æstan??)

Type d1(c.1A*1a)

arode þe ofer ealle gesceafte 1382a[80] (allit. *þ*e??)

Type e1(a.2A1a)

Hyge wearð mongum blissad 1162b

Type e1(b.2A1a)

deorc on þam dome standeð 1560a w. 3B1a

læg ic on heardum stane 1424b

[78] Compare p. 47 above, where it is suggested that this verse, with *uppe* moved into the introductory dip of the next line, might be a second A3 type in the off verse.

[79] This half-line is not in Bliss's summary; it appears with a question mark beside it in Pope's list.

[80] For Bliss a two-stress verse, with *arode* in the introductory dip.

Type e1(c.2A1a)
earm ic wæs on eðle þinum 1496a (allit. *ic*??)
Type a1(b.2A1a)
wite to widan ealdre 1514a
Type a1a(b.2A1a)
biþeahte mid þearfan wædum 1422a
Type a1(b.2A1a)
hloþe of ðam hatan hreþre 1162a (triple allit.)
ðystra þæt þu þolian sceolde 1385a (allit. *þæt* or *þu*??)
eadig on þam ecan life 1427a
Type a1(c.2A1a)
egeslic of þære ealdan moldan 888a
Lytel þuhte ic leoda bearnum 1424a
æleð hy mid þy ealdan lige 1546a[81]
Type a1a(2A1a)
geseoð sorga mæste 1208a[82] w. 3B1b
Type d1a(a.2A1a)
biwundenne mid wonnum claþum 1423a
Type e1c(3E1)
nysses þu wean ænigne dæl 1384b
Type e1(b.3E*2)
welan ofer widlonda gehwylc 1384a

Old English verse has, over the last century and a half, been subjected to varied straitjackets, some highly complex. Of the authoritative analyses of the last few decades, perhaps the most influential are those of Pope and Bliss. Whereas Pope taught us to listen for significant silence, Bliss gave us a Sievers retread that has become a valued norm against which editorial and critical assumptions are tested. Neither has shirked the necessary task of confronting the hypermetric lines, but, as Bliss points out, 'No satisfactory explanation of the reason for their appearance has yet been found.'[83] So, by comparison with the finely tuned theories that allow the close examination of variety within what are termed normal lines of Old English poetry, the expanded lines tend to be tucked away tidily into a separate appendix, almost as an embarrassment. Despite attempts made to accommodate these longer verses within patterns devised as the norm for the more usual shorter lines, through fusions, doublings, and replacements, the hypermetric lines

[81] For Bliss a two-stress verse, with *æleð* in the introductory dip.
[82] Alternatively, and without decontraction, this half-line might be described as eia(2Aia). Lucas ('Aspects of *Genesis B*', 168 n. 89) takes its paired *hu he sylfa cyning* 1208b as ending in an A type and therefore hypermetric.
[83] Bliss, *Metre of 'Beowulf'*, 88.

remain different. It is easy enough to gain a sense of some minimal scansion-apparatus for use when reading *Beowulf*, where the twenty-three hypermetric verses it contains can be put out of mind, almost as if anomalous. Statistically in *Beowulf* they seem scarcely significant, although stylistically, we dimly sense, they may serve to focus attention or generate tension. And no matter if the appearance of such verses has not been satisfactorily explained, they are already present within those few short poems and fragments securely dated as early as the eighth century and they occur in significant numbers in *Judith*, a poem generally agreed to be late. Most often the hypermetric lines scattered throughout the corpus are treated together, but I shall here look at their distribution only in *Christ III*. I shall attempt no theoretical explanation for their existence. Rather I shall look to see how they coexist, and in what forms, with some of the poem's shorter verses.

The Group 1 verses of Table 3 have two stresses. The number of lead-in syllables preceding the first stress is indicated by a small letter. Thus, Bliss's a1b(1A1a) appears here as b.1A1a, a simplification that serves to indicate how very little, formally, such hypermetric verses differ from normal verses with anacrusis. The number of syllables of the initial dip varies from two to six.[84] An analogy may be drawn between the introductory dips of the verses presented in Table 1 and these dips. The patterns are listed in order of weight, which shows that two-stress hypermetric verses most typically end in the commonest of all verse types, 2A1a (Sievers A type). Such a distribution appears virtually to be complementary with the occurrence of anacrusis in normal half-lines. The three-stress Group 2 verses are again represented as ending in a normal two-stress pattern, with the preceding syllables noted for convenience in the terminology used for light verses. The presence of brackets indicates that Group 2 hypermetric half-lines are heavier than Group 1 ones. The expedient of prefixing a letter to the pattern described within brackets makes it possible to see that, unlike heavy verses, three-stress hypermetric verses tend to have more than one unstressed syllable before the second stress.[85] Moreover, where Group 1 verses resemble the A3 type in having what can be termed a lengthy introductory dip, Group 2 verses usually have only one syllable of anacrusis.[86] The three syllables of anacrusis in

[84] Bliss (ibid. 94) states that the recorded range of variation overall is between one and eight syllables. Interestingly, the indication given in Tables 1 and 3 of accidental alliteration points to a greater use of deitic elements in *Christ III* than in *Beowulf*.

[85] See n. 48 for the apparent restriction of unstressed syllables to one before the second stress in heavy verses.

[86] The four examples, all in the first half-line, are: *geseoð sorga mæste* 1208a; *Of lame ic þe leoþu gesette* 1381a; *biþeahte mid þearfan wædum* 1422a; and *biwundenne mid wommum claþum* 1423a.

nysses þu wean ænigne dæl 1384b

are atypical, both for their number and their presence in the second half of the line.

Three further verses should be considered here:[87]

þinre alysnesse 1473a

to hynþum heofoncyninge 1513a

lif butan endedeaðe 1652b.[88]

These resemble the verse *in Hierusalem* 1134a, discussed above in relation to Table 2, but differ in their greater weight. Of them only 1513a keeps company with a hypermetric half-line: that it does might make it possible to add the other two to the already lengthy list of singleton hypermetric verses in *Christ III*.

It can be seen from Table 3 that the *Christ III* poet uses Group 1 and Group 2 verses indiscriminately in either half-line. By contrast, in *Guthlac A* both Group 1 and Group 2 types occur in the first half-line, but the two-stress variety only in the second half-line. And what may have been a stricter convention is found in *Guthlac B*, where Group 2 verses appear in the first half-line and Group 1 verses in the second half-line.[89] Among the longer poems *Christ III* is, as has been noted above, unusual in having so many single hypermetrical verses. In Table 3 the scansion of any hypermetric singleton's accompanying half-lines is given (w. = pairs with).

The adjoining half-line for a singleton is most often a B type (lines 921, 1049, 1107, 1377, 1383, 1409, 1463, 1560) and twice a C type (lines 1163 and 1359), patterns which share with the two-stress Group 1 hypermetric verses the likelihood of two or more introductory syllables. Three of the singletons are accompanied by heavy verses (lines 1304, 1425, and 1426), and only the first of these is outside a hypermetric cluster. It is noteworthy therefore that the singleton of line 1380b should be accompanied in the first half-line by a normal A type:

ærest geworhte,   ond þe ongiet sealde.

[87] Unless *Neorxnawonges wlite* 1405a be deemed a heavy verse, it should be noted here as also containing a compound that would, in *Beowulf*, stand on its own as a full measure. G. Russom, *Old English Meter and Linguistic Theory* (1982), seems not to allow for such verses, possibly because they are not found in *Beowulf*. Compare two *Andreas* verses cited by Stevens, 'Metre of . . . *Andreas*', 20, as possibly hypermetric: *manige missenlice* 583a (or 1D*1 with syllabic consonant suppressed) and *drohtigen dæghwamlice* 682a.

[88] Emendation, leaving out either *ende* or *deaðe*, has been proposed: for details, see Krapp and Dobbie, *The Exeter Book*, 261. This half-line does not appear in the lists of hypermetric verse of either Pope or Bliss.

[89] See Roberts, 'Metrical Examination', 114.

Were it not that a group of hypermetric lines follows, two syllables of anacrusis might be assumed in the b-verse. As well, two half-lines in Group 1 accompany light verses. The first accompanying light verse,

þonne iu hongade 1488,

may well have lost a subject pronoun.[90] For the second,

in byrgenne' þæt þu meahte beorhte uppe 1467,

I have already suggested that *uppe* might more naturally stand in the dip at the head of the following line, producing a second A3 pattern in the b-verses of *Christ III*. A possible third accompanying light verse,

For hwon ahenge þu mec hefgor 1487a,

is discussed above in the context of Table 1, where the likelihood of metrical stress on the finite verb is noted; it is now, despite the resulting infringement of Kuhn's first law, classified as a Group 1 hypermetric half-line.

Despite the small number of lines under discussion, certain tendencies may be glimpsed: the hypermetric singletons do not generally pair with 'normal' verses other than B and C types. There may therefore be some consistency in the sort of company kept by the single hypermetric verses of this poem. However, two half-lines from Table 2, where they are noted as possibly hypermetric, contrast interestingly in the light of this generalization:

Þonne wihta gehwylce 981b w. 1D*1

þe no geendad weorþeð 1639b w. a1c

They are to be compared with

Þæt bið foretacna mæst 892b w.1A*1a(1)

It would be convenient to term the first and the third of these half-lines normal with anacrusis and the second hypermetric because of the company they keep, but the poem's length is scarcely sufficient to allow such an assumption. It is at least plain from the numbers of hypermetric half-lines it contains that, metrically at any rate, *Christ III* is less than 'strict'.[91]

Overall the most striking feature of the half-line in *Christ III* is the frequency with which its patterns repeat themselves. This is evident very obviously in the homiletic enumeration of lines 1061–8, a passage Cook

[90] Compare n. 77 above.

[91] Compare Stanley, 'Prosaic Vocabulary', 388–9: 'Absence of a general statement about a poem indicates that, though there may be some prosaic words in the poem, I have not felt able to conclude that the poem fails to conform to the practice normal in "strict" verse.'

compares with a longer enumeration in the Old English anonymous homily *In die iudicii*:[92]

Đonne sio byman stefen   ond se beorhta segn,
ond þæt hate fyr   ond seo hea duguð,
ond se engla þrym   ond se egsan þrea,
ond se hearda dæg   ond seo hea rod,
ryht aræred   rices to beacne,
folcdryht wera   biforan bonnað,
sawla gehwylce   þara þe sið oþþe ær
on lichoman   leoþum onfengen.

(1061–8)[93]

The homily cited by Cook has recently been examined closely by Stanley, who claims from it an 'edited, newly won poetic text', nearly forty lines long, which he names 'The Judgement of the Damned'.[94] These are the opening lines of his C text:

La, hwæt þence we þæt we us ne ondrædað þone toweardan dæg þæs micclan domes:

Se is yrmþa dæg   7 ealra earfoða dæg.

on ðam dæge us bið æteowed

seo geopnung heofona   7 engla þrym
7 ealwihtna rire   7 eorðan forwyrd,
treowleasra gewinn   7 tungla gefeal,
þunorrada hlinn   7 se þistra storm,
þara lyfta leóma   7 þara liggetta gebrastl,
þara granigendran gesceaft   7 þara gasta gefeoht,
þa grymman gesihðe   7 þa godcundan miht,
se hata scúr   7 helwara ream,
þara beorga geberst   7 þara bimena sang,
se brada bryne ofer ealworld   7 se bitera dæg,
se miccla cwealm   7 þara manna mán,
seo sare sorh . . .[95]

Undoubtedly the *Christ III* poet is an able manipulator of what Stanley

[92] Cook, *The Christ of Cynewulf*, 189. More recently Biggs, 'Sources of *Christ III*', 40, has usefully drawn together a summary of the Old English homiletic analogues proposed for *Christ III*.

[93] This is by far the most striking run of matching verses; compare also lines 1642 ff.

[94] E. G. Stanley, '*The Judgement of the Damned*, from Corpus Christi College Cambridge 201 and Other Manuscripts, and the Definition of Old English Verse', *Learning and Literature in Anglo-Saxon England: Studies Presented to Peter Clemoes on the Occasion of his Sixty-Fifth Birthday*, ed. M. Lapidge and H. Gneuss (Cambridge, 1985), 363–91; repr. in E. G. Stanley, *A Collection of Papers with Emphasis on Old English Literature* (Toronto, 1987), 352–83.

[95] Stanley, *The Judgement of the Damned*, 382.

terms the 'affective rhythms' of the Old English homily.[96]

Perhaps it is the exploitation of such rhythms that makes *Christ III* so distinctive. The poet is obviously indebted to the vernacular homiletic tradition: the similarity of some of his materials to Vercelli Homily 8 has often been remarked.[97] In such passages *Christ III* is not fully heteromorphic; the lines do not pursue that continual matching of unalike verse patterns which McIntosh has reminded us is general to Old English poetry. Rather the mode is homomorphic when the poet switches into using lines and larger units made up of a continuous succession of examples of the same unit.[98] Nevertheless he has a firm grasp of the alliterative controls customary in Old English poetry, and, as I hope to have demonstrated, those aspects of his metre that are least in line with the conventions to be glimpsed in *Beowulf* have a certain self-consistency. Moreover, when presented in terms that allow comparisons to be drawn, they prove to be not without parallel in the larger corpus of Old English poetry.

[96] Ibid. 380. Compare D. R. Letson, 'The Poetic Content of the Revival Homily', in *The Old English Homily and Its Backgrounds*, ed. P. E. Szarmach and B. F. Huppé (Albany, NY 1978), 139–56. Letson singles out the Vercelli homily II variant for discussion of an 'affection for rhyme and alliteration . . . present to some extent in a large number of Old English homilies' (141–2).

[97] In particular, see R. Willard, 'Vercelli Homily VIII and the *Christ*', *PMLA* 42 (1927), E. B. Irving, 'Latin Prose Sources for Old English Verse', *Journal of English and Germanic Philology*, 56 (1957), 593–94, and M. R. Godden, 'An Old English Penitential Motif', *Anglo-Saxon England*, 2 (1975), 235.

[98] A. McIntosh, 'Early Middle English Alliterative Verse', *Middle English Alliterative Poetry and its Literary Background*, ed. D. A. Lawton (1982), 21–2. Compare Bliss, *The Metre of 'Beowulf'*, 2nd edn. (Oxford, 1967), 138: 'The poet combines his pairs of verses in such a way as to achieve greater variety, both of rhythm and of phrasing, than chance would dictate'.

A Grammarian's Greek–Latin Glossary in Anglo-Saxon England

HELMUT GNEUSS

Our knowledge of Anglo-Saxon culture and learning largely depends on the surviving manuscripts known to have been written or owned in early England; their close study remains a rewarding subject. Among them, books containing grammatical treatises and glossary materials are of particular interest as they yield valuable insights into the study and teaching of language in this period.[1] In the present article I propose to edit and discuss a glossary of literary, grammatical, and metrical terms, preserved in MS BL Harley 3826—into which it was copied at about the time when Ælfric wrote his *Grammar*—and hitherto almost completely ignored by Anglo-Saxonists. I have chosen the title 'Grammarian's Glossary' in view of the nature and range of Roman and medieval grammar, and of the close links between this discipline and poetics, rhetoric, and prosody.

The Manuscripts

1. H London, British Library, Harley 3826

MS Harley 3826 was written in Anglo-Caroline minuscule in the late tenth or early eleventh century, possibly at Abingdon. It consists of 168 small folios (12 × 9 cm). The collation is $1–8^8$, 9^6, $10–11^8$, 12^8 (wants 8), $13–19^8$, 20^{10} (fos. 153 and 156 are singletons), 21^4, 22^6 (wants 5); stubs after fos. 153, 156, and 167, but no loss of text.

Contents:

folios $1^r–24^v$ Alcuin, *De orthographia.* The text represents version I, as in Keil, *Grammatici Latini*, VII. 295–312 (see n. 18), but ends at 309.12. Cf. Anna Carlotta Dionisotti, 'On Bede, Grammars and Greek', *Revue Bénédictine*, 92 (1982), 111–41, at

[1] For an introductory survey of this subject, see H. Gneuss, 'The Study of Language in Anglo-Saxon England', *Bulletin of the John Rylands University Library of Manchester*, 72 (1990), 3–32.

130–1 and 138. This manuscript was neither recorded nor used in the edition of Alcuin's *Orthographia* by Aldo Marsili (Pisa, 1952).

24^{v}–70^{r} Beda, *De orthographia*, collated as H in the edition by C. W. Jones in *Bedae Venerabilis Opera. Pars I: Opera didascalia*, CCSL 123A (Turnhout, 1975), 1–57; for the textual affiliation see ibid. 4.

70^{v}–71^{r} A Latin (Greek)–Latin glossary.

71^{v}–84^{r} Abbo of Saint-Germain, *Bella Parisiacae Urbis*, Book III, with numerous interlinear Latin glosses, collated as H in the edition of Paul von Winterfeld, *MGH, Poetae Latini Aevi Carolini*, IV. i (Berlin, 1899), 116–21, with a note on the glosses on p. 77. Cf. Patrizia Lendinara, 'The Third Book of the *Bella Parisiacae Urbis* by Abbo of Saint-Germain-des-Prés and its Old English Gloss', *ASE* 15 (1986), 73–89.

84^{r}–86^{v} Further glossary entries, Latin (Greek)–Latin.

87^{r}–149^{r} Martianus Capella, *De nuptiis Philologiae et Mercurii*, Book IV, 'De dialectica'. Cf. Claudio Leonardi, 'I codici di Marziano Capella', *Aevum*, 34 (1960), 78–9; this manuscript has not been collated in *Martianus Capella*, ed. James Willis (Leipzig, 1983).

149^{v} (blank)

150^{r}–152^{v} The Grammarian's Glossary, printed below from this manuscript.

152^{v}–167^{v} Further glossary materials, continuing without break after the end of the Grammarian's Glossary: Greek and Latin terms explained in Latin. Those on fos. 152^{v} and 153^{r} (lines 1–3) correspond to the terms for parts of a Roman house in the Antwerp–London Glossary,[2] but the interpretations differ. The glosses on fos. 165^{r}–166^{v} may be a continuation of those on fos. 70^{v}–71^{r}. Cf. Michael Lapidge, 'The Hermeneutic Style in Tenth-Century Anglo-Latin Literature', *ASE* 4 (1975), 67–111, at 75 and 88 n. 1. Fos. 161^{r}–164^{v} contain glosses to Satires V-VIII of Juvenal; see Patrizia Lendinara, 'Le glosse secondarie', in *Studi linguistici e filologici offerti a Girolamo Caracausi* (Palermo, 1992), 269–81, at 269–70 n. 3.

[2] L. Kindschi, 'The Latin–Old English Glossaries in Plantin-Moretus MS 32 and British Museum MS Additional 32, 246' (unpublished diss., Stanford University, 1955), 235.11–236.5; cf. T. Wright, *Anglo-Saxon and Old English Vocabularies*, 2nd edn. by R. P. Wülcker (London, 1884), i. 183.36–184.10.

For MS Harley 3826 see Leonardi, *Aevum*, 34 (1960), 78–9; N. R. Ker, *Catalogue of Manuscripts Containing Anglo-Saxon* (Oxford, 1957), no. 241; T. A. M. Bishop, *English Caroline Minuscule* (Oxford, 1971), 13.

2. Manuscripts of the Grammarian's Glossary written on the Continent[3]

B Bologna, Biblioteca Universitaria, 797 (458), fo. 81^r–81^v.

A collection of texts on Latin grammar, metre and rhetoric, written in France, probably in the Rheims region, in the third quarter of the ninth century. The best and most recent description of this manuscript is by Simona Gavinelli, 'Un manuale scolastico carolingio: Il codice Bolognese 797', *Aevum*, 59 (1985), 181–95. The Glossary has been edited from this manuscript by Angela Maria Negri, 'De codice Bononiensi 797', *Rivista di filologia e di istruzione classica*, 87 (1959), 260–77, at 276–7.

D Berlin, Staatsbibliothek der Stiftung Preussischer Kulturbesitz, Diez. B Sant. 66, p. 349.

A collection of texts on Latin grammar and metre, written *c.*790, probably at the court of Charlemagne. E. A. Lowe, *Codices Latini Antiquiores* [= *CLA*], I–XI and Supplement (Oxford, 1934–71), VIII. 1044. Facsimile edition: *Sammelhandschrift Diez. B Sant. 66: Grammatici Latini et Catalogus Librorum.* Einführung Bernhard Bischoff, Codices Selecti xlii (Graz, 1973)—for the Grammarian's Glossary see p. 37 of the introduction; Louis Holtz, *Donat et la tradition de l'enseignement grammatical* (Paris, 1981), 358–61. The Glossary breaks off after item 95 because a quire has been lost after p. 349.

F Florence, Biblioteca Medicea Laurenziana, San Marco 38, fo. 3^r.

Grammatical treatises, Eucherius, Junilius; written at Corbie in the first quarter of the ninth century. The contents of this manuscript are listed in the unpublished 'Index MSS Bibliothecae FF. Ordinis Praedicatorum Florentiae ad S. Marcum' (1768) [= MS San Marco 945], cols. 111–12.

L Leiden, Bibliotheek der Rijksuniversiteit, Voss. lat. O. 74, fos. 146^r–147^r.

Glossaries, written in France, probably in the Paris region, in the first quarter

[3] I am deeply grateful to the late Professor Bernhard Bischoff, who generously supplied information about the dates and places of origin of manuscripts BFLRSXZ. I am also grateful to Miss Inge Milfull, who inspected MS San Marco 38 at Florence (and the unpublished catalogue) for me. I wish to thank the following libraries which sent me photographs of manuscripts in their possession: Real Monasterio de El Escorial; Florence, Biblioteca Medicea Laurenziana; Leiden, Bibliotheek der Rijksuniversiteit; Montpellier, Bibliothèque Interuniversitaire, Section Médecine; Oxford, Bodleian Library; Paris, Bibliothèque Nationale; Savignano sul Rubicone, Rubiconia Accademia dei Filopatridi; Biblioteca Apostolica Vaticana; Venice, Biblioteca Nazionale Marciana; Wolfenbüttel, Herzog-August-Bibliothek.

of the ninth century. See K. A. de Meyier, *Codices Vossiani Latini, Pars III: Codices in Octavo* (Leiden, 1977), 128–9.

M Montpellier, Bibliothèque de la Faculté de Médecine, H. 212, fos. 79^{v}–80^{v}.

A manuscript containing the works of Persius and Nonius Marcellus, written in France (Auxerre?) in the first half of the tenth century. The Grammarian's Glossary is followed on fos. 80^{v}–81^{v} by a glossary of rhetorical terms identical with that in MS S.

O Oxford, Bodleian Library, Add. C.144 (SC 28188), fo. 71^{r}–71^{v}.

A collection of grammatical and metrical treatises and extracts, and including the *Synonyma* ascribed to Cicero, copied in the early eleventh century in central Italy from a Beneventan exemplar (Monte Cassino?); it reached the Low Countries in the sixteenth century and was bought by the Bodleian in 1825. The manuscript and its contents have been frequently described and discussed; see Colette Jeudy in *Viator*, 5 (1974), 120–3; Holtz, *Donat*, 409–12 and *passim*; Martin Irvine, 'Bede the Grammarian and the Scope of Grammatical Studies in Eighth-Century Northumbria', *ASE* 15 (1986), 15–44. For a glossary with Old English glosses on fo. 153^{v}, going back to an Anglo-Saxon exemplar of the eighth century, see Ker, *Catalogue of Manuscripts Containing Anglo-Saxon*, Appendix no. 22.

P Paris, Bibliothèque Nationale, lat. 7530, fos. 145^{r}–146^{v}.

A collection of texts mainly on Latin grammar, metre and rhetoric, written between 779 and 796 at Monte Cassino. *CLA* V. 569. The manuscript has been described and discussed in great detail by Louis Holtz, 'Le Parisinus Latinus 7530, synthèse cassinienne des arts libéraux', *Studi Medievali*, serie terza, 16 (1975), 97–152.

R Rome, Biblioteca Apostolica Vaticana, Reg. lat. 215, fos. 120^{v}–121^{v}.

A miscellaneous collection, including a version of the *Synonyma* ascribed to Cicero and the *Scholica Graecarum Glossarum*, written in France (in the Tours region?) in the second half of the ninth century. For the contents see André Wilmart, *Codices Reginenses Latini*, I (Vatican City, 1937), 507–12; for the glossaries in the manuscript see M. L. W. Laistner, 'Notes on Greek from the Lectures of a Ninth Century Monastic Teacher', *Bulletin of the John Rylands Library, Manchester*, 7 (1923), 421–56. The Grammarian's Glossary is printed by Laistner, 450–1; in the manuscript it is preceded and followed by other glosses, mainly Greek–Latin, and it consists of only 64 items in the following order (for the numbering see the edition below): 62–74, 44b, 45–59, 61, 3–10, 12, 14, 19, 20, 124, 126–8, 88, 90, 100, 101, 103, 105, 110, 112–17,

119–24, with interpretations different from those of the other manuscripts for 88 and 90 (see the 'Notes', below). The manuscript is no. BF 1357 in Marco Mostert, *The Library of Fleury: A Provisional List of Manuscripts* (Hilversum, 1989), 259.

S Rome, Biblioteca Apostolica Vaticana, Reg. lat. 1587, fos. 22^{v}–25^{v}.

Fos. 1–64 of this manuscript were written in Western France in the first half of the ninth century (at the top of fo. 24^{v} is a Fleury *ex libris* s. ix/x); they include grammatical treatises by Maximus Victorinus and Sergius, and a copy of the conflated text of Alcuin's and Bede's *De orthographia.* On fos. 25^{v}–27^{r}, the Grammarian's Glossary is immediately followed by a Greek–Latin glossary of 80 rhetorical terms, inc. *BARBARISMOS: corruptus sermo,* expl. *anachefaleosis: recapitulatio.* See Elisabeth Pellegrin, *Les Manuscrits classiques Latins de la Bibliothèque Vaticane,* II. i (Paris, 1978), 311–14, and Mostert, *The Library of Fleury,* 284–5.

T Rome, Biblioteca Apostolica Vaticana, Ottobon. lat. 1354, fo. 48^{r}–48^{v}.

A collection of treatises and extracts on grammar and metre, written in the late eleventh or early twelfth century, probably in Italy. See Pellegrin, *Les Manuscrits classiques Latins,* I (Paris, 1975), 524–9, and Paul F. Gehl, in *Revue d'histoire des textes,* 8 (1978), 303–7.

U Rome, Biblioteca Apostolica Vaticana, lat. 623, fo. 84^{r}–84^{v}.

A copy of Isidore's *Etymologiae,* written in Italy in the late thirteenth or early fourteenth century. See M. Vatasso and P. F. de Cavalieri, *Codices Vaticani Latini,* I (Rome, 1902), 469–70.

V Venice, Biblioteca Marciana, Lat. Z. 497 (1811), fo. 13^{v}.

A collection of texts dealing with grammar—including a florilegium from Latin authors—rhetoric, logic, medicine, music, geometry, arithmetic, and astronomy, written in Italy about the middle of the eleventh century and based on a South Italian exemplar. For the manuscript and its contents see Pietro Zorzanello, *Catalogo dei codici latini della Biblioteca Nazionale Marciana di Venezia non compresi nel catalogi di G. Valentinelli, vol. I: Fondo Antico, Classi I–X, Classe XI, Codd. 1–100* (Trezzano, 1980), 109–22; Francis L. Newton, 'Tibullus in Two Grammatical *Florilegia* of the Middle Ages', *Transactions and Proceedings of the American Philological Association,* 93 (1962), 253–86; Holtz, *Donat,* 416.

W Wolfenbüttel, Herzog-August-Bibliothek, Weissenburg 86, fo. 145^{r}–145^{v}.

A collection of texts on Latin grammar and metre, written at Tours around the middle of the eighth century. *CLA* IX. 1394. For the contents see Hans Butzmann, *Kataloge der Herzog-August-Bibliothek Wolfenbüttel. Die neue Reihe, 10. Band: Die Weissenburger Handschriften* (Frankfurt am Main, 1964), 248–50. The Grammarian's Glossary was printed from this manuscript by Johann Friedrich Heusinger, in the second edition of his *Fl. Mallii Theodori de metris liber* (Leiden, 1766), 81–5. Heusinger's edition, including his introduction and notes, was reprinted word for word by Thomas Gaisford, *Scriptores Latini rei metricae* (Oxford, 1837), 574–6.

X Leiden, Bibliotheek der Rijksuniversiteit, B. P. L. 67D, fos. 1–2.

A copy of the *Liber glossarum*, written probably in France in the third quarter of the ninth century; the Grammarian's Glossary, on added leaves, was written towards the end of the ninth century. The order of the leaves is reversed, fo. 2 should precede fo. 1. See *Bibliotheca Universitatis Leidensis: Codices Manuscripti, III. Codices Bibliothecae Publicae Latini* (Leiden, 1912), 36.

Y Savignano sul Rubicone, Rubiconia Accademia dei Filopatridi, Camera I,1,1,9, fos. 80^{v}–81^{v}.

A collection of texts on grammar and versification, written in Northern Italy about the middle of the fifteenth century and described by Gavinelli, *Aevum*, 59 (1985), 193–5.

Z El Escorial, Real Biblioteca, B.I.12, fo. 109^{r}–109^{v}.

A copy of Isidore's *Etymologiae*, written in the thirteenth century, probably in Italy. The Glossary follows after the end of Book IX of the *Etymologiae*.

Another copy of the Glossary was contained in Chartres, Bibliothèque Municipale, MS 90 (fo. 56^{r}), destroyed in 1944. After this article had been finished, Professor Patrizia Lendinara kindly drew my attention to three further versions of the Grammarian's Glossary and generously supplied me with transcripts:

Paris, Bibliothèque Nationale, lat. 4883 A, fos. 26vb–27ra.

From south-west France, possibly St Martial at Limoges, late tenth or early eleventh century. The same version as in MS R, but nos. 100 and 101 have been omitted.

Barcelona, Archivo de la Corona de Aragón, Ripoll 74, fo. 55va–55^{vc}.

From the Benedictine abbey at Ripoll, written in the third quarter of the tenth century. Contains only items no. 21–44.

Erfurt, Wissenschaftliche Bibliothek der Stadt, Ampl. 8° 8, fos. 125^{v}–126^{r}.

Written in the twelfth century; origin unknown. The glossary comprises items 1–106 as in MS H; no omissions.

3. English glossaries incorporating entries from the Grammarian's Glossary

C Cambridge, Corpus Christi College, 144, fos. 1^r–3^v.

A manuscript with two glossaries, written probably in the South of England in the second quarter of the ninth century; on fo. ii is the late thirteenth-century shelfmark and *ex libris* of St Augustine's, Canterbury. The second of the two glossaries is the well-known 'Corpus Glossary' (fos. 4^r–64^v) with over 8,700 entries, more than 2,000 of them with Old English interpretations. The first is an alphabetic collection of 341 entries, most of them Hebrew or Greek names or words, with Latin interpretations; the sources for these entries are Jerome's *Liber interpretationis Hebraicorum nominum*, and the *Instructiones* of Eucherius. But a number of entries come from other sources, and these (as has not been realized previously) include fifty items from the Grammarian's Glossary, here arranged in batches under their respective initial letter, and within these batches still mostly in the order they have in their source; thus Corpus items 72–9 correspond to Grammarian's Glossary items 43, 66, 114, 116, 122–4, while Corpus items 253–63 represent entries 110, 1–4, 61, 65, 70, 75, 108, 124 in the source. The first Corpus Glossary was edited by J. H. Hessels, *An Eighth-Century Latin–Anglo-Saxon Glossary* (Cambridge, 1890), 3–8; a recent facsimile edition of the manuscript, with important introduction, is *The Épinal, Erfurt, Werden and Corpus Glossaries*, ed. Bernhard Bischoff, Mildred Budny, Geoffrey Harlow, M. B. Parkes, J. D. Pheifer, Early English Manuscripts in Facsimile, XXII (Copenhagen, 1988). See also *CLA* II. 122, Ker, *Catalogue of Manuscripts Containing Anglo-Saxon*, no. 36, and Thiel (see n. 4 below), 176.

E Cambridge, Corpus Christi College, 356, part iii.

An unpublished alphabetic Latin(Greek)–Latin glossary, taking up fos. 1^r–42^r of a manuscript of 42 leaves, with *c.*360 entries, written towards the end of the tenth century, probably at St Augustine's, Canterbury. The alphabetic sequence is interrupted on fo. 17^v by a list of synonyms for ships, and on fo. 28^r by 21 A-glosses inserted among P-glosses. On fo. 42^r is a list of the names of the Hebrew letters, with Latin interpretations.[4] The following

[4] These interpretations correspond almost exactly to type III (taken from the section on the psalms in Jerome's *Liber interpretationis Hebraicorum nominum*) of the alphabets listed by Matthias Thiel, *Grundlagen und Gestalt der Hebräischkenntnisse des frühen Mittelalters* (Spoleto, 1970; orig. diss. Munich, 1961), 90–3.

items of the Grammarian's Glossary occur (items with differing interpretations are in parentheses): 86, 9, (54), 16, 17, 100, 12, (10), 108, (124), (3), 4, 3, (11), 61, 107, (48), 47, 127, 90. For the manuscript see M. R. James, *A Descriptive Catalogue of the Manuscripts in the Library of Corpus Christi College, Cambridge* (Cambridge, 1912), II. 189–90; T. A. M. Bishop, 'Notes on Cambridge Manuscripts', *Transactions of the Cambridge Bibliographical Society*, 2 (1955–7), 188 and 334–6.

K London, British Library, Harley 3376.

An alphabetic glossary, written about the turn of the tenth and eleventh centuries, probably in the West of England. The glossary, with 5,563 entries—about one-third of them with Old English glosses—covers only the initial letters A–F. The remainder was lost.[5] The existing glossary includes nine items that may have come from the Grammarian's Glossary, corresponding there to items 5, 41, 43, 57, 104, 114, 115, 122, 123. A different interpretation is given for item 74 (Harley 3376, item D 486). The glossary was edited by Robert T. Oliphant, *The Harley Latin–Old English Glossary* (The Hague, 1966); for the shortcomings of this edition see Hans Schabram's review in *Anglia*, 86 (1968), 495–500. For the manuscript and the glossary see especially N. R. Ker, *Catalogue of Manuscripts Containing Anglo-Saxon*, no. 240, and J. D. Pheifer, *Old English Glosses in the Épinal-Erfurt Glossary* (Oxford, 1974), pp. xxxv–xxxvi.

The Glossary

The Grammarian's Glossary comprises 128 entries in the version of MS H. In this version, two original entries (44b and 64a) may have been accidentally omitted, while seven entries appear to be a later addition (81–7). If we disregard faulty copying or individual alterations in the early MSS BDFLPSWX, or—in the case of MS D—loss of leaves, we may assume that the original glossary had 123 entries, and that MS H is a late but fairly reliable representative of the original compilation. Eleven further items occur in MSS OPTUVXZ, or in most manuscripts of this group (12a, 14a, 28a, 35a, 44a, 74a–c, 104a–b, 121a); these may have been added at some stage in the early history of the text.

The Glossary is arranged according to subjects, as follows:

(i) *Poetry*

1–14 The poet, poetry, its genres and elements

[5] Two surviving fragments appear to be Oxford, Bodleian Library, Lat.misc.a.3, fo. 49, and Lawrence, Kansas, University of Kansas, Spencer Research Library, Pryce MS. P2A:1.

(ii) *Grammar*

15–20 Grammar

21–28 The parts of speech

29–54 The noun:

- 29–34 Gender
- 35–38 Declension
- 39–44 The cases
- 45–51 The number of formally different cases; comparison
- 52–54 Species

(iii) *Versification*

55–60 The syllable; quantity

61–67 Prosody and accent

68–70 Aspiration and spiritus marks

71–74 Special marks; the digamma

75–87 Types of feet according to the number of syllables

88–99 Types of feet

100–109 Metre, verse; further genres of poetry

110–113 Caesuras in the dactylic hexameter

114–117 Catalexis

(iv) 118–128 *Punctuation and the sentence*

As can be deduced from the contents of most of the manuscripts in which our Glossary is extant, it was apparently meant as a supplement to one or more of the standard treatments of Latin grammar and versification. The arrangement of the entries is on the whole systematic, but completeness does not seem to have been the compiler's aim: we do not find basic concepts of grammar like *vox* (apparently later supplied in the ancestor of MSS OPTUVXZ), like *vocales* and *consonantes*, and it is somewhat surprising to see that the categories of the noun have been treated rather fully, but the categories of the verb not at all.

Each entry consists of a Greek lemma, transliterated in letters of the Latin alphabet (often with various spellings and misspellings, as is to be expected), and of a Latin gloss; the only exception, where the lemma is a Latin word, occurs in item 15 (*ars*). The gloss may be either a translation or a definition, usually rather brief. In a few cases (items 51–4), the definition has been illustrated by one or two examples, while two entries supply etymological explanations (15, 88); it seems doubtful, however, if that of *ars* (15) was understood by all the scribes.[6]

The Grammarian's Glossary combines two basically different types of

[6] The derivation of *ars* from Greek *aretê* may explain why there is a Latin entry among the lemmata.

lemmata: the majority are Greek words that had been taken over as loan-words into Latin, especially those employed in prosody; they had become household words in the teaching of the *trivium.* In contrast to these, about three dozen of the lemmata, especially those denoting grammatical concepts (items 21–44), are words that had not been received into Latin because the Roman grammarians very early had chosen to render them by means of semantic loans and loan-formations (like *nomen* for *onoma, coniunctio* for *syndesmos*), which then became the standard terms in their language and also in the modern languages to our own day.

To identify the sources of a glossary is notoriously difficult, and it must become even more difficult when we realize that the Grammarian's Glossary largely consists of such terms as form the core and common stock of the technical vocabulary of grammar and versification in the early Middle Ages. The entries of our Glossary could have been excerpted from numerous grammars, grammatical commentaries, and treatises on metre, or could have been taken over from glossaries such as may be well known and accessible to scholars today, or may remain unpublished, or may have been lost. While it is impossible, then, to produce a reliable and complete analysis of our Glossary's sources, a few points seem clear. If we recognize that a genuine source of an entry can only be established where lemma *and* interpretation are the same, or nearly the same in source and glossary, then it is evident that the compiler of the Grammarian's Glossary made extensive use of Isidore's *Etymologies.* It appears certain that nearly fifty entries are based on this work, and early readers of the Glossary will have been well aware of this, as is shown by the rubric in MS W (see the 'Notes' section, below). As for the remaining entries, it is doubtful whether another, single source was utilized, or whether the compiler could build on a wider range of materials. It would seem, however, that most of these entries were supplied from glossaries rather than from grammars; for quite a number of entries, especially 21–44, this is likely because—as was mentioned above—the Roman grammarians had developed their own, vernacular terminology for the basic concepts of grammar and so did not normally employ, or explain, the corresponding Greek terms. I have found more than thirty items that can be traced back to glossaries of the *Hermeneumata* type, collections that are based on an original Greek–Latin compilation of the second century AD.[7] Also, I have found more than a dozen entries whose sources seem to

[7] The *Hermeneumata* glossaries have been printed in vol. III of G. Goetz, *Corpus Glossariorum Latinorum,* 7 vols. (Leipzig, 1888–1923) [= *CGL*]; cf. A. C. Dionisotti, 'Greek Grammars and Dictionaries in Carolingian Europe', in *The Sacred Nectar of the Greeks: The Study of Greek in the West in the Early Middle Ages,* ed. M. W. Herren and S. A. Brown, King's College London Medieval Studies, II (London, 1988), 1–56, at 26–31. The bilingual glossaries

be glossary materials going back to a sixth-century compilation ascribed to one Placidus, printed in volume V of the *Corpus Glossariorum Latinorum*. References to these sources will be found in the 'Notes' section; but I do not claim to have examined or exhausted all possible sources, whether they are glossaries or grammars.

When one considers the complicated and often confusing textual history of medieval glossaries, the manuscript versions of the Grammarian's Glossary appear remarkably uniform.[8] Yet there are numerous individual peculiarities and cross-connections between the various manuscripts that make it impossible for us to reconstruct the history of its transmission, let alone to establish a stemmatic relationship. However, an examination of the variant readings, of common errors, additions, and omissions yields some interesting results. Already in the eighth century, presumably in France, the textual transmission split into three branches or hyparchetypes:

1. A branch represented by the French MSS BLW; because of the date of MS W, this must have come into existence in the first half of the eighth century. The branch is marked by the omission of items 8–38 and 76–80, and by ordering items 56–73 as in the manuscripts of branch 3 (except MS D). The late Italian MS Y belongs in this group; it is very closely related to MS B.

2. A branch represented by MSS PX, which is characterized by a number of additional items (see above, p. 67), and by ordering items 56–73 differently from all the other manuscripts. Items 8–35 are present, but 36 and 37 have been omitted. Apart from MSS PX, this branch includes all the later Italian manuscripts (OTUVZ) except Y, and as MS P was written at Monte Cassino, branch 2 might be considered a specifically Italian text. But, as is clear from MS X, which shares most of this group's peculiarities, here too we witness a development that must have taken place in France, and not later than the third quarter of the eighth century, because of the date of MS P, which may well be the ancestor of all the later Italian manuscripts. Among these, MSS U and Z show close affinities.

3. This branch is represented by MSS DFS, which do not form a textual 'family' in the strict sense, since each of them has individual readings or shares some readings with branch 1 and some with branch 2. However, the members of this group appear to be closer to the original glossary than the other hyparchetypes: they do not omit items 8–38 (but F leaves out 36–8),

ascribed to Philoxenus and Cyrillus—both printed in *CGL*, vol. II—may also have been available to our compiler; in any case, a considerable number of entries in the Grammarian's Glossary are found in the *Hermeneumata* collections *and* in Philoxenus or Cyrillus.

[8] For the evidence underlying the following discussion, see the 'Notes' section, below.

as does branch 1, and they do not include the innovations (items 12a etc.) of branch 2. On the other hand, MSS D and F omit items 76–80, as does branch 1. The later MS M is closely connected with MS S, but M omits items 36–44a.

Of the Anglo-Saxon copies and excerpts of the Glossary, C—the oldest—cannot be derived exclusively from one of these three hyparchetypes. It does agree, however, in a few significant variant readings with B (116, 117, 120, 121); equally important seems the fact that a number of readings in C differ from those in H (cf. items 64a, 68, 69, 117, 120, 121). Even if we take into account the selective character of C, it is clear, therefore, that an 'English' branch of the Glossary text cannot be established on the basis of significant common readings of C and H, nor can the items in E and K that are probably derived from the Grammarian's Glossary throw more light on its transmission in Anglo-Saxon England, with the exception perhaps of item E 65 in MS K (= our item 5), whose peculiar spelling *Edulion* may link K with C.

Although it was written about three centuries after the compilation of its ultimate ancestor, H is a remarkably full and reliable copy of our Glossary and appears to belong in the third branch of its transmission: it neither has the additional items of the PX group, nor does it omit the items missing in the BLW group (8–38, 53, 76–80), while in ordering items 56–73 it agrees with FS and the BLW group. It shows individual readings shared by none of the other Continental manuscripts or by C (items 6, 13, 42, 60; 64a omitted; 81–7, 93, 117) but has a number of significant variants in common with MS D or groups of manuscripts that include D, a member of the third branch: 5, 31, 32, 36, 37, 61, 69, 94, 95, and cf. the omission of 44b and 64a only in D and H. This does not mean, however, that H and its presumable exemplar point back to a pure D-type ancestor or even a manuscript closely related to D. For D orders items 56–75 differently and omits a considerable number of entries contained in H that—with the exception of 81–7—must have been part and parcel of the original compilation: 17, 45–55, 60, 62, 63, 66, 67, 70, 71–3, 76–87; moreover, D and H differ clearly in nine readings (13, 24, 38, 56, 68, 74, 88, 91, 93), while nothing definite can be said about entries from 96 onwards, which are lost in D.

It may seem idle to speculate about the date and place of origin of the anonymous Grammarian's Glossary. As to the date, we have as a *terminus a quo* the time when Isidore's *Etymologies* became available outside Spain,[9] and

[9] See B. Bischoff, 'Die europäische Verbreitung der Werke Isidors von Sevilla', in his *Mittelalterliche Studien*, I (1966), 171–94, and M. Lapidge, 'An Isidorian Epitome from Early Anglo-Saxon England', in *Studi sulla cultura Germanica dei secoli IV–XII in onore di Giulia Mazzuoli Porru*, ed. M. A. d'Aronco *et al.*, *Romanobarbarica*, 10 (1988–9), 443–83.

as a *terminus ad quem* we can fix the dating of the earliest manuscript (W) which, however, on account of its gap between items 7 and 39, must be considered a copy of the ancestor (or a member) of the BLW family, which itself is at least at one remove from the original compilation. As a consequence, we should place the origin of the Glossary at some time in the second half of the seventh century, or in the first half of the eighth century, preferably early rather than late.

To determine the country, region, or place of origin of our Glossary may seem a hopeless task. Was it possibly a place where there was some interest in Greek studies? One might then be tempted to suggest Canterbury in the later seventh century, where, as we know, Greek as well as (Latin) grammar and metrics were taught in the school of Archbishop Theodore (669–90) and Abbot Hadrian (670–709/710).[10] But there is some weighty evidence against such a seemingly attractive hypothesis: (1) The provenance of nearly all the extant manuscripts, particularly the early ones, points to an origin on the Continent, probably in France. (2) If the early school of Canterbury, perhaps Theodore himself, had had a hand in the compilation of the Glossary, one would expect a reflection of this in what has been called the 'original English collection' of glosses, or in one of the glossaries derived from it, or related to it.[11] But there is no trace of this. The famous Leiden Glossary, the Épinal Glossary (and its copy, the Erfurt Glossary), and the second Corpus Glossary[12] all include a number of lemmata that occur in the Grammarian's Glossary, but their interpretations in nearly all cases differ essentially from those in our compilation, while the few closely corresponding entries—like the three[13] entries in the second Corpus Glossary

[10] For Greek taught at Canterbury, see M. Lapidge, 'The School of Theodore and Hadrian', *ASE* 15 (1986), 45–72; for grammar, W. Berschin, *Greek Letters and the Latin Middle Ages: From Jerome to Nicholas of Cusa*, rev. edn., trans. J. C. Frakes (Washington, DC, 1988), 121–5; for metrics, see N. Wright, 'Introduction to Aldhelm's Prose Writings on Metrics', in *Aldhelm: The Poetic Works*, trans. M. Lapidge and J. L. Rosier (Cambridge, 1985), 183–9.

[11] For the history and sources of this early glossary material in England, see W. M. Lindsay, *The Corpus, Épinal, Erfurt and Leyden Glossaries*, Publications of the Philological Society, VIII (London, 1921); J. D. Pheifer, *Old English Glosses in the Épinal–Erfurt Glossary* (Oxford, 1974), 'Introduction', esp. p. lvii; Lapidge, 'The School of Theodore and Hadrian'; J. D. Pheifer, 'Early Anglo-Saxon Glossaries and the School of Canterbury', *ASE* 16 (1987), 17–44.

[12] *A Late Eighth-Century Latin–Anglo-Saxon Glossary Preserved in the Library of the Leiden University*, ed. John Henry Hessels (Cambridge, 1906); 'The Épinal Glossary Edited with Critical Commentary of the Vocabulary', by A. K. Brown (unpublished diss., Stanford University, 1969); *CGL* V. 337–401 [the (first) Erfurt Glossary]; *The Corpus Glossary*, ed. W. M. Lindsay (Cambridge, 1921).

[13] Épinal has 18 lemmata in common with the Grammarian's Glossary, but only two interpretations are identical; Leiden has 15 such lemmata, with two common glosses; the second Corpus Glossary shares 29 lemmata with the Grammarian's Glossary, of which three show the same glosses.

(*epigramma* E 242, *brachus* B 184, *dactylus* D 7)—may well go back to other sources.

Moreover, an interest in Greek grammatical terminology may have been more general than we are inclined to think.[14] In MS Cotton Cleopatra A.vi, an English manuscript of the second(?) half of the tenth century, of unknown provenance and origin, the only known Anglo-Saxon copy of Donatus's *Ars maior* is followed by three anonymous grammatical treatises. The second of these (fos. 37^{v}–47^{r}) is an introduction to the grammar of Donatus in question-and-answer form, in which *gramma, grammatice,* and *prohemium* are interpreted as in the Grammarian's Glossary, and where the Greek names of the parts of speech—with the exception of that for the article—are supplied in one of the answers:

'Quomodo nominabant partes orationis apud Grecos?'

'Ita nominantur: onoma, antenoma, rema, epirema, metoche, sindesmos, prothesis, parenthesis.' (fo. 42^{v})

We should conclude from these considerations that the Grammarian's Glossary must have found its way to England in the course of the eighth century, or very early in the ninth. It was then drawn upon by the compiler of the first Corpus Glossary, unless we are to assume that this glossary as a whole was copied from a Continental exemplar. That C and possibly one or more near relatives survived the vicissitudes of the ninth century and were then again utilized might appear from the spelling *Edulion* in K. The version of the Glossary in H follows another line of transmission; the exemplar of H or one of its forerunners may have been a pre-Alfredian English copy, but it seems more likely that it came to England as part of one of the numerous French books imported in the course of the tenth century.[15] More may be known about this when all the glossary material in H has been thoroughly studied. Apart from K, the glossaries produced or copied in England in the tenth and eleventh centuries do not seem to have used the Grammarian's Glossary.[16]

[14] For the study of Greek in the early Middle Ages, see especially B. Bischoff, 'Das griechische Element in der abendländischen Bildung des Mittelalters', in his *Mittelalterliche Studien*, II (Stuttgart, 1967), 246–75; Berschin, *Greek Letters and the Latin Middle Ages*; M. C. Bodden, 'Evidence for Knowledge of Greek in Anglo-Saxon England', *ASE* 17 (1988), 217–46.

[15] Cf. H. Gneuss, 'Anglo-Saxon Libraries from the Conversion to the Benedictine Reform', *Settimane di studio del Centro italiano di studi sull'alto medioevo*, XXXII (1986), 678 and n. 110, and 'King Alfred and the History of Anglo-Saxon Libraries', in *Modes of Interpretation in Old English Literature: Essays in Honour of Stanley B. Greenfield*, ed. P. R. Brown *et al.* (Toronto, 1986), 37.

[16] For the later English glossaries see A. Cameron, 'A List of Old English Texts', in *A Plan for the Dictionary of Old English*, ed. R. Frank and A. Cameron (Toronto, 1973), 248–54, and Pheifer, *Old English Glosses*, pp. xxxi–xxxix.

The textual history of the Grammarian's Glossary suggests an origin in France. From there, at an early stage, copies were taken not only to England but also to Italy: the exemplar of MS P must have been available at Monte Cassino in the later eighth century. Was it possibly Paulus Diaconus himself who procured the Glossary for his monastery?

The Grammarian's Glossary was first published by Johann Friedrich Heusinger in 1766, from MS W, and again by Thomas Gaisford in 1837; Heusinger also knew the version in MS P. In 1876, Gustav Loewe mentioned the Glossary (he knew MSS W and X), and in 1923 Georg Goetz included a paragraph with remarks on the manuscripts and sources in his monumental *De glossariorum Latinorum origine et fatis*. More recently, attention has again been drawn to our Glossary by Bernhard Bischoff, Simona Gavinelli, and Walter Berschin.[17]

Text

The edition reproduces the text of MS Harley 3826 as faithfully as possible, but is arranged in columns, while in the manuscript the Glossary is written in run-on lines. Abbreviations are indicated by means of italics. No emendations have been made; where these would be called for, the pertinent information will be found in the 'Notes' following the edition. Entries in one or more of the Continental versions of the Grammarian's Glossary that may have been omitted in H (or its exemplar), or may have been added in those versions, are enclosed in square brackets. Lemmata with glosses corresponding to entries in Harley 3826 that occur in other Anglo-Saxon manuscript glossaries are recorded by the respective sigla (C, E, K, see above) to the right of the Harley entry.

	[fo. 150r] GRAMMATICĘ ARTIS NOMINA GRECE ET LATINE NOTATA.	
	Poeta. i. uates.	C
	Poeticus. liber.	C
3	Poema. i. uni*us* libri op*us*.	CE
	Poesis. i. op*us* multor*um* libror*um*.	CE
	Ydillion. paucor*um* uersuu*m*.	CK
6	Disticon. duor*um* locutio.	C
	Monosticon. uni*us* u*er*sus.	C
	Epodon. clausula*m* i*n* poemate.	

[17] For Heusinger and Gaisford see p. 65 above; G. Loewe, *Prodromus Corporis Glossariorum Latinorum* (Leipzig, 1876), 231–2; Goetz, *CGL* I. 102; Bischoff and Gavinelli, see p. 62 above; Berschin, *Greek Letters and the Latin Middle Ages*, 106 and 110.

9	Epigra*m*ma. titulus.	E
	P*ro*emion. dicendi initiu*m*.	
	P*ro*logus. seq*ue*ntis op*er*is p*rae*fatio.	
12	P*ro*blema. q*uae*stio.	E
12a	[Prothesis. propositio]	
	Thema. norma siu*e* mat*er*ia.	
	Tragoedia. luctuosu*m* carm*en*.	
14a	[Comoedia. laus in canticis dicta]	
15	Ars. apo tes. aretis .i. . . . disciplina siu*e* scientia.	
	Gra*m*ma. littera.	E
	Gra*m*matica. litteratura.	E
18	Gra*m*matic*us*. doctor lib*er*aliu*m* *uel* litteraru*m*.	
	Profora. int*er*rogatio.	
	Antifora. responsio.	
21	Onoma. nom*en*.	
	Antenoma. p*ro*nom*en*.	
	Rema. u*er*bu*m*.	
24	Epyrema. adu*er*biu*m*.	
	Methoche. participiu*m*.	
	[fo. 150^{v}] Arthron. articulus.	
27	Sindesmos. c*on*iunctio.	
	P*ro*tesis. p*rae*positio.	
28a	[Parathesis. interiectio]	
28b	[Schediasmos. interiectio]	
	Genos. gen*us*.	
30	Arsenicon. masc*u*linu*m*.	
	Telicon. femininu*m*.	
	Deteron. neutru*m*.	
33	Kynon. co*m*mune.	
	Epikenon. p*ro*miscuu*m*.	
	Piptosis. declinatio.	
35a	[Ptosis. casus]	
36	Anomala. inæqualia.	
	Analogia. c*om*p*ar*atio.	
	Euphonia. suauitas bene sonandi.	
39	Onomastike. no*min*atiuus.	C
	Genike. genit*iuus*.	C
	Dotike. datiuus.	CK
42	Eutike. acc*us*at*iuus*.	C
	Cletike. uocat*iuus*.	CK
	Afferetike. abl*at**iuus*.	C

44a	[Plithyntice. pluraliter]	
44b	[Aptota. in quibus nulla est inflexio casuum]	
45	Monoptota. eiusde*m* casus.	
	Diptota. in q*ui*b*us* similitudo duor*um* tantu*m* casuu*m*.	
	Triptota. triu*m* casuu*m* uarietas.	
48	Tet*r*aptota. iiii. casuu*m* uarietas.	E
	Pentaptota. u. casuu*m* inflexio.	
	Exaptota. ui. casuu*m* declinatio.	
51	Anomala. no*mina* q*uae* in co*mpar*atione mutant*ur*. ut bon*us*. melior. optimus.	
	Thetica. possessiua. ut euandrius a possidendo dicta.	
	Patronomica. a paren[fo. 151^{r}]tib*us* dicta uocabula. ut eacides. agame*m*nonides.	
54	Epitheta. adiectiua quę no*min*ib*us* apponunt*ur*. ut magn*us* homo. doctus philosophus.	
	Syllaba. co*mp*r*e*hensio litterar*um*.	
	Macra. longa.	
57	Brachia. breuis.	K
	Monocronon. uni*us* te*m*poris.	
	Dicronon. co*m*munis te*m*poris.	
60	Diptongon. uocalis duplicatio.	
	P*ro*sodia. accentus. *uel* son*us*.	CE
	Arsis. eleuatio.	C
63	Thesis. positio.	
	Oxia. accuta.	C
64a	[Baria. grauis]	C
	P*er*istomene. circu*m*flexus.	C
66	Cronos. longitudo *uel* te*mpus*.	C
	Ton*us*. accent*us*.	C
	Crisesma. crassitudo.	C
69	Dapsia. sipidu*m* *uel* asp*er*u*m*.	C
	Psile. lene *uel* purum.	C
	Apostrophos. regressio.	
71a	[Yphen. copulatio]	
72	Diastole. sep*ar*atio.	C
	Ypodiastole. subseparatio.	C
	Digra*m*mos. duplex litt*er*a.	C
74a	[Phoni. uox]	
74b	[Aphona. sine uoce]	
74c	[Phonienta. uocales]	
74d	[Imiphonas. semiuocales]	

75	Pos. pes.	C
	Monosyllaba. una syllaba.	
	Dyssillabos. duar*um* syllabar*um.*	
78	Trisillabos. triu*m.*	
	Tetrasillabos. iiii.	
	[fo. 151v] Pentasyllabos. u. syllabar*um.*	
81	Exasyllabos. u. syll*abarum.*	
	Eptasyll*abos.* ui. sill*abarum.*	
	Ogdosyll*abos.* uiii.	
84	Niasyll*abos.* uiiii.	
	Diasyllabos. x.	
	Undecasyll*abos.* xi.	E
87	Dodecasyllabos. xii.	
	Pyrrichi*us.* a pyrro filio achillis.	
	Spondeus. tract*us.*	
90	Trocheu*s.* celer.	E
	Iamb*us.* maledic*us.* *uel* libid*us.*	
	Dactilus. digitus.	
93	Anapest*us.* dactilo c*ont*rari*us* siue rep*er*cussus.	
	Amphimacr*us.* hinc inde long*us.*	
	Amphibrachis. hinc inde breuis.	
96	Tribrachis. triu*m* breuiu*m.*	
	Corios. coris apt*us.*	
	Ionicos. ineq*u*alis.	
98a	[Bacchios. conueniens baccicis cantibus]	
99	Pali*m*bachius. c*ont*rarius bachio.	
	Metron. m*en*sura.	E
	Rithmos. numerus.	C
102	Heroicon metron. uiror*um* fortiu*m* carm*en.*	
	Monometron. u*er*sus uni*us* pedis.	C
	Bucolicon. pastorale carm*en.*	CK
104a	[Georgica. agricultura uel rusticana]	
104b	[Epos. carmen]	
105	Dimetron. duor*um* pedu*m* uersus.	C
	Trimetron. triu*m* pedu*m.*	C
	Tetrametron. iiii. pedu*m.*	CE
108	Pentametron. u. pedu*m.*	CE
	Exametron [fo. 152r] .i. senariu*m.*	C
	Pentimemeren. syllaba remanens post duos pedes.	C
111	Eptimemeren. syllaba remanens po*st* t*er*tiu*m* pede*m.*	C
	Tritos trocheos. syllaba po*st* .iiii. pedes remanens.	C

	Tetobucolicos. syllaba po*st* q*u*intu*m* pede*m* remanens.	C
114	Catalecticos. ubi i*n* pede u*er*suu*m* una syllaba de*est*.	CK
	Brachiacatalectos. ubi duę min*us* s*unt*.	CK
	Acatalectos. ubi u*er*sus legitimo fine co*n*cludit*ur*.	C
117	Asp*er*catalectos. ubi sup*er* legitimos pedes syllaba crescit.	C
	Thesis. positurę.	C
	Telia. distinctio.	C
120	Ypostigme. subdistinctio.	C
	Mesi. media distinctio.	C
121a	[Stigmi. i. distinctio seu diastixis]	
	Cola. m*em*bru*m*.	CK
123	Co*m*ma. incisu*m*.	CK
	P*er*iodos. clausula siue circuit*us*. na*m* cola tot*us* u*er*sus *est*. co*m*mata *autem* ipse i*n*cisiones pedu*m*. p*er*iodos u*er*o tota sententia.	CE
	Monocolon. unim*em*bris sententia.	
126	[fo. 152^{v}] Dicolor. bime*m*bris.	
	Tricolon. trime*m*bris.	E
	Tetracolon. quadrim*em*bris.	
128a	[Pentacolon. quinquemembris]	

Notes

The following notes include all significant variant readings from MSS BCDEFKLPRSVWX, references to corresponding interpretations in Isidore's *Etymologies*, in grammars and glossaries, and references (marked 'cf.') to passages that help to explain terms and concepts of the Grammarian's Glossary. Among the variants, minor variations in spelling and scribal errors have not normally been recorded, but I have tried to give the reader an idea of how the scribes managed to cope with difficult Greek terms transliterated into Latin. The variant readings are also meant to provide corrections where the scribe of H—or one of his forerunners—has obviously blundered, as in items 18, 42, 52, 113, 117, 126. Variant readings from the later MSS MOTUYZ have not been recorded except where these add or omit a whole item (i.e. lemma and gloss). References to grammars and glossaries have had to be selective;[18] the Roman grammarian's name is always followed by

[18] Full references to the grammars can now be found in the computer concordance by V. Lomanto and N. Marinone, *Index Grammaticus: An Index to Latin Grammar Texts*, 3 vols. (Hildesheim, 1990); for the glossaries, see the index in vols. VI and VII of *CGL*. With few exceptions, all references to the grammarians are to the edition by H. Keil, *Grammatici Latini*, vols. I–VII (Leipzig, 1856–80), even though a few texts are now available in more recent

volume, page, and—in most cases—line in Keil's *Grammatici Latini.* 'Etym.' refers to the edition of Isidore's work by W. M. Lindsay (Oxford, 1911), while 'CGL' stands for Goetz, *Corpus Glossariorum Latinorum* (see n. 7); 'Beda AM' refers to *De arte metrica*, ed. C. B. Kendall, in *Bedae Venerabilis Opera. Pars I: Opera didascalia*, CCSL 123A (Turnhout, 1975). For 'Byrhtferth', see *Byrhtferth's Manual*, ed. S. J. Crawford, EETS 177 (1929). The best systematic treatment of the grammatical terms (items 15–55) is still that by Ludwig Jeep, *Zur Geschichte der Lehre von den Redetheilen bei den lateinischen Grammatikern* (Leipzig, 1893).

Rubric *GRAMMATICĘ]* FLPSV *INCIPIUNT GR.*; W *ESIDORI IUNIORIS PALESTINENSIS EPISCOPI GR.* (with *PALESTINENSIS* no doubt as a copyist's error for *HISPALENSIS*); *NOTATA*] D *praenotata*; Rubric in X: *Incipiunt glosae.*

1–14 Poetry and its genres

1 om. P; *uates*] om. V; *.i.* (= *id est*) in 1, 3 and 4 only in H; Etym. VIII. vii. 13, CGL V. 93. 17.

2 S *liber uel cantus*; cf. CGL V. 93. 18.

3–9 Etym. I. xxxix. 21–3.

3 BR *poema: opus unius libri* (R adds *metrici*).

5 DH *Ydillion*, R *ydilion*, F *idlion*, LVWX *edilion*, S *edyllion*, P *edilyon*, CK *edulion*, B *dilion*; CGL V. 104. 2.

6 *locutio*] BVX *uersuum*, P *uersurum*, R *uersum*, om. DFLSW; in OPVX, 6 follows item 7.

8–38 om. BLWY.

8 DHR *Epodon*, PV *ephodon*, X *epodhon*, F *ypodon*; *clausulam*] DRS *clausula*, X *clausa*; *in*] om. X. Cf. Diomedes I. 485.

9 *titulus*] O *super litteras titulus* (TV similar), cf. Etym. I. xxxix. 22. H reads at end of line 7 *titulus. Proemi*, but begins again line 8 *Proemion.*

10 PV *proymion*, X *proymon*; cf. E *proemium: praefatio libri prologum* (see item 11), and CGL V. 323. 10, Etym. VI. viii. 9.

11 om. F; CGL IV. 148. 42, 556. 16, V. 137. 48.

12 F *quaestio siue materia uel forma*, cf. item 13. CGL II. 416. 33, V. 137. 8 and 12; cf. E *problema: parabola. enigma. questio*, Etym. VI. viii. 14.

12a only in PUVXZ; UV *prepositio.*

editions. I am grateful to Professor Patrizia Lendinara for reading a draft of this article and for a number of valuable suggestions.

13 *norma*] DPSV and CGL V. 101. 22 *norma uel forma siue materia*, X *norma uel forma*; for F see item 12. Items 13 and 14 precede 12 in UZ.

14 Etym. XVIII. xlv, CGL V. 426. 50.

14a only in OPUVXZ.

15–20 Grammar

15 H *c.* five letters erased at end of line 11 and five letters at beginning of line 12; *aretis .i.*] FPV *aretes* (V *arestes*) *id est uirtus*; D reads: *Ars apo tes siue scientia*; X reads: *Apo tes. ars. Aretes. uirtus disciplinę siue scientiae; apo tes* is written as one word in all MSS; Etym. I. i. 1–2; cf. Diomedes I. 421. 8 f., Cassiodorus, *Institutiones*, ed. Mynors (Oxford, 1937), ii. 4, etc.

16 om. F; CGL III. 71. 4; Etym. I. v. 1.

17 om. FD; cf. Etym. I. v. 1.

18 om. F; *uel*] om. DPSVX; CGL IV. 84. 1, 521. 14; cf. E *grammati: litterati*; cf. Diomedes I. 421. 9–13.

19–20 PV *prophora*; PRV *antiphora*. These entries may refer to a grammar of the question-and-answer type, like the *Ars minor* of Donatus, or the *Excerpta* of Audax.

21–28 The parts of speech

Corresponding lists in Charisius, ed. Barwick (Leipzig, 1964), 470, and CGL III. 327 f., 375. 72–9; also, numerous occurrences of individual items in CGL II and III.

22 DFPSV *antonoma*, X *ontonoman*.

23 UZ *rima*.

24 om. F; VX *epirrema*, PS *epyrrema*, X *expirrema*.

25 PSV *metoche*, D *methoce*, X *Inethoche*.

26 MS *archon*; in OUVX follows after 28a, in P follows after 28b.

27 cf. Quintilian, *Inst. orat.* I. iv. 18.

28 FPVX *prothesis*; om. UZ.

28a only in OPTVX; 28b only in PT.

29–34 The noun: gender

29–32 CGL III. 376. 2, 8–10, etc.

31 DFS *thelicon*, V *thilicon*, PX *thylicon*; CGL V. 101. 17.

32 D *deceron*, F *detheron*(?), OPV *udeteron*, MS *undetheron*, X *udetheron*; in X follows after 33.

33–4 CGL III. 147. 38, 461. 23; etc.; cf. Priscianus II. 140, Donatus III. 375, etc.

33 S *chynon*.

34 D *epykenon*, S *epychenon*, P *epicynon*, V *epikynon*, X *EPKINωN*; in X follows after 35.

35–51 The noun: declension, the cases

35 FPX *pipthosis.*

35a only in OPTVX.

35–6 om. FOPUVXZ; for the position in this section see Etym. I. xviii, Probus IV. 48 f. In T, 36–8 follow 50.

36 CGL III. 488. 73. Items 36–44a om. M.

37 Etym. I. xxviii. 1, Pompeius V. 197. 24.

38 om. FOPUVZ; D *eophonia: suauitas sonorum;* X *eufonia: bene sonans oratio*; in X follows after 75; for the relation to *analogia* (item 37), see Cledonius V. 47. 12–18, etc.

39 ff. BLW resume again.

39–44 For corresponding lists of cases see CGL III. 376 and 382; also, individual entries in CGL.

39 *nominatiuus*] C *genitiuus.*

40 X *geratice.*

41 D *doctice.*

42 BDPSVX *etiatice* (V *etiatici*), F *epiatice*, C *ethiantike*, LW *atiatike*; LW *accusatiuum.*

43 V *cletici*, BX *eletice*; LW *uocatiuum*; 43 om. UZ.

44 DSW *aferetike*, PX *apheretice*, V *apheretici*, L *afaretike*, F *aferitice*, C *afertice*, B *auestice.*

44a only in OPTUVXZ; CGL III. 376. 13.

44b–50 cf. Etym. I. vii. 33, Donatus IV. 377. 23–5.

44b not in DH; *est*] om. W; follows 45 in BFLMSTWY.

45–55 om. D.

45 FPVWX *casui*, L *causa.*

46 *in ... casuum*] BFR *duorum casuum; casuum*] V *casuum uarietas*, SW *casuum est.*

47, 48 *uarietas*] om. FORX; cf. E *tetraptota: nomina quae tantum in quatuor casibus declinantur.*

49 *inflexio*] B *uarietas*, om. FR.

50 *ui. casuum*] BLPSVWX *omnium casuum uaria* (B om. *uaria*); *declinatio*] om. FOR.

51 *nomina*] B *nomina inequalia*; *quae ... optimus*] om. DF; *in comparatione*] om. B; *optimus*] BLPSVWX add *malus. peior. pessimus*; R reads *anomalia nomina sunt inaequalia*; Pompeius V. 154. 24–6, etc.

52–54 The noun: species

52 *Thetica*] B *De elitica*; S *possessiui*; *ut ... dicta*] om. FORW; *euandrius*] BPSVX(L?) *euandrius ensis*, correctly, see Etym. I. vii. 21, Donatus IV. 374. 1, Priscianus II. 68. 16; *dicta*] BLPSV *utique dicta*; cf. Priscianus II. 68–82.

53 om. BLWY; *Patronomica*] FHPSVX; *a ... uocabula*] S *parentibus uoc. ducta; dicta ... agamemnonides*] om. F; *dicta ... eacides*] X *uocabula ducta ut alcides; agamemnonides*] V *agamemnon*, X *agamemnon qui et herculus*; in OPUVZ follows after 54; cf. Priscianus II. 62–8 (*Aeacides*: 62.17).

54 *adiectiua*] *id est adiectiua* BLPW; *quę*] S *id est quae; quę ... philosophus*] om. FORW; *ut*] BPSV *utputa; doctus*] PV *doctor; philosophus*] BLPSV add *magnus et doctus epitheta* (V *epithete*, B *aphiteta*) *sunt*; in X 54 precedes 52; Etym. I. vii. 22, CGL V. 19. 10, 65. 6; cf. E: *Epiteta: nomina aliis nominibus adicta.*

55–74 The order of entries in OPUVXZ differs: 55–7, 64, 64a, 65, 69–73 (72 om. PVX), 66, 58–63, 67, 68, 74.
The order of entries in D is: (45–55 om.), 74, 75, 61, 56–9, 64, 65, 68, 69, 88–95 (60, 62, 63, 66, 67, 70–3, 76–87 om.)

55–60 The syllable; quantity

55 BFLPSVWX *litterarum congregatio*; Priscianus II. 44. 2, Donatus IV. 368. 18, CGL IV. 285. 14, V. 99. 2, 558. 5: *comprehensio*; CGL V. 99. 2: *congregatio*; Diomedes I. 427. 4: *congregatio uel comprehensio.*

56–7 DR *macron: longa*; DR *brachin*; Etym. I. xix. 4–5, CGL V. 114. 39.

58–9 BX *monochron*, LW *mochron*; X *dicron*, W *dischronon*; 59 om. BMY; cf. Sergius IV. 533.

60 om. D; *Diptongon*] PV *diphthongon*, X *diptonga; uocalis duplicatio*] PV *uoglis id est duplex sonus*; S *duplex uocalis*; X *duplex sonus siue uocalis*; F *dualis sonus*; BL *duae uocales* (B adds *iunctae*); W *geminatio uocalium.*

61–67 Prosody and accent

61 om. F; *uel sonus*] om. C; *uel*] all except DHR *siue*; Etym. I. xviii. 1.

62–3 om. D; *positio*] L *propositio*; Etym. I. xvii. 21, CGL V. 101. 27.

64–6 Etym. I. xix. 1–3; Byrhtferth 182.31–184.2.

64a all except DH; *Baria*] X *baruch*; *grauis*] CL *breuis*, F *breuis uel grauis.*

65 V *perispomeni*, BS *perispomene*, X *perismomens*, C *pistomine.*

66 om. D; *longitudo uel*] om. C and CGL III. 524. 57, IV. 224. 10.

67 om. D; Etym. I. xviii. 1, CGL V. 102. 8.

68–70 Aspiration and spiritus

Etym. I. xix. 9–10, Priscianus III. 520. 14–17, etc.

68 HW *Crisesma*, R *Chrisesma*, DFPSV(X?) and CGL V. 102. 15 *trisesma*, L *trissesma*, B *trissisma*, C *trissima*; DUZ and CGL V. 102. 15 *grassitudo*; cf. Sergius IV. 526. 1–3: *crassitudo autem in spiritu est, unde etiam Graeci adspirationem appellant*; an alternative term used by Priscianus (II. 6. 22) is *latitudo*. For *trisesma* see CGL VII. 368; for *chrisesma*, Laistner (edition of R, see above, p. 63) suggests *chrisma*.

69 *Dapsia*] D *dapsya*, R *dapsid*, BCFLPRSVW *dasia*, X *basia; sipidum*] BCDFLPWX *hispidum*, V *ispidum*; S *spidum; uel asperum*] D *uel aspex*, F *uel aspersum*, C om., BLSVW add *unde et aspiratio* (V *aspitio*); BY follows after 70; CGL III. 514. 3.

70 om. D; S *phyle; lene uel purum*] LW *leue u.p.*, B *leuem u.p.*, X *lenę uel purae*, C *purum*; CGL V. 95. 17–18.

71–74 Special marks; the digamma

71 om. D; B *egressio*; cf. Etym. I. xix. 8, Priscianus III. 520. 11–14, etc.

71a only in H.

72 om. DPVX; Etym. I. xix. 7, Priscianus III. 520. 10, etc.; CGL IV. 229. 39.

73 in H at the foot of the page, with *signe de renvoi* after 72; om. BDY; W *spondiastole*, X *separatio*; CGL V. 104. 8.

74 BCDR *digammos; littera*] S *gramma*; Etym. I. iv. 8; cf. Pompeius V. 105, etc., and K (entry D 486) *Digamma. .i. uau uel f.*

74a–b only in OPTUVXZ.

74b in X follows after 38 (both after 75); *uoce*] X *uoce id est muta*; cf. CGL II. 254. 15, etc.

74c only in OPTUVZ.

74d only in OUZ.

75–87 Types of feet (i)

75 *Pos*] PV *pus*, S *pes*; CGL V. 94. 2.

76–87 om. in BDFLWY; 81–7 om. in MOPSTUVXZ, and so 81–7 only in H, where they may represent a later addition. Otherwise, the PX branch may have omitted 81–7 because they were considered inappropriate; cf. Diomedes I. 474–82, Sergius IV. 480 f.,

Pompeius V. 122 f., Beda AM ix. 4–11, and especially Mallius Theodorus VI. 588 and Etym. I. xvii. 1 and 28.

76 om. SV; follows after 80 in PX; P *monosyllabon: unius syllabe.*

77 V *duo syllabe.*

78 om. V; X *trium syllabarum*; cf. CGL III. 522. 65.

79 PSVX *quattuor syllabarum*; cf. CGL III. 522. 63.

80 *syllabarum*] V *syllabe*, S om.

86 cf. E *Endeca: uersus decem sillabarum.*

88–99 Types of feet (ii)

88 *pyrro*] om. X; *achillis*] W *achelli*, X *achillo*; PX(L?) add *nominatus*, S *nominatos*, VW *nominatur*; Audax VII. 334. 8 f.; different explanations in R and Etym. I. xvii. 2.

89 om. L; Etym. I. xvii. 2, CGL V. 100. 5.

90 Etym. I. xvii. 3, quoted more fully in E; R *trochaeus: rotatilis* (cf. Prudentius, ed. Cunningham, CCSL 126, p. 401, 'Epilogue', line 8).

91 D *iambicus*; *uel libidus*] F *siue libidus*, BPSVW *siue liuidus*, F *uel liuidus*; Etym. I. xvii. 4; cf. Diomedes I. 485. 11.

92 Etym. I. xvii. 8.

93 *siue repercussus*] only in H; Etym. I. xvii. 7 (manuscript B).

94 *hinc*] *hinc et* BFLPSVWX; Etym. I. xvii. 10.

95 om. X; *hinc*] *hinc et* FLPSVW; *et* om. in BDH and CGL III. 488. 31; Etym. I. xvii. 9. D ends after *breuis*.

96 CGL V. 102. 11; Etym. I. xvii. 5: *Tribrachys, qui et chorius appellatur* . . ., cf. item 97.

97 *Corios*] X *corius*, PSVW *chorios*, L *chorius*, F *coriambi*, B *coriambus*. All except B and F erroneous, as is clear from Etym. I. xvii. 5 (see item 96), and I. xvii. 16: *Choriambus uero, quia ex hoc pede compositum carmen choris aptissimum sit.*

98 Etym. I. xvii. 17.

98a only in H.

99 Audax VII. 335. 12.

100–109 Metre, verse, genres of poetry

100 Etym. I. xxxix. 1.

101 VX *arithmos*; Etym. I. xxxix. 3.

102 *uirorum*] om. F; *carmen*] om. B; Etym. I. xxxix. 9; cf. Diomedes I. 494. 32 f.

103 PV *unius pedis uersum*; in BFLMSWY follows after 104, in OPTUVXZ follows after 104b.

104 FLPVW *pastoralem*; Etym. I. xxxix. 16, Diomedes I. 486. 17.

104a only in OPTUVZ.

104b only in OPTUVXZ.

105–9 cf. Etym. I. xxxix. 6, Diomedes I. 506 f.

105 *pedum*] B *uersuum;* *uersus*] L *uersurum*, W *uersuum*, BCRX om.

106 *pedum*] BFW *pedum uersus*, L *pedum uersum.*

107 .iiii.] BPVW *quattuor*, X *iiiior*, L *quinque* (cf. item 108); *pedum*] E *pedum uersus*; 107 om. UZ; CGL V. 101. 29.

108 om. LUZ; CGL IV. 270. 32; E and CGL IV. 139. 44, 550. 12: *pentametrum: uersus quinque syllabarum.*

109 cf. CGL V. 66. 6.

110–113 Caesuras

Cf. Diomedes I. 497 f., Servius IV. 457, Sergius IV. 523, Maximus Victorinus VI. 240, etc; Beda AM xii, Byrhtferth, 98–100.

110 *syllaba . . . pedes*] R *post tres pedes remanens.* W places *post duos pedes* to the right of *eptimimeren* (item 111), and from here until item 120 each gloss in W interprets the lemma of the preceding line.

111 *syllaba . . . pedem*] BLPSVX *syllaba post tertium pedem* (S: *pedum*, BX: *tres pedes*) *remanens;* (*rem.* om. B) *tertium pedem*] C *iii. pedes.*

112 FHPV *tritos trocheos*, BC *tritus trocheus*, LSWX and CGL V. 102. 4 *titos trocheus* (L *chroceus*), R *tetratrochaeos;* *.iiii.*] RX *quattuor*, LPV *quartum*, W *ter*, B *tres*, C *.uii.;* *pedes*] PV *pedem*, S *pedum*, L om.; *remanens*] om B.

113 *Tetobucolicos*] C *terte bocolicon*, S *tetarcos bucholicos*, LW *tetarto buccolicon*, R *texobucolicos*, B *tetartecobilicon*, PV *tetartos* (V *tetrartos*) *trocheos*, X *tardos trocheus*; *syllaba*] om. R; *quintum*] CRX *quinque*, B *quattuor*, LPVW *quartum*; *pedem*] BCRX *pedes;* *remanens*] om B. For the terminology cf. Iulius Severus VI. 645. 30 *tetarte bucolicon* (*t. bucolice*, Audax VII. 333. 15); Servius IV. 457. 12 *tetartum trochaeum*; Diomedes I. 497. 10 *tetrapodia bucolice*; Maximus Vict. VI. 240 and Beda AM xii. 35 *bucolice tome.* For the confusion about item 113 in the glossary versions (and in several grammars) of what are in fact two different types of caesura, see Neil Wright in Lapidge and Rosier, *Aldhelm: The Poetic Works*, 267 n. 40.

114–117 Catalexis

Cf. Servius IV. 457, Marius Vict. VI. 61, Audax VII. 333, etc.

114 *uersuum*] BCR *uersus*, L *uersu.*

115 PRVW *brachicatalectos*, CLX *brachicatalecticus*, B *bracchicatalecticon;* *duę*] PVX *due syllabe*, B *duo.*

116 B *catalecticus*, C *catalectus; uersus*] L *uersu; concluditur*] X *concluduntur*, R *clauditur*; Servius IV. 457. 16, CGL IV. 22. 44.

117 LPRSVX(W?) *Ypercatalectos*, BC *Ypercatalecticus; super*] BC *sub; crescit*] B *adcrescit*.

118–128 Punctuation and the sentence

118–24 Etym. I. xx, II. xviii. 1, Diomedes I. 437. 39, 465. 23 f., Donatus IV. 372, Sergius IV. 533 f.

118 om. L; *positurę*] C *positura*; PVX *positure uel stigme*.

119 BCFLPRVX *thelia* (V *thelza*); CGL V. 101. 16.

120 S *yposticme*, BCLW(F?) *yposticen* (L *yposticem*), V *yposticma*, R *ypostigma*; Audax VII. 324. 18, etc.; CGL V. 104. 9.

121 BL *mes*, C *mec*; W with gloss for 120 and 121; Diomedes I. 437. 17 f.

121a only in OPTUVXZ; X *stiema: distinatio* (*seu d.* om.).

123 X *comata: incisiones pedum*, cf. Etym. I. xx. 6, Marius Vict. VI. 53 f., etc., and item 124.

124 BLPW(F?) and CGL V. 92. 4 as H; *circuitus*] X *circuitus uel tota sententia*; X ends with *uersus est*, V with *uersus*; R splits 124 into two entries (ed. Laistner nos. 46 and 58); C no. 78: *commata ... pedum*, C. no. 263: *Periodos clausula uel tota sententia est*. The gloss (except in C) does not properly distinguish between the senses of *comma* and *colon* as applied to prose and verse; cf. Pompeius V. 133 f., Beda AM xii. 42–51.

125–8 om. BLVY.

125 *unimembris*] FWX *unius membri*.

126 PRSW *dicolon*, F *discolon*, X *bicolon*; *bimembris*] R *dimembris*, X *bimembri sententia*.

127 *trimembris*] X *trimembri sententia*; CGL V. 102. 12.

128 om. BLVXY; CGL V. 101. 28.

128a only in W. X adds after 127 definitions of *Ecloga* and *Hyperbaton*; M and S continue with glosses of rhetorical terms.

Poetic Words in Late Old English Prose

ROBERTA FRANK

Imagination is to reality what poetry is to prose: the former will always think of objects as massive and vertical; the latter will always try to extend them horizontally.

Goethe, *Italian Journey* (Messina, 18 May 1787)

Theorists since Isocrates have tried to epigrammatize the essential difference between poetry and prose. Prose is bread, sweet new wine, a stately walker; poetry is a wreath of flowers, heady mead, a swift runner.[1] Prose is conceptual, intellectual, judicious, informative; verse is imagistic, emotional, playful, attitudinal. Prose raises the walls, poetry lays the roof; prose extends horizontally, poetry, vertically.[2] Baffled, we suspect the worst, that nothing fundamental separates the two modes.

Not that they are interchangeable. We want our prose not too regular in its rhythm, not too fond of patterns of repetition. But how many are too many? Where do we draw the line? At what point on the stylistic spectrum does prose turn into poetry? In the late twentieth century, it is not subject or diction or rhyme that screams 'verse' but typographical convention. A ragged right margin tells readers to adopt a particular stance, to look at words, not through them. 'Print it as poetry and it is poetry.'[3]

[1] These metaphors, among others, are used by Anglo-Latin authors to explain why they wrote on one subject in prose and verse. See Gernot Wieland, '*Geminus Stilus:* Studies in Anglo-Latin Hagiography', in *Insular Latin Studies*, ed. M. Herren, Papers in Mediaeval Studies, 1 (Toronto, 1981), 113–33. Also E. R. Curtius, *European Literature and the Latin Middle Ages* (1945), trans. W. R. Trask (New York, 1953), 147–54 ('Poetry and Prose' and 'System of Medieval Styles').

[2] Aldhelm, *De virginitate*, ed. R. Ehwald, Monumenta Germaniae Historica Auct. Ant. 15 (Berlin, 1919), 321: 'The rhetorical foundation stones were now laid and the walls of prose were built, so I shall—trusting in heavenly support—build a sturdy roof with trochaic slates and dactylic tiles of metre'; trans. M. Lapidge, in M. Lapidge and M. Herren, *Aldhelm: The Prose Works* (Cambridge, 1979), 131. For poetry as 'up' and prose as 'across', see the epigraph.

[3] R. A. Lanham, *Style: An Anti-Textbook* (New Haven, Conn. and London, 1974), 99. Cf. the 1960s phenomenon of Found Poetry, in which doctors' prescriptions, IRS bulletins, and airline instructions to passengers were set out on the page as verse: Ronald Gross and George Quasha, *Open Poetry: Four Anthologies of Expanded Poems* (New York, 1973), 431–526.

But Old English verse is written out as prose, without line divisions and largely unpointed. What oral-culture equivalent to the printed page alerted Anglo-Saxon audiences to put on a poetic hat, to prepare to hear words sing? They certainly distinguished between verse and prose. Ælfric calls Bede's prose life of Cuthbert an *anfeald gereccednys* 'straightforward narrative', the verse life, a *leoðlic gyddung* 'poetic recitation'; the preface to Alfred's *Boethius* describes the king's prose paraphrase of the metres as *spell* 'speech', his subsequent verse rendition as *leoð* 'song'.[4] Practised in applying Latin categories to their own language and literature, Anglo-Saxon authors, unlike M. Jourdain, knew when they were speaking prose. It is we who are not quite certain where they drew the boundary.[5]

In two recent essays, Eric Stanley has reminded us that the rhythmical stringing together of parallel phrases linked by alliteration, a feature of several kinds of Old English rhetorical prose, does not in itself make 'poetry'. To be considered verse, a piece of rhythmic, alliterative prose 'must contain some items . . . from the language of Old English poetry'; when these are located, 'we may then go on, if we wish, and allege that the author too recognized, and intentionally used, these items as a sign that his discourse here is poetical'.[6] Like make-up and dress, poetic words invite a certain attitude, a particular sort of attention. But one robin does not make a spring, and quantitative definition again raises its hoary head. How many poetic words have to be present to push Old English prose over the edge, into the leafy-green region of poetry? Who decides? And under what circumstances

[4] *Ælfric's Catholic Homilies: The Second Series, Text*, ed. M. Godden, EETS ss 5 (London, 1979), 81 (Homily X, St Cuthbert); *King Alfred's Old English Version of Boethius' De consolatione philosophiae*, ed. W. J. Sedgefield (Oxford, 1899; repr. Darmstadt, 1968), 1. Ælfric's *Grammar* defines prose (negatively) as 'plain Latin composed and ordered without poetic art': *Ælfrics Grammatik und Glossar: Text und Varianten*, ed. J. Zupitza (Berlin, 1880; repr. 1966), 295.

[5] Thus Ælfric's alliterative and rhythmic discourse, initially assumed to be verse (e.g. J. Schipper, 'Metrische Randglossen', *Englische Studien*, 9 (1886), 184–94), looks more like prose to twentieth-century readers: e.g. K. Luick, 'Englische Metrike: Geschichte der Heimischen Versarten', in *Grundriss der germanischen Philologie*, ed. H. Paul (2nd edn., Strassburg, 1901–2), II. ii. 141–80, at 142–3; G. Gerould, 'Abbot Ælfric's Rhythmic Prose', *Modern Philology*, 22 (1924–5), 353–66; O. Funke, 'Studien zur alliterierenden und rhythmisierenden Prosa in der älteren altenglischen Homiletik', *Anglia*, 80 (1962), 9–36. But the contrary view, that Ælfric was writing poetry, still has supporters: e.g. S. Kuhn, 'Was Ælfric a Poet?', *Philological Quarterly*, 52 (1973), 643–62.

[6] *The Judgement of the Damned*, from Corpus Christi College Cambridge 201 and Other Manuscripts, and the Definition of Old English Verse', in *Learning and Literature in Anglo-Saxon England: Studies Presented to Peter Clemoes on the Occasion of his Sixty-Fifth Birthday*, ed. M. Lapidge and H. Gneuss (Cambridge, 1985), 363–91; repr. *A Collection of Papers with Emphasis on Old English Literature*, Publications of the Dictionary of Old English, 3 (Toronto, 1987), 352–83, at 357. See also 'Alliterative Ornament and Alliterative Rhythmical Discourse in Old High German and Old Frisian compared with Similar Manifestations in Old English', *Beiträge zur Geschichte der deutschen Sprache und Literatur*, 106 (1984), 184–217.

was it permissible for prose writers to reach out and 'quote' from the other register, plucking for their own pleasure both 'the mud-flowers of dialect | And the immortelles of perfect pitch'?[7]

Anglo-Saxon England is far enough distant for its stylistic etiquette to be based on rules very different from our own; it is clear, however, that literary good manners mattered. Authors tell us again and again of their concern for tone and register, for choosing the right word. The chronicler Æthelweard interrupts his account of a Viking defeat to 'correct' his diction: 'There fell three of their kings in that same "storm" (or "battle" would be the right thing to say).'[8] Vernacular writers would have possessed at least as delicate a sense of appropriateness, of the distinctions between synonyms. Some Old English words seem to have been confined to prose (e.g. *pytt, borg, cnapa, bradnes, þoden, bibliođece*), others to poetry (e.g. *frod, wicg, eoh, guđ, beadu, tir, hruse, geofon, dreor*);[9] still others had different meanings, depending on whether they are used in poetry or prose (e.g. *bord, bill, mæl, blæd (m.), mere, gewinn, rand*).[10] A fourth group of words, catalogued over twenty years ago by Eric Stanley, occurs almost exclusively in prose and only rarely in verse (e.g. *digollice, ege, gedrefednes,*

[7] Seamus Heaney, *Field Work* (London, 1979), 56 ('Song').

[8] *The Chronicle of Æthelweard*, ed. Alistair Campbell (London, 1962), 53: 'Ibidemque ruunt reges tres eorum turbine in eodem (uel certamine dicere fas est).' 'Storm' is a natural metaphor for battle (cf. Gm. *Sturm*, OE *storm, scur* [of arrows]). But Æthelweard had an interest in Old Norse names and words (see pp. lix–lx), and *turbo*, esp. in the context of a Viking assault at Wodnesfeld, recalls the skaldic kenning for 'battle': 'storm, gust, whirlwind, eddy, shower (of Woden or missiles)'. See Rudolf Meissner, *Die Kenningar der Skalden* (Halle, 1921), 176–202. At least one chronicler in late Anglo-Saxon England shows a similar tendency to use Old English poetic words to portray Viking ships and Viking warfare: see R. I. Page, '"A Most Vile People": Early English Historians on the Vikings', *The Dorothea Coke Memorial Lecture in Northern Studies* (University College London, 1986), 3–25, at 26–7.

[9] This split has been acknowledged for over 150 years: 'The language of poetry is as distinct from that of prose among the Anglo-Saxons as any two dialects' (J. M. Kemble, *The Poetry of the Codex Vercellensis with an English Translation* (London, 1843), p. ix). A number of poetic words that never occur in prose do appear in glosses and glossaries (e.g. *mece, breahtm, gecringan, gar*); these texts cannot simply be handed over to the register of prose, since sometimes the Old English word glosses a Latin poetic expression. Figures from *The Dictionary of Old English: D*, ed. A. Cameron *et al.* (Toronto, 1986), reveal the extent of the prose/poetry division. Of the 897 headwords in 'D', 118 are used in poetry only; of these, the vast majority (100) are compounds, most of which are *hapax legomena* or nearly so.

[10] Words in this group tend, in poetry, to be generalizing and metaphorical ('this is that'); in prose, particularistic ('this is put for that'), treating local variations in size, hue, material as distinct entities: cf. *mere* 'sea, water' vs. 'small lake'; *mæl* 'time' vs. 'specific time (for eating)'. Theoretically, the poetic word favours speakers, whose ideal 'economy' consists of a few general terms, the prose word, auditors, whose ideal 'economy' consists of a vast, precise vocabulary. See G. K. Zipf, *Human Behavior and the Principle of Least Effort: An Introduction to Human Ecology* (Cambridge, Mass., 1949), 19–20.

gladian, mildheort, spellian, gewiss, cafertun, hwilwende).[11] A fifth group, made up of words frequent in verse but not totally lacking in prose, has yet to receive official recognition.[12]

This essay looks at some of the circumstances under which poetic words were admitted into prose. It has, however, some wider implications. With a few notable exceptions, our scholarship has tended to treat as interchangeable adjectives like 'poetic', 'early', 'Anglian', 'archaic', 'dialectal', and 'obsolescent'.[13] Texts with 'poetic' and 'Anglian' symptoms and no named author are likely to end up quarantined in ninth-century Mercia.[14] When a pillar of Winchester usage like Ælfric publicly indulges in poetic language (nos. 5, 6, and 15), these 'deviations' can be explained 'by his concern for style'.[15] But a poetic word in an anonymous homily tends to be looked upon as a lonely, passive survivor, to be interrogated solely for genealogical or linguistic information: 'interesting occurrence of the poetical and Anglian word in a prose homily' is the inevitable professional diagnosis.[16] Even an 'archaism', however, lives in the present, if it lives at all.

Where in the literature, for example, do poetic words 'hang out'? The fifteen terms surveyed below tend to cluster in rhetorical set-pieces: a prose soul and body address (no. 1), a description of the tumult of Judgement

[11] 'Studies in the Prosaic Vocabulary of Old English Verse', *Neuphilologische Mitteilungen*, 72 (1971), 385–418.

[12] Identifying these words has been greatly facilitated by the *Microfiche Concordance of Old English* (= *MCOE*), ed. A. diP. Healey and R. L. Venezky (Toronto, 1980). Kenneth Sisam notes their existence in *Studies in the History of Old English Literature* (Oxford, 1953), 68–9: '*Sigor* "victory", occurring once [in *St Christopher*], is usually reckoned poetical and Anglian, but Ælfric has it, and at this date well-known poetical words may be expected in elevated prose'. Defining 'poetic' is, as Bunyan said of life, 'a hard matter, yea, a harder matter than many are aware of'. For the purposes of this essay, 'poetic word' designates a simplex more than 70% of whose total occurrences (in poetry and prose) are in verse; such a word is labelled 'mainly poetic' in the Toronto *Dictionary of Old English*. (In '*D*', only 16 out of 897 headwords fit into this category.) Since poetic texts comprise barely 6% of the corpus of OE literature, the 70% cut-off ensures a generous safety margin. In addition, to be eligible for inclusion the word must occur in at least two poems and more than four times. I have not counted glosses in my statistics (see n. 9); their number is sufficient, however, to affect the 'poetic' status of only two of the words examined (see nos. 14 and 15 below). 'Late prose' means, in practice, almost all OE prose, for most of the time we have no secure way of distinguishing between anonymous works composed after 950 and any that are earlier. Moreover, some of the prose texts that can be assigned with certainty to the early period are extant only in modernized copies of the 11th and 12th centuries.

[13] J. Bately, 'Old English Prose Before and During the Reign of Alfred', *ASE* 17 (1988), 93–138, casts a critical eye on this tradition.

[14] See ibid. on the lack of evidence for any tradition of vernacular prose in Mercia before Alfred and his collaborators set to work.

[15] W. Hofstetter, 'Winchester and the Standardization of Old English Vocabulary', *ASE* 17 (1988), 139–61, at 161.

[16] R. Willard, 'Address of the Soul to the Body', *PMLA* 50 (1935), 957–83, at 962 n. 27.

Day (nos. 4, 5d, 12a, and 13b), and an *ubi sunt* catalogue (nos. 5c and 13c), three themes well represented in Old English verse; some words occur in passages that closely parallel extant poems (nos. 5d, 7a, and 13a). Poetic words apparently prefer direct or reported speech to straight narrative (nos. 1, 2a, 5a, 5e, 6c, 7c, 8, 14b, 14e, and 15a); homilists in oral performance may have found it easier to put poetic words in the mouths of others (just as Chaucer only repeats what the coarse Miller says). God, Christ, saints, angels, souls, and scripture speak more poetically than ordinary men; and the attributes of holiness attract poetic language (nos. 2b, 3a, 6a–b, 7c, 10, 11, and 12).[17] Poetic words twice advertise the English past, a kind of lexical 'ye olde' sign (nos. 2b and 3b).[18] They often occur as variation, in apposition to a prosaic near-synonym (nos. 2a, 4, 6c, and 13c–d). Sometimes their appearance signals closure: it is in the final sentence of a peroration that Ælfric twice uses *metod* in his First Series of *Catholic Homilies*; and it is in the final sentence of a prayer that poetic *swegl* occurs for the first and only time in prose (no. 8).

Late copies of early works add and subtract poetic words with apparent freedom. Three eleventh-century manuscripts of the *OE Bede*, a text also preserved in copies from the early tenth century, substitute a poetic word for the 'unmarked' term of the original (no. 9); while the 'late-West-Saxon corrector' of Werferth's translation of Gregory's *Dialogues* is responsible for expunging at least one poetic word from that Alfredian text (no. 3). Such changes may be attributed to the teachings of a particular school, to traditions of interlinear glossing of Latin texts, to a reviser's idiosyncratic taste, even to an author's second thoughts. Malcolm Godden has shown how Ælfric, shortly after completing the Second Series of *Catholic Homilies*, changed his mind about the suitability of poetic *metod*, replacing it with an 'equivalent' expression.[19] Scribal literary criticism appears to have cleansed some anonymous homilies of their poeticisms (nos. 4, 5b–c, 10, 11, 12a, and

[17] Verse is similarly an attribute of kingship in Shakespeare's *Henry IV*: Prince Hal uses prose in the taverns to hide his real nature, reverting to poetry when he addresses his father and other members of the royal court.

[18] For 'ye olde' signs in early Middle English, see E. G. Stanley, 'Laȝamon's Antiquarian Sentiments', *Medium Ævum*, 38 (1969), 23–37, at 27.

[19] 'Ælfric's Changing Vocabulary', *English Studies*, 61 (1980), 206–23. But Ælfric did not expunge the poetic formula *roderes wealdend* (var. *rodera*) 'ruler of the skies' (ÆCHom II.14.1 146.253), an expression occurring sixteen times in verse and only this once in prose. The expression *metoda dryhten* 'lord of fates' occurs five times in Ælfric's Second Series, twice in the First Series. *Metod* appears about 260× in verse, 8× in prose; the only non-Ælfrician prose use is in Alfred's translation of a metre in the *Boethius* (IV. 6): *se metod eallra gesceafta* (ed. Sedgefield, p. 136, line 19). Alfred permitted himself the occasional poetic word in his prose paraphrase of the metres, something he never did when rendering Boethius' prose: see items 2a and 13a below.

15b). Yet the passing of centuries did not always make a text less poetic: a scribe writing in transitional English in the second half of the twelfth century managed twice to insert a poetic word avoided in earlier versions of the homily (no. 13d).[20]

Not all poetic words seem equally able to pass into the everyday world of prose. If they have already 'intermarried' with a prosaic word, either as a collocation (nos. 12, 13b, and 13d) or as a 'composed' form, their path into prose appears smoother. The existence of prosaic *hygeleas* 'thoughtless' and *hygeleast* 'folly' probably improved *hyge*'s chances of assimilation (no. 7). There are many poetic simplices for 'man' or 'lord' that never appear in prose (e.g. *bealdor, beorn, secg, hæle, firas, frea, hyse, freca, hleo, rinc,* and *scealc*); three that cross over—*brytta, guma,* and *wiga*—are also found in prose compounds denoting specific occupations (e.g. *fodderbrytta, brydguma,* and *rædewiga*), a fact that may not have hurt their prosaic careers.[21] Numerous appearances in glosses, especially in manuscripts with Kentish associations, may be another sign of potential acceptability in prose (nos. 14 and 15); but we still have much to learn about this neglected aspect of Old English literary history.[22]

Poetic words occurring in prose include *ætberan, afysan, agalan, andsaca, ansyn* ('lack'), *aswebban, atol, awa, bæl, bealu* (adj.), *befæðman, bemurnan, benc, beþringan, bewitian, gebiden, geblanden, brego, brim, clam* ('bond, grip'), *gecost, demend, eafora, fæðm* ('bosom, embrace'), *fus, fysan, geomor, hador, hæleð, hwearft, leod* ('prince'), *linnan, liss, mæðel, metod, nergend, opþringan, scriþan, sigor, sliþen, swæse, torht, torn, þeoden, þrag, upheofon, wadan,* and *waþ*. For reasons of space, the analysis that follows has been limited to fifteen such simplices, selected solely for their capacity to surprise, puzzle, and delight. There are some principles behind the ordering of items, and not all are lexical. In honour of the scholar to whom this piece is dedicated, the list begins with three words meaning 'man, prince', for he,

[20] This manuscript, Bodley 343, is sometimes given credit for another 'poeticism': the hapax legomenon *imetodlice* 'inevitably, certainly' (see J. R. Clark Hall, *A Concise Anglo-Saxon Dictionary* (4th edn., Cambridge, 1960), s.v. *gemetodlice; Middle English Dictionary*, s.v.). In the four earlier copies of the text in question (B 3.2.11), the homilist mentions eight capital sins 'without some of which no man can easily be found': [*un*] *eaðlice gemet* [*ed*] *bion* (Max Förster, *Die Vercelli-Homilien: I.–VIII. Homilie*, Bib. ags. Prosa 12 (Hamburg, 1932; repr. Darmstadt, 1964), 55, lines 21–2); the Bodley 343 reading 'without ... which no man can inevitably (?) be' is not felicitous, and *imetodlice* is as likely to be a false conflation of *eaðlice* and *gemeted* as an adverbial form of poetic *metod*.

[21] But cf. poetic *brego* 'ruler, lord', which occurs thirty-four times in verse and once in Ælfric's prose; it never forms part of a prose compound, yet crosses over all the same.

[22] See E. G. Stanley, 'The Scholarly Recovery of the Significance of Anglo-Saxon Records in Prose and Verse: A New Bibliography', *ASE* 9 (1981), 223–62, at 249; repr. in *A Collection of Papers*, 3–48, at 33.

too, is *gumena se getyddusta* 'the most learned of men', *godes brytta* 'a generous dispenser of good', and, not least, *strang wiga* 'a strong warrior'.[23]

1. *Brytta* m. 'lord, prince, dispenser' (36× verse, 1× prose)

Soul and Body address: HomM 14.2 (Healey) 34 (B 3.5.14.2) Bodleian, Junius 85 and 86 (Ker 336 art 2) s. xi med.
The soul says: 'Geherstu, goda lichoma and þu geleaffulla, þu wære godes brytta, forðon ðu Godes willan worhtest' ('Hear ye, good body and you faithful one, you were a dispenser/prince of good, because you carried out God's purpose').

A few sentences earlier, another soul had castigated its body in equally rhythmic and alliterative phrases: 'Þu eart deofles hus, forðan ðu deofles willan worhtest. Þu wære yrres hyrde and oferhydig' ('You are a house of the devil, because you carried out the devil's purpose; you were a guardian/prince of anger and proud').

Brytta parallels *hyrde*, here used in its poetic sense 'guardian, prince', not 'herdsman, shepherd', and provides a vehicle for the homilist's paronomastic linkage of *goda, god,* and *God.* An abbreviated paraphrase of this address occurs in HomS 6 (Ass 14) 81 (B 3.2.6) Cambridge, Corpus Christi College (hereafter CCCC) 302 (Ker 56, art 11, s. xi/xii) and BL, Cotton Faustina A. IX (Ker 153 art 5, s. xii[1]); this late homily retains *deofles hus* but omits both *yrres hyrde* and *godes brytta.* Like *brytta,* poetic *andsaca* 'adversary' (18× verse; 1× prose) occurs only once in the extant prose, in a Soul and Body address in which a sinful body is apostrophized as *Godes andsaca*: HomU 9 (VercHom 4) 294. It is curious that—while the Vercelli *prose* Soul and Body pieces exhibit poeticisms—the Vercelli version of the *Soul and Body* poem seems less 'poetic' than its Exeter Book counterpart, the former presenting, for example, common *æht* and *frofor* where the latter has poetic *geahð* and *hroðor* respectively.

2. *Guma* m. 'man, lord, hero' (159× verse, 3× prose in 3 MSS)

   (a) *Alfred's Boethius,* Bk IV, met 7: Bo 40.139.5 (B 9.3) BL, Cotton Otho A. VI (Ker 167) s. x med.; Bodleian, Bodley 180 (Ker 305) s. xii[1].
   'Wella, wisan men, wel; gað ealle on þone weg ðe eow [læráð] þa

[23] Each prose text in which the poetic word occurs is normally identified by its (1) *MCOE* short title and line number, (2) Cameron number, (3) manuscript, and (4) Ker number and date. (For manuscripts of Ælfric's *Catholic Homilies, Second Series,* see edn. by M. Godden, pp. xxv–lxxiv.) Editions and abbreviations are those cited in the *MCOE: The List of Texts and Index of Editions.* For Cameron number, see A. Cameron, 'A List of Old English Texts', in *A Plan for the Dictionary of Old English,* ed. R. Frank and A. Cameron (Toronto, 1973), 25–306; for Ker number and date, see N. R. Ker, *Catalogue of Manuscripts containing Anglo-Saxon* (Oxford, 1957).

f[oremæran bisna] þara godena gumena & þara weorðgeornena wera þe ær eow wæron' ('Ah, ye wise men, walk, all of you, on that path shown to you by the famous examples of those good lords and honour-seeking men who lived before you'). Cf. *Ite nunc fortes ubi celsa magni | Ducit exempli uia.*

(b) Byrhtferth's *Manual* (1008–11): ByrM 1 (Crawford) 44.1 and 158.10 (B 20.20.1) Bodleian, Ashmole 328 (Ker 288 art 1) s. xi med.

(i) Introducing Bede's verses concerning the months: 'Beda þus giddode, gumena se getyddusta ... ' ('Bede thus recited, the most learned of men').

(ii) Introducing a passage from Bede's *De natura rerum*: 'Beda cwyð, gumena se getiddusta on Angelcynne ...' ('Bede says, the most learned of men among the English people').

Metre IV.7 is one of the nine not translated into Old English verse in Cotton Otho A. VI. Alfred's alliterative prose never mentions Agamemnon, Ulysses, and Hercules, whose deeds take up most of Boethius' poem; instead, he speaks more generally of the example of good men of the past, the *guman* 'heroes' of ancient days.

Byrhtferth twice names Bede 'the most learned of men', as if repetition might drill the epithet into his pupils' heads and the resonant *guma* recall for them a distant, golden age in the north of England.[24] The first occurrence (b.i) is in an alliterative long line: cf. 'þæt gyddedon gumena mænigeo' (*Dan* 727); 'guma gilphlæden gidda gemyndig' (*Beo* 868).

3. *Wiga* m. 'warrior, man' (42× verse, 2× prose in multiple MSS, 3× gloss: note [*heros*] ÆGram 57.9)

(a) Werferth's translation of Gregory's *Dialogues*: GD 2(C) 3.110.13 (B 9.5.4) CCCC 322 (Ker 60) s. xi², BL, Cotton Otho C. I vol. 2 (Ker 182 art 1) s. xi in.

'And swa se Godes stranga wiga sanctus Paulus nolde beon gehæfd binnan þære byrig Damasco, ac sohte þone feld þæs campes' ('and thus the strong warrior of God, St Paul, wished not to be confined within the city of Damascus, but sought the battlefield'). Cf. *praeliator Dei teneri intra claustra noluit, certaminis campum quaesivit.*

Cf. GD 2(H) 3.110.12 (B 9.5.10.2) Bodleian, Hatton 76 (Ker 328A art 1) s. xi¹: 'Soþlice se stranga Godes fyhtling nolde beon gehæfd binnon clysingum þære burge Damasci, ac sohte þone feld þæs gecampes.'

[24] Byrhtferth also calls Bede 'se *æglæca* lareow' ('the awesome teacher', 74.15), using a term otherwise found only in poetry. See now A. Nicholls, 'Bede "Awe-Inspiring" not "Monstrous": Some Problems with Old English *aglæca*', *Notes and Queries*, 236 (1991), 147–8.

(b) *OE Bede*: Bede I 12.50.27 (B 9.6.3) Bodleian, Tanner 10 (Ker 351) s. x[1].
'& hi þa sona hider sendon maran sciphere strengran wighena [CCCC 41, s. xi[1]: *strangra wigena*]' ('And then they at once sent here a larger fleet with a stronger force of warriors'). Cf. *mittitur confestim illo classis prolixior, armatorum ferens manum fortiorem.*

Werferth completed his translation by 893 at the latest; sometime between 950 and 1050, an anonymous reviser, whose vocabulary corresponds to that of the 'Winchester school', made many minor modifications, including the change of *wiga* to *fyhtling*.[25] Poetic *wiga* was known in Æthelwold's Winchester, as Ælfric's gloss suggests, but for some, presumably contextual, reason, the Hatton reviser preferred to depict Paul as a 'soldier', not 'warrior'.

In the *OE Bede*, the invading Saxons of 449 are depicted as *wigan*, the poetic word perhaps heroicizing and distancing these ancestral pirates. The Anglo-Saxon chronicler used another poeticism, equally rare in prose, to describe how the same founding fathers arrived in three *ceolum* 'ships', a learned echo perhaps of Gildas who reports in the *De excidio Britanniae* 23 (sixth century in s. xi MS) that the Anglo-Saxons came to Britain in *cyulis—ut lingua eius exprimitur.*

4. *Blæst* m. 'flame, blaze, gust' (6× verse, 1× prose in 3 MSS, 1× gloss; *blast* in PsCaG 6.13 is in hand of s. xiii)

Judgement Day homily in four copies (= VercHom 2 with additions in style of Wulfstan): HomU 32 (Nap 40) 71 (B 3.4.32) CCCC 419 (Ker 68 art 8) s. xi[1]; Bodleian, Hatton 114 (Ker 331 art 82) s. xi (3rd quarter); BL, Cotton Cleopatra B. XIII (Ker 144 art 1) s. xi (3rd quarter).

'In þam dæge us byð æteowed ... þæra ligetta blæst' ('On that day will be revealed to us ... a blaze of lightnings').

Cf. *liggetta gebrastl* 'crackling of lightnings' CCCC 201 (Ker 49B art 15) s. xi med.

HomU 8 (VercHom 2) 46 (B 3.4.8) Vercelli, Biblioteca Capitolare CXVII (Ker 394 art 2) s. x[2]: *liga blæstm* 'flash of flames'.

HomM 13 (VercHom 21) 223 (B 3.5.13) as above, art 26; *liga gebrasl* 'crackling of flames'.

The text of rhythmical, alliterative prose in which *blæst* appears has been

[25] On the 'Winchester school' see H. Gneuss, *Hymnar und Hymnen im englischen Mittelalter*, Buchreihe der Anglia, 12 (Tübingen, 1968), 186–7, and 'The Origin of Standard Old English and Æthelwold's School at Winchester', *ASE* 1 (1972), 63–83, at 78–81. Hans Hecht early connected the reviser of Werferth's translation with this school: *Bischof Wærferths von Worcester Übersetzung der Dialoge Gregors des Grossen*, Bib. ags. Prosa 5 (Leipzig and Hamburg, 1900–7), ii. 131.

published by E. G. Stanley (n. 6) who observes the connections among the related pieces in Hatton 113/114, CCCC 201, and Vercelli. The unique *blæstm* seems to have inspired creativity in later adapters of Vercelli 2. Three of the four surviving MSS of Napier 40 use the poetic word *blæst*; CCCC 201 shares with Vercelli 21 the reading *gebras(t)l*, a term that, with the exception of one gloss, occurs only in the related *Judgement Day II* (in CCCC 201) and Napier 29 (in Hatton 113). Both poetic *blæst* and prosaic *gebrastl* (Ælfric uses *gebrastlian* with some frequency) appear to be separate 'updatings' of a perhaps no longer comprehensible *blæstm*.

5. *Folde* f. 'earth, land, world' (192× verse, 6× prose in multiple MSS, 3× gloss)
   (a) Ælfric's St Martin homily: ÆCHom II.39.1 292.164 (B 1.2.42) Pagans challenge the saint to stand under a tree as it is *feallende to foldan* 'falling to the earth'.
   (b) Vercelli 2/Napier 40: HomU 8 (VercHom 2) 80 (B 3.4.8); HomU 32 (Nap 40) 100 (B 3.4.32) [MSS as no. 4 above]
   The body decays in *þære cealdan foldan* 'in the cold earth'. Cf. *foldan* in Hatton 114 and Cleopatra B. XIII; *eorðan* in Vercelli 21 and CCCC 419; *moldan* in CCCC 201.
   (c) Vercelli 10/Napier 49 and 30
      (i) HomS 40.3 (VercHom 10) 317 (B 3.2.40)
      Hwær com foldan fægernes? ('Where has the earth's beauty gone?') HomS 40.1 (Nap 49) 291: *foldan* in CCCC 421 (Ker 69 art 9) s. xi[1], CCCC 302 (Ker 56 art 33) s. xi./xii, CCCC 302 (Ker 56, art 12), and (HomS 7.156, B 3.2.7) Cotton Faustina A. IX (Ker 153 art 6) s. xii[1]; cf. *folce* (HomU 3 [Belf 12] 132, B 3.4.3) Bodleian, Bodley 343 (Ker 310 art 80) s. xii[2]; *eorðan* (HomU 27 (Nap 30) 184 (B 3.4.27) Bodleian, Hatton 113 (Ker 331 art 23) s. xi (3rd quarter).
      (ii) HomS 40.3 (VercHom 10) 281
      mountains *hrioseð to foldan* 'fall to earth'; cf. *eorðan* in Napier 49 (all MSS); *eorðe* in Bodley 343.
   (d) Napier 29/*Judgement Day II*
   HomU 26 (Nap 29) 100 (B 3.4.26) Hatton 113 (Ker 331 art 22) s. xi (3rd quarter).
   'eall Adames cynn eorðbugjendra, þe on foldan wearð æfre gefeded' ('all the race of Adam, of earthdwellers, who were ever reared in the world'); cf. *JDay II*: 'eal Adames cnosl eorðbuendra | þe on foldan wearð feded æfre'. Neither is a close translation of the Latin poetic source (*De die judicii*, attributed to Bede).

(e) Prose Solomon and Saturn dialogue
Sol I 9.1 (B 5.1) BL, Cotton Vitellius A. XV (Ker 215 art 3) s. xii med.
Of the elements from which Adam was created, 'þæt æroste wæs foldan pund of ðam him wæs flesc geworht' ('the first was a pound of earth, from which his flesh was made'). Cf. *pondus limi inde factus est caro* (U. Lindelöf, ed. *Rituale ecclesiae Dunelmensis*, Surtees Society 140 (London, 1927), 192).

Folde is the poetic, *eorðe* the prosaic word for 'earth' in Old English, as in Old Norse, where an eddic poem announces that the earth is called *jǫrð* by men, *fold* by the gods (*Alvíssmál* 10.1). *Folde* occurs in both early and late prose; when multiple manuscripts exist, we find *eorðe* freely if inconsistently substituted. The most tenacious *folde* is in item c.i, an *ubi sunt* catalogue based on a passage found in Isidore's *Synonyma* and Defensor's *Liber Scintillarum* (neither of which, however, includes this particular image).[26] Only Hatton 113 'corrects' to *eorðe*; but the same manuscript admits *folde* into a preceding prose piece that corresponds to parts of *JDay II* (item d). The mid-twelfth-century manuscript that describes how God created Adam's flesh from *folde* (item e) uses another poetic word for the first man's 'mind' (see 14e). In both instances, the Old English gloss to the Latin of the *Durham Ritual* employs non-poetic terms.

6. *Folm, folme* f. *folma* m. 'hand, palm' (59× verse, 4× prose in multiple MSS, 5× gloss [1x for 'palm branch'], 3× plant name *Fornetesfolm*)
   (a) Ælfric's Invention of the Cross homily: ÆCHom II.19 175.46 (B 1.2.22).
   Elene brings to Constantine 'ða isenan næglas þe wæron adrifene þurh Cristes folman ða ða he gefæstnod wæs' ('the iron nails that were driven through Christ's hands when he was fastened').
   (b) Werferth's translation of Gregory's *Dialogues*
      (i) GD 2(C) 32.166.5 (B 9.5.4) (see no. 3a above)
      Benedict, to revive a dead child, 'aþenode his folmas upp to heofonum' ('stretched out his hands to heaven'). Cf. *ad caelum palmas tetendit.*
      (ii) GD Pref 3(C) 15.208.18 (B 9.5.5)
      Florence, to rid the land of serpents, 'ahof his eagan up to heofonum & his folme aðenede' ('lifted his eyes up to heaven and stretched out his hands'). Cf. *ad caelum oculos et palmas tetendit.*

[26] See J. E. Cross, '*Ubi Sunt* Passages in Old English—Sources and Relationships', in *Vetenskaps-societeten i Lund Årsbok* (1956), 25–44.

(c) Prose Solomon and Saturn dialogue: Sol II (Menner 1941) 65 (B 5.3) CCCC 422 (Ker 70A) s. x med.
The arms of the Pater Noster are longer than the whole world, 'ðeah ðe hie sien mid þe beorhtestan wyrhtan folmum tosomne gefeged' ('though they may be joined together by the hands of a most excellent craftsman').

The 'Winchester' reviser of Gregory's *Dialogues* accepts *folm*, at least in Werferth's second book (which is as far as he 'corrected'). Ælfric's alliterative pairing of Christ's *folman, gefæstnod* by nails to the cross, parallels that of *Elene* 1062 and *Christ* 1454. Werferth's translation of Gregory's Latin is faithful to a fault. Like an 'early Mercian' Grimm, he glosses the *palma* of his original as *folm*, its Old English cognate.[27] In the prose *Solomon*, which separates fragments of two verse dialogues, *folm* elegantly varies the Pater Noster's *earmas* and *handa* in the same sentence.

7. *Hyge* m. 'thought, intention, desire' (132× verse, 4× prose in 5 MSS, 2× gloss)

(a) Rogation homily: HomM 13 (VercHom 21) 176 (B 3.5.13) (see no. 4).
'Ac uton bliðum mode on haligum hige wæccan lufian & gebedum fylgian on þisse hwilwendan tide' ('But let us with happy heart in holy intention love vigils . . . ')
HomU 27 (Nap 30) 87 (B 3.4.27) (Worcester; see no. 5.c.i).
'And bliðum mode on halgum hige wæccan lufjan and ure cyrican secan and urum gebedum fyljan . . .'
Cf. *An Exhortation to Christian Living*, ASPR VI, p. 67, lines 4b–6 (A 18) CCCC 201 (Ker 49A art 2b) s. xi. med.: 'and wæccan lufa | on hyge halgum on þas hwilwendan tid | bliðe mode, and gebedum filige'.

(b) Sunday Letter homily: HomU 46 (Nap 57) 297.17–19 (B 3.4.46) Lambeth Palace 489 (Ker 283 art 4) s. xi (3rd quarter) (Exeter).
'swa hwa swa hæfð ænigne hyge to gode, he wile hlistan þissera worda' ('whosoever has any thought to goodness, he will listen to these words').

(c) Life of St Margaret: LS 14 (MargaretAss 15) 298 (B 3.3.14) CCCC 303 (Ker 57 art 23) s. xii[1] (Rochester?).
God's voice announces to the saint: 'Þine hande and þinne hige clæne gehylde and for minre lufa mycel geþrowedest' ('Your hands and your thought you kept pure and for love of me endured much').

[27] *Folm* glosses *palmas, palmi, palmites* in, respectively, LorGl 1 (Grattan-Singer) 29, OccGl 45.1 (Meritt) 224, and PsGlE (Harsley) 79.12. 'Grimm's-law' correspondences between *fisc/pisc-, faðir/pater, fell/pell-, for-/per-, fot/ped-*, etc. are likely to have been noticed by Anglo-Saxon students of Latin, if only because the vernacular was so poor in p-words.

(d) Prayer: Lit 4.5 (Banks) 1 (B 12.4.5) BL, Cotton Galba A. XIV (Ker 157 art iv) s. xi[1] (Winchester?).
Penitent to God: 'Ic bebiode minre sawle gehealdnesse & mines lichoman, min word & weorc & mine geþohtas, mine heortan & minne hyge, min leomu & mine lic, ðu min fell & flæsc, min blod & ban min . . . ' ('I commit the keeping of my soul and of my body, my words and deeds and my thoughts, my heart and my desire, my limbs and my body, you my skin and flesh, my blood and my bones . . .').

Poetic *hyge* occurs in prose passages with strong alliterative and rhythmic patterning. In item (a), the homily may have taken the word from the poem (as usually argued) or the borrowing could have gone the other way: *hyge* suggests the former, and prosaic *hwilwende*, with which it alliterates, the latter.[28] (Napier 30 rejects the poetic epithets for God preceding this passage in Vercelli and thought to derive from another, this time unknown, verse source.) In item (b), the homilist uses *hyge* and an old ploy to ensure his audience's attention: if you are going to be good (and saved) you'll sit quietly and listen to me. God's poetical commendation in item (c) stands out from its prosaic context and recalls in its choice of words the versified psalms of the Paris Psalter (e.g. *þa ðe heortan gehygd healdað clæne*, 83.12; cf. 61.8, 72.17, 89.14, 118.30). The balanced phrasing of the prayer in item (d) seems to be striving for a liturgical majesty as it praises God. (Some of its alliterating collocations—e.g. 'blood and bones', 'fell and flesh'—survived into early modern English.) *Hyge* and its seat, the *heorte*, are also paired in the poetic psalms and once, memorably, in *Maldon* 312.

8. *Swegl* n. 'sky, heaven' (85× verse, 1× prose in 2 MSS)
Prayer: Lit 4.3.3 (Hallander) 25 (B 12.4.3.3) BL, Royal 2 B. V [Regius Psalter MS] (Ker 249 art e) s. xi med.; BL, Cotton Tiberius A. III (Ker 186 art 9f) s. xi med. (Christ Church, Canterbury).
The speaker in the final sentence of the prayer recalls Christ's invitation to enter his father's kingdom where the blessed live 'mid dreame butan deaþe on swegle butan susle' ('joyously without death in heaven without misery').

The eleventh-century corrector of the Old English text in Royal 2 B. V, who

[28] The most recent contribution to the debate maintains the priority of the prose: 'I suspect that the . . . prose has been turned with a little difficulty into verse, not that the prose is a "dilution" of the verse': J. E. Cross, *Cambridge, Pembroke College MS. 25: A Carolingian Sermonary Used by Anglo-Saxon Preachers*, King's College London Medieval Studies, 1 (London, 1987), 150.

modernized many words to the late West Saxon standard of Tiberius A. III, left poetic *swegl* alone, restricting himself to 'updating' the preceding preposition (*in* to *on*). The two poeticisms (*dream* is here used in its poetic sense of 'joy', not prosaic 'music') describe heaven, the two prose words, life on earth.

9. *Ferhð* mm. 'life, mind' (85× verse, 1× prose in 3 MSS)
   OE Bede: Bede 5 8.406.25 (B 9.6.7) Bodleian, Tanner 10 (see 3b).
   Bede, quoting scripture, says of Archbishop Theodore and his peers that 'their bodies are buried in peace, and their name will live *wide ferh in ecnesse* 'forever in eternity'. Cf. Ecclesiasticus 44: 14: *in generationes et generationes.*
   feorh BL, Cotton Otho B. XI (Ker 180 art 1) s. x med. (Winchester).
   færð (with *a* in *æ* partly erased) Oxford, CCC 279 pt. II (Ker 354) s. xi in.
   ferhð CCCC 41 (Ker 32 art 1) s. xi[1]; CUL Kk. 3.18 (Ker 23) s. xi[2].

Ferhð is substituted in three late manuscripts of the *Bede* for the synonymous, more common, and probably cognate *feorh*; both nouns combine in verse with *wid (widan feorh/ferhð, wide feorh/ferhð, widefeorh/wideferhð*). An eleventh-century scribe, not recognizing smoothed *ferh* as *feorh*, may have supplied a final -*ð*; it is also possible that poetic *ferhð* was chosen to close the scriptural quotation.

10. *Ðryð f.* 'strength, majesty, glory' (18× verse plus 8 nominal compounds, 0× prose); *ðryðful* adj. 'strong, glorious' (2× verse, 1× prose)

    HomS 40.3 (VercHom 10) 41 (B 3.2.40.6) (see 5c).
    Before the coming of Christ, men were orphans, deprived of the heavenly kingdom and blotted out from *þam þryðfullan frumgewrite* 'the glorious original charter'.
    HomS 40.1 (Nap 49) 291 (see 5c): *frymþelican* 'primeval, original', CCCC 302 (Ker 56 art 33) s. xi/xii; *frymþlican*, Blickling Homily 9 (Ker 382 art 9) s. x/xi; *frumsceapenan* 'first created', CCCC 421, s. xi[1].

Both *þryðful* and *frymþlic* are appropriate modifiers for the unique *frumgewrit*, which refers to the divine charter granting heaven to man as a homeland; *frumsceapen*, frequent in Ælfric who applies it to Adam (and once Eve), is perhaps less successful. In Old English verse, *þryðful* designates devils and persecutors, and the *þryðfullod* 'proud, puffed up' in the Regius Psalter gloss to *elati* (130.1) are eyes; *þryðful* with reference to a document may presuppose a certain degree of personification.

11. *Wrætlic* adj. 'artistic, beautiful, wonderful' (48× verse, 1× prose)

Nativity of Mary: LS 18.2 (NatMaryAss 10J) 362 (B 3.3.18.3) Bodleian, Hatton 114 (see 4) s. xi (3rd quarter).
[She was] *on ðam dauidtidiscum sangum wrætlicre* 'more wonderful in psalmody' [than anyone was before]; cf. Ps–Mt 6.63.14 *in carminis Davidicis elegantior.*
Cf. LS 18.1 (NatMaryAss 10N) 359, Bodleian, Bodley 343, s. xii[2] (see 5c.i): *on þam dauidisce sange wræstlicre* 'more able, excellent, delicate'; CCCC 367 pt II, 14[r].26 (Ker 63 art 6) s. xii[1] *on þam dauitidiscum sangum wærlicre* 'more careful, circumspect'.

Wrætlic had a short prosaic life. All three adjectives are possible synonyms for *elegans* 'fastidious, cultivated, punctilious, graceful, skilful with words', and there is no deciding between them. Poetic *wrætlic* is used of God's voice in *Andreas* 93 and 630, of angels' speech in *Christ* 509, and of the saint's words in *Andreas* 1200.

12. *Blican* vb. st. 1 'shine, glitter' (26× verse, 2× prose in 3 MSS, 1× gloss)

(a) Wednesday in Rogationtide
HomS 33 (Först) 104 (B 3.2.33), Bodleian, Hatton 116 (Ker 333 art 26) s. xii[1].
On the seventh day of the Last Week 'drihten cymð þonne on micclum megenþrimme, & fyr on his ansyne scineþ & blyceð' ('the Lord will come then in a great heavenly host and fire will shine and glitter in his sight').
Cf. HomS 44 (B 3.2.44) CCCC 162 (Ker 38 art 37) s. xi in.: 'drihten cymð þonne on micclum mægenþrymme and fyr on his onsyne scinð'.

(b) Invention of the Cross
LS 6 (InventCrossMor) 238 (B 3.3.6) Bodleian, Auctarium F.4.32 (Ker 297 art a) s. xi[2].
'& þær com mycel leoht up of þære stowe þe seo halige rode on afunden wæs & þær ætywedon þa næglas & on þare eorþan scinan & blican swa þæt seloste gold' ('And there came a great light up from the place where the holy cross was found, and there were revealed the nails—shining and glittering in the earth like the best gold'). Cf. *tamquam aurum fulgens in terra.*
Cf. CCCC 303 (Ker 57 art 18) s. xii[1] (Rochester), as above.

In verse, *blican* is used of the sun, glittering metals, cliffs, and heavenly presence and glory. It often signals an 'end', the completion of a journey of discovery, possibly one of its connotations in the two homilies cited above. The homilist's description of divinity at the Last Judgement (item (a)) echoes Ps. 49: 3 'A fire will shine in his sight'. The Hatton 116 scribe writes *scineþ* and *blyceð* (using the unsyncopated form characteristic of verse) in contrast to the preceding *cymð*, as if signalling a shift in register and rhythm. The earlier CCCC 162 text of the same homily, almost certainly not the copy from which Hatton 116 descends, has only *scinð*. In item (b), the nails of the cross attract poetic diction as they did in Ælfric's homily on the same subject (6a). *Blican* appears both times in the company of *scinan*, as if it were good form in late Anglo-Saxon England to use the poeticism in conjunction with a clarifying synonym.

13. *(Ge)dreosan* vb. st. 2 'to fall, perish' (26× verse, 5× prose in multiple MSS)

  (a) *Alfred's Boethius*, Bk 2, met 4: Bo 12.26.28 (B 9.3.2) (see 2a).
  'Forðam swa swa sigende sond þone ren swylgð, swa swylgð seo gitsung þa dreosendan welan þisses middangeardes' ('Just as the sinking sand swallows rain, so avarice swallows the falling/perishing riches of this earth'). Cf. *Met.* 7.13: *dreosendne welan* 'perishing wealth'.

  (b) Last Judgement: HomU 26 (Nap 29) 82 (B 3.4.26) (see 5d).
  'And ealle duna dreosað and hreosað' ('And all mountains fall and sink'). Cf. *JDay II*, 99: 'þa duna dreosað and hreosað'; and *De die judicii*, 51: *montesque ruent*.

  (c) *Ubi sunt* catalogue in Vercelli 10/Napier 49 and 30.
  HomS 40.3 (VercHom 10) 319 (see 5c.i).
  '... gelice rena scurum þonne <hie> of heofenum swiðost <dreosað>' (MS *dreoseð*) ('like rain showers when they fall most violently from heaven').
  HomS 40.1 (Nap 49) 295: *dreosað*, CCCC 302 art 33, s. xi/xii; *hreosað*, Cotton Faustina A. IX, s. xii^{1}, CCCC 302 art 12, s. xi/xii, and CCCC 421, s. xi^{1}; *reoseð*, Bodley 343 (= HomU 3 [Belf 12] 135), s. xii^{2}.
  HomU 27 (Nap 30) 189: *dreoseð* (em. to *dreosað*).

  (d) *Ubi sunt* catalogue in Bodley 343
  HomU 3 (Belf 12) 110 (see 5c.i).
  'swa eac þa heagæ mihtæ her on worlde fællæð & drosæð' ('so too the great powers here in the world fall and fail'). Cf. *hreosað & feallað*, VercHom 10, Nap 49; *afeallað and ahreosað*, Nap 30.
  Cf. HomU 3 (Belf 12) 121.
  The world is 'hwilwendlic & feallendlic & brosnodlic & drosendlic & brocenlic & yfellic & forwordenlic' (*dreosendlic* not in VercHom 10, Nap 49 or 30).

(e) Blickling homily 10
HomU 20 (BlHom 10) 119 (B 3.4.20) (see 10).
'Mine welan þe ic io hæfde sindon ealle gewitene & gedrorene' ('My riches that I formerly had are all departed and perished').

Once again King Alfred's diction shows poetic symptoms when he translates a metre into prose; and once again Napier 29 employs a poetic word found in the corresponding lines of *JDay II*. But where Napier 49 and Vercelli 10 shared a poetic reading in item 5c, and Napier 30 went its own way, here Vercelli 10 and Napier 30 agree on *dreosan*, while Napier 49, with one exception, substitutes *hreosan*. And Bodley 343, which avoids *dreosan* in 13c, may have done so out of exhaustion rather than distaste, for it uses that verb twice in an earlier section of the same exhortation (13d): its paired verbs *fællað & drosað* recall similar collocations in Old English verse (e.g. *Wan* 63 and *Beo* 1753), as do the linked *gewiten and gedroren* in 13e (e.g. *Sea* 86). The need for synonyms in rhetorical prose seems to have encouraged words normally confined to poetry to perform their magic on a broader stage.

14. *Sefa* m. 'understanding, heart, mind' (93× verse plus 62 nominal compounds, 6× prose in 6 MSS, 15× glosses [lemma always *sensus*])

(a) Pentecost homily
HomS 47 (BlHom 12) 101 (B 3.2.47) (see 10).
'Hie ðam Halgan Gaste onfengon on heora sefan' ('They received the Holy Spirit in their understanding/heart').

(b) Life of St Margaret
LS 16 (MargaretHerbst) 53 and 219 (B 3.3.16) BL, Cotton Tiberius A. III (Ker 186 art 15) s. xi med. (Christ Church, Canterbury).

(i) She prays to God for angels to help her, 'to ontynenne mine sefan and to answariende mid bylde' ('to reveal my heart/mind and to respond with boldness'). Cf. *ad aperiendos sensus meos et os meos ad respondendum cum fiducia.*

(ii) The Devil says, 'Ic heo[m] ableonde hera sefan & ic hi gedyde ofergeotan þa heofenlican snyttro' ('I blinded their understanding and I caused them to forget heavenly wisdom'). Cf. *et occaeco oculos eorum et obscuro sensus eorum et facio eos oblivisci omnem caelestem sapientiam.* MS *hera sefan* underlined and corrected (s. xi^2) to *fram geleafan.*

(c) Life of Machutus
LS 13 (Machutus) 38.14–15 (B 3.3.13) BL, Cotton Otho A. VIII, Otho B. X (Ker 168) s. xi in.
'Ne mæg na ure sefa areccean . . .' 'Our understanding is not at all able to relate . . .'). Cf. *noster sensus explicare non valet.*

(d) Heading/Introduction for Latin Office
Lit 5.3.2.4 (Fehr) 15 (B 12.5.3.2.4) CCCC 422 (Ker 70B art p) s. xi med.; also Lit 5.11.6 (Fehr) 11 (B 12.5.11.6) Bodleian, Laud Misc. 482 (Ker 343 art 18) s. xi med.
Priest tells penitent: 'Đu most þa digelnysse ðines modes sefan [Laud Misc. *seofan*] ðurh soþe andetnisse geyppan' ('You must those hidden things in the understanding of your heart disclose in true confession').

(e) Prose Solomon and Saturn dialogue
Sol I 911 (B 5.1) (see 5e).
'Fifte wæs gyfe pund, þanon hym wæs geseald sefa and geðang' ('the fifth was a pound of grace, from which was given his understanding and thought'). Cf. *pondus gratiae inde est sensus hominis (Durham Ritual*, 192).

At least four of the six occurrences of *sefa* in prose are in texts that closely translate a Latin original. There seems to have been no inclination to edit the word out: the 'correction' of *hera sefa* to *fram geleafan* in b(ii) probably has less to do with the poetic word than the reviser's conviction that the sentence with its two accusative objects (MS *heo, sefan*) made no sense as it stood. The appearance of 'Anglian' *sefa* in prose and glosses, particularly in manuscripts with Kentish associations, was noted by Helmut Gneuss in 1968 and most recently by Walter Hofstetter.[29] *Sefa* translates *sensus* 4× in metrical hymns of the Durham Ritual (Canterbury); 3× in the interlinear glosses to prayers in MS Arundel 155 (probably Canterbury); 2× in the St Margaret life in Tiberius A. III (Christ Church, Canterbury); 1× in the St Machutus life in Otho A. XIII (probably Canterbury); it also occurs 1× in Psalter D (Canterbury connection), 2× in E (Eadwine's Canterbury Psalter), once each in K and M, and in CleoGl (St Augustine's, Canterbury), SedGl 2, and BrGl. Although it is predominantly poetic (and its Old Norse cognate is exclusively poetic), *sefa* at some particular moment and place in Anglo-Saxon England became a rival to *andgiet* as the 'agreed-upon' translation of *sensus*. It is never used by Ælfric or Wulfstan; and, unlike *hyge*, it never graces passages of rhythmic, alliterative prose.

15. *Heolstor* m. 'place of hiding, darkness' (14× verse plus 6 nominal compounds, 4× prose in multiple MSS, 22× glosses)

(a) Ælfric's St Cuthbert homily: ÆCHom II 10.88.231 (B 1.2.11).
The saint tells an abbess that no one escapes (*forfleon*) God's power

[29] *Hymnar und Hymnen*, 180 and 188; *Winchester und der Spätaltenglische Sprachgebrauch: Untersuchungen zur geographischen und zeitlichen Verbreitung altenglischer Synonyme* (Munich, 1987), 108–9, 233–4.

'on nanum heolstrum. heofenan. oþþe eorðan. oþþe sæ ðriddan' ('in any hiding-place, heaven or earth or sea third').

(b) Vercelli homily 23 (St Guthlac): LS 10 (Guth) 345 (B 3.3.10) (see no. 4).
The devils tormenting the saint 'hie sylfe in heolstre hyddon' ('hid themselves in darkness'). Cf. Bodleian, Laud Misc. 509 and BL, Cotton Vespasian D. XXI fos. 18–40 (Ker 344 art 5) s. xi^2: 'ac hi sylfe on þeostre gehyddon'.

(c) Life of St Machutus: LS 13 (Machutus) 23^r. 16 (see no. 14).
A nobleman 'fleonde heolster gesohte' ('fleeing, sought a hiding-place'). Cf. *fugiens latebram expetiit.*

(d) Easter Day homily: HomS 28 82 (B 3.2.28) Bodleian, Junius 121 (Ker 338 art 33) s. xi (3rd quarter) (Worcester).
The devils 'on þam heolstre geflymde wæron' ('were banished in that darkness').

Heolstor is by definition a 'poetic word', for 78 per cent of its combined occurrences in poetry and prose are in verse. But it is even more frequent in glosses, occurring in manuscripts dating from s. viii/ix (Corpus Glossary in CCCC 144, St Augustine's, Canterbury) to s. xi^2 (Arundel psalter glosses). The greatest single concentration (8×) is found in two related Abingdon MSS containing Aldhelm glosses. The anonymous prose texts containing *heolstor* are usually classified on the basis of vocabulary as early and Anglian/Mercian; the replacement of the poetic word by *þeostru* in the Cotton Vespasian Guthlac text is regarded as scribal modernization. Yet 'poetic' and 'Anglian' *heolstor* is employed by Ælfric in a homily that was probably his first piece wholly in the alliterative style.[30] We can only guess why he chose it, and be sure that he did not do so absentmindedly. Despite a life spent in Wessex and among Wessexmen, Ælfric went 'poetic', confident that his intended audience was practised in the separate dictions of verse and prose, *utriusque linguae peritus.*

Since such 'bilingualism' is not a constitutive feature of our own literary language, we barely notice when Old English poetic words stray into prose. Current English registers as comic the clash of colloquial and 'fancy' language in, for example, the *New Yorker* cartoon of the criminal testifying before the judge: 'So den I got piqued and bashed him one.' But the poeticisms that adorn Old English prose seem to have been neither parodic nor 'artificial'; and the settings in which they glitter would not have struck anyone as

[30] See J. C. Pope, *Homilies of Ælfric: A Supplementary Collection,* 2 vols., EETS 259–60 (London, 1967–8), i. 113; Godden, 'Ælfric's Changing Vocabulary', 219 and 221.

vulgar. To appreciate the distance between our expectations and those of an Anglo-Saxon audience is a first step in increasing our sensitivity to a minor but still undervalued aspect of Old English style.

There are a few practical benefits to the kind of analysis performed here. Sometimes light is shed on the meaning of an individual word or on the interpretation of a puzzling passage.[31] Sometimes the local effects that a prose writer sought with his poeticisms become a little clearer.[32] And sometimes awareness of the distribution of competing synonyms can stop us from introducing a poetic word editorially into prose.[33]

More often, however, the findings of this study make cloudy what was formerly clear. The frequency of poetic words in prose, at least in the sample tested here, is on the whole unrelated to date or dialect: *guma*, bridging a gap of some six-score years, occurs in Alfred and Byrhtferth; *folm*, in Werferth and Ælfric. Before *c.*950, poetic words occur both in 'early-Mercian' and early-West-Saxon prose texts; after *c.*950, in 'Anglian' (= late-non-West-Saxon) and 'Winchester-School' writings. And various kinds of late prose, not only that composed in a rhythmic, alliterative style, have and hold the occasional poetic word.

The question of priority raised twenty years ago by Eric Stanley remains unanswered. Which came first, *Judgement Day II* or the corresponding section of Napier 29? Does *An Exhortation to Christian Living* underlie the prose of Vercelli homily 21 and Napier 30, or is it the other way around? The two poems admit prosaic words freely, words that seem at home in the homilies; but the prose itself has an unusual concentration of poetic words

[31] Once the unusually 'poetic' style of Ælfric's St Cuthbert homily is recognized, for example, the saint is heard to order his attendant seals back to the 'sea' (the poetic meaning of *sund*), and not, more puzzlingly, to 'swimming' (its prose meaning). Poeticisms already identified in this homily include *heolstor* and *siplice* (Godden, 'Ælfric's Changing Vocabulary', 217–19 and 221–2) and *fremde* (Hofstetter, *Winchester*, 39). Pope (*Homilies*, 115) observes that Ælfric is here 'imitating the poetical verse a little more closely with respect to number of syllables and even stress-patterns'.

[32] See discussion of *guma* (no. 2) and *wiga* (no. 3).

[33] For example, poetic *lixende* has been tentatively inserted in Ælfric's Nativity homily as a translation of *lucens* in John 5: 35 *erat lucerna ardens et lucens*: 'leo[htfæt wære beorhte lixende]'(ÆHom 1 312 [B 1.4.1] Pope 1, 196–216). *Lixende* occurs 26× in verse (including *Metres of Boethius*), 4× in 'Anglian' prose, as well as in late glosses (see Franz Wenisch, *Spezifisch anglisches Wortgut in den nordhumbrischen Interlinearglossierungen des Lukas-evangeliums* (Heidelberg, 1979), 181–2). In the Lindisfarne and Rushworth Gospels, *lucens* (John 5: 35) is glossed by *lixende*; in the West-Saxon Gospels, by *lyhtende*. But even the Lindisfarne glossator adds *vel scinende*; and the late-West-Saxon reviser of Gregory's *Dialogues* 'corrects' Werferth's *lixende* to *scinende* (see David Yerkes, *The Two Versions of Wærferth's Translation of Gregory's Dialogues: An Old English Thesaurus* (Toronto, 1979), §992). Ælfric employs *scinende* many times (twice with *leohtfæt*) and *lixende* never; he had little incentive to use the latter poetic word to translate *lucens* when two acceptable synonyms (including one, *lyhtende*, with *l*-alliteration) existed.

(e.g. *folde* (9d), *dreosan* (13a), *þeodcyningas*, and *hyge* (7a)), all found as alliterative counters in the corresponding lines of the poem. The tumbling mountains (*montesque ruent*) of *De die judicii* (51) would in Old English poetry have had to be dressed in alliteration and rhythm; but a prose writer, intent on transforming Bede's hexameters into a rhythmical and sonorous *Kunstprosa*, could still have been the first to come up with *duna dreosað and hreosað*. And although *þeodcyningas* is not a close, prosaic rendering of 'the mighty' (*pauperque potensque*, 80), its willingness to alliterate with *þearfan* might have made it appealing to homilist and poet alike. At particular moments in Anglo-Saxon England, poetry and prose seem to have moved, temporarily, closer together on the stylistic spectrum. Some Old English poets welcomed prosaic words, valuing their particularism, allusiveness, and metonymy; they recuperated poetry for another kind of mental process. And Old English prose writers for their part never ceased courting the pleasures of language—the noun burnished by time, the gleaming verb, the aged but unwithered adjective—knowing, with Xerxes, that the way to men's hearts was through their ears.[34] When they chose poetic words, they engaged powerful and significant 'others', 'icebergs in the linguistic history of our poetry, whose visible contours have been transformed, but whose bases were broad and deep in Cædmon's time'.[35]

[34] Herodotus 7.39. On 'unpoetic' poetry and the development of rhythmic prose, see now M. S. Griffith, 'Poetic Language and the Paris Psalter: The Decay of the Old English Tradition', *ASE* 20 (1991), 167–86.

[35] Geoffrey Shepherd, 'Scriptural Poetry', in *Continuations and Beginnings: Studies in Old English Literature*, ed. E. G. Stanley (London, 1966), 21. Walter Goffart and Scott Gwara read an earlier (1990) draft of this paper and made a number of valuable corrections and suggestions for which I am grateful.

Old English Weak Genitive Plural -an: *Towards Establishing the Evidence*

TERRY HOAD

Old English morphology and its evolution have been among the most intensively studied aspects of that language, and the progressive simplification of the inflectional system has been recognized as one of the most fundamental structural developments in the history of English.

Nevertheless, there is much that remains to be explained, and even much data yet to be assembled and analysed. My purpose here is to examine one feature of Old English morphology that seems to have been inadequately dealt with thus far—the ending *-an* as possibly occurring in the genitive plural of weak adjectives and substantives—and to make a contribution towards a better account of it. A full treatment of the feature in question still remains to be undertaken, but I hope in what follows at least to have outlined the problem and to have gone part of the way towards its resolution.

The two current standard handbooks[1] of Old English grammar report that in late Old English the ending *-an* is found in the genitive plural of the weak declension of adjectives:

> W-S develops d.p. *-an* earlier in the weak adj. than in the noun and the strong adj . . . it is already as frequent as *-um* in weak adjs. in eW-S. lW-S sporadically extends *-an* to gen. pl.[2]

> Gen. Pl. auf *-ena* (selten auch *-ana*, *-na*), *ʒȳdena* [*sic*; read *ʒōdena*?] usw., finden sich frühws. in der gelehrten Übersetzungsliteratur wie Cura past. Daneben finden sich vereinzelte Ansätze zu Bildungen auf *-an* (nach Analogie zu den übrigen Kasus auf *-an*), oder auf *-a* (nach der vokal. Substantivdeklination). Auch Mischformen wie *hāliʒrana* und *hāliʒran* begegnen ganz vereinzelt in Urkunden.[3]

I here express my warm thanks to Professors Carl Berkhout and Roger Dahood, who each kindly read and commented on a draft of this article, much to its benefit.

[1] A. Campbell, *Old English Grammar* (Oxford, 1959), and K. Brunner, *Altenglische Grammatik* (3rd edn., Tübingen, 1965). A new handbook, R. M. Hogg's *Grammar of Old English*, has begun to appear, but so far only volume 1, *Phonology*, has been published (Oxford, 1992). Volume 2 is to deal with morphology.

[2] Campbell, *Old English Grammar*, §656.

[3] Brunner, *Altenglische Grammatik*, §304 Anm. 2.

One of these handbooks makes a similar claim with regard to the genitive plural of the weak declension of substantives:

Vereinzelt finden sich für *-(e)na* spätws. auch *-an,* wie *ēastran, cǣȝean* (zu *cǣȝ* stf. Schlüssel), oder *-enan,* wie *ēaȝenan,* und stark *-a,* wie *bæcistra, prica, nama.*[4]

A slightly earlier authority alludes to the 'mixed' adjectival forms:

In den g.pl. is de uitgang *-ra* de meest gebruikelijke, *-ena* komt meer uitsluitend in de geleerde taal voor. Een zeer enkele maal vinden wij compromis-vormen; dit kunnen ook wel schrijffouten zijn, bv. *-rana, -ran.* Laat treedt ook, evenals in het sterke adjectief, *-a* op[5]

and reports of the genitive plural of weak substantives:

In het l.ws. treedt soms *-an* op voor *-ena,* bv. *wǽtan* g.pl. 'vloeistof', voorts *-a* naar de sterke declinatie, bv. *bæcestra* van *bæcestre* 'bakker', en zelfs *-enan,* bv. *éagenan* van *éage* 'oog'.[6]

The development of the use of *-an* in such functions would be in keeping with the move towards loss of case-distinctive inflections in later Old English, and the claims of the handbooks will therefore in themselves seem plausible enough. Editors and others, apparently for the most part following the lead of the grammarians,[7] have on various occasions accepted the existence of a genitive plural ending *-an* and have invoked it for the interpretation of what are often ambiguous or otherwise difficult forms. This has been the case with a number of verse texts. For example, at *Beo* 525:[8]

Đonne wene ic to þe   wyrsan geþingea

the adjectival form *wyrsan* has been explained as probably or possibly genitive plural,[9] as has *wyrsan* at *Prec* 7.[10] So too have the substantival forms *banan*

[4] Ibid., §276 Anm. 5. Campbell appears to be silent on this point.

[5] R. Girvan, *Angelsaksisch Handboek* (Haarlem, 1931), §307 Aanm. 1.

[6] Ibid., §285 Aanm. 2.

[7] But see also n. 31, below.

[8] In references to Old English texts I use the short titles adopted in R. L. Venezky and A. diP. Healey, *A Microfiche Concordance to Old English* (Newark and Toronto, 1980).

[9] See C. W. M. Grein, *Sprachschatz der angelsächsischen Dichter,* Bibliothek der angelsächsischen Poesie, 3–4, 2 vols. (Cassel and Göttingen, 1861–4), ii. 765 (similarly in the revision of this work by J. J. Köhler, Heidelberg, 1912, 847); A. J. Wyatt, *Beowulf with the Finnsburg Fragment* (Cambridge, new edn. rev. by R. W. Chambers, 1914), 29; E. A. Kock, 'Interpretations and Emendations of Early English Texts, V', *Anglia,* 43 = NF 31 (1919), 298–312 (see 301); J. Hoops, *Kommentar zum Beowulf* (Heidelberg, 1932), 80; F. Klaeber, *Beowulf and the Fight at Finnsburg* (Boston, 3rd edn. with Supplements, 1950), 150; E. V. K. Dobbie, *Beowulf and Judith,* Anglo-Saxon Poetic Records, 4 (New York and London, 1953), 145; C. L. Wrenn, *Beowulf with the Finnsburg Fragment* (2nd edn., London, 1958), 306 (so in the 3rd edn. rev. W. F. Bolton, 1973, 118); E. von Schaubert, *Heyne-Schückings 'Beowulf',* 3 vols (17th/18th edn., Paderborn, 1961–3), ii. 51; B. Mitchell, *Old English Syntax,* 2 vols. (Oxford, 1985), §1335.

[10] See Grein, *Sprachschatz,* ii. 765 (also Grein-Köhler, *Sprachschatz,* 846, s.v. *ge-wyrht,*

and *guman* at *Dream* 66 and 146,[11] *brogan* at *Beo* 583,[12] *flotan [and Sceotta]* at *Brun* 32,[13] *gingran, sceaðan,* and *welan* at *And* 894, 1133, 1159, and 1291,[14] and *sceaþan* at *Christ A, B, C* 775.[15] None of these forms requires by its context to be read as genitive plural. The supposed existence of a substantival genitive plural ending *-an* has also quite recently been brought into the discussion of the form *granigendran* at *HomU 32* 90 (MS C).[16]

Matti Rissanen, in his study of the uses of *one* in Old and Early Middle English, also speaks of *-an* as a weak genitive plural ending, with a reference to Brunner.[17]

-weorht); E. A. Kock, *Jubilee Jaunts and Jottings* (Lund and Leipzig, 1918; Lunds Universitets Årsskrift, N. F. Avd. 1, Bd 14, Nr 26), 28; G. P. Krapp and E. V. K. Dobbie, *The Exeter Book*, Anglo-Saxon Poetic Records, 3 (New York, 1936), 293. For a different interpretation see T. A. Shippey, *Poems of Wisdom and Learning in Old English* (Cambridge and Totowa, NJ, 1976), 5 and 49.

[11] For *banan* 66 see e.g. A. S. Cook, *The Dream of the Rood* (Oxford, 1905), 33–4, and Kock, 'Interpretations, V', 301, and for both *banan* 66 and *guman* 146 see e.g. Grein, *Sprachschatz*, i. 75 ('*gen.pl.* . . . on banan gesyhðe (?) *Kr.* 66') and 532–3 (also Grein-Köhler, *Sprachschatz*, 34 and 282); C. L. Wrenn, review of *The Dream of the Rood* (ed. B. Dickins and A. S. C. Ross), *Review of English Studies*, 12 (1936), 105–8 (see 106), and Wrenn, *Beowulf* (2nd edn.), 306, s.v. *wyrsa.* M. Swanton, *The Dream of the Rood* (Manchester, 1970), 123–4 and 134, takes both *banan* and *guman* as genitive singular, but refers to their having been thought by others to represent 'a known late WS gen. pl. form' (p. 124).

[12] See E. A. Kock, 'Interpretations and Emendations of Early English Texts, VI', *Anglia* 44 = NF 32 (1920), 97–114 (see 100–1).

[13] See Grein, *Sprachschatz*, i. 305 (also Grein-Köhler, *Sprachschatz*, 202); Kock, 'Interpretations, V', 301 (note to *And* 893–5); Wyatt (rev. Chambers), *Beowulf*, 29 (also A. J. Wyatt, *An Anglo-Saxon Reader* (Cambridge, 1919), 278). A. Campbell, *The Battle of Brunanburh* (London, 1938), 108, gives no consideration to the possibility of *flotan* being a good genitive plural form; according to him, *flotan* is to be emended to *flotena*, or else we must emend *Sceotta* to *Sceottas* (with both words then being treated as nominative forms). E. Ekwall, in a review of Campbell's edition (*English Studies*, 21 (1939), 218–20; see 220), takes *flotan* as a genitive singular form: '*flota* also means "fleet" and "crew of a fleet". The correct explanation is in Bosworth-Toller (Suppl.).' Ekwall is followed by E. V. K. Dobbie, *The Anglo-Saxon Minor Poems*, Anglo-Saxon Poetic Records, 6 (New York, 1943), 148.

[14] See Kock, 'Interpretations, V', 301 (on *gingran* 894), and K. R. Brooks, *Andreas and the Fates of the Apostles* (Oxford, 1961), 101 (on *sceaðan* 1133), 102 (on *welan* 1159), and 109 (on *sceaðan* 1291). Brooks (p. 93) takes *gingran* 894 as the subject of *gehyrdon*, and therefore as nominative plural.

[15] See Kock, 'Interpretations, VI', 100–1, and Brooks, *Andreas*, 101 (note to line 1133).

[16] See E. G. Stanley, '*The Judgement of the Damned* (from Cambridge, Corpus Christi College 201 and Other Manuscripts), and the Definition of Old English Verse', in M. Lapidge and H. Gneuss (eds.), *Learning and Literature in Anglo-Saxon England: Studies Presented to Peter Clemoes* (Cambridge, 1985), 363–91 (the form *granigendran* is discussed on p. 387).

[17] M. Rissanen, *The Uses of 'One' in Old and Early Middle English*, Mémoires de la Société Néophilologique de Helsinki, 31 (Helsinki, 1967), 83 n. 1. Rissanen is illustrating the construction '*one* + genitive/possessive pronoun + noun', and in most of his examples there is apparent concord between the form of *one* and the noun (e.g. *Bede 5* 1.384.11 *gif ic aan his wundor asecgo; Exod* 2.5 *sende heo ane hire þinene þider 7 het hine feccan*). For three of his examples, Rissanen admits the alternative possibility that a form in *-an* may be a genitive plural: *Mt(WSCp)* 26.51 *asloh of anys þæra sacerda ealdres þeowan eare; ÆCHom I,33* 492.34

It is always desirable in such matters to have the evidence firmly established. I will consider first the supposed adjectival genitive plural ending *-an* and then the supposed substantival ending.

As may be seen from the passages cited above, the only evidence offered in the handbooks for weak adjectival genitive plural *-an* is that of the 'Mischformen wie *hālizrana* und *hālizran*' mentioned by Brunner. It may be noted that whereas Campbell restricts his statement to late West Saxon, Brunner's formulation seems to imply that he believes the forms in question to occur more widely in Old English.

The basis for Brunner's statement is to be found in notes published by Sievers in 1884 to correct and supplement the first edition of his *Angelsächsische Grammatik*:

Im gen. pl. [*sc.* of weak adjectives] findet sich bisweilen auch das *-an* der übrigen casus: *his unnytan færelta* Cura past. 257, 9, *heora yfelan dǣda* Aelfr. N. T. 21, 22, *ðāra ylcan zerihta* C. D. 3, 138 . . . Eine mischung von starker und schwacher declination [zeigt] endlich der sonderbare genetiv *ðǣre hâlizrana* und *ðǣre hâlizran* in der urkunde C. D. 2, 5 (Sweet O. E. T. 454, 9 und 20).[18]

Brunner's grammar is in origin a revision of that of Sievers, and indeed the note under discussion is scarcely changed from the one which appeared in the second edition of the *Angelsächsische Grammatik*:

Gen. pl. auf *-ena*, wie *zódena*, finden sich wol nur in der gelehrten übersetzungsliteratur, wie Cura past. Daneben finden sich vereinzelte ansätze zu bildungen auf *-an* (nach der analogie der übrigen casus auf *-an*) oder *-a* (nach der substantivdeclination). Auch mischformen wie *hálizrana* und *hálizran* begegnen ganz vereinzelt in urk.[19]

In assessing the evidence for weak adjectival genitive plural *-an*, therefore, we should look first at the examples assembled by Sievers.

They prove on examination not to be uniformly convincing. The alleged example from the *Cura pastoralis* translation was questioned by Cosijn just two years after Sievers' article appeared.[20] Cosijn's grounds were that such an ending would be without parallel in the early West Saxon texts, and that a genitive plural would not be appropriate in the context:

Sua mon oft let[t] fundigendne monnan, & his færelt gælð, sua gælð se lichoma ðæt

cwæð se hælend to anum his gecorenan; ÆLS (Martin) 36 *betæht to þam gewinne mid anum his þeowan þe his gesiðe wæs.* Since these examples are ambiguous as to case they will not be discussed further here.

[18] E. Sievers, 'Miscellen zur angelsächsischen Grammatik', *Beiträge zur Geschichte der deutschen Sprache und Literatur*, 9 (1884), 197–300 (see 260).

[19] E. Sievers, *Angelsächsische Grammatik* (2nd edn., Halle, 1886), §304 Anm. 2. (The first sentence appears in almost identical form in the 1st edn. (Halle, 1882).)

[20] P. J. Cosijn, *Altwestsächsische Grammatik*, 2 vols. (The Hague, 1883–6), ii. 13.

mod, oððæt he gebrocad wierð mid sumre mettrymnesse, & ðon*ne* ða mettry*m*nesse getacnað se lichoma ðæm mode ðone ungesewenan engel ðe him togenes stent, & him wiernð his unnyttan færelta ðurh ðæs lichoma mettrymnesse.[21]

Cosijn takes *færelta* as a *u*-stem genitive singular, which is also the explanation offered by Campbell.[22]

Sievers' example *ðara ylcan gerihta* comes from a charter purporting to record the confirmation of land to Winchester Cathedral by King Edgar in the second half of the tenth century:

Her ys geswutelod on þysum gewrite hu Eadgar cyning mid geþeahte his witena geniwode Tantunes freols þære halgan þrynnesse 7 sc̄e Petre 7 sc̄e Paule into Wintanceastre to þam biscopstole ealswa Eadweard cyning hit ær gefreode 7 geuþe ꝥ ægþer ge twelfhynde men ge twyhynde weron on þam Godes hame þara ylcan gerihta wyrþe þe his agene men sindon on his agenu*m* cynehamu*m*.[23]

The text, however, survives only in a twelfth-century cartulary, and its authenticity is not above suspicion.[24] It is therefore poor evidence on which to base a linguistic argument with regard to Old English.

The alleged 'mixed' forms *haligrana* and *haligran*, which were transformed between 1884 and 1886 from peculiarities occurring in a single text to a type found 'ganz vereinzelt in urk[unden]', are not very securely attested and present problems with regard to their interpretation. Sievers cited them from a ninth-century charter of Berhtwulf of Mercia, following Kemble's text:

Ic berhtwulf. rex. ðas mine gesaldnisse trymme 7 faestna in cristes rode tacne 7 in his ðaere haligrana 7 in his wotona gewitnisse

7 we aec alle bibeodað ðe aet ðisse gewitnisse werun ...... on cristes noman 7 on his ðaere haligran gif aenig monn. ðas ure gewitnisse in-cerre on owihte ðaet he aebbe ðaes aelmaehtigan godes unhli .... 7 his ðaere haligran ....[25]

The dots are Kemble's. For comparison, I give the corresponding portions of the text as I printed them in the revised edition of Sweet's *Second Anglo-Saxon Reader*:

[21] *CP* 36.257.5; H. Sweet, *King Alfred's West-Saxon Version of Gregory's Pastoral Care,* EETS OS 45, 50, 2 vols. (London, 1871), i. 257 (Bodleian MS Hatton 20, dated '890–7' by Ker (*Catalogue*, 384 (item 324)); the reading *his unnyttan færelta* is shared by British Library MS Cotton Tiberius B.xi, also dated '890–7' by Ker (*Catalogue*, 257 (item 195))).

[22] Campbell, *Old English Grammar*, §614.

[23] *Ch 806(Rob 45)* 1; A. J. Robertson, *Anglo-Saxon Charters* (Cambridge, 1956), 92 (no. 45).

[24] See the references cited by P. H. Sawyer, *Anglo-Saxon Charters: An Annotated List and Bibliography* (London, 1968), 256–7 (no. 806).

[25] *Ch 204(HarmD 3)* 8 and 11; J. M. Kemble, *Codex diplomaticus aevi saxonici*, 6 vols. (London, 1839–48), ii. 5–6 (no. 243). The charter is reckoned to be an authentic document, and is preserved in a manuscript dated 's.ix. med.'; see Sawyer, *Anglo-Saxon Charters*, 122–3 (no. 204).

Ic Berhtwulf *rex* ðas mine gesaldnisse trymme 7 faestna in Cristes rodetacne 7 in his ðaere haligran a [footnote: *prec. by two unexplained marks*] 7 in his *wotona gewitnisse

7 we aec alle bibeodað ðe aet ðisse gewitnisse werun on Cristes noman 7 on his ðaere haligra[n], gif aenig monn ðas ure gewitnisse incerre on owihte, ðaet he aebbe ðaes aelmaehtgan Gode[s unhlis . . 7] his ðaere haligran up in heofnum ðaes we him [ge]beodan maege.[26]

None of the principal editors of this charter other than Kemble has printed *haligrana* as one word in the first passage cited above, and the interpretation of *in his ðaere haligran a* is quite uncertain.[27] In the second passage, the first of the two examples of the phrase *his ðaere haligran* is today not to be read with certainty, and the interpretation of neither is without problems.

Of the examples given in Sievers' note we are left, therefore, with the Ælfrician one, which is harder to dismiss. At the end of his *Letter to Sigeweard*, Ælfric discusses the wrong-doings of the Jews and the retribution which befell them, concluding:

7 þis wæs þ*æt* edlean heora yfelan dæda 7 eac hellewite, þæt þ*æt* him hefegore ys.[28]

Crawford prints the text from Bodleian MS Laud Misc. 509, dated 's. xi²' by Ker,[29] although the same reading is found in British Library MS Harley 3271, which Ker dates 's. xi¹'.[30] There is therefore no apparent reason to doubt the reliability of *yfelan*, at least, as an Old English form.

[26] H. Sweet, *A Second Anglo-Saxon Reader* (2nd edn. rev. T. F. Hoad, Oxford, 1978), 219–20. The square brackets 'enclose letters supplied because missing from or not legible in the MSS.', single points are 'used to indicate lost or illegible letters', and the asterisk indicates 'an erroneous or anomalous form, being thus equivalent to "sic" ' (pp. [xi]–xii).

[27] W. B. Sanders, in *Facsimiles of Anglo-Saxon Manuscripts*, 3 vols. (Southampton, 1878–84), i, item 8, prints *haligranna*. W. de G. Birch, *Cartularium saxonicum*, 3 vols. (London, 1885–93), ii. 35 (no. 452), prints 'in his ðaere haligran √√ a'. J. Earle, *A Hand-Book to the Land-Charters, and Other Saxonic Documents* (Oxford, 1888), 122–3, prints 'in his ðaere haligran 7 in his wotona gewitnisse', with the note: '*haligrana*, K[emble]; *haligranna*, S[anders]:-but two subsequent instances seem to justify *haligran*, and the added *-a* or *-na* looks rather like the attempt of a διορθωτής to fill in a gap left by the scribe'. F. E. Harmer, *Select English Historical Documents of the Ninth and Tenth Centuries* (Cambridge, 1914), 5f (no. 3), prints 'in his ðaere haligran √√ a 7 in his wotona gewitnisse', with the note (pp. 81–2): 'cf. 1.25 and 1.27 below. Sievers (*Angelsächs. Gramm.* § 304, n.2) seems to regard *haligran* as an isolated gen.plur., but is it not more probable that the explanation is to be found in a misunderstanding of some Latin formula? The hieroglyphics following *haligran* are unexplained. They can hardly be a later insertion to fill a blank space, since they are in exactly the same ink as the rest of the text.'

[28] *ÆLet 4(SigeweardZ)* 8; S. J. Crawford, *The Old English Version of the Heptateuch, Ælfric's Treatise on the Old and New Testament and his Preface to Genesis*, EETS OS 160 (London, 1922), 74.

[29] N. R. Ker, *Catalogue of Manuscripts Containing Anglo-Saxon* (Oxford, 1957), 422 (item 344).

[30] Ibid. 309 (item 239).

With regard to *-an* as a genitive plural ending of weak substantives in late Old English (which if it were to be established might lend support to such evidence as there is for a similar ending in the adjectives), the origin of Brunner's remark lies once again in Sievers' article of 1884:

Im gen. pl. erscheint eine starke form in *bæcistra* Gen. 40, 16. 29. 41, 10; vereinzelt spät *-enan* statt *-ena*, *ê3enan* Ld. 1, 72 O, *mâ heofenan* Ld. 3, 232 (für **heofenenan*, wie *teóna* Haupt gl. 506ᵇ für *teónena*); vgl. auch *þâra cǽ3ean* L. Cnut 2, 77 s. 180; *ðâra hâl3ena eástran* Beda 118; *ǽlcra liman* Ld. 2, 314 (zu dem stf. *limu* glied, dat. *ǽlcre lime* Ld. 2, 288, acc. pl. *leome* Ld. 3, 20).[31]

Once again, Sievers' examples are not entirely satisfactory. Of those from the *Leechdoms* one, *egenan*, from the later-twelfth-century or thirteenth-century British Library MS Harley 6258 B,[32] is too late to stand as reliable evidence for Old English (the ending *-enan* is in any case beyond the scope of the present discussion), while *ælcra liman*, which appears to be misreported from the sentence:

he is god wiþ ælcre liman untrumnesse[33]

is dubious as an example of a genitive plural form *liman*. It seems likely that *ælcre* is in agreement with *untrumnesse*, and so is of no help in determining the number and case of *liman*. Sievers recognizes a strong feminine noun *limu*, but 'limb' is usually a strong neuter in Old English.[34] The form *liman* could perhaps be explained as a spelling for strong genitive plural *lima* in a

[31] Sievers, 'Miscellen', 246. Once again, Brunner's note follows closely that in the second edition of Sievers' grammar: 'Vereinzelt findet sich spät *-an* [*sc.* for the genitive plural of weak substantives] wie *éastran, cǽ3ean,* oder *-enan*, wie *éa3enan,* und stark *-a*, wie *bǽcistra, prica, nama*' (Sievers, *Angelsächsische Grammatik* (2nd edn.), §276 Anm. 1; the form *bǽcistra* is corrected to *bæcistra* in the 'Nachträge und berichtigungen' (see p. 228)). It may be noted here that Grein's interpretation of a number of substantival forms in *-an* in verse texts, as well as adjectival *wyrsan* at *Beo* 525 (see nn. 9–11 and 13, above), antedates this article by more than twenty years.

[32] On the date see Ker, *Catalogue*, p. xix, and H. J. de Vriend, *The Old English Herbarium and Medicina de Quadrupedibus*, EETS 286 (Oxford, 1984), p. xxx. The passage corresponds to *Lch 1(Herb)* 1.6.2, where the reading (in the 11th-cent. manuscript Cotton Vitellius C.iii) is *eagena*; de Vriend, *The Old English Herbarium*, 32 (with the form *e3enan* printed p. 33, line 2).

[33] *Lch II(3)* 12.2.6; O. Cockayne, *Leechdoms, Wortcunning, and Starcraft of Early England*, 3 vols. (1864–66), ii. 314; G. Leonhardi, *Kleinere angelsächsische Denkmäler: 1* (no more published), Bibliothek der angelsächsischen Prosa, 6 (Hamburg, 1905), 96. The manuscript is British Library Royal 12 D.xvii, dated 's. x med.' by Ker (*Catalogue*, 332 (item 264)).

[34] There is at least one occurrence, noted by Sievers, of 'limb' with apparent feminine gender: *gif mon eac of his gewitte weorðe þonne nime he his dæl 7 wyrce cristes mæl on ælcre lime, butan cruc on þam heafde foran se sceal on balzame beon 7 oþer on þam heafde ufan (Lch II(2)* 64.1.10; Cockayne, *Leechdoms*, ii. 288 (Cockayne suggests emendation to *ælcum*)). On the manuscript, see the preceding note. If in the phrase presently under discussion *liman* is to be taken as an advanced spelling for a feminine form, it could equally well be singular or plural on formal grounds.

variety of Old English in which final *-n* had been lost from at least some inflectional endings. There is, however, some evidence for possible weak declension for 'limb':

Ne mihte nan wana beon þam welwillendan Hælende ænig his limena æfter his æriste[35]

þa eodan hi mid miccle gefean to him & hi cyston his leoman & ofslogan hine þa[36]

And forðan men þa leofestan, weorþiað eow selfe betweonan eow forðan we syndan ealra anra leoman and crist is ure heafod[37]

bregdeð sona
feond be ðam feaxe, læteð flint brecan
scines sconcan; he ne besceawað no
his leomona lið, ne bið him læce god[38]

If *liman* can be a weak form in the phrase *wiþ ælcre liman untrumnesse*, it may seem more natural to take it as a singular (translating 'for each infirmity of [a] limb').[39]

It seems that nothing exactly like Sievers' *þæra cægean* occurs in the manuscripts of II Cn 76, 1a (using Liebermann's numbering[40]). The readings recorded by Liebermann are *þære cægean*,[41] *ðara cægan*,[42] and *þære cægen*.[43] The context may suggest that the phrase is plural:

And gyf hwylc man forstolen þingc ham to his cotan bringe 7 he arasod wurðe, riht is, þ*æt* he hæbbe þ*æt* he æft*er*eode.
7 butan hit under þæs wifes cæglocan gebroht wære, si heo clæne.
Ac þære cægean heo sceal weardian, þ*æt* is hyre hordern 7 hyre cyste 7 hyre tege: gif

[35] *ÆHom 7* 156; J. C. Pope, *Homilies of Ælfric*, EETS 259, 260, 2 vols. (Oxford, 1967–8), i. 347. Pope says of *limena*: 'This form, unless merely scribal, may have been preferred for its extra syllable. Another instance of the weak form of the genitive plural is cited in B[osworth-] T[oller] from *Solomon and Saturn*, I.102a, where the extra syllable is metrically necessary' (i. 351, note to line 157).

[36] *LS 30 (Pantaleon)* 477. The *Microfiche Concordance* cites this text from the unpublished edition by P. M. Matthews (dissertation, University College London, 1965–6), with minor corrections by J. Söderlind.

[37] *HomM 5 (Willard)* 213 (but this part of the text is not included in the partial edition by R. Willard, *Two Apocrypha in Old English Homilies*, Beiträge zur englischen Philologie, 30 (Leipzig, 1935)).

[38] *MSol* 99; Dobbie, *The Anglo-Saxon Minor Poems*, 35.

[39] Cockayne translates 'for every ailment of limb' (*Leechdoms*, ii. 315).

[40] F. Liebermann, *Die Gesetze der Angelsachsen*, 3 vols. (Halle, 1903–16), i. 362. I have not ascertained to which edition of the Anglo-Saxon laws Sievers' reference applies.

[41] MS G, i.e. British Library MS Cotton Nero A.i. fos. 3–57, dated 's. xi med.' by Ker (*Catalogue*, 210 (item 163)).

[42] MS B, i.e. Corpus Christi College, Cambridge, MS 383, dated 's. xi/xii' by Ker (*Catalogue*, 110 (item 65)).

[43] MS A, i.e. British Library MS Harley 55, dated 's. xii med.' by Ker (*Catalogue* 302 (item 226)).

hit under þyssa ænigum gebroht byð, þonne byð heo scyldig.[44]

This is the view towards which Liebermann inclines, translating:

Dagegen auf folgende (-den?) Schlüssel muss sie Acht geben, nämlich ihre Vorrathskammer und ihre Kiste und ihren Schrein [beaufsichtigen][45]

The singular cannot be entirely ruled out, however.

If the phrase is plural, the only case possible is the genitive. The verb *weardian* is said to govern both the accusative and the genitive,[46] although there appears to be little certain evidence for the latter.[47] It must be said that the interpretation of *þære cægean* in this passage remains somewhat uncertain.

Sievers' example *eastran* is evidently taken from Wheloc's edition of the Old English Bede,[48] the base manuscript of that edition being Cambridge University Library Kk. 3.18.[49] The same reading is found a little earlier in Corpus Christi College, Oxford, MS 41.[50] The earliest manuscript of the Old English Bede,[51] however, reads *Eastrana*:

Forðon he ongeat þæt heo on monegum þingum Godes cirican ungeþwærodon, ond ealra swiðust þæt heo þa symbelnesse Eastrana 7 þone dæg þære drihtenlecan æriste ne weorðodon mid rihtre tide.[52]

The inflectional forms of the 'Easter' word are exceptional in various ways, as is noted by Campbell and Brunner,[53] and this example is therefore not a particularly good one for establishing the existence of an Old English genitive plural ending *-an* of substantives.

The phrase *ma heofenan*, from *ÆTemp* 1.8:

[44] *LawIICn* 76–76.1; Liebermann, *Gesetze*, i. 362–4 (II Cn 76–76,1a; MS G).

[45] *Gesetze*, i. 363. In the notes he says '*þære* und *cægean* können spätwestsächs. Gen. plur. sein. Der Plural, den Lateiner annehmen, passt besser in den Zusammenhang' (iii. 213, note to II Cn 76,1a).

[46] See e.g. Mitchell, *Old English Sytax*, §1092. Liebermann suggests that in this passage '*weardian* regiert erst Gen., dann Acc.' (*Gesetze* iii. 213, note to II Cn 76,1a).

[47] The example cited in J. Bosworth and T. N. Toller, *An Anglo-Saxon Dictionary* (Oxford, 1898), s.v. *weardian, Ia.*, is from the *Peterborough Chronicle* annal for 1088: *Ac þa englisce men þe wærdedon þære sæ gelæhton of þam mannon* [*r* in *wærdedon* is added above the line]; C. Clark, *The Peterborough Chronicle 1070–1154* (2nd edn., Oxford, 1970), 16. The writing of this part of the *Peterborough Chronicle* is thought to be datable to shortly after 1121 and the scribe to be the same as the one responsible for the First Continuation, working up to 1131 or shortly thereafter (see Clark, *Peterborough Chronicle*, p. xvi). It therefore provides good evidence only for a very late variety of what might still be called Old English.

[48] Abraham Wheloc, *Historiæ Ecclesiasticæ Gentis Anglorum Libri V* (Cambridge, 1643), 118 (*HE*. II.iv).

[49] Dated 's. xi[2]' by Ker (*Catalogue*, 36 (item 23)).

[50] Dated 's. xi in.' by Ker (*Catalogue*, 432 (item 354)).

[51] Bodleian MS Tanner 10, dated 's. x[1]' by Ker (*Catalogue*, 428 (item 351)).

[52] *Bede 2* 4.106.30; T. Miller, *The Old English Version of Bede's Ecclesiastical History of the English People*, EETS os 95, 96, 110, 111, 2 parts (London, 1890–8), i. 106–8.

[53] Campbell, *Old English Grammar*, §619.1; Brunner, *Altenglische Grammatik*, §278 Anm. 3.

Sind swa ðeah mâ heofenan · swa swa se witega cwæð; Celi celor*um* · þ*æt* is heofena · heofenan[54]

may be better evidence, if we demand a partitive genitive after *ma*.[55] The unambiguous forms from Ælfric in the citations in the *Microfiche Concordance*, s.v. *ma*, suggest that in his works *ma* is usually followed by a genitive form. A possible exception, however, is *ma oðre* at *ÆLS* (*Agatha*) 220:

Se munt byrnð æfre . swá swá má oþre doð.[56]

We might also note that Pope, in the *Glossary* to his edition of *Homilies of Ælfric*, records *ma* as occurring both as a substantive and as an adjective (it not being always certain which).[57] Since his example of adjectival *ma*[58] is itself in combination with a substantival form in *-an*, however, we are no further on.

It is perhaps significant that in the close vicinity of *ma heofenan* we apparently find distinctive forms *heofena* gen. pl. ~ *heofenan* nom. pl.[59] Does this make it less likely that *heofenan* can be a genitive plural form?

In his *Glossary*, Pope reports the form *heofon* (strong masculine or strong feminine) as occurring in the texts he edits over seventy times in the plural but just once in the singular, but *heofone* (weak feminine) as occurring exclusively in the singular in the twenty-eight places in which it is used.[60] Only one of the examples seems unambiguously singular, however.[61] Given

[54] H. Henel, *Ælfric's De temporibus anni*, EETS os 213 (London 1942), 6. The base manuscript is Cambridge University Library Gg. 3.28, dated 's. x/xi' by Ker (*Catalogue*, 13 (item 15)).

[55] If Sievers' explanation of *heofenan* as a shortening of **heofenenan* were correct, the ending (*-enan*) would not fall within the scope of the present article. However, it does not seem necessary to explain it in that way. It is simpler to assume that it is a form of the weak feminine substantive *heofone*.

[56] Skeat, *Ælfric's Lives of Saints*, i. 208. Mitchell, *Old English Syntax*, appears not to discuss explicitly the case governed by *ma*, although constructions with *ma* are presumably parallel to those with *fela*, on which see Mitchell's §1299 (showing examples of *fela* both followed by a genitive plural form and by an accusative plural form).

[57] Pope, *Homilies of Ælfric*, ii. 886.

[58] *ÆHom 3* 122; see p. 125 and n. 107, below.

[59] The alternative possibility, that *heofena* is a nominative plural form of strong feminine *heofon* and *heofenan* a genitive plural form of weak feminine *heofone*, seems less likely. Feminine *seo heofon* occurs at e.g. *ÆTemp* 1.5: *Seo heofon belicð on hire bosme ealne middaneard* (Henel, *Ælfric's De temporibus*, 4), and 5.3: *Seo heofen 7 sæ 7 eorðe sind gehatene middangeard* (Henel, *Ælfric's De temporibus*, 42), and elsewhere in Ælfric. According to Pope, however, 'it is apparently Ælfric's substitute for the weak *seo heofone* in the nominative singular, since he uses *heofonan* for the singular in the other cases, as the Glossary shows; and in all probability he uses the strong masculine word only in the plural, *heofonas*, etc.' (*Homilies of Ælfric*, ii. 717 (note to XXI.186)).

[60] Ibid. ii. 873. Cf. Pope's comments quoted in the preceding note.

[61] *ÆHom 11* 508 *on ðære niwan heofonan*; Pope, *Homilies of Ælfric*, i. 444 (line 516).

the apparent general rarity of *-an* as a genitive plural ending of weak nouns in Ælfrician texts, it seems unlikely that all the twenty examples in the pieces edited by Pope of a genitive form *heofonan* (seventeen of which are in the phrase *heofonan rice*) are plural. Some may be, however (and we may note beside the examples of *heofonan rice* just mentioned the occurrence of the unambiguously plural forms of 'heaven' at *ÆHom 3* 179 *heofona rice* and *ÆHom 28* 10 *heofena rice*).

It was earlier noted that Girvan cites a form *wætan* as an example of genitive plural *-an*.[62] The only place at which such a form appears to be attested with that function is *ÆCHom II, 3* 19.17, as preserved in MS K (Cambridge University Library MS Gg. 3.28):

ne dránc hé [*sc.* John the Baptist] naðor ne wín. ne beor. ne ealu. ne nan ðæra wǽtan ðe menn of druncniað.[63]

Malcolm Godden, in his edition of the Second Series of *Catholic Homilies*, notes the similar passage at *ÆCHom II, 17* 171.64:

Ne dránc he [*sc.* St James the Apostle] wines drenc. ne nan ðæra wætena þe druncennysse styriað[64]

and there is a further parallel passage at *ÆCHom I, 25* 352.4 [Luke 1]:

He [*sc.* John the Baptist] bið mære ætforan gode: ne abyrigð he wines ne nan þæra wætana þe men of druncniað.[65]

Godden believes that the form *wætan* at *ÆCHom II, 3* 19.17 is 'almost certainly an error, since the genitive plural is always *wætena* in the *Catholic Homilies* and that is the BR reading [*sc.* the reading of Bodleian MS Bodley 343 and Corpus Christi College, Cambridge, MS 178] here'.[66] He therefore prints *wætena* in his text. However, the only occurrences of *wæte* in Ælfric in which the genitive plural is required appear to be the three mentioned above, which is too few for us to be able to draw conclusions about the validity of the forms. Cambridge University Library MS Gg. 3.28, dated 's. x/xi' by Ker,[67] cannot easily be set aside as a witness in such matters. The example remains unreliable, however.

Can the existence of genitive plural *-an* be more firmly established? It is

[62] See p. 109, above.

[63] M. Godden, *Ælfric's Catholic Homilies: The Second Series*, EETS SS 5 (Oxford, 1979), 19.

[64] Ibid. 171.

[65] The *Microfiche Concordance* cites *ÆCHom I* from the unpublished edition by P. A. M. Clemoes (dissertation, Cambridge, 1955–6); the passage is not printed in B. Thorpe, *The Homilies of the Anglo-Saxon Church: The First Part, Containing the Sermones Catholici, or Homilies of Ælfric*, 2 vols. (London, 1844–6), i. 352.

[66] Godden, *Ælfric's Catholic Homilies*, 347 (note to III.18).

[67] See n. 54, above.

not an easy matter to determine how many other forms of this type have been identified, or exist but remain unidentified, in Old English texts. References to such forms appear to be generally lacking in the scholarly literature. I have looked at a considerable number of forms in *-an* in the *Microfiche Concordance* in an attempt to locate examples of that ending in the genitive plural of weak adjectives and substantives, but since the ending occurs with extremely high frequency in the Old English corpus I have only been able to examine a fairly small proportion of the total number.

I will consider first the weak adjective. Since Sievers' only good example[68] is from Ælfric, it is reasonable to start the search for further examples in the works of that author.[69]

There is frequently considerable difficulty in determining the case or number of a given form, since the ending *-an* occurs at a number of places in the familiar paradigms of weak adjectives and nouns in Old English, and since the forms of accompanying demonstratives are also often ambiguous as to case or number. Thus while the form *heofonlican* at *ÆCHom I, 6* 90.6 is possibly genitive plural:

Se godspellere lucas beleac þis dægþerlice gospel mid feawum wordum. ac hit is mid menigfealdre mihte þæra heofonlican gerinu afylled[70]

the phrase *þæra heofonlican gerinu* may equally well be singular.[71]

Rather clearer are two examples similar to that in the *Letter to Sigeweard* and found at *ÆCHom II, 30* 238.104 (*fulan*):

Þæt meox is þæt gemynd his fulan dæda. on ðære dædbote[72]

and *ÆCHom II, 33* 251.55 (*godan*):

Nis gode nan neod ure godan dæda.[73]

Another apparently reliable example from Ælfric is *foresædan* at *ÆCHom I, 40* 610.11:

þære sæ gemencgednys. and þæra yþa sweg ungewunelice gyt ne asprungon: ac

[68] That is, *yfelan* at *ÆLet 4(SigeweardZ)* 8; see p. 113, above.

[69] In addition to the reverse index in the *Microfiche Concordance* I have had the benefit of the use of a print-out of a reverse index to the vocabulary of Ælfric's *Catholic Homilies* kindly lent to me by Professor Malcolm Godden.

[70] For the corresponding passage see Thorpe, *Homilies*, i. 90.

[71] For *þæra* as a genitive singular form, cf. e.g. *ÆLS (Basil)* 143 *ealle ða þenunga þæra halgan mæssan*; 353 *ac let þa godas þeowas þæt godes templ bugian and þæra are brucan þe him geahnod wæs; ÆCHom I,24* 348.6 *ða oþre werod þe him mid wuniað brucað ðæra incundan ymbwlatunge his godcundnysse; ÆCHom II,33* 251.50 *ac we sceolon geriman ure misdæda mid woþe and geomerunge and þæra miltsunge gebiddan.*

[72] Godden, *Ælfric's Catholic Homilies*, 238. On the base manuscript see n. 54, above.

[73] Ibid. 251. On the base manuscript see n. 54, above.

þonne fela þæra foresædan tacna gefyllede sind nis nan twynung þæt ða feawa þe ðær to lafe sind witodlice gefyllede beoð.[74]

Among non-Ælfrician texts I have found a few additional possible examples. Some of these are questionable on grounds of ambiguity as mentioned above, or because the variety of language they seem to represent is a rather late one.

The form *godcundlican* at *LS 23 (MaryofEgypt)* 2.226:

Ða æfter manega tída fæce cw*æð* þ*æ*t wíf to Zosime; Ðe gedafenað abbud Zosimus to biddenne and to bletsigenne . forþan þu eart underwreðed mid þære sacerdlican lare . and þu eart tellende Cristes gerýnu mid þam gyfum þæra godcundlican æt his þam halgan weofode manegum gearum þeowigende[75]

is possibly genitive plural. Skeat translates:

It befitteth thee, Abbot Zosimus, to pray and to bless, because thou art authorised by the sacerdotal dignity, and thou preachest Christ's mysteries with the gifts of divine things, serving at his holy altar for many years.[76]

However, it would seem at least as plausible to take *þæra godcundlican* as genitive singular, with *lare* understood from the previous clause (translating: 'with the gifts of divine instruction').[77]

The form *heofonlican* at *LS 13(Machutus)* 19.R.1:

Utan agan þone halga<n> gast · þæt sie on ús geedniwad · se willa · þara heofonlican gefeana[78]

does not appear to be ambiguous as to case or number. Furthermore, the manuscript (British Library MS Cotton Otho A.viii) is dated 's. xi in.' by Ker,[79] and the written language of the *Life of Machutus* seems in principle to be what a scribe writing 'late West Saxon' towards the close of the Anglo-Saxon period would have found acceptable.

In what sense this example can be taken to show that *-an* was a possible genitive plural ending of adjectives is not entirely clear, however. Yerkes notes forms such as 25.R.12 *weran* (genitive plural) and 32.R.6 *lichoma*[80] (dative singular) which seem to suggest a more general loss of distinctions

[74] Thorpe, *The Homilies of the Anglo-Saxon Church*, i. 610, prints *ðæra foresædra tácna.*

[75] W. W. Skeat, *Ælfric's Lives of Saints*, EETS os 76, 82, 94, 114, 2 vols. (London, 1881–1900), ii. 16. As Skeat recognized (see ii. 446), the text is not by Ælfric. The base manuscript is British Library Cotton Julius E. vii, dated 's. xi in.' by Ker (*Catalogue*, 206 (item 162)).

[76] Skeat, *Ælfric's Lives of Saints*, ii. 17.

[77] For *þæra* as a genitive singular form see n. 71, above.

[78] D. Yerkes, *The Old English Life of Machutus*, Toronto Old English Series, 9 (Toronto, Buffalo, and London, 1984), 104.

[79] *Catalogue*, 218 (item 168).

[80] Yerkes, *The Old English Life of Machutus*, p. xxvii; *weran* occurs on p. 43, line 12, of Yerkes's edition and *lichoma* on p. 19, line 6.

between inflectional endings than is helpfully dealt with by formulations of the type 'lW-S sporadically extends *-an* to the genitive plural'.

Also undoubtedly genitive plural is *erran* at *LS 3(Chad)* 190:

7 þa dydon hi swa hit halgu*m* gedafnade. sprecon be þa*m* life þera erran hæhfædera.[81]

The *Life of St Chad*, however, is preserved only in Bodleian MS Hatton 116, of the first half of the twelfth century,[82] and its modern editor is of the opinion that alongside some 'late West Saxon' linguistic features the text shows 'a number of Transitional elements better termed E[arly] M[iddle]E[nglish] than L[ate]O[ld]E[nglish]'.[83] Forms from this text are therefore of limited value for establishing whether *-an* was a genuine Old English genitive plural ending.

LawIICn 1 (II Cn Prol, by Liebermann's numbering) reads:

Þis is seo woruldcunde gerædnes, þe ic wylle mid minan witenan ræde, þ*æt* man healde ofer eall Englaland.[84]

The form *witenan* seems to be a substantival genitive plural of the type mentioned by Brunner and Sievers in the notes cited earlier,[85] but is not within the scope of the present discussion. Liebermann appears to take *witenan* as genitive plural but *minan* as dative singular (in agreement with *ræde*).[86] Robertson, however, is inclined to take *minan* too as genitive plural:

In spite of the difficulty of explaining *minan* as a gen. pl. adjectival form (except, perhaps, as due to the influence of the following noun), I am inclined to think that the whole phrase is simply equivalent to *mid witena geþeahte*, cf. II Edm. Pre.; II Edg. Pre.; VIII Atr. Pre.; I Cn. Pre.[87]

The form is therefore perhaps to be considered a further example of a weak adjectival genitive plural in *-an*, with the additional anomaly that the possessive adjectives normally follow the strong declension. It is not, for our present purpose, a very secure example.

[81] R. Vleeskruyer, *The Life of St Chad* (Amsterdam, 1953), 180. Cf. p. 135: 'Weak plural genitives in *-an*, of which *erran* is an example, appear sporadically in other MSS also (S[ievers-]B[runner] §304, n. 2).'

[82] Ker, *Catalogue* 403 (item 333): 's. xii¹'.

[83] Vleeskruyer, *St Chad*, 67.

[84] Liebermann, *Gesetze*, i. 308 (MS G; the other manuscripts share the reading *mid minan witenan ræde*).

[85] See pp. 109 and 114, above.

[86] See *Gesetze*, iii. 202 (note 2 to II Cn Prol): 'Über späten Gen.pl. *s.* Sievers *Gram.* 276¹', and Liebermann's translation 'Dies ist nun die weltliche Verordnung, die ich mit meinem Witanrathe will, dass man über ganz England hin halte' (*Gesetze*, i. 309).

[87] A. J. Robertson, *The Laws of the Kings of England from Edmund to Henry I* (Cambridge, 1925), 351. Robertson translates: 'This is further the secular ordinance which, by the advice of my councillors, I desire should be observed over all England' (p. 175).

Among verse texts, *miclan* at *KtHy* 7 might appear to be unambiguously genitive plural:

We ðe heriað   halgum stefnum
. . . .
and þe þanciað,   þioda walden,
ðines weorðlican   wuldordreames
and ðinra miclan   mægena gerena.[88]

However, *ðinra* in the edited text is an emendation of MS *ðare*, and it is at least possible that *ðare miclan gerena* is genitive singular (with *gerena* being a form of feminine *gerynu*).[89]

Two other not entirely clear-cut verse examples are at *MCharm I* 51:

Erce, Erce, Erce,   eorþan modor,
geunne þe se alwalda,   ece drihten,
æcera wexendra   and wridendra,
eacniendra   and elniendra,
sceafta hehra,   scirra wæstma,
and þæra bradan   berewæstma,
and þæra hwitan   hwætewæstma,
and ealra   eorþan wæstma.[90]

The phrases *þæra bradan berewæstma* and *þæra hwitan hwætewæstma* have usually been taken as genitive plural, parallel to *æcera wexendra* (etc.), *sceafta hehra*, and *scirra wæstma*.[91]

[88] Dobbie, *The Anglo-Saxon Minor Poems*, 87. The manuscript is British Library Cotton Vespasian D.vi, dated 's. x med.' by Ker (*Catalogue*, 268 (item 207)). A facsimile of the manuscript text is now available in Fred. C. Robinson and E. G. Stanley, *Old English Verse Texts from Many Sources*, Early English Manuscripts in Facsimile, 23 (Copenhagen, 1991), plates 21.1–3 (the relevant passage is on plate 21.1).

[89] For this and other proposed readings of the line see Dobbie, *The Anglo-Saxon Minor Poems*, 190.

[90] Ibid. 117–18. The text is in British Library MS Cotton Caligula A.vii, in a hand dated 's. xi¹' by Ker (*Catalogue*, 172(item 137)). For a facsimile of the manuscript see now in Robinson and Stanley, *Old English Verse Texts from Many Sources*, plates 19.4.1–5 (the relevant passage is on plate 19.4.4).

[91] The text is edited, translated, and discussed by G. Storms, *Anglo-Saxon Magic* (The Hague, 1948), 172–86. Storms translates the relevant portion:

Erce, Erce, Erce, mother of earth,
may the omnipotent eternal Lord grant you
fields growing and thriving,
flourishing and bountiful,
bright shafts of millet-crops,
and of broad barley-crops,
and of white wheat-crops,

The manuscript text, it may be noted, has the reading *þære* (rather than *þæra*) in both the relevant phrases, as well as the readings *hen se* and *scire* (rather than *hehra* and *scirra* as in the edited text). While the edited text as reproduced above and the interpretation of the phrases *þæra bradan berewæstma* and *þæra hwitan hwætewæstma* as genitive plural may be the best that can be done by modern readers, the piece at this point raises enough questions for it not to be an ideal witness to grammatical forms.

An apparently better prose example than those mentioned above is *mæstan* at *HomU 9 (VercHom 4)* 286:

þa earnode he me þære mæsta ȝestynþo 7 þara mæstan benda.[92]

The phrase *þære mæsta gestynþo* raises some questions,[93] and the form *mæsta*—apparently for *mæstan*—may suggest that we should be cautious about taking the form *mæstan* itself at face value. However, this can probably be accepted as a relatively safe example of genitive plural *-an.*

In turning to substantival forms, we may first of all note the study by Connie C. Eble of the substantival inflections in one of the main manuscripts containing the First Series of Ælfric's *Catholic Homilies.*[94] This study includes a table[95] indicating that *-an* occurs five times in the manuscript in question as the ending of the genitive plural of substantives. These five occurrences of weak genitive plural *-an* appear to be identifiable as follows.

First, Eble mentions two forms of masculine weak substantives which 'appear to indicate extension of *-an* to gen.pl.'.[96] These are *yldran* at *ÆCHom I, 4* 60.21:

on ðam oðrum dæge eode se apostol be ðære stræt þa ofseah he hwær sum uðwita lædde twegen gebroðru, þe hæfdon behwyrfed eall heora yldran gestreon on deorwurðum gymstanum[97]

and *gefan* at *ÆCHom I, 15* 226.26:

Ac se stranga samson aras on midre nihte: and gelæhte þa burhgeatu and abær hi uppon anre dune. to bismre his gefan.[98]

and of all the crops of the earth.

[92] M. Förster, *Die Vercelli-Homilien: I.–VIII. Homilie,* Bibliothek der angelsächsischen Prosa, 12 (Hamburg, 1932), 97. The manuscript (Vercelli, Biblioteca Capitolare MS CXVII) is dated 's. x^{2}' by Ker (*Catalogue,* 460 (item 394)).

[93] See Förster, *Die Vercelli-Homilien,* 97 (nn. 143 and 144).

[94] C. C. Eble, 'Noun Inflection in Royal 7 C. XII, Ælfric's First Series of Catholic Homilies' (dissertation, University of North Carolina at Chapel Hill, 1970). The manuscript is dated 's. x ex.' by Ker (*Catalogue,* 324 (item 257)).

[95] Eble, 'Noun Inflection', 19.

[96] Ibid. 35.

[97] For the corresponding passage see Thorpe, *Homilies,* i. 60. Thorpe prints *yldrena.*

[98] For the corresponding passage see ibid. 226.

The latter example may, however, be a dative plural form with *-(a)n* instead of *-(u)m.*[99]

Eble claims further that 'genitive plurals *namana* and *wætana* appear' in which 'the spelling *-ana* instead of *-ena* is probably an attempt to rectify an incorrect gen.pl. in *-an* by simply adding an *-a*'.[100] Her example *wætana* is that discussed above.[101] The form *namana* to which she refers is apparently at *ÆCHom I, 38* 586.8:

nu wille we eow secgan þa getacnunge þæra feowera apostola namana þe crist ætfruman geceas[102]

although it does not seem to be explicitly identified in the course of the dissertation.[103]

Finally, Eble says of the feminine weak substantive form *culfran* at *ÆCHom I, 28* 412.10:

Se lareow bið culfran cypa þe nele ða gyfe þe him god forgeaf buton his gegearnungum: oþrum mannum buton sceattum nyt don[104]

that it is 'probably a genitive plural in which the *-an* has been extended from the other cases'.[105]

It is not easy to know how to assess the examples provided by Eble since the manuscript is, in Ker's words,

faultily written, containing miswritings such as 'naman' for 'monan' (f. 53), incomplete words, e.g. 'witeg' for 'witegan' (f. 35ᵛ), 'middan' for 'middaneard' (f. 72ᵛ), 'mað' for 'maðmas' (f. 146), and many examples of homoioteleuton.[106]

I have located a few additional possible occurrences of *-an* as a genitive plural ending of substantives, several of the examples being not wholly reliable for the kinds of reasons that have already been discussed.

To begin with Ælfrician examples, one is in the passage referred to at n. 58 above:

99 Cf. Pope, *Homilies of Ælfric*, i. 184: '*-an* sometimes replaces *-um* in the dative plural of weak nouns'.

100 Eble, *Noun Inflection*, 35.

101 See p. 118, above.

102 For the corresponding passage see Thorpe, *Homilies*, i. 586.

103 A similar view regarding *namana* had already been expressed in N. Eliason and P. Clemoes, *Ælfric's First Series of Catholic Homilies: British Museum Royal 7 C.XII*, Early English Manuscripts in Facsimile, 13 (Copenhagen, 1966), 32: 'Grammatical revision which had been imperfectly carried out seems to lie behind . . . such spellings as *namana* (fol. 206v/2).'

104 For the corresponding passage see Thorpe, *Homilies*, i. 412.

105 Eble, *Noun Inflection*, 50.

106 *Catalogue*, 324.

He send eft ma þeowan to ðam manfullan tilian, and hi swa him þenedon swa swa þam oðrum.[107]

Further examples of *ma* followed by a noun form in *-an* are *ma wyrhtan* at *ÆCHom II,5* 41.13:

Æt nextan twa tída ofer none eode se hláford and gemette má wyrhtan standan[108]

and *ma naman* at *ÆGram* 94.2:

Ne synd na ma naman speliende butan þas fiftyne.[109]

In these examples, the interpretation of the form in *-an* depends on whether or not it is assumed that *ma* will always govern a genitive form in Ælfrician Old English.[110]

An apparently somewhat better Ælfrician example is *gelican* at *ÆHomM 4(Ass 5)* 135:

Nu is heora witeȝunȝ *and* heora ȝelican him sylfu*m* to forwyrde, forþam þe hi wiðsocon Criste, be þam ðe hi witeȝodon, þeah þe hi næron wyrðe.[111]

Also probably to be taken as genitive plural is *halgan* at *ÆLS (Julian & Basilissa)* 432:

Þæra halgan líc . þurh geleaf-fulle menn . wurdon gebyrigde sona mid blisse . binnan Godes cyrcan.[112]

Skeat translates this passage as 'the saints' bodies by believing men were soon buried . . .'.[113] It is conceivable that in this passage *þæra* is to be taken as an independent use of the demonstrative pronoun, equivalent to Modern English 'their'.[114] However, there is a change of subject at this point, which may make that a less likely possibility.

There are also a few possible non-Ælfrician examples, some of which are again open to question. The form *wisan* at *Solil 1* 37.13 has been claimed to be a genitive plural:

[107] *ÆHom 3* 122; Pope, *Homilies of Ælfric*, i. 253. See p. 117, above. The base manuscript is Corpus Christi College, Cambridge, 162, dated 's. xi in.' by Ker (*Catalogue*, 51 (item 38)).

[108] Godden, *Ælfric's Catholic Homilies*, 41. On the base manuscript see n. 54, above.

[109] J. Zupitza, *Ælfrics Grammatik und Glossar* (Berlin, 1880; Sammlung englischer Denkmäler, 1), 94. The base manuscript is St John's College, Oxford, 154, dated 's. xi in.' by Ker (*Catalogue*, 436 (item 362)).

[110] Cf. p. 117 and n. 56, above.

[111] B. Assmann, *Angelsächsische Homilien und Heiligenleben*, Bibliothek der angelsächsischen Prosa, 3 (Kassel, 1889), 70. On the base manuscript see n. 107, above.

[112] Skeat, *Ælfric's Lives of Saints*, i. 114. On the base manuscript see n. 75, above.

[113] Ibid. 115.

[114] On 'independent *se*' see Mitchell, *Old English Syntax*, §§316–27, although none of the examples there cited seems to function as the equivalent of a possessive pronoun. Cf. also pp. 126–7, below.

hys me lyst swâ læng swâ lǽs, and *si*mle swâ îc ma wilnige þæt leoht to geseônne swa me lǽs lest þara wisan.[115]

However, if *þara wisan* is here genitive, it is at least as likely that it is singular. It is also possible that it is dative rather than genitive, in which case it must be singular. For *þara* as a dative singular form in this text, cf. *Solil 1* 22.14:

Eaðre me þincð þeah myd scêðpe [= scipe?] ôn drigum lande to farande þonne me þynce mid ðam eagum buta[n] þara gescea[d]wisnesse æ[ni]gne creft to geleornianne.[116]

The form *deadan* at *GDPref 3(C)* 21.224–5:

hwylc wundor is þ*æt* forðon, þeh þe hwylce ʒodes ʒecorenra, þa hwile þe hi in lichaman beoð ʒ*e*sette, maʒon wyrcan maniʒe wundra, eac swilce we witon, þ*æt* full oft þara deadan ban lifiað 7 mære weorðað mid maniʒum wundrum?[117]

looks at first glance like a genitive plural, the phrase *þara deadan ban* then meaning 'the bones of the dead'. We should, however, also look at the source (*Dialogi* iii. 21):

quid autem mirum, si electi quique in carne positi multa facere mirabiliter possunt, quorum ipsa quoque ossa mortua plerumque in multis miraculis vivunt?[118]

It might appear from this, especially since the Old English translation of the *Dialogues* 'adheres quite strictly to the Latin and is a literal (though not error-free) rendering',[119] that *deadan ban* is here to be taken as an adjective plus substantive phrase in the nominative plural. The Latin (*quorum . . . ossa mortua*) refers to the bones of the *electi* just mentioned, not to 'the dead' in general. In the Old English translation, *þara* seems not to be a relative

[115] W. Endter, *König Alfreds des Grossen Bearbeitung der Soliloquien des Augustinus*, Bibliothek der angelsächsischen Prosa, 11 (Hamburg, 1922), 37; T. A. Carnicelli, *King Alfred's Version of St Augustine's 'Soliloquies'* (Cambridge, Mass., 1979), 73. The manuscript is British Library Cotton Vitellius A.xv fos. 4–93, dated 's. xii med.' by Ker (*Catalogue*, 281 (item 216)). On *wisan* see Endter 85 (note to p. 37, line 15); '*þara wisan* = *þara wisena* . . . oder = *þære wisan*', and Carnicelli 73 (note to line 8): '*wisan*, gen.pl.'. H. L. Hargrove, *King Alfred's Version of St. Augustine's Soliloquies Turned into Modern English*, Yale Studies in English, 22 (New York, 1904), 23, translates: 'Ever the less is my desire for it, and ever the more I wish to see the light, even as I lust after this manner'; but he identifies *wisan* as genitive plural in *King Alfred's Old English Version of St. Augustine's Soliloquies*, Yale Studies in English, 13 (New York, 1902), 118.

[116] Endter, *König Alfreds des Grossen Bearbeitung der Soliloquien*, 22; Carnicelli, *King Alfred's Version of St Augustine's 'Soliloquies'*, 20.

[117] H. Hecht, *Bischof Wærferths von Worcester Übersetzung der Dialoge Gregors des Grossen*, Bibliothek der angelsächsischen Prosa, 5, 2 parts (Leipzig, 1900 and Hamburg, 1907), i. 224. The manuscript is Corpus Christi College, Cambridge, 322, dated 's. xi[2]' by Ker (*Catalogue*, 106 (item 60)).

[118] U. Moricca, *Gregorii magni dialogi* (Rome, 1924), 190.

[119] S. B. Greenfield and D. G. Calder, *A New Critical History of Old English Literature* (New York and London, 1986), 43.

pronoun, however. Can it here be an example of 'independent *se*', to be translated 'their'?[120]

Janet Bately, in her edition of *The Old English Orosius*,[121] hesitantly labels '*gpl.* (?)' the form *legian* at *Or 4* 1.160.8:

Þa ne getruwade se eahteþa dæl þara legian þæt Romane Pirruse wiðstondan mehte.[122]

However, this foreign word does not seem reliable evidence for Old English morphological patterns.

The form *gelican* at *Conf 3.1.1(RaithY)* 1.8:

Þis synt þa idelnessa þisse worlda: ærost is ofermetta 7 nið 7 æfesta 7 hatheortnes 7 stala 7 druncennes 7 galscipe 7 dyrne geligro 7 lyblac 7 gytsung 7 reaflac 7 scincræft 7 manslihtas 7 feala oðra þissa gelican[123]

is another which may be a partitive genitive plural, but may also be nominative plural.

A second substantive form in *-an* in the Old English translation of the *Soliloquies* is a rather better example than *wisan*, discussed above. This is the form *eagan* at *Solil 1* 35.16:

Ðu geþencst ða hǣle þara eagan ðinre sawle.[124]

Another apparently good example is *Egyptiscan* at *Exod* 12.36:

7 Drihten his folc wurðode Israhela bearn, mid þara Egyptiscan gestreone.[125]

The translation at this point does not follow exactly the wording of the Vulgate:

dedit autem Dominus gratiam populo coram Aegyptiis ut commodarent eis

but the sense of the Old English seems clear enough.

Finally, there seems little reason to doubt that *timan* at *ByrM 1(Crawford)* 120.18 is a genitive plural form:

[120] Cf. p. 125 and n. 114, above.

[121] J. Bately, *The Old English Orosius*, EETS ss 6 (Oxford, 1980), 374.

[122] Ibid. 86; H. Sweet, *King Alfred's Orosius*, EETS os 79 (London, 1883), 160. The base manuscript is British Library Additional 47697, dated 's. x^1' by Ker (*Catalogue*, 165 (item 133)).

[123] J. Raith, *Die altenglische Version des Halitgar'schen Bussbuches*, Bibliothek der angelsächsischen Prosa, 13 (Hamburg, 1933), 6. The base manuscript is Bodleian Laud Misc. 482, dated 's. xi med.' by Ker (*Catalogue*, 419 (item 343)).

[124] Endter, *König Alfreds des Grossen Bearbeitung der Soliloquien*, 35; Carnicelli, *King Alfred's Version of St Augustine's 'Soliloquies'*, 72. Cf. Endter 84 (note to p. 35, line 16): '*þara eagan* ist später Gen. pl. = aws. *þara eagena*', and Carnicelli 72 (note to line 5): '*eagan* shows lOE extension of *-an* to the genitive plural'.

[125] Crawford, *The Old English Version of the Heptateuch*, 247. The base manuscript is British Library Cotton Claudius B.iv, dated 's xi^1' by Ker (*Catalogue*, 178 (item 142)). The translation of Exodus is not thought to be by Ælfric.

Seofon daga ryne ys seo wucu, 7 feower wucan wyrcað anne monð, 7 þry monðas wyrcað þryfeald gewrixlunge þæra feower timan, þæt ys lengtenis 7 sumoris 7 hærfestis 7 wintres, þ*æt* heora ælc hæfð þry monðas.[126]

It is evident from this discussion that there is a certain amount of evidence for *-an* as a genitive plural ending of weak adjectives and substantives in at least late Old English. About ten of the forms I have discussed[127] have been seen to be reasonably good examples, and there are no grounds for thinking that others would not come to light if my initial and incomplete search were extended. What is needed in order to establish the position satisfactorily is a more thorough and systematic examination of the material than I have been able to carry out, with attention given to variant readings and their significance in the light of the particular textual history of each work.

Eric Stanley pointed out over twenty years ago that

> anyone now embarking on the study of any aspect of the Old English vocabulary must be aware of what is required. The whole corpus of Old English writings has to be gone through, for though Grein-Köhler and B[osworth-]T[oller] are fairly comprehensive for verse, the lexicography of prose is insufficient for detailed surveys.[128]

Although he was speaking of lexical studies, similar requirements attend the investigation of morphological features, especially those that are attested relatively infrequently in the surviving materials. The invaluable results of the work so far done on the *Dictionary of Old English*, in which Eric Stanley has himself played a very significant role, have amongst other things been to enhance to a very high degree our ability to scan much of the existing body of Old English. The sheer bulk of data now quickly accessible, however, means that some investigations will be immensely time-consuming. And even now there remain variant readings to be tracked down and analysed.

In view of all this, I offer the above discussion of possibly genitive plural

[126] S. J. Crawford, *Byrhtferth's Manual*, vol. i [no more published], EETS OS 177 (London, 1929), 120. The manuscript is Bodleian Ashmole 328, dated 's. xi med.' by Ker (*Catalogue*, 349 (item 288)). Crawford translates: '... and three months form the three-fold rotatory change of the four seasons' (p. 121). The likely source for this passage is printed by P. S. Baker, 'Byrhtferth's *Enchiridion* and the Computus in Oxford, St John's College 17', *Anglo-Saxon England*, 10 (1982), 123–42: '.vii. dies ebdomadam faciunt. Quattuor ebdomade mensem complent. Tres menses uicissitudinem triformem quattuor temporum, id est ueris, estatis, autumni, hiemis' (p. 137).

[127] *ÆLet 4(SigeweardZ)* 8 *yfelan; ÆCHom II,30* 238.104 *fulan; ÆCHom II,33* 251.55 *godan; ÆCHom I,40* 610.11 *foresædan: HomU 9 (VercHom 4)* 286 *mæstan: ÆHomM 4(Ass 5)* 135 *gelican; ÆLS (Julian & Basilissa)* 432 *halgan; Solil 1* 35.16 *eagan; Exod* 12.36 *Egyptiscan; ByrM 1(Crawford)* 120.18 *timan.*

[128] E. G. Stanley, 'Studies in the Prosaic Vocabulary of Old English Verse', *Neuphilologische Mitteilungen*, 72 (1971), 385–418 (see 385).

-an to a much respected colleague and generous friend with no claim that it is in any way conclusive. I do so bearing in mind his own prudent warning that 'hasty conclusions may be worse than none'.[129]

[129] Ibid. 388.

Apocalypse and Invasion in Late Anglo-Saxon England

MALCOLM GODDEN

The moral and theological problems posed by successful invasion, and particularly invasion of a sophisticated Christian civilization by heathen barbarians, were a recurrent issue in Anglo-Saxon writings. Bede took up the issue briefly in his *Historia Ecclesiastica*, suggesting that the Anglo-Saxon invaders were agents of the divine wrath against the slothful and sinful Britons: 'the fire kindled by the hands of the heathen executed the just vengeance of God on the nation for its crimes'.[1] Alcuin touched on the issue again in his letters on the sack of Lindisfarne by the Vikings, suggesting a parallel with the earlier Anglo-Saxon invasions and hinting that the attack might have been divine punishment for fornication, adultery, incest, avarice, robbery, or perhaps bad judgements.[2] It was a major concern in Alfredian prose, and seems to have influenced the choice of Latin works to translate. Alfred hinted at the idea of divine punishment as an explanation for the Vikings in his preface to the *Pastoral Care* but explored the issue much more fully and profoundly in his version of Boethius: he introduced the discussion with his own account of the barbarian invasion of Italy and the imprisonment of Boethius, and then used that as a basis for questioning the apparent dominance of evil in a world supposedly ruled by a benevolent God.[3] The Old English version of Orosius's history of the world engaged centrally with the same topic, taking as its starting point the barbarian sack of Rome and trying to place both it and the whole history of empires and warfare in the context of a Christian scheme: the translator, following but modifying his source, noted the possibility that barbarian invasion of Christian communities could be seen as divine punishment for their sins,

[1] *Bede's Ecclesiastical History of the English People*, ed. B. Colgrave and R. A. B. Mynors (Oxford, 1969), I. xv.

[2] Letter to Ethelred of Northumbria, in *Alcuini Epistolae*, ed. E. Dümmler, Monumenta Germaniae Historica, Epistolae Carolini Aevi, II, 1895, 42–4; translated in *English Historical Documents*, vol. i, *c.*500–1042, ed. D. Whitelock (2nd edn., London, 1979), 842–4.

[3] *King Alfred's West-Saxon Version of Gregory's Pastoral Care*, ed. H. Sweet, EETS os 45 and 50 (London, 1871), 5, lines 5–13; and *King Alfred's Old English Version of Boethius De Consolatione Philosophiae*, ed. W. J. Sedgefield (Oxford, 1899).

but argued more strongly that the comparative mildness of such invasions in the Christian era was evidence of the ultimate benevolence of the Christian dispensation: 'It is disgraceful for us to complain, and call it warfare, when strangers and foreigners come to us and rob us of some little thing and immediately leave us again.'[4]

When Viking raiding resumed at the end of the tenth century it prompted writers such as Ælfric and Wulfstan to take up this issue once again, no doubt in awareness of all their predecessors. Both became increasingly involved in advising the king and his council, as well as attempting to offer guidance to a wider public, and their writings show them exploring and adapting a number of different ways of coming to terms with the Viking problem. Not the least of their intellectual problems was that they wrote in the shadow of eschatological expectations, and had somehow to face the question of the relationship between those two very different kinds of threat.

1. Ælfric

A recent historical study remarks of Ælfric that 'for the most part he wrote for monks, and his view looks inward to the monastery not outwards to the larger kingdom'.[5] If the first statement was never true of Ælfric, the second both reflects a common view of him and has a degree of justice for his early career. But however cloistered he may have been at Cerne, his election as abbot of Eynsham in 1005 would have brought him into close contact with national politics and external events even if he had not needed to care about them before. Recent work by historians has increasingly emphasized the political roles played by his patrons Æthelweard and Æthelmær.[6] The fact that Ælfric's new community at Eynsham included Æthelmær himself might suggest it had a role as a place of pastoral or cloistered retreat from the political turmoil. But Barbara Yorke argues that Eynsham was designed by Æthelmær as a place of temporary exile rather than permanent retreat.[7] Æthelmær was back in political life a few years later. Conversation between Ælfric and his patron may have been entirely about the doctrine of the Trinity and the knottier aspects of predestination theory; but it is just as likely that it was about the concept of the three estates and the precedents for warfare. Certainly Ælfric's writings show an increasing concern with

[4] *The Old English Orosius*, ed. J. Bately, EETS ss 6 (London, 1980), 83.

[5] J. Campbell, E. John, and P. Wormald, *The Anglo-Saxons* (Oxford, 1982), 202.

[6] See especially B. Yorke, 'Aethelmaer: The Foundation of the Abbey at Cerne and the Politics of the Tenth Century', in *The Cerne Abbey Millennium Lectures*, ed. K. Barker (Cerne Abbas, 1988), 15–25.

[7] Ibid. 20.

political and national issues, even before he went to Eynsham; and by the end of his life he had become strikingly outspoken on such matters. That it involved a shift of emphasis for himself is evident from the way in which he reinterpreted, in a more political way, biblical texts and stories which he had earlier treated in a far less topical sense.

There are two main points to make about his early work: first, its use of an apocalyptic setting; secondly, the absence of reference to the Viking threat. In the preface to his first series of *Catholic Homilies*, written around 990, Ælfric announces the approaching end of the world and the coming of the reign of Antichrist, as a context for his own writing.[8] The series ends with a homily on the signs that are to accompany the ending of the world—of which some, Ælfric insists, have already been seen and the others are not far distant. One of these signs, according to the Bible, is that nation shall rise up against nation and kingdom against kingdom. Ælfric notes that this has happened in recent times, more severely than in previous ages, but gives no more detail and passes on immediately to other signs.[9] He may not in fact have been thinking of particularly recent events: the next sign which he discusses is earthquakes, and his examples of recent occurrences are actually from the time of the emperor Tiberius. Certainly there is no explicit reference to the Vikings. Similarly, when he returns to that biblical verse in the context of a different Gospel reading, in the homily on martyrs in his second series of *Catholic Homilies*, written probably two or three years later, he gives it the briefest of comments and moves on to the evidently more interesting subjects of the early persecution of the martyrs and the possibilities for a kind of spiritual martyrdom within the security of the monastic cloisters.[10] When he does engage with the question of why God might permit a heathen *here* to oppress His followers, it is primarily to introduce a series of comforting stories from Old and New Testament times showing how God has in fact saved and protected his people:

Oft hwonlice gelyfede menn smeagað mid heora stuntan gesceade, hwi se Ælmihtiga God æfre wolde þæt þa hæðenan his halgan mid gehwilcum tintregum acwellan moston; ac we wyllað nu eow gereccan sume geswutelunge of ðære ealdan æ, and eac of ðære niwan, hu mihtiglice se Wealdenda Drihten his halgan wið hæðenne here . . . gelome ahredde. (CH I. 566)

[8] *The Homilies of the Anglo-Saxon Church: The First Part, containing the Sermones Catholici or Homilies of Ælfric*, ed. B. Thorpe, i (London, 1844), 2–6. (Subsequent references to this text will be in the form CH I (= First Series of Catholic Homilies) and page number in Thorpe's edition.)

[9] CH I. 608.

[10] *Ælfric's Catholic Homilies: The Second Series, Text*, ed. M. Godden, EETS ss 5 (London, 1979), 311. Subsequent references to this text will be in the form CH II (= Second Series of Catholic Homilies) plus homily number and line number.

Often people of little faith ask with their foolish reasoning why the Almighty God would ever allow the heathens to kill his saints with every kind of torment; but we will now give you some demonstrations, both from the old law and the new, of how mightily the powerful lord has often protected his saints from the heathen *here*.

By the time he completed the Second Series however, probably in 994–5, the Viking threat had already begun to impinge on his writing and the apocalypse becomes less prominent. The preface to this series, evidently written after the work was completed, says nothing of the world's ending but does mention the Vikings, if only as a hindrance to writing. And in subsequent works the Vikings and the problem of invasion become important issues. They are particularly frequent in his next major collection, the so-called *Lives of Saints*.[11]

The key discussion here, though a deeply puzzling one, is a homily called *De Oratione Moysi*, 'On the Prayer of Moses' (LS xiii), in which Ælfric attempts to place the Viking attacks in terms of the divine will and the end of the world. This is one of the most politically charged of all Ælfric's writings, though much of the charge is just below the surface and the implications are at times puzzling and at times naïve. The collection in which it appears was begun after 995 and completed by 1002, and textual and linguistic evidence suggests that this item was composed earlier than most of the others in the collection; one should perhaps think of a date not long after 995, though a little earlier is possible.[12]

The text begins, appropriately and positively enough, by describing how the Hebrews defeated their enemies in battle. Joshua led the army and Moses prayed; as long as Moses lifted his arms in prayer Joshua was successful, but whenever Moses' arms drooped Joshua was driven back. The story evidently offers a paradigm for the relations between military power and the Church: the military success of the general is entirely dependent on the intercessory efforts of Moses, whose contemporary equivalent were the clergy, or perhaps more specifically the monks; and this is a theme to be developed later. But at this point Ælfric limits himself to a more restricted message:

> Be þisum we magon tocnawen þæt we cristene sceolan
> on ælcere earfoðnisse æfre to gode clypian .
> and his fultumes biddan mid fullum geleafan .
> gif he ðonne nele his fultum us don
> ne ure bene gehyran . þonne bð hit swutol

[11] *Ælfric's Lives of Saints*, ed. W. W. Skeat, EETS os 76, 82, 94, 114 (London, 1881–1900, reprinted as two volumes 1966). References to this text will be in the form LS plus item and line number.

[12] See P. Clemoes. 'The Chronology of Ælfric's Works', in *The Anglo-Saxons: Studies presented to Bruce Dickins*, ed. P. A. M. Clemoes (London, 1959), 212–47, at 222–5; and M. R. Godden, 'Ælfric's Changing Vocabulary', *English Studies*, 61 (1980), 206–23, at 211.

þæt we mid yfelum dædum hine ær gegremedon .
ac we ne sceolon swaðeah geswican þære bene .
oðþæt se mild-heorta god us mildelice ahredde .
(LS xiii. 30–7)

From this we can recognize that we Christians should in every distress call to God and ask for his help; if he will not give us help nor hear our petition it will be clear that we have angered him previously with our evil deeds. But nevertheless we should not cease from prayer until the merciful God mercifully saves us.

In his earlier homilies Ælfric had offered much more complex analyses than this, recognizing that there were many reasons why God might allow his people to be afflicted, and anger with them for their sins was only one of those.[13] But the emphasis on divine anger turns out to have a part to play in contemporary polemic later in the text. Ælfric then steers away from the topical implications of the Joshua and Moses story and draws a spiritual meaning out of it: 'Now we have warfare against the fierce devil' (line 41). He then drifts into a rather rambling discussion of prayer, fasting, penance, and the twelve abuses of the world. But then he suddenly introduces the contemporary situation:

Wel we magon geðencan hu wel hit ferde mid us .
þaða þis igland wæs wunigende on sibbe .
and munuc- lif wæron mid wurð-scipe gehealdene .
and ða woruld-menn wæron wære wið heora fynd .
swa þæt ure word sprang wide geond þas eorðan .
Hu wæs hit ða siððan ða þa man towearp munuc-lif .
and godes biggengas to bysmore hæfde .
buton þæt us com to cwealm and hunger .
and siððan hæðen here us hæfde to bysmre .
Be þysum cwæð se ælmihtiga god . to moyse on þam wæstene .
Gif ge on minum bebodum farað . and mine beboda healdað .
þonne sende ic eow ren-scuras on rihtne timan symble .
and seo eorðe spryt hyre wæstmas eow .
and ic forgife sibbe and gesehtnysse eow .
þæt ge butan ogan eowres eardes brucan .
and ic eac afyrsige ða yfelan deor eow fram .
Gif ge þonne me forseoð and mine gesetnyssa awurpað .
ic eac swyðe hrædlice on eow hit gewrece .
ic do þæt seo heofen bið swa heard eow swa isen .
and seo eorðe þær-to-geanes swylce heo æren sy .
Þonne swince ge on idel . gif ge sawað eower land
ðonne seo eorðe ne spryt eow nænne wæstm .
And gif ge þonne git nellað eow wendan to me .
ice sende eow swurd to and eow sleað eowre fynd .
and hi þonne awestað wælhreowlice eower land .

[13] See e.g. CH I. 470–6 and 574.

and eowre burga beoð to-brocene and aweste .
Ic asende eac yrhðe into eowrum heortum .
þæt eower nan ne dear eowrum feondum wið-standan .
Þus spræc god gefyrn be þam folce israhel .
hit is swa ðeah swa gedon swyðe neah mid us .
nu on niwum dagum and undigollice.

(LS xiii. 147–77)

We can well consider how well things fared with us when this island was living in peace, and monasteries were treated with honour and the laity were vigilant against their enemies, so that our fame sprang widely throughout this world. What happened then afterwards, when people overthrew the monasteries and treated God's services with contempt, but that disease and hunger came upon us, and afterwards a heathen army treated us with contempt. Almighty God spoke to Moses about this in the wilderness: 'if you walk in my commandments and keep my commandments, I will send you rain at the right time and the earth will produce its crops for you, and I will give you peace and harmony, so that you may enjoy your land without fear and I will drive the evil beasts from you. If you scorn me and reject my laws, I will very swiftly avenge it on you. I will cause the heavens to be as hard as iron to you, and the earth beneath it like brass. Then you will toil in vain if you sow your land, and the earth will produce no crops for you, and if you will still not turn to me, I will send a sword to you and your enemies will strike you, and they will savagely lay waste your land, and your cities will be ruined and laid waste. I will send cowardice into your hearts so that none of you will dare to resist your enemies.' Thus said God of old concerning the people of Israel, but it has now very nearly happened to us, in recent times quite openly.

Hunger, pestilence, and the heathen *here* are here seen as divine punishment for the English nation's destruction of the monastic life and their contempt for the monks' services to God. Ælfric's nostalgic reference in another text to the times of Edgar when the monastic life flourished and no foreign *sciphere* was seen, makes it clear that his reference here is not to the distant past but to the very recent Viking raids, of the 980s and early 990s, which he interprets as a divine punishment for English attacks on the monastic movement occurring since the time of Edgar, presumably in the reign of Ethelred himself.

Ælfric is clearly drawing here on a long tradition of viewing invasion as divine punishment, but in a particularly personal form. It is a thoroughly monastic, one might say cloistered, point of view. He then gives a long series of Old Testament examples of God punishing sinners in his anger but being willing to spare them if proper intercession is made. The contemporary and political resonance of his argument is again hard to miss:

Be ðysum man mæg tocnawan þæt micclum fremiað
þam læwedum mannum . þa gelæredan godes ðeowas .
þæt hi mid heora ðeow-dome him ðingian to gode .

nu god wolde arian eallum ðam synfullum .
gif he þær gemette tyn riht-wise menn.
(LS xiii. 216–20)

From this one can see that the learned servants of God[14] greatly benefit the laity when they by their offices intercede for them with God, now that God was willing to spare all the sinful if he met ten righteous people there [that is, in Sodom].

Both by their intercession and by their mere presence in the kingdom the monks save the laity from the divine anger that they have deserved. That part of the message is clear enough. But what are we to make of the story Ælfric then tells of David, whose people are destroyed by God because of the king's own sin (240–72)? Is there a suggestion that the Viking attacks relate to the specific sins of Ethelred or Edgar? The political bite of this text is striking.

Finally at the end of the text Ælfric introduces the topic of the end of the world:

Fela ungelimpa beoð on ende ðissere worulde .
ac ge-hwa mot forberan emlice his dæl .
swa þæt he ðurh ceorunge ne syngie wið god .
and for ðære woruld-lufe him wite ge-earnige .
Þes tima is ende-next and ende þyssere worulde .
and menn beoð geworhte wolice him betwynan .
swa þæt se fæder winð wið his agenne sunu .
and broðor wið oþerne to bealwe him sylfum .
(LS xiii. 290–9)

There will be[15] many misfortunes at the end of this world, but everyone must bear his lot patiently, so that he does not sin against God by complaining and earn punishment for his love of this world. This time is last and the ending of this world, and people will be made evil towards each other, so that the father fights with his own son and brother with his brother, to their own destruction.

It is not clear how if at all Ælfric meant this apocalyptic note to relate to the earlier mention of Viking armies or to the general theme of divine wrath and mercy. The final words draw on Christ's words foretelling the last days in Mark 13: 12:

Tradet autem frater fratrem in mortem, et pater filium.

But Ælfric does not use the earlier verses from Mark foretelling wars and the rising of nation against nation as signs of the approaching end, and makes no reference here to warfare or invasion. His emphasis is rather on misfortunes that must be patiently born, and on internal conflict. It is

[14] By *gelæredan*, 'learned', Ælfric probably means specifically the monks.
[15] *Beoð* is present in form but probably future in meaning.

indeed hard to see how his interpretation of the Vikings could have been fitted into an apocalyptic framework. The listing of historical precedents, and the suggestion that monastic intercession can ward off the danger, are at odds with any notion that the invasions might be part of a final and inevitable apocalypse. We seem to be dealing here with two different paradigms for explaining the contemporary situation.

This is clearly an important and politically significant text, but the different ways of explaining invasion are hard to reconcile: there is first the biblical paradigm of divine aid against the foreign enemy; then the alternative biblical paradigm of divine wrath and punishment for sins; and finally the apocalyptic paradigm of tribulations marking the end of the world. The need to find a way of comprehending and explaining Viking attacks in a context of religious belief and institutions is strongly felt; but the answers are as yet unclear and Ælfric seems to be trying out several different historical models.

This piece, as I have said, is possibly an early one within the *Lives of Saints* collection. Elsewhere in that collection Ælfric seems to have been developing a very different and more positive view of the situation, associated with a search for a different kind of historical model or analogue. The paradigm which offered itself immediately was Abbo of Fleury's account of the martyrdom of St Edmund at the hands of the Vikings in 871.[16] Abbo wrote his version in 985–7 and a few years later Ælfric produced his own English version of it, which he included in the *Lives of Saints* collection (LS xxxii). The gap in time was short, but enough for Viking raids to have become a much more typical and urgent issue; Ælfric recalls that for us when he remarks that the Danes in 871 went with their *scip-here* harrying and killing widely throughout the land, *swa heora gewuna is* ('as their custom is', line 28). Edmund and his subjects are here seen not as sinners but as innocent victims—the Danes killed men and women and simple children, says Ælfric, and shamefully treated the innocent (*bilewitan*, 42) Christians. The Vikings are the bloodthirsty agents of the devil—*geanlæhte þurh deofol.* The attack is conceived as a religious conflict culminating in an act of martyrdom: Edmund's rejection of Viking political domination is closely identified with his refusal of the Viking demands to forsake his God, and his murder imitates the deaths of Christ and St Sebastian. While God apparently permits the heathen persecution, He is seen to be protecting the king's body from a succession of attempted violations of his sanctity, as an explicit guarantee and symbol of Edmund's spiritual salvation. As a model for comprehending the Viking troubles it is strikingly different from the piece

[16] Edited by M. Winterbottom in *Three Lives of English Saints* (Toronto, 1972).

De Oratione Moysi: neither the wrath of God nor the approach of apocalypse has any place here, and the emphasis is on heroic resistance or patient endurance of afflictions instigated by the devil and his heathen agents rather than monastic intercession to ward off an attack instigated by a wrathful God.

The theological implications of this narrative are explored in a discursive passage in another text from this collection, *Natale Quadraginta Militum* (LS xi). After telling the story of the forty soldiers who were martyred in the days of the emperor Licinius for their refusal to sacrifice to pagan gods, Ælfric adds a long discussion of the implications. One of the main points that he makes is that though God permits the heathens to persecute his followers it is the devil who incites them and God will punish them; the use of present tense suggests that he is thinking of his own time:

> þa hæðenan hynað and hergiað þa cristenan
> and mid wælhreowan dædum urne drihten gremiað.
> ac hi habbað þæs edlean on þam ecum witum .
> (LS xi. 353–5)

The heathens oppress and harry the christians and anger our lord with cruel deeds, but they will have their repayment for this in eternal torments.

There is divine anger here, but it is directed against the heathen raiders not their victims. What Ælfric seems to be developing here is a way of viewing the Viking raids quite different from that seen in the *De Oratione Moysi*, one that uses the paradigm of martyrdom: the Viking attacks reflect neither divine wrath nor apocalypse but the age-old conflict between the forces of the devil and the followers of God, and can be paralleled by all the stories of heathen persecutions of the early Church which form the bulk of the *Lives of Saints* collection, and indeed by some Old Testament stories. That, perhaps, is the major point of the collection, apparently instigated as it was by two leading members of the military aristocracy, ealdorman Æthelweard and his son Æthelmær.

This way of placing the Viking troubles is developed further in one of the latest of Ælfric's writings, a homily dated approximately around 1009.[17] In the midst of an exposition of the Gospel story of the disciples' fishing, Ælfric launches into a sudden attack on those Englishmen who sided with the Danes, arguing that this was the work of the devil and a betrayal of their own nation:

[17] *Homilies of Ælfric: A Supplementary Collection*, ed. J. A. Pope, EETS os 259, 260 (London, 1967–8), no. xiv (pp. 511–27).

Swa fela manna gebugað mid ðam gecorenum
to Cristes geleafan on his Gelaðunge,
þæt hy sume yfele eft ut abrecað,
and hy on gedwyldum adreogað heora life,
swa swa þa Engliscan men doð þe to ðam Deniscum gebugað,
and mearciað hy deofle to his mannrædene,
and his weorc wyrcað, hym sylfum to forwyrde,
and heora agene leode belæwað to deaðe.

(128–35)

So many people turn with the elect to the faith of Christ within his church that some of them, the evil ones, break out again, and live their life in false doctrine, as do those English people who turn to the Danes, and mark themselves with the devil, in allegiance to him, and do his works, to their own destruction, and betray their own nation to death.

There is nothing to prompt this outburst in the sources and the sharpness is perhaps rather surprising, but the perspective is that developed earlier in the *Lives of Saints*: once again the Vikings are the agents of the devil rather than divine wrath, and national and political opposition to them is identified with the true faith. The connection with the *Lives of Saints* is underlined when Ælfric goes on to draw a parallel with the victims and traitors of the early persecutions of the Church:

Swa dydon eac hwilon sume þa Cristenan
on anginne Cristendomes: þa ða man acwealde
þa halgan martiras huxlice mid witum,
for Cristes geleafan, þa cyddon wel fela
heora ungetrywðæ, and wiðsocon Criste,
and hine forleton, þæt hy libban moston,
ac heora lif wæs syððan wyrse þonne deað.

(140–6)

So did also formerly some Christians at the beginning of Christianity: when the holy martyrs were shamefully killed with torments for their faith in Christ, those showed well their untruth, and forsook Christ, and abandoned him, so that they might live, but their life was afterwards worse than death.

One of the important implications of this hagiographic model for the Viking raids is the political one that resistance is imperative. For if we look back at the life of Edmund, one can note how the question of military resistance is delicately worked out. Edmund's first impulse is to resist the Vikings in battle and it is only when the bishop convinces him that military resistance is impossible that he turns to the Christian ideal of passive endurance. There is also possibly a hostile allusion to the contemporary issue of Danegeld: Hinguar's demand that the royal or national treasure-hoard be opened to him is coupled with his demand for political submission, and the two are linked by Edmund with the concept of submission to heathen domination. This implicit concern with justifying military resistance to the Vikings in a religious context is also explored further in a digression in his account of the Maccabees (LS xxv); Ælfric enunciates the concept of the just war and defines it as war against the cruel seamen (*reðan flotmen*). The point is then developed further with a discussion of the doctrine of the three estates of society, identifying the landowning class as a warrior class, the *bellatores.*

Ælfric's later writings also show him exploring further the possibilities of Old Testament narrative as a paradigm for the Viking problem. When he produced his prose rendering of the story of Judith, perhaps around 1002–5, he offered a variety of ways of interpreting the story, or seeing its contemporary relevance, such as taking Judith herself as a type of the Church in conflict with the devil, or as a type of the nun, but he did not propose a political or military reading.[18] When, however, he wrote his long treatise on the Old and New Testaments some time after he became abbot of Eynsham in 1005, it was the military and political implications of the Judith story that he emphasized:

Iudithe seo wuduwe, þe oferwann Holofernem þone Siriscan ealdormann, hæfð hire agene boc betwux þisum bocum be hire agenum sige; seo ys eac on Englisc on ure wisan gesett eow monnum to bysne, þæt ge eowerne eard mid wæ[p]num bewerian wið onwinnendne here.

Judith the widow who overcame the Syrian ealdorman Holofernes has her own book among the others, about her victory; this is also set down in English in my fashion, as an example for you people, that you should defend your land with weapons against the invading *here.*[19]

The shift of emphasis is perhaps partly to be explained by the fact that the treatise is formally addressed to a secular landowner, Sigeweard of East Heolon, and a member of what Ælfric would call the class of *bellatores.* But as a note at the head of the text explains, the work was read, and no doubt intended, as an address to a wider readership than just one, and the passage itself uses *eow monnum* in the plural. The shift of readership is itself significant. When Ælfric wrote his version of Judith he thought of a religious-minded readership including nuns; now it was the fighting class that was on his mind, and he was looking to the Old Testament for historical parallels to the Viking attack.

[18] *Angelsächsische Homilien und Heiligenleben,* ed. B. Assmann, Bibliothek der angelsächsischen Prosa, 3, reprinted with a supplementary introduction by P. A. M. Clemoes (Darmstadt, 1964), 102–16.

[19] *The Old English Heptateuch,* ed. S. J. Crawford, EETS OS 160 (London, 1922), 49, lines 772–80.

It would have been easy, perhaps natural, for someone in Ælfric's position to find in the Judith story support for the argument which he had made much earlier in the piece *De Oratione Moysi*, that God lets the heathen army oppress his people when they fail to honour him and that intercession by the Church is what will save them, rather than military means. For in the biblical Book of Judith Achior tells Holofernes that the Israelites have in the past only been defeated when they angered their God; Judith's intercession with God is an important theme of the biblical story, and, as we have seen, Ælfric had previously interpreted her as the Church. But that is not in fact the way he invites Sigeweard to read the story: his suggestion is much more in line with the Old English poem on Judith, which presents her as a heroic figure and emphasizes the importance of warfare. Ælfric's decision to read the story in a topical sense, and with militaristic implications, is an interesting straw in the wind.

It is, though, with reference to the Maccabees that he reserves his sharpest comments on the national and political scene. When he produced his *Lives of Saints* collection, perhaps around 1000, the longest single item was his account of the wars of the Maccabees against the heathen invaders of Israel, and in his comments on the just war and the three classes of society he implicitly drew out the relevance to his own time. Now, writing in 1006 or later, he draws Sigeweard's attention sharply to the lessons of their story:

hig wunnon mid wæ[p]num þa swiðe wið þone hæðenan here, þe him on wann swiðe, wolde hig adilegian and adyddan of þam earde, þe him God forgeaf, and Godes lof alecgan. Hwæt, þa Mathathias, se mæra Godes þegen, mid his fif sunum, feaht wið þone here miccle gelomlicor, ðonne þu gelyfan wylle, and hig sige hæfdon þurh þone soðan God, þe hig on gelyfdon æfter Moyses æ. Hig noldon na feohtan mid fægerum wordum anum, swa þæt hi wel spræcon, and awendon þæt eft, þe læs ðe him become se hefigtima cwyde, þe se witega gecwæð be sumum leodscipe þus: *Et iratus est furore Dominus in populo suo et abhominatus est hereditatem suam, et cetera*: "Drihten wearð yrre mid graman his folce, and he onscunode his yrfwerdnisse, and he betæhte hig on hæþenra handum, and heora fynd soðlice hæfdon heora geweald, and hig swiðe gedrehton þa deriendlican fynd, and hig wurdon ge-eadmette under heora handum." Nolde Machabeus, se mæra Godes cempa, habban þisne dom ðurh his Drihtenes yrre, ac him wæs leofre, þæt he mid geleafan clipode on his eornost to Gode þisne oðerne cwyde: *Da nobis, Domine, auxilium de tribulatione, quia uana salus hominis, et cetera*: 'Syle us, leof Drihten, þinne soðan fultum on ure gedrefednisse and gedo us strengran, for þan ðe mannes fultum ys unmihtig and idel. Ac uton wyrcean mihte on þone mihtigan God, and he to nahte gedeð urne deriendlican fynd.' Machabeus þa gefylde ðas foresædan word mid stranglican weorcum, and oferwann his fynd, and sint for ði gesette his sigefæstan dæda on ðam twam bocum on biliothecan Gode to wurðmynte, and ic awende hig on Englisc and rædon gif ge wyllað eow sylfum to ræde! (Crawford, 49–50, lines 785–838)

They fought fiercely with weapons against the heathen *here*, which assailed them strongly, seeking to destroy them and drive them from the land which God had given them, and suppress the praise of God. Then Machabeus the great thegn of God with his five sons fought with the *here* much more frequently than you will believe, and they won the victory through the true God, in whom they believed according to Moses' law. They did not want to fight just with fair words, speaking well but changing it afterwards, lest they should be struck by the heavy words which the prophet spoke about a nation thus: 'And the Lord was enraged with anger against his people and rejected his inheritance, and gave them into the hands of the heathens, and their enemies truly had power over them, and the cruel enemies oppressed them sorely and they were humbled under their hands.' Machabeus that great champion of God did not want this judgement upon him, through God's anger, but preferred to call earnestly with faith to God, saying: 'Give us, dear Lord, your true help in our troubles and make us strong, because man's help is weak and in vain. But let us show strength through the almighty god and he will bring to nothing our cruel enemies.' Machabeus then fulfilled those words with mighty deeds, and overcame his enemies, and therefore his victorious actions are set down in two books in the Bible, to the honour of God, and I turned them into English; read them if you wish as counsel for yourselves.

The concept of divine wrath with the English is here, but what Ælfric now envisages is anger not for failing to support the monasteries, but for failing to honour promises to fight. His reference to promising much and performing little brings us very close to the tones of the anonymous Londoner or East Anglian who wrote the *Chronicle* account of the period, and indeed to Offa's remark in *Maldon* that many who spoke bravely in the meadhall would not fight when battle came. Old Testament story here provides a model for fusing national and religious interests in a resolute and military defence against the Danes.

When Ælfric wrote this he was probably in close contact with ealdorman Æthelmær, who seems at this time to have been out of favour with the court and taking shelter in Ælfric's monastery at Eynsham. Perhaps this plea for firm resistance reflects his influence. If so, even Æthelmær had eventually to change his mind: it was he who led the south-western thegns in submission to Sweyn in 1013, while Ethelred and London fought on.[20] If, as is generally assumed, Ælfric died before that crisis, he never had to face the failure of his paradigm and the difficulties which his view of the Vikings as the forces of the devil would have posed.

2. Wulfstan

Wulfstan was heavily influenced by Ælfric's writings and the influence is evident in his views both on apocalypse and on the Old Testament parallels

[20] Yorke, 'Aethelmaer', 20.

for the Vikings. But Wulfstan lived on to face greater crises than Ælfric had seen, and his writings show him being driven by circumstance to develop new perspectives.

Like Ælfric, Wulfstan's earliest writings engage centrally with the question of apocalypse and have very little to say about the Viking threat. A closely related sequence of five sermons, probably dating from around the year 1000, deal with the Gospel passages on the end of the world and with the approaching reign of Antichrist, which Wulfstan now sees as imminent.[21] The third of these seems to allude in passing to the Viking raids. Wulfstan argues here that some of the tribulations which are to mark the imminent end of the world are already afflicting the English, and are the consequence of sin, by which, he says, 'we anger God more than we need to'. He speaks of people's disloyalty to God and to each other, and goes on:

And ðy us deriað and ðearle dyrfað fela ungelimpa, and ælþeodige men and utancumene swyðe us swencað, ealswa Crist on his godspelle swutollice sæde þæt sceolde geweorðan. He cwæð: *Surget gens contra gentem, et reliqua.* Ðæt is on Englisc, upp ræsað þeoda, he cwæð, and wiðerræde weorþað and hetelice winnað and sacað heom betweonan for ðam unrihte þe to wide wyrð mid mannum on eorðan. (Bethurum iii. 20–6)

Therefore many misfortunes harm and afflict us, and foreigners and people from overseas greatly harass us, just as Christ in his Gospel clearly said it should happen; he said: Nation shall rise up against nation. That is in English, nations shall rise up and become opposed and fiercely contend and struggle with each other, because of the wrongfulness that will happen too widely amongst people in the world.

Wulfstan's major discussion of the Viking threat, the *Sermo ad Anglos quando Dani maxime persecuti sunt*, did not appear until 1014 however. It was a text which Wulfstan repeatedly rewrote in radical ways, and we cannot begin to comprehend his treatment of the issue until we have clarified the processes of rewriting.

The sermon exists in five manuscripts but these clearly reflect three very distinct versions of the text: a short version running to about 130 lines; a longer version running to 178 lines; and a still longer version of about 202 lines. Dorothy Whitelock and Dorothy Bethurum both argued that Wulfstan was responsible for producing and issuing all three versions, beginning with the shortest and gradually expanding it into the form of the longest and latest.[22] Some problems in that view were pointed out by John

[21] *The Homilies of Wulfstan*, ed. D. Bethurum (Oxford, 1957). The five sermons are numbers i–v.

[22] D. Whitelock, *Sermo Lupi ad Anglos* (3rd edn., London 1963), 3–5; Bethurum, *Homilies of Wulfstan*, 22–4.

C. Pope in a review of Bethurum's edition,[23] and a series of objections were put forward in 1975 by Stephanie Dien, who argued instead that the longest version represented Wulfstan's original, that the intermediate version was a subsequent abridgement by him, and that the shortest version was an independent abridgement of the original by someone else unidentified.[24] There has been no subsequent discussion of that argument, but it seems to have been accepted in the recent authoritative critical history of the period by Greenfield and Calder.[25] Yet there remain strong arguments for the earlier view. The positive points are as follows:

1. The longest version is clearly Wulfstan's own work throughout, since one of the two manuscripts in which it survives, British Library MS Cotton Nero A.i, is annotated and corrected in Wulfstan's own hand.[26]

2. Successive expansion through a series of versions is a well-documented characteristic of his work, seen in a number of other texts.

3. The Nero MS in fact preserves traces of the process of expansion in its text of a passage on sexual abuses which is unique to the longest version: the scribe seems initially to have missed the additional passage he was meant to copy but then saw his mistake, stopped and copied the new passage, and then continued with the original text.[27]

4. The short version seems internally coherent as an autonomous text, and in its concerns and emphases relates closely to Wulfstan's own earlier eschatological homilies, as we will see; one of the surviving copies occurs in a manuscript produced very close in time to Wulfstan's lifetime.

5. The close relation of this short version to the original form of the sermon is demonstrated by its unique inclusion of a clause referring to Ethelred's expulsion, which must have been in the original Wulfstan text that lies behind all three versions, since the preceding sentences in all of them lead up to it.

The objections to the earlier view can readily be disposed of. Pope's objection stemmed from his acceptance of a somewhat misleading hypothesis of Whitelock and Bethurum, viz. that one of differences between the

[23] *Modern Languages Review*, 74 (1959), 333–40.

[24] S. Dien, '*Sermo Lupi ad Anglos*: The Order and Date of the Three Versions', *Neuphilologische Mitteilungen*, 64 (1975), 561–70. The theory is developed a little further in her later article, published as S. Hollis, 'The Thematic Structure of the *Sermo Lupi*', *ASE* 6 (1977), 175–95.

[25] S. B. Greenfield and D. G. Calder, *A New Critical History of Old English Literature* (New York and London, 1986), 90.

[26] See N. R. Ker, 'The Handwriting of Archbishop Wulfstan', in *England before the Conquest: Studies in Primary Sources presented to Dorothy Whitelock*, ed. P. Clemoes and K. Hughes (Cambridge, 1971), 315–31.

[27] See Whitelock, *Sermo Lupi*, 5 n. 2.

first and the second version, the deletion of the reference to Ethelred's exile, was a change made by Wulfstan in the reign of Cnut. As Pope pointed out, the other changes in the second and third versions must date from before Cnut's accession. But there is in fact no reason for dating the omission so late and the objection disappears if the change is dated to Ethelred's reign instead.[28] The further objections raised by Stephanie Dien, though cogently argued, do not carry sufficient weight when considered more closely. Her main positive point was a literary one, that there is much verbal repetition and structural patterning in the fullest version, binding the unique passages to the rest of the sermon: but that seems evidence only that the same person wrote the unique passages, not that they were all written at the same time. She also questioned the attribution of the correcting hand in the Nero manuscript to Wulfstan, but gave no reasons and seems in a subsequent article to have accepted the attribution.[29] Her assumption that once Cnut became king Wulfstan would necessarily have deleted the passage on Gildas which is unique to the longest version seems not to be borne out by the evidence of the manuscripts, as we will see later. But the real weakness of her argument is that it requires an exceedingly complex and implausible alternative hypothesis to account for all the detailed variations amongst the manuscripts. She proposed that they resulted from a series of different activities in a variety of archetypes: first scribal error in a Wulfstan archetype causing the accidental omission of the Ethelred clause without Wulfstan noticing the mistake; then expansion by Wulfstan, adding the passage on sexual abuses; then abridgement by Wulfstan, removing the Gildas passage to meet the sensibilities of Cnut – but not, apparently, removing the far more offensive passage on the atrocities of the Vikings which appears in both the intermediate and the longest version—and also the passage on sexual abuses; and finally abridgement by someone else who was working from a different archetype which had preserved the Ethelred clause and who coincidentally removed the Gildas passage as well as other passages. Her argument assumed two major improbabilities: first that the omission of the Ethelred reference was an accidental error by one of Wulfstan's scribes and that Wulfstan himself failed to notice the error despite the fact that, on her account, he subsequently revised the sermon at least three times (and despite the fact that it is a prominent part of his argument and there is nothing in the text to prompt accidental omission); and secondly that the anonymous reviser who produced the shortest version happened to light independently on precisely the same passage to omit as Wulfstan himself had chosen to

[28] See further below.
[29] Hollis, 'Thematic Structure', 176–7.

omit earlier in a different archetype. The traditional view, that Wulfstan steadily expanded the sermon in response to changing events and attitudes, remains the best explanation of the manuscript testimony and surely deserves to be re-established as the scholarly consensus. I will discuss Wulfstan's rewriting of the sermon on that basis.

In tracing the history of the text we can see how Wulfstan's engagement with the issue of the Vikings gradually evolves and the problems which arise in the process, as he explores different paradigms for explaining disaster. The shortest version of the sermon survives in two manuscripts, Cambridge, Corpus Christi College 419 and Oxford, Bodleian Library MS Bodley 343. This version of the sermon runs to about 130 lines and deals with the crimes and troubles of the English, in the context of the approaching end of the world. The reference within the text to Ethelred's expulsion, as one of the major crimes of the English, shows that it must have been composed after 1013 (Ethelred left at the very end of that year, and returned early in 1014). The theme is clearly announced in the opening words:

> ðeos woruld is on ofste, and hit nealæcð þam ende, and þy hit is on worulde aa swa lencg swa wyrse, and swa hit sceal nyde ær Antecristes tocyme yfelian swyðe. (Bethurum xx (BH) 1–6)

> This world is in haste and it approaches the end and things in the world are worsening all the time and so it must necessarily grow more evil before Antichrist's time.

The sermon in this form is best seen as the last in the line of Wulfstan sermons on the end of the world and the reign of Antichrist, Bethurum i–v, and indeed seems to refer back to them in significant ways. In Bethurum v, composed possibly soon after the year 1000, Wulfstan had said of the future reign of Antichrist:

> Nis se man on life þe mæge oððe cunne swa yfel hit asecgan swa hit sceal geweorðan on þam deoflican timan. Ne byrhð þonne broðor oðrum hwilan ne fæder his bearne ne bearn his agenum fæder ne gesibb gesibban þe ma þe fremdan. (Bethurum v. 97–100)

> There is no one alive who can or knows how to describe how evil it shall be in that devilish time. Then brother will not protect brother nor father his child nor child his own father nor kinsman his kinsman any more than a stranger.

The second sentence is an adaptation of Christ's warning of future persecution, heralding the coming of the new kingdom, in Mark 13: 12, where the future tense is also used: 'the brother shall betray brother to death, and the father his son; and sons will rise up against parents and deliver them to death'. But in the *Sermo ad Anglos* the same words occur in the past tense:

on þysan earde wæs . . . nu fela geara unrihta fela and tealte getreowða æghwær mid mannum. Ne bearh nu foroft gesib gesibban þe ma þe fremdan, ne fæder his suna, ne hwilum bearn his agenum fæder, ne broðer oðrum. (Bethrum xx (BH) 56–8)[30]

For many years there have been in this land many injustices and wavering loyalties everywhere amongst people. Kinsman has not protected kinsman any more than the stranger, nor father his sons, nor at times the child his own father, nor brother his brother.

The anarchy and strife which Wulfstan had earlier foretold as marks of the turmoil that would come at the end of time are now seen as events that have already come to pass—perhaps reflecting the gap of ten years or so between the two sermons. Though the millennium is now well past, the apocalyptic expectations in this version are if anything more intense. Wulfstan locates the text internally, at a moment when the signs of the approaching end are all around him and the reign of Antichrist is almost upon him.

The concern of the sermon is with the crimes of the English against family, kindred, lords, and Church, and the sufferings that are the consequences of those crimes. It clearly draws a little on Christ's description of the signs that will precede the end in the Gospels; but in its emphasis on sin rather than external signs and tribulations, its real source and inspiration is probably St Paul's account of the vices that will mark the closing stages of the world in his epistle to Timothy (2 Tim. 3: 1–5, 13):

Know this also, that in the last days perilous times shall come. For men shall be lovers of their own selves, covetous, boasters, proud, blasphemers, disobedient to parents, unthankful, unholy, without natural affection, trucebreakers, false accusers, incontinent, fierce, despisers of those that are good, traitors, heady, swollen up, lovers of pleasures more than lovers of God; having a form of godliness, but denying the power thereof . . . evil men and seducers shall wax worse and worse.

The only hint of a reference to the Viking troubles in this version is in the general account of the turmoil of the times: 'ne dohte hit nu lange inne ne ute, ac wæs here and hunger, bryne and blodgyte' ('it has not prospered now for a long time internally or externally, but there was raiding army and hunger, burning and bloodshed', 50–1). That too is in fact an adaptation of an apocalyptic passage in the earlier sermon on the last days, one which again used future tense where Wulfstan now uses the past: 'Eac sceal aspringan . . . here and hunger, bryne and blodgyte' (Bethurum v. 102–4). That apart, the Vikings become an almost obtrusive absence in this version. There is

[30] There is a curious mistake here in Whitelock, *English Historical Documents*, i. 931, which unaccountably translates this as present tense—'kinsman does not protect kinsman etc.'—though all manuscripts of all versions have indisputably past tense *bearh*—'did not protect or has not protected'. A similar mistranslation occurs in M. Swanton, *Anglo-Saxon Prose* (London and Totowa, NJ, 1975), 118, where *bearh* is rendered 'will not protect'.

something perverse in citing the expulsion of Ethelred as an example of lord-betrayal without even hinting at the Viking invasions which, in the *Chronicle* account at least, seem to have played such an important part in Ethelred's departure. Possibly Wulfstan was writing at a time when he needed to be politic; possibly it was the crimes of the English rather than the pressures on them that seemed to him most striking at the time.

The second version of the sermon appears in a collection of Wulfstan texts copied into Cambridge, Corpus Christi College, MS 201, a manuscript produced around the middle of the eleventh century. It shows considerable expansion in the account of the failings of the English, but its most substantial addition is a passage of thirty lines on the Vikings:

La, hu mæg mare scamu þurh Godes irre mannum gelympan þonne us deð gelome for agenum gewirhtum? Ðeah þræla hwilc hlaforde ætleape and of cristendome to wicinge wurðe, and hit æfter þam eft gewurðe þæt wæpengewrixl wurðe gemæne þegne and þræle, gif þræl þone þegen fulice afille, licge ægilde ealre his mægðe; and gif se þegen þone þræl þe he ær ahte fullice afille, gilde þegengilde. Ful earhlice laga and scandlice nydgild þurh Godes irre us sind gemæne, understande se þe cunne, and fela ungelumpa gelumpð þisse þeode oft and gelome. Ne dohte hit nu lange inne ne ute, ac wæs here and hæte on gewelhwilcan ende oft and gelome, and Engle nu lange eal sigelease and to swiðe geyrgde þurh Godes irre, and flotmen swa strange þurh Godes þafunge þæt oft on gefeohte an fealleð tyne and twegen oft twentig, and hwilum læs, hwilum ma, eal for urum sinnum. And oft tyne oððe twelfe, ælc æfter oðrum, scændað and tawiað to bismore micclum þæs þegnes cwenan and hwilum his dohtor oððe nydmagan, þar he on locað þe læt hine silfne rancne and ricne and genoh godne ær þæt gewurde. And oft þræl þone þegn þe ær wæs his hlaford cnit swiðe fæste and wircð him to þræle þurh Godes irre. Wala þare yrmðe and wala þare worldscame þe nu habbað Engle, eall for Godes irre! And oft twegen sæmen, oððe þri hwilum, drifað þa drafe cristnra manna fram sæ to sæ ut þurh þas þeode gewilede togædere, us eallum to worldscame, gif we on eornost ænige scame cuðe oððe a woldan ariht understandan. Ac ealne þone bismor þe we oft þoliað we gildað mid weorðscipe þam þe us scændað. We him gildað singallice, and hi us hynað dæghwamlice. Hi hergiað and heaweð, bændað and bismriað, ripað and reafiað and to scipe lædað. And hwæt is, la, ænig oðer on eallum þam gelympum buton Godes irre ofer ðas þeode swutol and gesene? (Bethurum xx (C) 97–126)

Lo, how can greater shame befall people through God's anger than frequently does with us because of our own actions? If a serf should run away from his master and turn from Christianity to be a Viking, and it should fall out afterwards that there is armed conflict between the thegn and the serf, if the serf should kill the thegn he will lie without any wergild to all his kindred; and if the thegn should kill the serf that he previously owned, he will pay the wergild of a thegn. Very cowardly laws and shameful payments are common among us through God's anger, let him understand it who can, and many misfortunes befall this nation again and again. Things have not prospered at home or abroad for a long time now, but there has been raiding and persecution in every corner again and again, and the English have been entirely without victory for a long time and too greatly humiliated through

God's anger, and the Vikings so strong through God's permission that often in battle one fells ten and two often fell twenty, and sometimes less, sometimes more, all because of our sins. And often ten or twelve, one after the other, shame and greatly disgrace the thegn's wife and sometimes his daughter or kinsman, while he who thought himself bold and mighty and brave enough before that happened looks on. And often a serf binds very firmly the thegn who had been his master and makes him into a serf, through God's anger. Alas for the misery and also for the worldly shame that the English now have, all because of God's anger. And often two seamen, or sometimes three, drive the herd of Christians from sea to sea, out through this nation bound together, to the shame of us all, if we seriously knew any shame or could comprehend things properly. But all the disgrace that we often suffer we repay with honour to those who shame us. We continually pay them, and they daily humiliate us. They harry and kill, make captive and humiliate, plunder and steal and carry off to their ships. And what, lo, is there in all these events but the anger of God, clear and visible over this nation?

While preserving the original apocalyptic setting of the sermon, Wulfstan here also locates the text within the specific contemporary scene of Viking raiding and legal agreements with a settled Viking army. The particular humiliations and atrocities described seem to relate to the crimes which Wulfstan attributes to the English: the failure of the English to recognize the rights of social hierarchy and law finds its echo in the overturning of social hierarchies by the Vikings. The story of rape seems to be told not so much with sympathy for the female victims but rather in a tone of contempt for the thegn whose sense of his own power and importance is shattered when he has to watch helplessly while his own female kindred are abused. Wulfstan presents these humiliations as essentially a manifestation of God's anger with the English because of their crimes against morality and religion. Six times in the thirty-line passage he uses the phrase *þurh Godes yrre.*

A significant detail is the omission of the reference to Ethelred's expulsion, though the original lead-up to it is still there (the text now reads: 'it is a very great betrayal of a lord to conspire in his death or drive him living from the land, and both have happened in this land: Edward was betrayed and killed and afterwards burnt'). The reference is also missing from both copies of the third and latest version of the sermon, including a copy corrected by Wulfstan himself; as Dorothy Whitelock and Dorothy Bethurum have both argued, the omission must have been Wulfstan's work, or at least had his support. Dorothy Bethurum suggested that the deletion 'was probably political in nature, for if the homily was revised after Cnut's succession, it might have been unwise to refer in such a context to Ethelred's exile'.[31] Dorothy Whitelock made a similar point: 'Policy may have dictated this omission, if made in Cnut's reign, for the expulsion of Ethelred, which

[31] Bethurum, *Homilies of Wulfstan*, 22.

Wulfstan calls "a very great treachery", was in favour of Cnut's father'.[32] Both are hesitant about locating the revision in Cnut's reign, and surely rightly. The new passage on the Vikings is apparently written in the thick of Viking raiding. It is thoroughly English and anti-Viking in its perspective, and expresses strong antipathy to the payment of geld to buy them off. It cannot have been written after 1018, when Wulfstan played a major part in the reconciliation with Cnut, and does not look as if it could have been written after Cnut acceded in late 1016. But no reasons have ever been given for dating Wulfstan's deletion of the Ethelred phrase in Cnut's reign, and I cannot myself see any. If policy did dictate the deletion of the reference to Ethelred, it was surely connected with the return of that king early in 1014 rather than the accession of Cnut; presumably his return involved a reconciliation with those Anglo-Saxon leaders who had accepted Sweyn in 1013 and were therefore implicated in the king's expulsion. As we will see, there are reasons for thinking that this second version cannot have been produced later than 1014.

The third version survives in two copies, British Library MS Cotton Nero A.i and Oxford, Bodleian Library, MS Hatton 113, produced at Worcester in the third quarter of the eleventh century. It includes two more brief passages on the crimes of the English and another longer passage near the end on Gildas and the Anglo-Saxon invasion of Britain. The first of these new passages seems to reflect back upon the rape-scene added in the earlier version:

> And scandlic is to specenne þæt geworden is to wide and egeslic is to witanne þæt oft doð to manege þe dreogað þa yrmþe, þæt sceotað togædere and ane cwenan gemænum ceape bicgað gemæne, and wið þa ane fylþe adreogað, an æfter anum and ælc æfter oðrum, hundum gelicost þe for fylþe ne scrifað, and syððan wið weorðe syllað of lande feondum to gewealde Godes gesceafte and his agenne ceap þe he deore gebohte. (Bethurum xx (EH) 85–91)

> And it is shameful to report what has happened too widely, and it is horrible to know what is often done by too many men, who engage in a miserable practice, that they combine together and buy a woman between them as a common purchase, and with that one woman engage in a filthy act, one by one and each after the other, just like dogs who are not troubled by filth, and afterwards sell God's creature, his own purchase that he dearly bought, out of the country into the possession of enemies, in exchange for money.

The English are here seen to be appropriating the atrocities of the Vikings, abusing their own fellow-creatures; but their crime is far greater, since the woman whom they abuse is seen as the possession not just of a proud thegn but of God himself. It is, though, the Gildas passage which is important.

[32] Whitelock, *Sermo Lupi*, 6.

There is nothing explicit about the Vikings in this latter passage but the allusion could hardly be missed:

An þeodwita wæs on Brytta tidum Gildas hatte. Se awrat be heora misdædum hu hy mid heora synnum swa oferlice swyþe God gegræmedan þæt he let æt nyhstan Engla here heora eard gewinnan and Brytta dugeþe fordon mid ealle. And þæt wæs geworden þæs þe he sæde, þurh ricra reaflac and þurh gitsunge wohgestreona, ðurh leode unlaga and þurh wohdomas, ðurh biscopa asolcennesse and ðurh lyðre yrhðe Godes bydela þe soþes geswugedan ealles to gelome and clumedan mid ceaflum þær hy scoldan clypian. Þurh fulne eac folces gælsan and þurh oferfylla and mænigfealde synna heora eard hy forworhtan and selfe hy forwurdan. Ac utan don swa us þearf is, warnian us be swilcan; and soþ is þæt ic secge, wyrsan dæda we witan mid Englum þonne we mid Bryttan ahwar gehyrdan. And þy us is þearf micel þæt we us beþencan and wið God sylfne þingian georne. (Bethurum xx (EH) 176–90)

There was a historian in the times of the Britons called Gildas. He wrote about their misdeeds, how they had so excessively angered God through their sins that in the end he let the *here* of the English conquer their land and utterly destroy the British nobility. And that happened, as he said, through robbery by the powerful and through greed for wrongful treasures, through abuses of national law and through false judgements, through the sloth of the bishops and the wicked cowardice of God's messengers who were all too often silent about the truth and mumbled with their mouths when they should have cried out. Also through the foul indulgences of the people and through gluttony and various sins they forfeited their land and ruined themselves. But let us do as is needful, take warning from such events; and what I say is the truth, we know of worse deeds amongst the English than we heard anywhere amongst the Britons. And therefore there is great need that we take thought for ourselves and zealously conciliate God himself.

Wulfstan is here no longer talking about raids by small groups of Vikings or the problems of treaty agreements between the two sides but about the invasion and conquest of the whole country, and inviting us to see the parallel between the Anglo-Saxon conquest of Britain, as divine punishment for the sins of the Britons, and the threatened Viking conquest of England, as divine punishment for the sins of the English. The injunction which immediately precedes the Gildas passage—'let us protect ourselves lest we all perish'—and the final exhortation—'But let us do as is needful . . .'—show that this passage was written, at the very latest, before Cnut's accession in 1016–17. The conquest of the English by foreigners was still something that could be forestalled by repentance and reform when this final version was produced. The Nero copy has the famous rubric dating the text to 1014: *sermo ad anglos quando Dani maxime persecuti sunt eos, quod fuit anno millesimo xiiii ab incarnatione domini nostri Iesu Cristi.* This was at least approved, if not written, by Wulfstan, since the manuscript was corrected by him, and it cannot refer to the date of the original version of the sermon since that has no reference to the Viking troubles; there seems no reason to doubt that the date refers to this particular version, the third.

What the textual history suggests is the rapidity with which Wulfstan found himself rethinking his ideas and finding a framework for the Viking raids and invasions. The text seems to have originated early in 1014 as a short apocalyptic sermon, but twice within the next two years, probably within the same year, Wulfstan expanded it to take account of the Viking attacks. In the process, its emphasis gradually shifted from the apocalyptic crisis to the national one. The sense of an approaching end of all things, so strong in the earlier homilies on the last days and still very evident in the first version of the sermon, gives way to a sense of the longer and continuing movement of history. The successive stages of the text reflect both a diminishing concern with apocalypse and a growing concern with invasion, and the process of rethinking the crisis has left its marks on the text.

An association between apocalypse and Viking invasion had already been touched on by Wulfstan in his early eschatological sermon, Bethurum iii, but the nature of the link is far from clear, and it remains a deeply problematic issue with the *Sermo ad Anglos*. Stephanie Hollis has argued that Wulfstan identified the Vikings as the agents of Antichrist:

> The coming of the Vikings is the coming of the reign of Antichrist, predicted in the opening sentence. Wulfstan's presentation of the Vikings as antichrists whose victory establishes the reign of the arch-enemy appears to be without parallel in Old English homiletic literature, but to him the equation of Viking rule with the reign of Antichrist would have been a logical inference.[33]

If so, one might comment, he was able to change his mind about Viking rule very quickly, since by 1018 he was acting as a leading adviser to the Viking ruler Cnut. But there are a number of problems with this identification, even in the second version of the sermon. 'Nation shall rise up against nation' is one of the signs that will warn of the approaching end, rather than part of that end. In both Bethurum iii and v the attacks of foreigners are presented as precursors of the coming of Antichrist and that seems to be so in the *Sermo ad Anglos*: the Viking troubles are present and past, Antichrist is still future. It is certainly true that the Antichrist tradition included a belief, based on Revelation 17, that there would be a final battle between the good and the forces of Antichrist and that the latter would include the barbarian hordes of the tribes of Gog and Magog.[34] But this particular tradition is in fact not present in the *Libellus de Anticristo* of Adso, which seems to have been Wulfstan's main source for ideas on Antichrist.[35] There is the motif of

[33] Hollis, 'Thematic Structure', 185.

[34] See R. K. Emmerson, *Antichrist in the Middle Ages* (Manchester, 1981).

[35] Ibid. 88.

the four beasts of the Apocalypse, vividly described in the Old English adaptation of Adso which is preserved in Wulfstan manuscripts,[36] and they too were used to associate Antichrist with warfare. Yet neither Gog and Magog nor the four beasts seem to be what Wulfstan is invoking here.

Antichrist and the Vikings seem in fact to be very differently presented in Wulfstan's thought. Antichrist is the devil or is closely associated with him, and his role is to seduce Christians into unbelief or false belief. The Vikings do have a different religion, or some of them do (if it is they whom Wulfstan has in mind when he talks of the religion of the heathens), but Wulfstan speaks of it positively and does not suggest that the Vikings are concerned to seduce Christians into other beliefs. Nor does he identify them in any explicit way with the devil or Antichrist, or present them as tempters. His emphasis on the Vikings' role as agents of divine punishment for the sins of the English seems also to distinguish them from Antichrist and his agents. In his early apocalyptic homilies Wulfstan followed Ælfric in raising the question why Antichrist would be allowed to afflict mankind:

Ælcne mann he wile awendan of rihtan geleafan and of cristendome and bespannan to his unlarum gif he mæg; and God hit geþafað him sume hwile for twam þingum: an is ærest þæt men beoð þurh synna swa forð forworhte þæt hi beoð þæs wel wyrðe þæt deofol openlice þænne fandige hwa him fullfyligean wille; oðer is þæt God wile þæt ða þe swa gesælige beoð þæt hi on rihtan geleafan ðurhwuniað and ðam deofle anrædlice wiðstandað, he wile þæt þa beon raðe amerede and geclænsode of synnum þurh ða myclan ehtnesse and ðurh þæne martirdom ðe hy þonne þoliað. (Bethurum iv. 15–24)

He will seek to turn everyone from the true faith and from Christianity and seduce them to his false teachings if he can. And God will permit this for a while for two reasons: first because people will be so guilty through sins that they will thoroughly deserve that the devil should openly test who is willing to follow him; and secondly, because God will wish that those who are so blessed that they persevere in the right faith and resolutely resist the devil should be purged and cleansed of their sins through the great persecution and through the martyrdom which they then will suffer.

There is clearly an association here between the sins of humanity and the tribulations caused by Antichrist, but neither Wulfstan nor Ælfric presents this as divine punishment or anger, nor do they associate external tribulations with Antichrist's persecution of the faithful who will not forsake Christ. There is an important distinction here between the temptations and persecutions imposed on all Christians by Antichrist, which God in his goodness permits so that they may all be tried or purged before the final

[36] Ed. A. S. Napier, *Wulfstan: Sammlung der ihm zugeschriebenen Homilien* (Berlin, 1883), 191–205.

judgement, and the external tribulations which are imposed by God on the English in particular, in anger at their sins.

Wulfstan seems not to have been thinking of the Vikings as agents of Antichrist but rather to have been attempting to place the Viking raids within the apocalyptic framework in two other ways: first, as we see more clearly in Bethurum iii, by identifying them with the turmoil and tribulation which, according to the Gospels, or rather medieval interpretation of them, would precede Antichrist's time; and secondly, and more particularly, by interpreting them as divine punishment for the crimes and sins which St Paul saw as precursors of the end. Yet in a number of ways the traditional topos of divine punishment sits uneasily within this apocalyptic framework. It is not part of the New Testament tradition of apocalypse as presented in the sources which most influenced Wulfstan and his contemporaries, that is the synoptic gospels and St Paul's epistle. It is at odds with the Antichrist tradition, which conceives rather of a devil figure who is allowed to tempt or test mankind. And in both Wulfstan's and Ælfric's writings on the topos of divine punishment, its emphasis is tribal or national whereas apocalypse is universal: that is, divine anger is directed against a particular nation for particular sins, often employing other nations as agents; apocalypse involves the tribulations of the whole world, though more particularly of the faithful. One can already see the awkwardness in Bethurum iii, where Wulfstan tried to make the idea of wars between nations as an expression of universal sin fit the concept of invasion by others as a consequence of a particular nation's sins.

This emphasis on divine anger seems indeed to reflect less the traditions of apocalypse than the influence of another set of paradigms which Wulfstan was interested in, those of the Old Testament. Several sermons which Bethurum dates between the early eschatological pieces and the late *Sermo ad Anglos* hint at an identification of Old Testament events with the contemporary Viking situation. Thus, in his adaptation of Ælfric's first homily on salvation history, printed as Bethurum vi, Wulfstan added an allusive reference to the Babylonian captivity:

> And æt nyhstan þæt folc ða wearð swa wið God forworht þæt he let faran hæþenne here and forhergian eall þæt land; and ðone cyningc Sedechiam þe þa wæs on Iudea lande man geband, and ealle þa duguðe þe on þam earde wæs man ofsloh oðþon gebende and lædde hi ut of earde, and fullice .lxx. wintra syððan on an wæs se ðeodscype eall geðeowod under heora feonda gewealde, swa forð hy wæron wið God forworhte. (Bethurum vi. 115–22)

> At length the people became so sinful towards God that he let a heathen *here* come and harry all that land; and the king Zedechiah was taken captive and all the nobility were killed or taken captive and led from that land, and for fully 70 years that nation was enslaved under the control of their enemies.

Similarly, in his excerpts from Isaiah and Jeremiah, printed as Bethurum xi, Wulfstan selects God's warning to the people of Israel:

and for ðam sceal geweorðan ... eower eard weste and eac eowre burga mid fyre forbærnde. Ælðeodige men eow sculon hergian, and ðonne ge gebiddaþ and to me clypiað, nelle ic eow gehyran, forðam þe ge syndon mid mane afyllede. (Bethurum xi. 112–16)

Your land shall be laid waste and your cities destroyed by fire. Foreigners shall harry you and when you pray to me I will not hear you, because you are filled with sin.

And the sermon called 'Godly warning' is a series of excerpts from Leviticus giving God's warning to the Israelites:

And gif ge þonne fram me hwyrfað eowre heortan ... þonne sceal eow sona weaxan to hearme wædl and wawa, sacu and wracu, here and hunger; and scylan eowre heortan eargian swyþe and eowra feonda mægen strangian þearle, and ge tofesede swyþe afyrhte oft lytel werod earhlice forbugað. ... and ge beoð gesealde feondum to gewealde, þa eow geyrmað and swyþe geswencað. Land by awestað and burga forbærnað. (Bethrum xix. 59–68)

If you turn your hearts from me ... then poverty and misery will increase with you, conflict and vengeance, harrying and hunger; and your hearts will grow cowardly and your enemies' power strengthen and you will often flee in cowardly fashion from a little troop, routed and frightened ... And you will be given into the power of enemies who will oppress and humiliate you. They will lay waste the land and burn the cities.

As Dorothy Bethurum notes,[37] this passage seems to have prompted some of the vivid details in the account of Viking humiliations added in the second version of the *Sermo ad Anglos*—'the seamen are so strong, through God's permission, that often in battle one fells ten and two often fell twenty'.

In emphasizing the wrath of God for the sins of the English as the driving force behind the Viking raids in the second version Wulfstan seems to be drawing heavily on the Old Testament paradigms which he had been collecting earlier. But that tradition has the effect of unsettling the apocalyptic context with which he had started. The Old Testament parallels suggest the cyclic repetition of divine punishment and repentance rather than the once-only end of all things; they imply divine anger with the chosen people rather than the destruction of the whole world.

If the emphasis on divine wrath in the passage newly added to the second version seems to subvert the idea of apocalypse, that is still more true of the additions in the third version. As Nicholas Howe has pointed out,[38] the

[37] Bethurum, *Homilies of Wulfstan*, 355.

[38] N. Howe, *Migration and Mythmaking in Anglo-Saxon England* (New Haven, Conn. and London, 1989), 9.

apocalyptic reading is difficult to reconcile with the citation of Gildas and the Anglo-Saxon invasion of Britain; as he says, the citation of a historical precedent would be a curious way of accounting for aspects of the end of the world. Equally, when Wulfstan warns of the danger that such a precedent might be repeated if the English do not take care, this is curiously at odds with the notion of the promised end of all things, which the opening of the homily describes as imminent. Wulfstan's complaints about policies for dealing with the Vikings (such as paying geld) and his drawing of historical parallels suggest that he is already thinking of a longer-term historical framework rather than imminent apocalypse. Though a reading of the sermon in its longest form might invite one to think that the Vikings are part of the apocalypse, a review of the history of the text might suggest that the Viking invasions represent another layer of thought.

The paradigms drawn from Old Testament history and from national history are alike in questioning the idea of apocalypse, but there is an important development of thought that separates them. For the Old Testament stories had insisted on the exclusiveness of the Israelites: though God in his wrath might allow the heathens to conquer, they remained heathens eternally beyond the pale and the Israelites remained the chosen people. That seems to have been Ælfric's perspective on the Vikings. In turning finally to the Gildas paradigm, Wulfstan was, consciously or not, turning to a story which allowed for eventual acceptance of the invaders within the fold of religion and civilization. He was drawing a parallel between the Viking invaders and the earlier Anglo-Saxon invaders who had arrived as barbarians but rapidly established a new Christian civilization. It was no doubt because of that paradigm that he was able so quickly to achieve the frame of mind that enabled him to become Cnut's adviser.

The *Sermo ad Anglos* is, as we have seen, an intensely topical text, repeatedly revised in the space of a year or two, in response to the developing political situation, and its very title asserts its role as an address to the nation by a figure of great authority. But how was it promulgated? It is generally taken for granted that Wulfstan's sermons were essentially oral texts, records of or designs for oral performance, though there has been remarkably little discussion and even less evidence. One key piece of evidence is the sermon edited as Bethurum xiii. In Oxford, Bodleian Library, MS Hatton 113 it appears with the heading *Sermo ad Populum*, and in British Library MS Otho B.x it had the rubric *Sermo Item*. In its opening address and in its content and tone and style it shows the same marks of the sermon genre as Wulfstan's other texts. But in Cambridge, Corpus Christi College MS 201 it appears with no rubric and instead an introductory sentence which identifies it as a written text:

Wulfstan arcebisceop greteð freondlice þegnas on ðeode, gehadode and læwede, ealle gemænelice þa ðe him betæhte sindon for gode to wissianne. And ic bidde eow for Godes lufan þæt ge þises gewrites giman and on hwiltidum hit on gemynde habban, forðam þeah ðe hit leohtlic minegung þince, hit is þeah þearflic, gime se þe wille. (Bethurum xiii, note to line 3)

Archbishop Wulfstan greets in friendship the thegns in the nation, both clerical and lay, all together, who are entrusted to him to guide on behalf of God. And I urge you for God's sake that you pay heed to this writing and have it in your thoughts from time to time, because although it may seem a warning of little importance, it is however needful, let him who will take heed.

Evidently Wulfstan circulated this text as a separate written document, designed to be read, a kind of episcopal equivalent to the legal and administrative document known as a king's *gewrit*. Bethurum calls it 'A Pastoral Letter' but argues even so for its essential orality:

It is quite unlikely that this sermon was a letter in the literal sense, for it is addressed to the thanes, both clerical and lay, the latter of whom may not all have been able to read, and it is ... composed for oral delivery.... It may have been composed for delivery at a meeting of the Witan, where Wulfstan is known to have preached, and then sent to the principal noblemen of the York and Worcester dioceses. (Bethurum, 339)

It may have been, but there is no evidence that it was either preached at the outset or read aloud when it reached its destination. All we can say is that, for all its pretence of orality, it had an authentic life as a written text from the beginning. And though it may have been read aloud when it reached its addressees, it does not look as though it was read in what one might call a preaching context.

The copy of Bethurum xiii in CCCC 201 does not itself derive from one of these individual written copies circulated by Wulfstan. It appears here as part of a large collection of Wulfstan's writings evidently compiled and circulated by Wulfstan as a collection. This copy clearly derives from an in-house record of the *gewrit* which Wulfstan sent out, and the same is probably true of most, perhaps all, of the other copies, judging from their manuscript context. The separate versions would probably only have survived if they had been subsequently copied, or bound, into larger collections. Only the chance preservation of the introductory address in one manuscript reveals its history; from the other manuscripts one would have assumed it was just another sermon. But it seems quite possible that Wulfstan's other 'sermons' had a similar written promulgation. It may well be then that the *Sermo ad Anglos* had its origins not in a series of preaching occasions but in a series of writs. Indeed, the title *Sermo ad Anglos* seems to suggest more widespread promulgation than any preaching occasion could possibly give.

The *Sermo ad Anglos* must surely have had some form of immediate promulgation, whether orally or in the form of an episcopal writ. Yet that has probably left no trace and we are left with guesswork. What the manuscripts show is a second stage of promulgation, involving a very different status for the work. The evidence is clearest with the earliest of them, British Library MS Cotton Nero A.i, containing Wulfstan's *Institutes of Polity*, law-codes mostly written by Wulfstan himself, his sermon on Evil Rulers, and a number of similar texts by or closely associated with Wulfstan, as well as the third and longest version of the *Sermo ad Anglos*; it is a small format manuscript with passages and annotations in Wulfstan's own hand. The most interesting feature from our point of view is the rubric with which the Sermo begins: *Sermo Lupi ad Anglos quando Dani maxime persecuti sunt eos, quod fuit anno millesimo xiiii* . . . This, I take it, was certainly seen and approved by Wulfstan and I would think devised by him: we see his hand revising rubrics elsewhere in the manuscript. It was surely not a contemporary rubric belonging to the original promulgation of the sermon. It has all the signs of being written well after the event, explaining the circumstances of the sermon after the Danish persecutions had died down—after 1018, one would think. (One cannot refer to a time 'when the Danes most severely persecuted the English' unless those persecutions seem to have moderated or disappeared.) Even the phrase 'ad Anglos' seems to have dating implications: it reflects a time when 'ad Anglos' was no longer equivalent to 'ad populum', when Wulfstan needed to explain that the sermon had been addressed to the English before the institution of an Anglo-Danish hegemony. Wulfstan seems to be annotating the text for posterity, or perhaps for other contemporary readers, explaining its historical positioning after its moment had passed and the political situation from which the sermon had sprung had radically changed. That seems to suggest a date for the rubric, and hence the manuscript, no earlier than 1018.

Neil Ker says of this manuscript that it was 'perhaps in the nature of a hand-book for the use of Wulfstan', and Henry Loyn suggests that the manuscript was compiled by Wulfstan soon after Cnut's accession as 'a vast conversion document', and 'a commonplace book especially intended for a bishop's use in advising a king'—that is, I take it, for Wulfstan's own use in advising Cnut.[39] One wonders whether the *Sermo ad Anglos* was a very appropriate text to place before the king: though it does flatteringly suggest that the Vikings were agents of divine wrath against the English—that it was not the Danes' fault, as it were, if they went around raping and

[39] N. R. Ker, *A Catalogue of Manuscripts containing Anglo-Saxon* (Oxford, 1957), 211; H. Loyn, *A Wulfstan Manuscript containing Institutes, Laws and Homilies*, Early English Manuscripts in Facsimile, 17 (Copenhagen, 1971), 49.

pillaging—it still dwells on the shameful activities of the Vikings and records Wulfstan's appeal to the English to take measures against the invaders and his criticism of Danegeld. Nor does it really seem to be a collection designed for his own use. The careful provision of rubrics, like the one for the *Sermo ad Anglos*, suggests the preparation of texts for the use of others. What, we might ask, is the point of defining this text as 'Sermo Lupi', a sermon by Wulfstan, except to inform readers outside the Wulfstan circle? And though one might argue that the rubrics are simply copied from other versions designed for circulation, in the very next item we find Wulfstan's hand revising a rubric. This, surely, was a collection of his recent writings designed by Wulfstan to be sent out to others. And though it clearly has its religious and administrative uses, in its inclusion of such texts as the *Sermo ad Anglos* it seems to be edging in the direction of an anthology of Wulfstan's collected prose—a literary collection, one might say.

We have already seen that the scribe appears to have been working from a copy of the *Sermo ad Anglos* marked up by Wulfstan with additional passages, one of which he originally missed. Another Wulfstan addition is made in his own hand in the margin—an additional clause, *toeacan oðran ealles to manegan þe man unscyldgige forfor* ('apart from all too many others who were guiltlessly killed', 79–80), which also occurs in the Hatton copy but not in the earlier versions. The natural supposition would be that Wulfstan conceived of this additional clause when correcting the Nero version and that it was subsequently transferred to another copy. But why should he be trying to improve the sermon during Cnut's reign? Surely he was not still delivering it—not with its warning that the land will be overrun by foreigners if the English do not take care? Bethurum argues cogently that most of the additions in Wulfstan's hand in this manuscript suggest an attempt to update the texts by comparison with other, more fully revised copies.[40] That may well be what is happening in this case too: that Wulfstan was not here revising the text but copying in earlier additions from a more up-to-date copy. Even so, what it suggests is a continued interest in perfecting the text, even though its moment had passed. He is, presumably, imagining readers still interested in reading the text as the historical monument that the rubric identifies. Wulfstan seems to have been thinking of this copy as a cross between a historical record from the past and a literary text. By 1018 its moment had clearly passed and much that it said had ceased to be relevant, but even so he had it copied out again in a collection of his works, corrected it, and furnished it with an explanatory rubric so that readers would know how it came to be written and what its historical role was.

[40] Bethurum, *Homilies of Wulfstan*, 18–19.

The other manuscript of this third version of the sermon points in the same direction. Hatton 113 is a collection of homilies produced at Worcester, Wulfstan's own episcopal seat, some time between 1062 and about 1075, and the *Sermo ad Anglos* occurs within a collection of Wulfstan's sermons evidently put together by him and presumably preserved at Worcester: the set begins with the general rubric *Incipiunt sermones lupi episcopi.* The *Sermo* has a version of the rubric found in Nero: *Sermo Lupi ad Anglos quando Dani maxime persecuti sunt, quod fuit in dies æþelredi regis.* I think it likely that the dating clause is an alternative reading by Wulfstan himself, rather than a later simplification by scribes. As we will see, an echo of it occurs in another manuscript. Either way, the Hatton manuscript evidently draws on a Wulfstan collection in which the *Sermo ad Anglos* had been included and marked up by the archbishop for posterity, some time after 1018, in much the same way as Nero, but here within a collection of his sermons. The text shows quite a number of small additional clauses that are not in the main text of Nero. One of them at least is clearly the work of Wulfstan—the one which we have seen added in his hand in the margins of Nero. It seems quite likely that the others are too, as Dorothy Whitelock suggested:[41] they seem very much in his manner. Hatton then preserves an independent version of the *Sermo,* more fully revised by Wulfstan.

The only copy of the second version seems to reflect the same kind of promulgation. It appears in Cambridge, Corpus Christi College MS 201, produced at the New Minster in Winchester around the middle of the eleventh century and containing a collection of sermons and ecclesiastical laws and injunctions probably compiled by Wulfstan. The text of the *Sermo* begins with an erroneous version of the Wulfstan rubric, giving 1009 instead of 1014 as the date: *Sermo Lupi ad Anglos quando Dani maxime persecuti sunt, quod fuit anno millesimo VIIII.* Presumably the scribe misread an X as a V. More interesting is the intrusive comment after the first sentence:

> Þis wæs on Æðelredes cyninges dagum gediht, feower geara fæce ær he forðferde. Gime se ðe wille hu hit þa wære and hwæt siððan gewurde.

> This was composed in the time of King Ethelred, four years before he died. Let him who will take note how things then were and what happened afterwards.

The wording looks as though it may be in origin Wulfstan's own.[42] The opening words are an English version of the dating clause in the independent Hatton version, 'quod fuit in dies æþelredi regis', while 'gime se ðe wille' is a characteristic Wulfstan phrase, precisely the words in fact that Wulfstan

[41] Whitelock, *Sermo Lupi*, 5.

[42] Whitelock (ibid. 6) suggests that *feower* may be a mistake for *feawera* 'few'.

adds to the rubric of the item following the *Sermo ad Anglos* in the Nero manuscript. The scribe has perhaps incorporated into the text Wulfstan's own marginal comment, written in 1018 or later and pointing back to the original significance of this text.

That kind of post-crisis concern with copying and circulating the *Sermo* was not confined to Wulfstan himself. Whether in its original form as a sermon on the imminent end of the world, or in its later form as a text on the threatened conquest of England, the *Sermo ad Anglos* retained its interest for English readers long after both crises had faded away. The first version appears in a small collection of sermons by Wulfstan, Ælfric, and others, Cambridge, Corpus Christi College MS 419, produced approximately about the time of Wulfstan's death in 1023, probably at Canterbury. As we have already seen, the second and third versions were re-copied in collections of Wulfstan's work around the middle of the eleventh century and again a decade or so later. But the other manuscript of the first version is in some respects the most surprising of all. Bodley 343 was produced in the twelfth century, possibly in the West Midlands, though many of its contents seem to derive from south-eastern collections.[43] It contains a very large collection of Old English homilies and similar texts, many of them by Ælfric. The *Sermo* appears here in a small group of pieces that seem to draw yet again on a Wulfstan collection, containing items by him or written for him or for the use of a bishop. The status of this first version of the *Sermo* as essentially a sermon on the end of the world rather than the Vikings is clear in the manuscript, where it immediately follows three of Wulfstan's sermons on Antichrist and the last days. Whether that ordering reflects the form in which Wulfstan himself put the *Sermo* into circulation or the interests of the compiler of the Bodley 343 selection is, I think, impossible to say. It does, though, raise a question about the function of this manuscript. What was this twelfth-century compiler looking for when he selected these four Old English sermons announcing the imminent end of the world around the year 1000, especially Bethurum v which quotes the biblical reference to a thousand years and goes on: 'Þusend geara and eac ma is nu agan syððan Crist wæs mid mannum on menniscan hiwe, and nu syndon Satanases bendas swyðe toslopene, and Antecristes tima is wel gehende.' These sermons are in their own way almost as tied to a particular moment as the later versions of the *Sermo ad Anglos* with their emphasis on the Viking threat. Did the compiler recognize their historical status and prize it, or did he overlook the topical references and find their warning of apocalypse just

[43] There is a detailed account of the manuscript, together with a discussion of the possible functions of 12th-cent. copies of Old English texts, in *Old English Homilies from MS Bodley 343*, ed. Susan Irvine, EETS OS 302 (Oxford, 1993).

as relevant to his own time? And that is of course part of a larger question about the whole manuscript, for the compiler seems to have laboured to bring together a range of much older texts many of which to varying degrees proclaim their date in their contents and all of which must have announced their antiquity by their language. Similarly, if we look back at the Hatton manuscript we find the tremulous hand of Worcester glossing the *Sermo ad Anglos* as if its warning of possible Viking invasion were still as urgent as ever in the thirteenth century. Ælfric's *De Oratione Moysi* can also be found in a twelfth-century manuscript. As one crisis after another came and went—the millennium, the Viking conquest, the Norman Conquest—these highly topical texts retained their historical interest across the divide that apparently separated the Anglo-Saxon world from its successor.

The Englishness of Old English

BRUCE MITCHELL

§1. An Oxford professorial colleague of Professor E. G. Stanley, in whose honour this volume has been prepared, wrote in 1984:

One needn't get carried away with the similarities between the development of relativization in the post-creole continuum in Hawaii and in Old English and thus conclude on the basis of such parallelisms that Old English (or Middle English) was a creole. It would be futile, in my opinion, to launch a debate about the prospect of uncovering creole origins for Old and Middle English (or for that matter, proto-Germanic). Bailey (1973) and no doubt others would wish to push these similarities farther than I would. When referring to pidginization/creolization (and pidgins/creoles), we must be careful not to confuse the process with the entities which result from them. Hence the term 'creolization' should be reserved for a situation in which a creole results. There are however cases where conditions are conducive to simplification, reduction etc. (e.g. second language acquisition), but which do not give rise to a pidgin or creole.[1]

This warning from Romaine, however, came too late to prevent writers such as Bailey and Maroldt[2] and Poussa[3] importing the word 'creole' into the debate about the origins of Middle English. I therefore propose to recapitulate some of the salient points which have so far been made and to put forward some non-'linguistic' linguistic arguments and some literary considerations in support of my agreement with Romaine in her use of the word 'futile'.

§2. The question at issue, of course, is why the West-Saxon dialect of Old English—a Germanic language very similar to the ancestor of Modern German—was replaced by a descendant of the East Midland dialect, in the process becoming an SVO language dependent on prepositions and losing the inflexions, the three Germanic element orders, and such things as the

[Submitted 1990]

[1] S. Romaine, 'Relative-Clause Formation Strategies in Germanic', *Historical Syntax*, ed. J. Fisiak, Trends in Linguistics Studies and Monographs, 23 (Berlin, New York, and Amsterdam, 1984), 465.

[2] C.-J. N. Bailey and K. Maroldt, 'The French Lineage of English', *Langues en contact—Pidgins—Creoles—Languages in Contact*, ed. J. M. Meisel, Tübinger Beiträge zur Linguistik, 75 (Tübingen, 1977).

[3] P. Poussa, 'The Evolution of Early Standard English: The Creolization Hypothesis', *Studia Anglica Posnaniensia*, 14 (1982), 69–85.

strong and weak declensions of the adjectives—features which are all retained in Modern German. What may be called the traditional view, to which I subscribe, is that a major factor was the Scandinavian invasions and the consequent establishment of bilingual communities of speakers of English and Scandinavian dialects—all Germanic in origin. As a result, the inflexional endings (which differed from dialect to dialect) were confused and reduced so that they were no longer distinctive. Such reduction was possible only because Old English was already moving towards the SVO order—which replaces the nominative/accusative distinction—and already frequently used prepositions as well as the case-endings which they have almost completely replaced: for example, *of Scyttiscum cynne* and *mid hearpum.* Burchfield rejected the notion of Scandinavian influence:

> In passing I should mention that some scholars have inclined to the view that the mixing of the Scandinavian dialects and those of the Anglo-Saxons produced a kind of creolized (flexionless) English as the two sets of people sought to understand each other by ignoring inflexions, and that this mutilated kind of discourse led to the loss of grammatical gender and the emergence of new patterns of accidence in the post-Conquest period. This view, which supposes a period, however temporary, of creolized and virtually illiterate speech, cannot be sustained. It is much more likely that the linguistic changes of the period 900 to 1200 result from an increasing social acceptance of informal and unrecorded types of English, which, for convenience, I have called Vulgar Old English. These informal types of English emerged because of the instability of the Old English declensional system itself—it seems to have had too few clearly distinguishable case endings to bring out the necessary relationships between words. Moreover, lying ready at hand was a set of powerful but insufficiently exploited prepositions.[4]

We cannot deny the existence of 'Vulgar' or (as I prefer to call it in the passage which follows) colloquial Old English:

> That there were colloquial forms of Old English seems certain. But these are not recorded in our manuscripts, which are concerned on the whole with topics removed from everyday life—charters, wills, learned works of history and theology, sermons, and poems—and are mostly written by linguistically conservative scribes. There is the possibility that, in the words of Lebow, the Anglo-Saxon Chronicle 'was kept by men who wrote as they spoke and who spoke in a manner much more modern than the other writers of the time indicate' (see *OES* i, p. lviii). Some light might also be thrown on colloquial OE usages by working back from more nearly colloquial ME documents (ibid.). But these usages are largely irrecoverable.[5]

We cannot deny the influence of colloquial Old English, even though it is 'largely irrecoverable'. But I cannot believe that this influence alone was sufficient to trigger off or cause or speed up (however one cares to put it)

[4] R. Burchfield, *The English Language* (Oxford and New York, 1985), 13–14.

[5] B. Mitchell, *On Old English* (Oxford and New York, 1988), 341. (For *OES* see n. 11 below.)

the fundamental changes with which we are concerned. As Shippey wrote in his review of Burchfield's book, apropos of Burchfield's dismissal of the theory of Scandinavian influence, 'he simply disregards the phenomena that fit it—like the relative linguistic conservatism of the south and west, or the prominent irruption of Norse even into the English personal pronouns, like "she" or "they" . . .'.[6] This is a telling point. We cannot deny the relevance of Scandinavian influence.

§3. I would further argue that Burchfield oversimplifies—or indeed fails to state—what I have called the traditional view by concentrating on those expositions of it which introduce the concept of 'creole'. He is not to blame for introducing this concept. But the fact that those changes in the English language which did occur need not—or indeed, as will become plain below, could not—have involved creolization, does not dispose of the theory of Scandinavian influence. As I see it, Burchfield is to blame for not pointing this out.

§4. To adapt Romaine's remark (§1 above), it would be futile, in my opinion, to continue a debate about the prospect of uncovering creole origins for Old and Middle English; Görlach's article 'Middle English—a creole?' has put a decisive end to the discussion.[7] He rightly observed that

> a serious treatment of the question raised in the title is made difficult by the fact that the term 'creole' is used quite vaguely by some scholars; others have redefined it to make it satisfy the specific needs of their arguments. This appears to be the case, in particular, with one article which has caused some stir, but which, owing to poor organization, contradictory arguments, and selective data (often taken from inappropriate registers, and disregarding frequencies, chronological distributions and social functions of individual features), and finally owing to an idiosyncratic redefinition of the term 'creole', remains obscure even after repeated readings. I am speaking of Bailey and Maroldt's 'The French lineage of English' (1977).
>
> In order to test the validity of the claim that Middle English can be called a creole, one must therefore start afresh.[8]

This fresh start led Görlach to conclude that

> unless simplification and language mixture are thought to be sufficient criteria for the definition of a creole or creoloid (and I do not think they are, since this would make most languages of the world creoles, and the term would consequently lose its distinctiveness), then Middle English does not appear to be a creole.[9]

He gave short shrift to any possibility of creolization through Latin or the

[6] T. A. Shippey, *Times Literary Supplement* (22 Mar. 1985), 306.

[7] M. Görlach, 'Middle English—a Creole?', *Linguistics across Historical and Geographical Boundaries in Honour of Jacek Fisiak on the Occasion of his Fiftieth Birthday*, vol. i, ed. D. Kastovsky and A. Szwedek (Berlin, New York, and Amsterdam, 1986), 329–44.

[8] Ibid. 330.

[9] Ibid. 335.

Celtic languages. His examination of French as a possible candidate resulted thus:

> I am not aware of any texts that could justify the assumption that there was a stable pidgin or creole English in use in 13th-century French households. Even if such forms did exist as short-lived phenomena, they are very unlikely to have carried any prestige, an assumption that would be necessary to explain any possible adoption of such garbled English as a model for native speakers of English, and in consequence creolization of the language.[10]

I accept Görlach's dismissal of French influence. I have said elsewhere that Bailey and Maroldt 'seem to me guilty of both over-simplification and exaggeration in their assessment of that influence',[11] and in any event the real damage (if that is the right word) had been done before the thirteenth century.

§5. Görlach then turned his attention to what he calls 'the most plausible case ... the Scandinavian dialects in the Danelaw area'. On this subject he wrote:

> What is found in the development of English between the 10th and 14th centuries can be explained as a reduction of redundancy inherent in the Old English system (cf. Görlach 1974/1982: 61–62), but the geographical spread of innovative features illustrates that the special needs of communication in the Danelaw triggered off or speeded up changes in English that might otherwise have taken much longer to happen:
>
> 1. the loss of grammatical gender (which often diverged in Old English : Old Danish);
> 2. the expansion of the class of strong masculines in noun inflection (the class existed, and was well marked, in Old Danish);
> 3. the loss of inflection in articles and adjectives, but only a regularization of the inflection of nouns.
>
> All these developments are first recorded from the East Midlands, from where they spread south: Kent preserved traces of grammatical gender, inflection of articles etc. well into the 14th century. It is also significant that Middle English did not lose, as would be expected in a 'proper' creole, gender and case in pronouns, number in nouns, personal endings and tense markers in verbs; it retained the passive and did not replace tense by aspect. The development of Middle English is, then, in many cases away from the typical pidgin and creole features.[12]

If we add to this account the fact that SVO order and prepositions were waiting in the wings or already on stage (see §2 above), we have a useful statement of the traditional view. On this point Clark has written of the *Peterborough Chronicle* 1070–1154:

[10] Ibid. 337.
[11] *Old English Syntax* (Oxford, 1985), ii. 1007. Abbreviated in this article to *OES*.
[12] Görlach, 'Middle English—a Creole?', 340–1.

The syntax of the Peterborough Continuations is, then, at a very revealing stage: before our eyes English is beginning to change from a synthetic language to an analytic one. And what can be perceived of the chronological relationships between the various changes is significant. Contrary to the view that it was the previous existence of analytic machinery which brought about loss of inflexion, inflexional loss here seems to be more advanced than the procedures needed to replace it. Noun-inflexions are virtually reduced to the Modern-English level, whereas the analytic procedures destined to supply their place—fixed word-order, prepositional constructions—are only partially developed. It would be rash to deduce too much: this is only one text among many, and its evidence is not clear-cut. Such as it is, however, the evidence suggests that loss of the dative case, for instance, takes place rather in spite of a lack of substitute procedures than because its functions had already been usurped by them.[13]

This last statement is based on her findings that in this part of the *Chronicle* it is mainly sense, not inflexion or element order, which distinguishes between direct and indirect objects, e.g. 1070.11 ... *se cyng heafde gifen þet abbotrice an frencisce abbot* (is *-e* in *frencisce* a dative?), 1114.33 ... *þa geaf se cyng þone abbotrice an munec of Sæis (þone* accusative), and 1132.10 *7 Te king iaf ðat abbotrice an prior of Sancte Neod* (no inflexions);[14] *OES* §1210 is relevant to this problem. There is plenty of room here for solid work as opposed to hollow speculation about the underlying element order of Old English and Middle English.

§6. One final point remains to be made about creolization. In 1982 I wrote thus in *OES*:

With the book at press (October, 1982), I am happy to find myself in agreement with the fundamental conclusions (though not with all the terminology or all the details) of Poussa's important article on 'The evolution of early standard English' (*SAP* 14 (1982), 69–85):

It is argued that the fundamental changes which took place between standard literary OE and Chancery Standard English: loss of grammatical gender, extreme simplification of inflexions and borrowing of form-words and common lexical words, may be ascribed to a creolization with Old Scandinavian during the OE period. The Midland creole dialect could have stabilized as a spoken lingua franca in the reign of Knut. Its non-appearance in literature was due initially to the prestige of the OE literary standard. The influence of French to be seen in ME texts is less fundamental: mainly loanwords. Most of the French influence on syntax and word-formation probably came in during the standardization of the English written language, through the habits of scribes who were accustomed to writing standard Latin and French.[15]

Later, realizing the ambiguity of the phrase 'in agreement with the funda-

[13] *The Peterborough Chronicle 1070–1154*, 2nd edn., ed. C. Clark (Oxford, 1970), pp. lxxiii–lxxiv.

[14] Ibid., p. lxx.

[15] *OES* ii. 1007–8.

mental conclusions'—which could readily be taken to imply my acceptance of the concept of creolization—I wrote the following commentary on Poussa's article:

91 Poussa, Patricia, 'The evolution of early Standard English: the creolization hypothesis', *SAP* 14 (1982), 69–85.

In *OES* ii, pp. 1007–8 (in a passage written while the book was at press), I found myself 'in agreement with the fundamental conclusions (though not with all the terminology or all the details)' of this article. My main reservations can be explained more fully here. They are twofold. First, there is the use of the term, and the concept of, 'creolization'; see my comments on item 96. Second, the proposition that 'the Midland creole dialect could have stabilized as a spoken lingua franca in the reign of Knut' (Poussa, p. 84) remains to be established. But, *pace* Burchfield (item 96), the existence in England of bilingual speech communities involving two Germanic languages—*a phenomenon without parallel, as far as I know, on the Continent*—must have been a major factor in the loss in English of some linguistic phenomena which were common to Old English and Old High German but remain in German.[16]

I must now withdraw the phrase in italics, in view of this report by Görlach:

Haugen (1981: 104) states that Danish lost most of its inflections in the 13th to 15th centuries, the time when the Danes were more or less bilingual, i.e. speakers of Danish and Low German—languages that were largely identical in lexis, but widely divergent in inflections.[17]

Item 96 reads:

96 Burchfield, R. W., *The English Language* (Oxford, 1985).

Rvw: Not cited; see Introduction §v.

Has some valuable comments on colloquial or 'Vulgar' Old English (pp. 4, 13–14, and 138–9) but, by using the phrases 'a kind of creolized (flexionless) English' and 'creolized and virtually illiterate speech' (pp. 13–14), gives what seems to me an unfairly simplistic summary of the theory that 'the mixing of the Scandinavian dialects and those of the Anglo-Saxons' was a major influence in the disappearance of Old English inflexions. In my opinion, this problem might be better tackled without the use—by writers before and after Burchfield—of 'creole', 'creolized', and 'creolization', firstly because these words are used in different ways by different writers and therefore often lead to what are in effect terminological arguments, and secondly because of what I call 'the "Englishness" of English syntax'; see *OES* ii, p. 1007. Further on the possibility of Scandinavian influence see T. A. Shippey, *TLS* March 22 1985, p. 306.[18]

I agree with Görlach when he denied that any of the broken forms of English which may have existed during the relevant period developed into a pidgin

[16] B. Mitchell, *A Critical Bibliography of Old English Syntax* (Oxford, 1990), 28–9.
[17] Görlach, 'Middle English—a Creole?', 340.
[18] Mitchell, *Critical Bibliography*, 30.

and when he said that 'the assumption that Anglo-Scandinavian did, and even rose to become a quasi-standard under the Danish kings of the 11th century (as put forward by Poussa) cannot be substantiated'.[19] Poussa's summary, quoted in full in the passage from *OES* at the beginning of this section, reads in part:

It is argued that the fundamental changes which took place between standard literary OE and Chancery Standard English: loss of grammatical gender, extreme simplification of inflexions and borrowing of form-words and common lexical words, may be ascribed to a creolization with Old Scandinavian during the OE period.[20]

But the concept of creolization is not essential to her basic argument. Had she written (as she could have) at the end of the passage quoted above the words 'may be ascribed to the existence of bilingual societies of Anglo-Saxons and Scandinavians during the Old English period', she would have come close to stating what I have called the traditional view. Peter Hunter Blair's map delineating the Danish settlements in the ninth century[21] and Baugh and Cable's map delineating the East Midland dialect area of Middle English[22] coincide quite remarkably and, as the latter authorities put it,

out of this variety of local dialects there emerged toward the end of the fourteenth century a written language that in the course of the fifteenth won general recognition and has since become the recognized standard in both speech and writing. The part of England that contributed most to the formation of this standard was the East Midland district, and it was the East Midland type of English that became its basis, particularly the dialect of the metropolis, London.[23]

This may serve to explain what I meant by saying in 1982 that I found myself in agreement with Poussa's fundamental conclusions, though not with all the terminology or all the details.

§7. Continuity then—not discontinuity—is my theme. Acceptance of the proposition that Middle English is a creole runs contrary to what I call 'the Englishness of Old English' and 'the Englishness of English syntax'. For the proposition that Middle English is a creole involves acceptance of the idea of discontinuity between the spoken Old English language and the spoken language of later periods and between the language of Old English prose and verse and the prose and verse of later periods. As Görlach persuasively put it,

if Anglians and Scandinavians made successful attempts at communication, their

[19] Görlach, 'Middle English—a Creole?', 332.

[20] Poussa, 'Evolution of Early Standard English', 84.

[21] P. H. Blair, *An Introduction to Anglo-Saxon England* (Cambridge, 1956), 77.

[22] A. C. Baugh and T. Cable, *A History of the English Language* (3rd edn., London, Boston, and Henley, 1978), 190.

[23] Ibid. 191–2.

sons and granddaughters would not have had any difficulty in understanding them. Even in written language, in which the break is marked (the obvious reason for this being the loss of a written standard, which has nothing to do with creolization), there are indications of continuity, ranging from the continuation of the *Peterborough Chronicle* in the 'most progressive' East Midlands to a very smooth transition from written Old English to 13th-century Middle English in the diocese of Worcester. Knowledge of Old English was in fact never completely lost in England. While it is possible to stress the discontinuity in the development of English (and in consequence refuse, like Bailey, to speak of Old English, substituting for it the term 'Anglo-Saxon'), it is at least equally justifiable to stress the continuity of English—the spoken English that was the only means of communication for the majority of the English population, handed on from one generation to the next.[24]

Let me demonstrate this continuity, briefly for the written language and then with examples from the prose and the verse. The spoken language is beyond recall but it is hard to resist the feeling that in such passages as that from the Laud MS (§13) or from *Beowulf* (§16) one can hear the English voice.

§8. That there was continuity in the language itself—despite the replacement of West-Saxon by East Midland as the predominant dialect—cannot be gainsaid. The inflexional system of Modern English is not the same as that of Old English. But Burchfield was right to dismiss the notion that there ever was a stage when the English language was 'flexionless'.[25] Jones, in an important study, has recently shown that there was continuity in the processes involved in the loss of gender.[26] Clark (to name but one scholar) has made the same demonstration for the case and number inflexions of nouns, adjectives, and pronouns,[27] and for the inflexions of person, number, and mood, in verbs.[28] From *OES* §§1093–9 it is clear that the elaborate analytic verbal system of Modern English—including what Shippey called 'the bewildering quadrille of modal verbs and their meanings'[29]—was present in more than embryo in Old English; only those patterns which involve the participles 'being' and 'been' and the auxiliary 'do' were missing. Clark's study has demonstrated beyond doubt the East Midland basis of the language of the Peterborough Continuations:

> Unlike the inscrutably conventional copied annals, the Peterborough Continuations are, in spite of influence from the *Schriftsprache* both on spelling and on grammar, strongly marked by the East-Midland dialect of the district where they were written.

[24] Görlach, 'Middle English—a Creole?', 341.

[25] Burchfield, *English Language*, 13.

[26] C. Jones, *Grammatical Gender in English: 950–1250* (London, New York, and Sydney, 1988).

[27] Clark, *Peterborough Chronicle*, pp. xlviii–xlix, lii–lxii, and lxvi–lxviii.

[28] Ibid. pp. xlvii–xlviii, lii, and lxv.

[29] Shippey, *TLS* (22 Mar. 1985), 306.

This is no less true of the First Continuation than of the Final one, whose East-Midland character seems never to have been questioned....

Morphology shows the East-Midland basis of this language even more clearly than phonology does.[30]

It has also shown that, despite the change of predominant dialect, the word 'continuation' is just as applicable to the linguistic processes involved in the reduction of inflexions as it is to anything else.

§9. For continuity in element order, I am content to rest my case on the following observations which I made in 1965 about element order in the *Peterborough Chronicle*, before I had become convinced that 'word-order' was a term better avoided:

The word-order of the two Continuations therefore contains much which is common to Old and Modern English, much which cannot occur in Modern English, and nothing which cannot be paralleled in Old English. Any claim to modernity must therefore rest on the relative percentages of the different orders and on the extent to which the constructions which were to survive have ousted the others.[31]

I believe that, *mutatis mutandis*, the same could be said of the element order in any transitional or any Middle English text which was not affected by some external influence such as an original in another language.

§10. The syntactical differences between Old English and Modern English are minor compared to the syntactical similarities. Differences in the form of the conjunctions, numerous as they are, are matters of vocabulary. *A Guide to Old English* has this to say:

§141 Important differences between OE and MnE are found in the following:

the position of the negative (§§144.1 and 184.4);
the use of the infinitives (§205);
the uses of moods and tenses of the verb (§§195 ff.);
the resolved tenses and the function of the participles therein (§§199 ff.);
the meaning of 'modal' auxiliaries (§§206 ff.);
agreement (§187);
the meaning and use of prepositions (§§213–214).

§142 Features found in OE, but not in MnE, include

strong and weak forms of the adjective (§§63 and 64);
some special uses of cases (§§188–192);
some special uses of articles, pronouns, and numerals (§§193–194);
the use of a single verb form where MnE would use a resolved tense or mood (§195);
idiomatic absence of the subject (§193.7).[32]

[30] Clark, *Peterborough Chronicle*, pp. xlv and xlvii.

[31] *Neuphilologische Mitteilungen*, 65 (1964), 138.

[32] B. Mitchell and F. C. Robinson, *A Guide to Old English* (4th edn., Oxford, 1986), §§141–2.

It then goes on to observe that the main difficulty of Old English syntax lies, not in the differences described in §§141–2 above, but in the following (all of which it discusses in turn): element order;[33] three difficulties in sentence structure, namely recapitulation and anticipation,[34] the splitting of groups,[35] and correlation;[36] and the syntax of subordinate clauses.[37] But here too there is continuity, as my comment on a doctoral dissertation shows:

872 Armentrout, Ruth Evans, 'The Development of Subordinating Conjunctions in English' (Pennsylvania State diss., 1978; *DAI* 39 (1978), 846A).

The abstract includes the following:

> The purpose of this study is to trace the development in English of the subordinating conjunctions that introduce adverbial subordinate clauses which express relationships such as manner, purpose, and result. On the basis of data collected from approximately thirty Old English and forty Middle English prose texts, the specific linguistic forms used as subordinating conjunctions are described first and then analyzed within a transformational–generative framework. These two earlier stages of English are compared with Modern English to demonstrate that no major structural changes have occurred in the language with respect to the adverb clauses and the conjunctions that introduce them.

I have some sympathy with the idea expressed in the last sentence in that I think that the structure of the Modern English complex sentence—like that of other Modern English sentences—was shaped in the crucible of the Old English language. But I have some difficulty in accepting the phrase 'no major structural changes' as a description of those changes in the forms of conjunctions, in the use of negatives, in the mood of verbs, in element order, and in the arrangement of clauses, which I discuss in the course of chapter VII of *OES*.[38]

But I repeat the opening sentence of this section: 'The syntactical differences between Old English and Modern English are minor compared to the syntactical similarities.'

§11. In the light of what I have so far written, I now make what may seem the startling claim that the factor which above all makes Old English seem a foreign language to those trying to read it today is neither its inflexions nor its element orders nor its syntax but its vocabulary. Let me demonstrate the reason for this claim and for my title 'The Englishness of Old English' with the help of a selection of passages from prose and verse. I offer them first in the original and then in a literal translation which preserves the element order of that original; this will show that, after the vocabulary,

[33] Ibid., §§143–7.
[34] Ibid., §148.
[35] Ibid., §149.
[36] Ibid., §§150–3.
[37] Ibid., §§154–80.
[38] Mitchell, *Critical Bibliography*, 174–5.

the greatest difference between Old English and Modern English is that the former uses the VSO and SOV orders, as well as SVO, in statements. But the reader will also note that the definite or indefinite article is often not expressed. The passages are taken from some of the most studied texts and have been chosen more or less at random on the basis of personal interest and preference. The fact that most editors—wrongly, in my opinion—use modern punctuation may exaggerate the familiarity. But this does not hold for the first two passages in §13.

§12. R. W. Chambers's *On the Continuity of English Prose from Alfred to More and his School* was first published by the Early English Text Society in 1932. Not all the details of his exposition can be accepted. But the basic message is incontrovertible: 'the continuity of English prose'. I begin my demonstration with five passages in the early West-Saxon dialect of the time of King Alfred. The first, composed by the king and written down in his reign, is part of his preface to the *Cura Pastoralis*:

Swæ clæne hio wæs oðfeallenu on Angelcynne ðæt swiðe feawa wæron behionan Humbre ðe hiora ðeninga cuðen understondan on Englisc oððe furðum an ærendgewrit of Lædene on Englisc areccean; 7 ic wene ðæt[te] noht monige begiondan Humbre næren. Swæ feawa hiora wæron ðæt ic furðum anne anlepne ne mæg geðencean besuðan Temese ða ða ic to rice feng. Gode ælmihtegum sie ðonc ðæt[te] we nu ænigne onstal habbað lareowa.[39]

So cleanly she [learning] was fallen away in England that very few were on this side of Humber who their rituals knew how to understand in English or even a letter from Latin into English to translate; and I believe that not many beyond Humber were not. So few of them were that I even one single [one] not can remember south of the Thames when I to throne succeeded. To God Almighty be thanks that we now any supply have of teachers.

I now offer three passages from the Parker Manuscript of the *Anglo-Saxon Chronicle*:

[755] AN. .dcclv. Her Cynewulf benam Sigebryht his rices 7 Westseaxna wiotan for unryhtum dęedum buton Hamtunscire, 7 he hæfde þa oþ he ofslog þone aldormon þe him lengest wunode, 7 hiene þa Cynewulf on Andred adræfde, 7 he þær wunade oþ þæt hiene an swan ofstang æt Pryfetesflodan: 7 he wręc þone aldormon Cumbran. 7 se Cynewulf oft miclum gefeohtum feaht uuiþ Bretwalum. . . . [40]

Year 755. Here Cynewulf deprived Sigebryht of his kingdom, and West Saxons' wise men [*second half of subject*] for wrongful deeds except Hampshire, and he had her [Hampshire] until he slew the alderman [Cumbra] who [with] him longest remained, and him then Cynewulf into the Weald drove, and he there remained until him a

[39] *King Alfred's West-Saxon Version of Gregory's Pastoral Care*, ed. H. Sweet, EETS OS 45 (1871), 3.17–5.1.

[40] *The Anglo-Saxon Chronicle: A Collaborative Edition 3 MS A*, ed. J. M. Bately (Cambridge, 1986), 35.

swineherd stabbed to death at Privett's spring: and he avenged the alderman Cumbra. And that Cynewulf often in great battles fought against Britons.

[784] AN. .dcclxxxiiii. Her Cyneheard ofslog Cynewulf cyning, 7 he þær wearþ ofslægen 7 .lxxxiiii. monna mid him; 7 þa onfeng Beorhtric Wesseaxna rices, 7 he ricsode .xvi. gear, 7 his lic liþ æt Werham, 7 his ryhtfędren cyn gęþ to Cerdice.[41]

Year 784. Here Cyneheard killed Cynewulf king, and he there was slain and 84 men with him; and then received Beorhtric West Saxons' kingdom, and he ruled 16 years, and his body lies at Wareham, and his direct descent on his father's side goes [back] to Cerdic.

[877] AN. .dccclxxvii. Her cuom se here into Escanceastre from Werham, 7 se sciphere sigelede west ymbutan, 7 þa mette hie micel yst on sę, 7 þær forwearþ .cxx. scipa æt Swanawic, 7 se cyning Ęlfred æfter þam gehorsudan here mid fierde rad oþ Exanceaster 7 hie hindan ofridan ne meahte ær hie on þam fæstene wæron, þær him mon to ne meahte, 7 h[i]e him þær foregislas saldon, swa fela swa he habban wolde 7 micle aþas sworon 7 þa godne friþ heoldon; 7 þa on hærfeste gefor se here on Miercna lond 7 hit gedęldon sum 7 sum Ceolwulfe saldon.[42]

Year 877. Here came the enemy army into Exeter from Wareham, and the naval force sailed west about, and then met them a great storm at sea, and there were lost 120 ships at Swanage, and the king Alfred after the mounted army with English army rode as far as Exeter and them from behind ride down not could before they in the fortress were, where them one to not could, and they him there hostages gave, as many as he to have wished and great oaths swore and then firm peace held; and then at harvest time went the enemy army into Mercians' land and it [*object*] shared out some and some to Ceolwulf gave.

And fifthly, we have a powerfully ironical attack on Romulus by the Christian translator of Orosius' *Historia*, for which he is not (as far as I know) indebted to the original Latin:

Swa weorðlice 7 swa mildelice wæs Romeburg on fruman gehalgod, mid broðor blode 7 mid sweora 7 mid Romuluses eame[s] Numetores, þone he eac ofslog, ða he cyning wæs 7 him self siþþan to ðæm rice feng! Þuss gebletsade Romulus Romana rice on fruman: mid his broðor blode þone weall 7 mid þara sweora blode þa ciricean 7 mid his eames blode þæt rice. Ond siþþan his agenne sweor to deaðe beswac, þa he hiene to him aspon 7 him gehet ðæt he his rice wið hiene dælan wolde 7 hiene under ðæm ofslog.[43]

Thus honourably and thus graciously was Rome at beginning hallowed, with brother's blood and with father-in-laws' [blood] and with Romulus' uncle's Numetor's [blood], whom he also killed, when he [Numetor] king was and himself afterwards to the kingdom succeeded! Thus blessed [*verb*] Romulus Romans' kingdom at beginning: with his brother's blood the wall and with the father-in-laws' blood the church [temple] and with his uncle's blood the kingdom. And afterwards [he] his

[41] Ibid. 39.
[42] Ibid. 50.
[43] *The Old English Orosius*, ed. J. Bately, EETS ss 6 (1980), 39.16–24.

own father-in-law to death betrayed, when he him to him allured and him promised that he his kingdom with him share would and him by means of that slew.

§13. Five later prose passages will, I believe, further demonstrate the continuity of English prose. The homilist Ælfric, Abbot of Eynsham, wrote thus of Edmund King and Martyr in the last decade of the tenth century in the late West-Saxon dialect:

Sum swyðe gelæred munuc com suþan ofer sæ fram sancte benedictes stowe on æþelredes cynincges dæge to dunstane ærcebisceope þrim gearum ær he forðferde . and se munuc hatte abbo . þa wurdon hi æt spræce oþþæt dunstan rehte be sancte eadmunde . swa swa eadmundes swurdbora hit rehte æþelstane cynincge þa þa dunstan iung man wæs . and se swurdbora wæs forealdod man . Þa gesette se munuc ealle þa gereccednysse on anre bec . and eft ða þa seo boc com to us binnan feawum gearum þa awende we hit on englisc . swa swa hit heræfter stent. Se munuc þa abbo binnan twam gearum . gewende ham to his mynstre and wearð sona to abbode geset on þam ylcan mynstre.[44]

A very learned monk came from the south over sea from St Benedict's place in Æthelred's king's day to Dunstan archbishop three years before he died and the monk was called Abbo. Then were they in conversation until Dunstan told about St Edmund just as Edmund's swordbearer it told Æthelstan king then when Dunstan young man was and the swordbearer was aged man. Then set the monk all the account in a book and afterwards then when the book came to us within few years then turned we it into English just as it hereafter stands. The monk then Abbo within two years went home to his monastery and was soon to abbot appointed in that same monastery.

Another authentic piece of invective, no doubt nearly contemporary, appears in the early twelfth-century Laud MS of the Anglo-Saxon Chronicle. It enshrines the English voice raised in protest against authority:

1011. Her on þissum geare sende se cyng 7 his witan to ðam here. 7 georndon friðes. 7 him gafol 7 metsunga behetan. wið þam þe hi heora hergunga geswicon.

Hi heafdon þa ofergan East Engla ·i· and East Seaxe ·ii· 7 Middel Seaxe ·iii· 7 Oxena ford scire ·iiii· 7 Grantabrycge scire ·v· 7 Heortford scire ·vi· 7 Bucingaham scire ·vii· 7 Bedanford scire ·viii· 7 healfe Huntadun scire ·x· 7 be suðan Temese ealle Centingas. 7 SuðSeaxe. 7 Hæstingas. 7 Suðrig. 7 Bearruc scire. 7 Hamtun scire. 7 micel on Wiltun scire.

Ealle þas ungesælða us gelumpon þurh unrædes. ꝥmann nolde him to timan gafol bedan. ac þonne hi mæst to yfele gedon hæfdon. þonne nam man grið. 7 frið wið hi. 7 naðe læs for eallum þisum griðe 7 friðe 7 gafole. hi ferdon æghwider folc mælum. 7 hergodon. 7 ure earme folc ræpton 7 slogon.[45]

1011. Here in this year sent the king and his counsellors to the army and asked for

[44] *Ælfric's Lives of Saints*, vol. ii. ed. W. W. Skeat, EETS OS 114 (1900), 314.1–12.

[45] *Two of the Saxon Chronicles Parallel*, vol. i, ed. J. Earle and C. Plummer (Oxford, 1892), 141.

peace and them tribute and provisions promised on condition that they their ravaging should cease.

They had then overrun (i) East Anglia and (ii) Essex and (iii) Middlesex and (iv) Oxfordshire and (v) Cambridgeshire and (vi) Hertfordshire and (vii) Buckinghamshire and (viii) Bedfordshire and (ix) half Huntingdonshire [*other MSS*: and (x) much of Northamptonshire] and south of Thames all Kent and Sussex and Hastings and Surrey and Berkshire and Hampshire and much of Wiltshire.

All these disasters us befell through lack of policy,[46] in that one would not them in time tribute offer but when they most to injury done had then took one [*subject*] peace and truce with them and none the less for all this peace and truce and tribute they went everywhere in bands and harried and our wretched folk [*object*] plundered and killed.

The Parker MS offers the following annal for perhaps the most famous date in English history:

[1066] <AN> ..i^{m}.lxvi. Her forðferde Eaduuard king, 7 Harold eorl feng to ðam rice 7 heold hit .xl. wucena 7 ænne dæg, 7 her com Willelm 7 gewann Ængla land. 7 her on ðison geare barn Cristes cyrce. 7 her atiwede cometa .xiiii. kalendas Mai.[47]

Year 1066. Here died Edward King, and Harold Earl succeeded to the kingdom and held it forty weeks and one day, and here came William and conquered England. And here in this year burnt Christ Church [*subject*] and here appeared comet 18 April.

My last two prose passages come from the *Peterborough Chronicle*, a twelfth-century continuation of the Laud MS. The first of these, written in the East Midland dialect, is accepted as very late Old English:

Millesimo cxx. . . . Syððan heræfter sætte se cyng Henrig his castelas 7 his land on Normandi æfter his willan, 7 swa toforan Aduent hider to lande for. 7 On þam fare wurdon adr[u]ncene þæs cynges twegen sunan Willelm 7 Ricard, 7 Ricard eorl of Ceastre 7 Ottuel his broðor 7 swyðe manega of þæs cynges hired—stiwardas 7 burþenas 7 byrlas 7 of mistlicean wican—7 ungerim swyðe ænlices folces forð mid. Ðysra deað wæs heora freondan twyfealdlic sar: an þet hi swa fearlice þises lifes losedan; oðer þet feawa heora lichaman ahwær syððan fundena wæron.[48]

Year 1120. Then after this disposed the king Henry his castles and his land in Normandy according to his desire, and so before Advent hither to land came. And on that journey were drowned the king's two sons William and Richard, and Richard Earl of Chester and Ottuel his brother and very many of the king's court—stewards and chamberlains and cupbearers and of various offices—and a very great number of excellent people with [them]. Their death was to their friends double grief—one

[46] The word *unrædes*, translated 'lack of policy' (literally 'no counsel' or 'bad counsel'), contains a bitter play on words. The king during this disastrous period was *Æþelræd*, literally 'noble counsel'. So *Æþelræd Unræd*, now known as Ethelred the Unready, may have been 'Noble counsel, No counsel' or 'Noble counsel, Bad counsel' to his subjects.

[47] *The Anglo-Saxon Chronicle*, 83.

[48] *Clark, Peterborough Chronicle*, 40.4–41.13.

that they so suddenly this life lost; other that few of their bodies anywhere afterwards found were.

And finally we have an extract from the last entry in the Anglo-Saxon Chronicle, written in the East Midland dialect in what is unquestionably Middle English:

Millesimo cliiii. On þis gær wærd þe king Stephne ded 7 bebyried þer his wif 7 his sune wæron bebyried æt Fauresfeld; þæt minstre hi makeden. Þa þe king was ded, þa was þe eorl beionde sæ; 7 ne durste nan man don oþer bute god for þe micel eie of him. Þa he to Engleland com, þa was he underfangen mid micel wurtscipe, 7 to king bletcæd in Lundene on þe Sunnendæi beforen Midwintre Dæi, 7 held þære micel curt.[49]

Year 1154. On this year was the king Stephen dead and buried where his wife and his son were buried at Faversham; that minster they had made. When the king was dead, then was the earl beyond sea; and not dared no man do other but good for the great awe of him. When he to England came, then was he received with great honour, and as king consecrated in London on the Sunday before Christmas, and held there great court.

§14. Even though Old English metre, with its long line consisting of two half-lines or verses linked by alliteration, differs fundamentally from the metres of Modern English verse, we need not restrict the continuity of language to English prose. The passages which follow give striking testimony to the fact that Old English is English.

§15. *Cædmon's Hymn* is the first extant Old English poem which uses the alliterative line for Christian purposes. It was sung between 657 and 680, when Hild was Abbess of Whitby. Bede gives a Latin paraphrase of it in his *Ecclesiastical History* and the earliest Old English text—the Northumbrian version printed on the left—appears on the last page of the Moore manuscript, written *c.*737. A later West-Saxon version is given after it.

Northumbrian version

Nu scylun hergan   hefaenricaes uard,
metudæs maecti   end his modgidanc,
uerc uuldurfadur,   sue he uundra gihuaes,
eci dryctin,   or astelidæ.
He aerist scop   aelda barnum
heben til hrofe,   haleg scepen,
tha middungeard;   moncynnæs uard,
eci dryctin,   æfter tiadæ
firum foldu,   frea allmectig.[50]

[49] Ibid. 60.1–7.

[50] *The Anglo-Saxon Minor Poems*, ed. E. van K. Dobbie, Anglo-Saxon Poetic Records, 6 (New York, 1942), 105.

West-Saxon version

Nu sculon herigean   heofonrices weard,
meotodes meahte   and his modgeþanc,
weorc wuldorfæder,   swa he wundra gehwæs,
ece drihten,   or onstealde.
He ærest sceop   eorðan bearnum
heofon to hrofe,   halig scyppend,
þa middangeard;   moncynnes weard,
ece drihten,   æfter teode
firum foldan,   frea ælmihtig.[51]

Now [they] must worship Heaven-Kingdom's Guardian, Creator's might and His purpose, [they] the works of God, because He of wonders of each, Eternal Lord, origin ordained. He first shaped for men's sons [*W-S* earth's sons] heaven as a roof, Holy Creator, then earth; mankind's Guardian, Eternal Lord, after furnished for men earth, Lord Almighty.

The Ruthwell Cross, now generally dated late seventh or early eighth century, contains rune passages which go back to the same original as *The Dream of the Rood* or which were used by the author of that poem. I translate only those passages which offer some continuity. They should be compared with *The Dream of the Rood* ll. 39–56 in §17 below.

I

[..]geredæ hinæ ḡod alme3ttig,
þa he walde on ḡalḡu gistiḡa,
[.]o*d*ig f[. . . . . . .] men.
[.]u*g*[. . . . .]

II

[. . . .] ic riicnæ k̄yniŋc,
hêafunæs h*l*afard, *h*ælda ic ni dorstæ.
*B*ismæræ*d*u uŋk̄et men ba æt*g*ad[..];
ic [. . .] *m*iþ blodæ [.]ist*e*mi[.],
bi[. . . . .]

III

Krist wæs on rodi.
Hweþræ þer fus*æ* fêarran kwomu
*æ*þþilæ til anum. Ic þæt al bi[. . . .].
S[. . .] ic w[.]s mi[.] so[.]ḡum gi*d*rœ[..]d,
h[.]a*ḡ* [. . . . .]

IV

*m*iþ stre*l*um giwundad.
Alegdun hiæ *h*inæ limwœrignæ,
gistoddu[.] him [. . . . . .]i*c*æs [..]f[..]m;
[. . .]êa[.]du[..]i[.] þe[. . . . .
. . . .][52]

[51] Ibid. 106.
[52] Ibid. 115.

I

'[un]clothed him[self] God Almighty,
when He wished on gallows to climb,
. . .
. . .'

II

'[Raised] I powerful king [*object*],
Heaven's Lord, bow I not dared.
Mocked us two men [*subject*] both together;
. . .
. . .'

III

'Christ was on rood.
However there eager ones from far came
noble together. . . .
. . .
. . .

IV

'with arrows wounded.
Laid they him limb-weary,stood by him . . .
. . .
. . .'

§16. The *Beowulf* poet puts the following dramatic speech in the mouth of an old Heathobard warrior, a survivor of previous battles between the Heathobards and the Danes. The occasion is the feast to celebrate the marriage, designed to settle this feud, between Freawaru daughter of Hrothgar, King of the Danes, and the young Heathobard king Ingeld, son of King Froda, who had been slain in battle by the Danes. The old warrior feels shamed and dishonoured as he watches the carousing and skilfully increases the pressure phrase by phrase on the son of a friend and former comrade who was also slain by the Danes, until the young man revives the blood feud by killing one of the Danes at the feast.

'Meaht ðu, min wine, mece gecnawan
þone þin fæder to gefeohte bær
under heregriman hindeman siðe,
dyre iren, þær hyne Dene slogon,
weoldon wælstowe, syððan Wiðergyld læg,
æfter hæleþa hryre, hwate Scyldungas?
Nu her þara banena byre nathwylces
frætwum hremig on flet gæð,
morðres gylpeð, ond þone maðþum byreð
þone þe ðu mid rihte rædan sceoldest.'[53]

[53] *Beowulf and Judith*, ed. E. van K. Dobbie, Anglo-Saxon Poetic Records, 4 (New York, 1953), 63.

'Canst thou, my friend, sword recognize which thy father to battle bore under helmet for last time, precious weapon, where him Danes slew, controlled battlefield, when Withergyld lay dead, after fall of heroes, brave Danes [*subject of* controlled]? Now here of those slayers son of one or another, in trappings rejoicing in hall struts, of killing boasts, and that treasure wears which thou by right own shouldst.'

§17. I conclude with this starkly paratactic passage from *The Dream of the Rood* or (less traditionally and less misleadingly) *A Vision of the Cross.* It is part of the confession by the Cross of the part it played in the Crucifixion. The Cross sees Christ as a man, as a heroic king, and as the Son of God.

Ongyrede hine þa geong hæleð —þæt wæs god ælmihtig!—
strang ond stiðmod. Gestah he on gealgan heanne,
modig on manigra gesyhðe, þa he wolde mancyn lysan.
Bifode ic þa me se beorn ymbclypte. Ne dorste ic hwæðre bugan to eorðan,
feallan to foldan sceatum, ac ic sceolde fæste standan.
Rod wæs ic aræred. Ahof ic ricne cyning,
heofona hlaford, hyldan me ne dorste.
Þurhdrifan hi me mid deorcan næglum. On me syndon þa dolg gesiene,
opene inwidhlemmas. Ne dorste ic hira nænigum sceððan.
Bysmeredon hie unc butu ætgædere. Eall ic wæs mid blode bestemed,
begoten of þæs guman sidan, siððan he hæfde his gast onsended.
Feala ic on þam beorge gebiden hæbbe
wraðra wyrda. Geseah ic weruda god
þearle þenian. Þystro hæfdon
bewrigen mid wolcnum wealdendes hræw,
scirne sciman; sceadu forðeode
wann under wolcnum. Weop eal gesceaft,
cwiðdon cyninges fyll. Crist wæs on rode.[54]

Undressed himself then young hero—that was God Almighty!—strong and resolute. Climbed He on gallows high, brave in many [men]'s sight, because He wished mankind to save. Trembled I when me the warrior embraced. Not dared I however bow to earth, fall to ground's surface, but I had to stand fast. Rood was I raised. Raised I powerful king, Heavens' Lord, bow myself not dared [I]. Pierced they me with dark nails. On me are the wounds visible, open malicious wounds. Not dared I of them none injure. Mocked they us two both together. All I was with blood made wet, drenched from the man's side, after He had His spirit sent forth. Much I on the hill endured have of cruel events. Saw I hosts' God cruelly stretched. Darkness had covered with clouds Ruler's corpse, bright radiance; shadow went forth dark under clouds. Wept all creation, lamented king's death. Christ was on Rood.

§18. Old English is where the English language began. It is where English prose began. It is where one tributary of the great river of English poetry began. So its place in any university English syllabus ought to be assured. As William L'Isle said in 1623 in his preface to *A Saxon Treatise Concerning the Old and New Testament,*

[54] *The Vercelli Book*, ed. G. P. Krapp, Anglo-Saxon Poetic Records, 2 (New York, 1932), 62.

I hold the knowledge of this old English, and any good matter of humanity therein written, but diuinity above all, worthy to be preserued.... What Englishman of vnderstanding is there, but may be delighted to see, the prety shifts our tongue made with her owne store, in all parts of learning, when they scorned to borrow words of another? Albeeit now sithence wee haue taken that liberty which our neighbours doe; and to requite them more then for need, our language is improued above all others now spoken by any nation, and became the fairest, the nimblest, the fullest; most apt to vary the phrase, most ready to receiue good composition, most adorned with sweet words and sentences, with witty quips and ouer-ruling Prouerbes: yea able to expresse any conceit whatsoeuer with great dexterity; waighty in weighty matters, merry in merry, braue in braue.... But sure to neglect the beginnings of such an excellent tongue, will bring vpon vs the foule disgrace not onely of ignorance... but of extreme ingratitude towards our famous ancestors, who left vs so many, so goodly monuments in their old Dialect recorded.[55]

[55] Quoted from E. N. Adams, *Old English Scholarship in England from 1566–1800*, Yale Studies in English, 55 (1917), 144–5.

Line-End Hyphens in the Ormulum *Manuscript (MS Junius 1)*

ROBERT BURCHFIELD

The essay that follows is based on some work I did on the *Ormulum* about 1956, by which time I had completed a fresh transcription of MS Junius 1 and was preparing the text for publication by the Early English Text Society. The essential points were to form part of the Introduction to this edition and will do so when I resume work on the edition. It seems appropriate now to offer this fragment as a tribute to my oldest friend in Oxford.[1]

In what follows reference is made to the seventeenth-century Dutch scholar, Jan van Vliet. For further details of van Vliet's work on MS Junius 1 readers are referred to my article '*Ormulum*: Words copied by Jan van Vliet from parts now lost', in *English and Medieval Studies presented to J. R. R. Tolkien on the Occasion of his Seventieth Birthday*, ed. Norman Davis and C. L. Wrenn (London, 1962), 94–111.

The general picture

MS Junius 1 is one of the earliest vernacular manuscripts in which a hyphen is more or less regularly employed at the line-end to indicate that a word is incomplete. The scribes of Old English manuscripts generally observed the normal contemporary conventions of syllabic division at the line-end, but usually did not employ a hyphen. In Junius 1 it is used almost invariably, and when it is not, it is nearly always because there was insufficient room at the edge of the manuscript. In some places it has been removed when the edges of the sheets were trimmed. The remaining instances where a hyphen is lacking are relatively few—e.g.[2] *bru/kenn* 4191, *wi/terrliȝ* 4990, *hæ/þenn*

[1] Eric Stanley and I were contemporaries as undergraduates. He went on to edit *The Owl and the Nightingale* (1960), and then to embark on an ambitious series of articles and books on Old English. My work on *A Supplement to the OED* and other Oxford dictionaries took me almost completely away from medieval studies for more than thirty years. The dictionary work is done, and, when I have completed my new edition of Fowler's *Modern English Usage* (1926), I hope to resume work on the *Ormulum.*

[2] The oblique stroke signifies that *bru* occurs at the end of a line in the manuscript with no hyphen and that the remainder of the word, namely *kenn*, appears at the beginning of the next line in the manuscript. Similarly in the other examples.

5036, *stann/denn* 9013—and may safely be regarded as oversights. In a few cases it is possible that lightly made hyphens have simply faded out.

Hyphens inserted by van Vliet

In many instances where Orm did not use a hyphen, one has been added by van Vliet. His pale greenish ink is unmistakable; moreover, his hyphen is almost always short and straight, and not at all like the medieval hyphen with its long sweep and curved-up right-hand end. A few of these are obvious corrections, supplied where Orm against his usual practice had omitted one, e.g. *bi-limmpeþþ* 1657, *cwenn-kenn* 19531, *drihh-tin* 5237, *i-noh* 10426. But more important are those of van Vliet's which occur in places where medieval taste concerning word-division differed from modern taste (even that of the seventeenth century). Thus *inn till* and *all swa* were always written as two words by the original scribe, and no hyphen is used when they are separated by the end of a line in the manuscript. But van Vliet has several times inserted one in these words, no doubt because he wrote 'until' and 'also' himself, not 'un til' and 'al so'. The main words of this type in which van Vliet inserted a hyphen where Orm had none are *all swa*, *inn till*, *mann kinn*, and *onn ȝæn*.

A partial guide to word-division

The original medieval hyphens provide a useful partial guide for establishing word-division in this text. Its presence or absence enables us to ascertain whether Orm regarded such combinations as *affterrwarrd*, *soþfasst*, *himm sellf*, and *middell ærd* as one word or two, where the evidence of word-division within the line is ambiguous. Within the line he writes freely, usually running many words together, or leaving them apart, fairly arbitrarily. For example, it would not be possible to record in a modern transcription the varying amounts of space between the elements of such a combination as *all all swa summ*. Each of the groupings *allallswasumm*, *all allswasumm*, *allall swasumm*, and *allallswa summ* is found, and the space between them, where there is one, is by no means constant. In the same way it would be absurd to transcribe line 8042 (a line chosen almost at random) as

Allonnanoþerrwise

simply because in the manuscript each word is joined to the next. The regular absence of a hyphen when such a group as *all all swa summ* is divided by the end of a manuscript line (at any of the three possible places) is a safe guide to the scribe's intentions. The same consideration makes it plain that line 8042 should be transcribed as

All onn an oþerr wise

On this basis it has been possible to compile a list of words of at least two elements which are treated by Orm as one word (list A); a second one of words which later, or in other contemporary manuscripts, coalesced as one word but which are kept separate in Orm (list B); and finally a list of words in which the hyphen is used inconsistently (list C).

By adopting the divisions used by Orm himself, at least those in words in lists A and B, a more satisfactory text can be arrived at than those that have been printed in the past. White and Holt, the editors of the standard edition of 1878, simply followed nineteenth-century conventions of word-division. Similarly, J. A. W. Bennett, in *Early Middle English Verse and Prose* (1966), regularized Orm's word-division to follow modern conventions.

For the relatively few words which have inconsistent hyphenation in the manuscript, it seems best to adopt the form that is the more common. For example, *onn/ȝæn* is found sixteen times and *onn-ȝæn* only once. It therefore seems right to adopt *onn/ȝæn* as the regular form and to relegate the hyphen in *onn-ȝæn* 6414 to a footnote. Similarly, because the prefix *bi* is joined by a hyphen to its stem more than sixty times, and left separate only six times, it seems best to transcribe all compounds containing the prefix *bi* as one word not two.

Yet even in a large manuscript like Junius 1, some words do not happen to occur at the line-end a sufficient number of times for a norm to be established. In a few words, too, the hyphen is employed or omitted without any obvious preference. Words of these two types include:

(*a*) Insufficient evidence: *att* (prefix), *læs* (suffix), *miss* (prefix), *orr* (prefix), *shipe* (suffix), *to* (prefix), *ummbe* (prefix).

(*b*) Inconsistent: *all mahhtiȝ*, *crisstenn dom* (and a few other words with the suffix *dom*), *forr* (prefix), *full wel*, *oferr* (prefix), *þwerrt üt*. For these words I have so far usually adopted (or imposed) a norm (see list C), but a certain amount of inconsistency is inevitable.

The three lists

The three lists are as follows:

A. Words that are regularly hyphenated when they are divided at the end of a line in the manuscript include:

affterr-warrd
annd-swere
bi-forenn
bi-limmpeþþ
bi-tacnedd
bi-twenenn
brerd-full
brid-ȳume(ss)
forrþ-rihht
forrþ-warrd
-full (*suffix*)
ᵹodd-cunndnesse
ᵹodd-spell
ȝe-hatenn
inn-warrd (liȝ)
i-noh
i-whillc
-leȝȝc (*suffix*)
-liȝ/-like (*suffixes*)
-nesse (*suffix*)
onn-fasst
rihht-wis(e)
soþ-fasst
to-warrd (*unhyphenated* 5038)
unn- (*prefix*)
unnderr-fanᵹenn
unnderr-stanndenn
wiþþ-stanndenn

Note: The list is not quite watertight. For example, in line 10426 Orm wrote *i/noh* and van Vliet inserted the missing hyphen.

B. Words and phrases not hyphenated when divided by the end of a line in the manuscript include:

all + adverb
all alls
all all swa summ
all rihht
all swa
all swa summ
forr to
forr þatt
forþ wiþþ
full + adv. or adj.
inn till
læredd follc
læwedd follc
mann kinn
middell ærd
onn ȝæn
paterr nossterr
pron. + sellf(enn) (himm sellf(enn), hemm sellfenn, etc.)
swa summ
swa þatt
þær affterr
þær inne
þær þurrh
upp o(nn)
ut off
wha se
wiþþ utenn.

Note: Exceptions are rare, e.g. *forr þatt* is hyphenated once (15183) in error, as is *mann kinn* (6792).

C. Words and phrases inconsistently hyphenated when divided by the end of a line in the manuscript. It is not surprising to find that then, as now, hyphenation was not always settled. Examples include:

-dom (*suffix*): crisstenn-dom, hæþenn-dom, haliȝ-dom, kine-dom each written with and without a hyphen with approximately equal frequency.

forr- (*prefix*): forr-blendedd, forr-buȝhenn, etc. Such formations are written 35 times with a hyphen and 18 times with none.

forr þi: with hyphen 4 occurrences, no hyphen 19 occurrences.

full wel: with hyphen 3 occurrences, no hyphen 10 occurrences.

ꝺoddspell-wrihhte(ss): with hyphen 8 occurrences, no hyphen 2 occurrences.

By allowing frequency to be the governing factor the following forms are postulated as those most likely to be favoured by Orm:

all mahhtiȝ	onnfon
forr þi	onnꝺann
forr þi þatt	onn ȝæn
full wel	onn ȝæness
ꝺoddspellwrihhte	þwerrt üt
lerninnꝺcnihht	uppwarrd
oferrcumenn	werelldshipess
onnfasst	

In practice, in all cases where the reading in the text is not that in the manuscript itself, details will be provided in a textual footnote.

Notes on special cases

(*a*) In two places Orm divides a word (in both cases personal names) across two *verse*-lines: *a-Aroness* 487–8; *ele-Azar* 583–4.

(*b*) Orm's hyphen is almost always a single stroke. I have noted only two examples of a double hyphen: *Hæ=lennde* 9217, *þeȝȝ=re* 10317. In *crisstenn/dom* 5306 and *ꝺoddspell/boc* 5323, van Vliet has inserted a double hyphen; and in *hely-sew* 5210 he has added a second hyphen.

(*c*) Many of the hyphens originally written by the main hand have faded, and have been inked over by van Vliet: e.g. in *nico-dem* 17071, *trow-wenn* 17074, *ha-liȝ* 17120, etc. These examples will be noted in the textual footnotes at the appropriate places.

(*d*) In a few places the hyphen at the line-end serves as a warning of elision. Thus *7 baþe-/hemm fell to þolenn wa* 897 (note that *h* never prevents elision in Orm). Other examples occur in *son se-/himm* 9929 and *son se-/hiss*

12440. There is a similar use in *forr-/tunnbindenn* 12703, where *forr-* is perhaps a warning to the reader not to expect the normal form *forr to* but the rare *forr* + *t* prefixed to the infinitive.

(*e*) *þehhtenn-daȝȝ* 4372 (for *þehhtenn-de daȝȝ*) is a natural type of scribal error.

(*f*) *whær-/o lande summ* 17892: the hyphen is perhaps used because of the tmesis *whær . . summ.*

(*g*) There are a fairly large number of instances of the type *all-le, kinn-ne.* These are usually regarded as scribal errors, but it is possible that the doubled consonant at the line-end has a function analogous to that of a catchword at the page-end. Alternatively it may have been a convention adopted as a safeguard against false pronunciation: it is as well to bear in mind that in Orm's orthography *kin-* signified /ki:n/. He may therefore have adopted the device of writing *kinn-/ne* to emphasize the shortness of the stem vowel. In all such instances the normal forms will be given in the text, and details of the seemingly aberrant forms will be given in textual footnotes. One curiosity is that in four places *nnn* (i.e. triple *n*) is written in mid-line instead of *nn*, e.g. *mennnisscnesse* 7461.

Conclusion

It is not claimed that an analysis of Orm's practice at line-ends solves all the problems of word-division when transcribing the text of this most difficult and complicated manuscript. All that can be said is that it seems desirable to keep as close as possible to the plain intentions of the author. When his practice is either not clear or inconsistent these facts and their implications should be made clear in the textual footnotes and in the glossary. Meanwhile one can but hope that someone will soon produce a facsimile of the manuscript so that all the idiosyncratic details of MS Junius 1 will become freely available without resort to the precious manuscript itself.

The Paradox of the Archaic and the Modern in Laȝamon's Brut

DEREK BREWER

Story-telling is a human characteristic. In some circles nowadays all cognitive activity and explanation is summed up as story-telling: 'strange though this may seem, many able philosophers and sociologists now believe that scientific explanations can never be more than stories, and that notions of scientific "fact" and "discovery" are merely aids which scientists use in heightening the dramatic effect of their own theatrical performance'.[1] A good many scientists would hotly dispute this, and the very formulation of the proposition here suggests its dubiety. Literary historians will recall the long history of the struggle to distinguish 'fiction' from 'lies', a distinction in modern times rendered even more difficult by consciously distorted or supplemented 'documentaries' or 'factions'. The problem of the status of any kind of discourse in relation to the universe of non-discourse is at the heart of all intellectual activity, and consequently of how we live. Its ramifications are infinite, but the problem can be rapidly brought down to the particular case of literary narrative and so to what I have called traditional story.

Traditional stories, that is, stories repeated from one narrator to another, exist in all societies. They have a necessary social function, even in the advanced societies of today, but they are a specially noticeable element in the literary culture of earlier stages of society. Stories perform many different functions more or less related to deeper compulsions in the self or society, from religious myth taken as absolute truth to trivial anecdotes which make no truth-claim but establish certain social perceptions and interpersonal links. As history they are particularly important for articulating the sense of society and the individual's participation in it. Medieval traditional stories dealing with historical events are of special interest in literary history because they make some claim to deal with 'objective' events, and yet are so varied in telling and interpretation. Variation with repetition is a characteristic of traditional narrative of all kinds. The repetition is inherent in the nature of repeating a known story, or at least in the absence of any claim to invention

[1] L. Hudson and B. Jacot, *The Way Men Think: Intellect, Intimacy and the Erotic Imagination* (New Haven, Conn. and London, 1991), 14.

or originality in telling the story. Variation is inherent in the desire to explain or make more vivid. Here the inherent instability in the notion of a story has full play. Moreover, medieval authors consciously or otherwise played with the relation of their own version both to previous versions and to what some might think of as 'objective truth'. Of all this Laȝamon's *Brut* is a most interesting specific example. The description attributed above by Hudson and Jacot to what some 'able philosophers and sociologists' think scientists are up to might with little adjustment be applied to Laȝamon. He is undoubtedly a story-teller; he participates emotionally in the action; he invents and dramatizes; yet he, like the scientists, seems in his earnestness to be aiming at some kind of truth. Moreover, he is creating a new, contemporary truth because his story is about consciousness of the past.

Of course for modern readers there is no question of the historical truth of Laȝamon's story. For us it is historical fantasy, purely a work of art, a fiction. It is as such we consider it. We are well enough aware that works of fiction have their own truths, to estimate which involves consideration of the apparent and less apparent aims of the writer, the nature of the 'text' (itself an ambiguous entity), and so forth. For Laȝamon, he assures us, his story is 'true'. For us, one approach is to ask ourselves what kind of truth did it hold for Laȝamon? When we note how often he consciously alters his main and effectively only source, Wace's *Le Roman de Brut*, we naturally wish to understand what Laȝamon thought he was doing. The question becomes more and more complex when we consider the nature of translation, which can have so many different relations to the original. No text exists entirely on its own; a translation by definition is more or less closely related to another text. The 'intertextuality' of the *Brut* offers a series of fascinating problems and pleasures. At the heart of all these problems lies the unequivocal pleasure of the 'story', that multiple-layered, richly suggestive, elusive entity composed of unnumbered particulars, which generates all these other pleasures and problems. Laȝamon's *Brut*, rather neglected these days, is a fascinating nexus of narrative pleasures and the questions they raise.[2]

[2] The fundamental study is now F. H. M. Le Saux, *Laȝamon's 'Brut': The Poem and its Sources*, Arthurian Studies, 29 (Cambridge, 1989) which magisterially covers all the basic literary historical aspects, and a comprehensive bibliography up to 1988. The language is studied by G. C. Mercatanti, *Il 'Brut' di Laȝamon: Analisi Linguistica e Paleografica, condotta sul MS B.M. Cotton Caligula A IX*, Studi di Anglistica Collana Diretta da Luisa Conti Camaiora (Del Bianco Editore; no place of publication notified, 1988). J. S. P. Tatlock, *The Legendary History of Britain* (Berkeley and Los Angeles, 1950) remains indispensable. The problems of the relation of medieval historical narrative to 'truth' are learnedly discussed by Ruth Morse, *Truth and Convention in the Middle Ages: Rhetoric, Representation and Reality* (Cambridge, 1991). The problems of the nature of translation are discussed by Le Saux and Morse and even more elaborately by Rita Copeland, *Rhetoric, Hermeneutics and Translation in the Middle Ages*

The pleasures and the puzzles start at the very beginning of the *Brut* with its extraordinary Prologue, to which I can find nothing quite comparable in French or English vernaculars of its time, which I take to be, following E. G. Stanley, somewhere roughly in the first two-thirds of the thirteenth century.[3]

As is well known, the poem survives in two manuscripts. The first, fuller form, accurate but not autograph, is BL MS Cotton Caligula A.IX; the second, something of an abbreviation, is BL MS Cotton Otho C.XIII. The two manuscripts are now thought to have been written not far apart in time, and Mercatanti, the most recent commentator, agrees on a date for the writing of the Caligula manuscript between 1280 and 1300. She locates the dialect, as we might expect, since Laȝamon himself tells us that he was priest at Areley Kings in Herefordshire, to the area of the county of Hereford, north Worcestershire, and Shropshire.[4] The Caligula manuscript is therefore close in dialect, area, and in time to Laȝamon's own composition.

Laȝamon in his unique Prologue is charmingly enthusiastic, personal, frank, and pleased with himself. He writes well and confidently, telling us about himself, his job, his father's name, his place of residence, how he loved it; what an outstandingly good idea he had, to tell about the English nobles, and where they came from; how he has done research, travelling far amongst the people, and collecting three splendid books, one in English, one in Latin, and one in French; what pleasure he took in looking at and handling the vellum pages and fingering the pen; how he took the true words from each and wove them together. He then requests every noble man, 'æðele man' (*æðel* being a favourite word, symptomatic of Laȝamon's enthusiastic, generous, and idealizing turn of style, used five times in the thirty lines so far summarized), who reads this book, made of true words, to pray for the souls of Laȝamon's father and mother and even for his own, though by

(Cambridge, 1991), and in the collection of essays, *The Medieval Translator: the Theory and Practice of Translations in the Middle Ages*, ed. R. Ellis, assisted by J. Price, S. Medcalf, and P. Meredith (Cambridge, 1989). I am indebted to all of these, though Morse and Copeland are primarily concerned with the tradition of Latin writings. Laȝamon's work is interestingly outside the learned tradition and barely achieves a mention. Valuable direct accounts of the *Brut* are, however, found in D. Everett, *Essays on Middle English Literature*, ed. P. Kean (Oxford, 1955, 23–45); C. S. Lewis, Introduction to *Selections from Laȝamon's 'Brut'*, ed. G. L. Brook (Oxford, 1963), pp. vii–xvii; J. A. W. Bennett, *Middle English Literature*, edited and completed by D. Gray (Oxford, 1986), 68–89; D. Pearsall, *Old English and Middle English Poetry* (London, Henley, and Boston, 1977), 108–12). All quotations are from Laȝamon, *Brut*, ed. G. L. Brook and R. F. Leslie, vol. i, EETS 250 (1963), vol. ii, EETS 277 (1978).

[3] The poem 'would fit remarkably well into the second quarter even the middle third of the thirteenth century': review of *The Owl and the Nightingale reproduced in Facsimile*, *Notes and Queries*, 209 (1964), 192–3; 'some time not very early in the second half of the thirteenth century', *Notes and Queries*, 213 (1968), 85–8.

[4] Mercatanti, *Il 'Brut' di Laȝamon*, 134, 136.

definition he is not yet dead. For such personal self-presentation we must wait perhaps fifty years for the much less lively Robert Manning of Bourne on the other side of the country, and perhaps as much as a hundred years later for the self-presentations of Chaucer, Langland, and Gower, under Continental influence.

The alternative manuscript version in Otho C.XIII gives the impression of being written by someone impatient with La3amon's peculiarities though close to him in time and place. He cuts down La3amon's enthusiasm. For the 'merne þonke', the 'glorious thought' or 'glorious thinking' La3amon attributes to himself, he writes merely 'þonke'. All the occurrences of 'æðele' are cut. The best the grudging redactor can supply—once—is 'godne' (Caligula, l. 29). He even cuts out La3amon's mother in the request to pray for the souls of his parents. As well as dour simplification and modernization he gives a different name to La3amon's father, 'Leucais', which remains a puzzle, and adds that he lives at Areley 'wide þan gode cniþte', l. 3. This may well be a genuine reference to a somewhat shadowy patron for whom La3amon wrote, and who may account for the rare second-person-singular address 'ich wullen seggen þe' (l. 2996; cf. ll. 3014, 3803, 4975, 8728, 9691 and comments below) in a work which is also remarkable for the absence of orality and the insistence on reading.

The warmth and apparent sincerity, even naïvety, of La3amon's Prologue are equalled by the problems it raises. The only statement which we can check may well be largely untrue. This is his statement of his sources, discussed by numerous scholars, most notably by E. G. Stanley and F. Le Saux. Even Stanley appears to have come to an unnecessarily charitable conclusion, that there may have been some book in Latin which might have been thought to have been written by St Augustine (though of Hippo, contrary to La3amon's statement) and by Alcuin who occasionally went under the mistaken name of St Albin.[5] In such depth of learning I cannot wade and am tempted towards a simpler solution, by no means unparalleled in medieval writers, that despite his brave invocation of 'þa soþere word', La3amon invented his Latin source, just as Chaucer refers to Lollius, whom he certainly had not read, even if he believed his work existed somewhere. It is agreed by all that though La3amon says he used three works as sources, the English Bede, the Latin by 'Albin and Austin', and the French by Wace, and compressed them into one, in fact he used only Wace, plus a few subsidiary minor sources, and some local stories, summed up by Le Saux in her authoritative survey. Have we here the first instance of the 'unreliable narrator' much beloved of modern critics? In one sense surely yes. Are we

[5] E. G. Stanley, 'La3amon's Antiquarian Sentiments', *Medium Ævum*, 38 (1969), 23–37.

dealing with that other modern critical obsession, an ironical writer? Surely not. How are we to understand the problem of Laȝamon's truthfulness or reliability in terms that are not anachronistic and grossly misleading? It is a problem that affects our understanding of so many aspects of the poem, and of other medieval literature.

The essential scholarly philological basis has been established by Stanley in his analysis of Laȝamon's 'antiquarian sentiment' and archaistic style. From here, and with Le Saux's survey, it may be possible to further and sharpen our understanding of a poet more subtle, perhaps more devious, more self-conscious, than the Prologue at first suggests. A closer examination of some selected details of the poem's relation to Wace's *Le Roman de Brut* leads us to some conclusions. Such comparisons have already been made by numerous scholars, whom to list in detail would comprise at least half a bibliography of Laȝamon studies. Many are discussed by Le Saux and all are noted in her bibliography. My debt to these scholars is obvious and some specific obligations are noted below: my aims and conclusions are somewhat different.

In brief, my argument extends that of J. S. P. Tatlock, modified occasionally by Le Saux, that Laȝamon consciously invents almost all of what he changes in Wace. The significance of Laȝamon's inventions remains to be evaluated and then we may again return at the end to the Prologue, not illogically, because despite its introductory position it bears all the signs, like virtually every other Preface, of having been composed last. That will lead finally to some observations on the nature of a poem designed to be read, to its readership, and to Laȝamon as a writer.

Laȝamon might literally have had, as he claims he had, three books on the desk in front of him. He asks us to imagine an Old English Bede, on the left, shall we say; the mysterious Latin book on the right; and Wace's *Roman de Brut leide þer amidden* (l. 19). He would have needed an unusually large desk, but a French illustration of the compiler Vincent of Beauvais does suggest a possible, though clumsy, arrangement.[6] At all events, Laȝamon has given us a physical picture of what he wanted us to believe was a mental process of summary compression of sources, even if it did not in fact take place. It is clear from the closeness of much of the translation that he had a copy of Wace on his desk and that he worked from that, 'translating' as he

[6] M. T. Clanchy discusses the physical arrangements and needs for writing, *From Memory to Written Record* (London, 1979). The illustration referred to is reproduced by Alison Stones, 'Prolegomena to a Corpus of Vincent of Beauvais Illustrations', *Vincent de Beauvais intentions et receptions d'une œuvre encyclopédique au Moyen Age*, ed. Monique Paulmier-Foucart, Serge Lusignan, Alain Nadeau (Montreal, 1990), 302–44, fig. 2. The MS is Paris, Bibliothèque Mazarine, 753, fol. 24.

went, much as Chaucer must have had a copy of *Il Filostrato* on his desk beside his own 'boc felle'.

There seems no other word to use but 'translating' and Le Saux has ably defended the concept from the possible stigma of lack of originality, even if we apply modern requirements of a literally accurate rendition of a text from a different language and culture. Even in such modern cases, as she remarks, 'translation becomes conscious re-creation' (p. 58). But there is no sign that Laȝamon is in a modern sense translating Wace in order to try to give the effects Wace appears concerned to produce. It is well known, for example, that Wace presents his material, especially in the Arthurian section, but also everywhere else, in terms of his own contemporary culture. To quote C. S. Lewis's brief summary of Wace's version of Geoffrey of Monmouth's *Historia Regum Britanniae*, 'he feels himself quite free to touch up Geoffrey's narrative, describing scenes as if he had been an eyewitness and adding details from his own imagination. His poem is bright and clear, not without gaiety, and slightly touched with scepticism. In it the courtesy and pageantry and some of the love-lore of the High Middle Ages appear.'[7]

Lewis plays down Wace's alterations from his source, Geoffrey of Monmouth's *Historia Regum Britanniae*, about which I would raise the same questions as arise with Laȝamon's treatment of Wace, but Lewis well represents the tone and style of Wace. Laȝamon on the other hand, as is well recognized, and confirmed by Stanley, presents a picture of an archaic society of a very different kind.

A word must be said about the style, though lack of space here prevents detailed consideration of versification and diction. Every reader recognizes their archaic, or, as Stanley more accurately describes it, archaizing quality. Tatlock described the change long ago:[8] 'Lawman has translated not only his language and style, but also his cultural background, from those expected among mid-twelfth century Normans to those of more primitive people.' Such a view led Tatlock to a condescending view of Laȝamon as 'a man little acquainted with the advance of civilisation' (p. 514), and therefore as making his transposition unconsciously and in ignorance. He assumed that the 'primitive people' were Laȝamon himself and his readers. Another interpretation of the same facts, which I prefer, would attribute to Laȝamon a clear recognition that he was dealing with an earlier stage of history and a more primitive people than his own, to whom a more primitive presentation would be appropriate. In this interpretation Laȝamon has a more 'sophisticated' view of the past as past than has Wace.

[7] *Selections from Laȝamon's* Brut, ed. G. L. Brook, with a preface by C. S. Lewis (Oxford, 1963), p. viii.

[8] Tatlock, *Legendary History*, 488–9.

It is clear from the studies of Stanley and Le Saux and others that despite the Old English flavour of Laȝamon's diction, immediately apparent on reading, much of it is not true Old English. 'Laȝamon's use of compound nouns is fully conscious' (Le Saux, 191). Le Saux goes on to assume 'that compounds were also part of the vocabulary of Laȝamon's initial audience' (ibid.). In some sense this must be true, in that they were presumably recognizable, but it does not follow that they were in normal use. Everything points to the deliberate uniqueness of Laȝamon's poetic diction, but a uniqueness modelled on some acquaintance with an older style. He and his audience, or, as I shall later argue, his reader(s), must have had acquaintance with at least the descendants of Old English poems. This can easily be agreed on grounds of general likelihood, in view of the continuity of English styles especially in the west of England, and the later revival (if that is what it was) in the West Midlands of alliterative verse. Laȝamon can well be assumed to be imitating what he thought of as an archaic style. Many of his compounds (some 200 according to Oakden, quoted by Le Saux, p. 190) are unique to himself. He is *inventing* an archaizing style. Stanley makes the valuable comparison with Spenser's *Faerie Queene.* Spenser in Ben Jonson's opinion 'writ no language'. But everyone could understand Spenser's language, though they did not use it themselves, and they recognized it as evoking a fantasy of an ancient world. It seems likely that Laȝamon in the same sense writ no language. It may well have been that the decision to do so was not fully realized from the very first. I have the impression that the archaizing to some extent developed. It came to a climax in the Arthurian section, where, significantly, are grouped the celebrated long-tailed similes, no longer attributed to some specific source, and unlike anything in Old English poetry, but clearly aiming at a special effect (Le Saux, 206–11, citing Stanley, *Medium Ævum*, 38 (1969)).

Laȝamon can therefore be thought of as developing a practice of transposing Wace's anachronistically 'modern' presentation of the primitive early history of Britain into something more suitable. He adopts a modified form of ancient versification, avoids modern French words and concepts, creates his own archaizing diction as he goes along with his 'loft-songe' (l. 36). All these remarks are of course based on the text of the *Brut* written in Cotton Caligula A.IX, obviously closest to the original. The point here is that the other manuscript of the poem, Cotton Otho C.XIII, little if any later in date, is in part an abbreviation, but mainly a modernization, of the Caligula version. Caligula is a careful manuscript which preserves the oddity, as it may well have seemed, of the original. Otho gets rid of the deliberate archaizing. To take but one tiny example, the Caligula version frequently has a king calling a *husting*, a parliament. Every instance of this is removed in the Otho version, which, if it retains the line in which the word occurs, uses some such feeble equivalent as *speche*.[9]

Laȝamon develops a style and tone suitable to his ancient matter as he proceeds to translate Wace's *Brut* quite closely. It is clear throughout both these long poems that with very rare exceptions Laȝamon understood Wace's French perfectly. But the word and concept of 'translation' in the modern sense is a little misleading. Laȝamon takes liberties, for example with numbers in armies, and does so constantly throughout the poem. He adds emphases, heightens the highlights. For example the brutal toughness of the closing lines of the speech at ll. 499 ff. is his addition, and a few lines later he adds a favourite primitive threat—to draw someone with horses (l. 515)—a punishment never so far as I know practised in England but attributed to barbarous foreigners by Laȝamon as by Chaucer (*Prioress's Tale, CT* VII. 633).

Laȝamon's deliberate alterations and historical invention are the product of a deeper engagement in the subject-matter than that felt by Wace. From lines 528 onwards feeling more personal and more partisan than Wace's is expressed. When Brutus and his Trojans find the heathen temple, Laȝamon comes out much more strongly against it as the Devil's choice (l. 572), and characteristically expands the speech reported indirectly in Wace (ll. 661–8) as addressed to Diana into dramatic, urgent speech:

> Leafdi Diana, leoue Diana, heȝe Diana, help me to neode...
> (601–7)

Increasingly throughout the poem Laȝamon exploits his talent for vivid direct speech, eventually using it in part as a narrative device in a dramatic way. At any given point the suggestion may come from Wace. The expression and feeling are Laȝamon's.

He begins to add from his own knowledge. When Britain is divided and to Cambert falls Cambria, as in Wace, Laȝamon adds:

> þat is þat wilde lond þat Welsce men luuieð
> (1060)

He also adds in the next line that Wales took its name from Queen Galoes.

A number of studies, their results gathered together by Le Saux, have shown how Laȝamon often heightens his account with direct speech and

[9] Time and space have forbidden any consideration of the stylistic qualities of the Otho text, but even he may occasionally have been infected by Laȝamon's archaism to the extent of occasionally inventing his own, for example, perhaps, *bendhuse* (Otho, l. 525), (the only noted occurrence) on the analogy of *qualhuse* (Caligula, l. 365, retained in Otho), though in Caligula, l. 526 *maðmas* is abandoned for the pallid *godes* in Otho. Consistency is not to be looked for.

vivid emblematic detail. He occasionally corrects, and continuously alters Wace. He omits much in the way of explanation, especially the logistics of battle. He also omits many of Wace's cross-references to events contemporary with those he describes, such as events in the Bible and in Homer, although Laȝamon does include the reference to the birth of Christ (ll. 4524 ff.). In general, Laȝamon is interested neither in history as such, nor chronology, nor how things came about. His interest is dramatic, as seen most clearly by the great number of direct speeches he invents. At the same time he constantly invents concrete emblematic detail. He both summarizes and adds. To give one example from the plethora of instances, he summarizes to some extent the list of the great gathering after Arthur's nine years' stay in France. At the same time he adds the reference to story-telling, to harping and singing in hall and how they sang of Arthur the King (l. 12082) and the stories men told of their adventures. This cannot but remind one of the 'joy in hall' described in *Beowulf*. Although it would seem common to human nature (modern soldiers or college boat-clubs could testify to something like it, at any rate as far as singing goes), this may be part of Laȝamon's re-creation of archaic modes.

After this description of joy in hall we are told that Arthur proceeds to Caerleon for his curiously delayed coronation, and Laȝamon adds to Wace that 'some books say' that afterwards the town was bewitched (ll. 12113–14). Laȝamon adds to Wace's list of the gathering the names of some English earls, albeit curious ones, for example Gurguint of Herford, Beof of Oxford, Gursal of Bath, Vrgent of Chester, Ionatas of Dorchester. Laȝamon changes some of the names given in Wace, though this may be due to his exemplar since names in manuscripts are notoriously unstable. Then he summarizes the plenty of the feast, while adding the curiously specific detail, convincingly enough and rather charmingly, that among every good there was hay and grass (for the horses).

In the past there has been great reluctance on the part of scholars to believe that Laȝamon invents anything. J. S. P. Tatlock was for long almost alone in attributing the variations of the *Brut* to Laȝamon's own imagination (*The Legendary History*, 487). A. C. Gibbs, however, also considers that Laȝamon 'is not a responsible historian' (quoted Le Saux, 171). The tendency, common to medievalists, was to believe that anyone, especially if unknown and whose writings had disappeared, was more likely to have invented details, great or small, than the more significant author being studied. Hence over a century of source-hunting, now authoritatively criticized and contributed to by Le Saux. Her work makes clear Laȝamon's fundamental reliance upon Wace, supplemented by incidental borrowings from Geoffrey of Monmouth, and traces of hagiographical writing, Welsh poetry, West

Midland local oral traditions. She emphasizes that such sources were generally regarded as 'true' in some sense and that 'Laȝamon's poem is therefore a piece of literature nurtured by other literary works by a poet under the misconception that his *Brut* was a piece of historical writing based on dependable, historical sources' (Le Saux, 228).

A closer look at a specific addition by Laȝamon will clarify his concept of what he was doing. The poem progresses with many variants, many of which can be interpreted as attempts by Laȝamon to make his story 'truer' by adding convincing, often 'archaizing' details. We come to the murder of Constantine by the treacherous Pict, and the problem of the succession caused by his eldest son, Constance, having been made a Benedictine monk. In the original account Geoffrey then proceeds to the outcome with his usual brisk, clear, brief narrative, relating the essential core of the story, which is that the ambitious earl Vortigern persuaded Constance, though a monk, to accept coronation from Vortigern. Wace expands this to some extent. Laȝamon expands Wace considerably. By now Laȝamon, after some 6,000 lines, is really getting into his stride, and we are near the beginning of the Arthurian episode, for the youngest brother of Constance is Uther Pendragon, who will eventually succeed to the throne and beget Arthur.

In the *Brut*, after the murder of Constance's father Constantine the succession is debated and the second brother, Aurelius Ambrosius, is proposed as king. There is debate. The ambitious Vortigern opposes the election of Aurelius Ambrosius (ll. 6485 ff.). He asks for a fortnight in which to arrange another solution, which Laȝamon (nor of course Wace, who has little of this) does not for the moment disclose. Then Laȝamon really takes off. Vortigern, he says, pretended to go to his own country but in fact went to the abbey at Winchester where Constance was a monk. Vortigern asked the abbot very politely (*mid mildere speche*, l. 6504) if he might speak with Constance in the monastery 'speech-house'. There Vortigern persuaded the weak Constance, who anyway never wanted to be a monk, to accept the kingship, provided that Vortigern had complete control. There is a well-managed dialogue, stylized into speeches, vivid and convincing. Constance is said to hate his black clothes. Vortigern took a cape from one of his knights, put it on Constance, and led him thus disguised out of the monastery. Vortigern then put Constance's black habit on one of his men, brought the man back, and conversed with him as if he were the monk Constance. 'Monks went up, monks went down', says Laȝamon, and seeing the man in monk's clothes, with hood down hiding his crown (which of course would have been untonsured), thought he was their brother. Vortigern and his knights sat there talking all the daylight with the pretended monk. Eventually the monks came to the abbot and made a speech to him about their unease, saying that Vortigern was giving bad advice. The abbot denied this. At last Vortigern and his knights went, the monks ran to find Constance, and found instead his 'clothes lying by the walls'. They lamented, the abbot 'leaped on his horse', galloped after Vortigern, and cried,

> Seie me, þu wode cniht, whi dest þu swa muchel vnriht
> (6565)

and so forth. Vortigern turned, caught hold of the abbot,

> & swor bi his honden þat he hine wolde an-hongen
> (6571)

unless he agreed forthwith to release Constance from his vows. The abbot dared do no other, and as a reward

> & þat child ȝef þan abbede an hond twenti sulhene lond.
> (6576)

'Child' meaning 'warrior' may be another archaizing, or at least poetic, word. There follows a circumstantial account of the debate about the election of Constance as king.

None of this is in Wace. No convincing source has been suggested. This entertaining narrative of an ingenious trick is in a sense an enthusiastic participation, an account of what 'must have' happened—a device by no means unknown even to modern biographers and historians. The story bears all the marks of popular narrative, of the kind of ingenious story which pleases all levels of society. It portrays the characters of Vortigern and Constance very well in broad, entirely credible strokes, borne out in the general course of the actions that follow when Constance and eventually the treacherous Vortigern become in their turn king. Laȝamon must have known he was making it up. It even has a touch of implicit humour.

The outcome of Constance's reign was disaster, and though Laȝamon makes no explicit comment it would seem probable that the invented preliminary story aims in a sense to prepare us for the ultimate outcome. (It is notable that retellings of Arthurian stories sometimes expand them by adding preliminary accounts of the hero's origins, his *enfances*, in a somewhat analogous way, to account for the hero's later eminence. The most obvious example is the French prose *Lancelot*, but on a different plane of seriousness the birth stories in the gospels of Matthew and Luke, absent in Mark and John, probably owe something to the same purpose.) Laȝamon wishes to engage us more deeply in the unfolding history of events in a manner common to traditional story-tellers at all periods.

It is worth remarking here, however, that though there may be a light veil of archaizing and anglicizing diction (*speche-hus*, for example) cast over the narrative, the narrative structure of this little episode, its directness and significant realistic detail, are 'modern' in spirit. The marks of oral delivery and traditional 'epic' style, such as G. V. Smithers finds in *Havelok*, are missing.[10] It is impossible to avoid 'modernity' when re-creating the past.

This example is clear cut because short and self-contained. Any sustained comparison of Laȝamon's text with that of Wace, especially from this section onwards, illustrates the same fertility of invention. The aim is to make the narrative more interesting and effective. When we come to the long section concerned with Arthur, the aim is in addition to aggrandize Arthur. In this attempt 'truth' in any historical sense both is and is not the issue. Laȝamon is creating an archaic king and society, surely consciously imposing an ethos quite different from what he found in his source, but which he must have decided was more authentic. Obvious examples are the mystifications associated with Arthur's birth and death, too well known to need repetition here, and the increased mystery of Merlin. Although the sources of the *aluen* who carry off the apparently dying Arthur may well come from diffused folklore traditions, oral, Welsh, French, or whatever, the *aluen* are clear evidence that Laȝamon is deliberately creating a myth of antiquity for which there is no documentary evidence. Other examples are his frequent evocations of feasts and voyages, well discussed by Ringbom,[11] including the many references to 'gleemen' and the songs in hall. Some of these references are suggested by Wace, but most are original. Laȝamon does not scruple to alter details found in Wace to create his conception of a great archaic king, a champion in his own right, as he must have felt, a truer conception of what Arthur was actually like.

A curious example of Laȝamon's creativity is provided by the two episodes of the arming of Arthur. 'The arming of the hero' is an ancient and wide-spread topos from antiquity to the late Middle Ages which I have examined extensively elsewhere. It follows a set pattern, and there is an elaborate first arming of Arthur before the battle with Childric at Bath (ll. 10543–57) which has a strange mixture of names.[12] Calibeorne, Pridwen, and Ron come from Wace, who took them from Geoffrey, who presumably took them from Celtic sources, since they are Celtic. Wygar the *aluisc smith* who made the birnie is obviously an English name, as is Goswhit, the name of the helmet.

[10] G. V. Smithers, 'The Style of *Hauelok*', *Medium Ævum*, 57 (1988), 190–218.

[11] H. Ringbom, *Studies in the Narrative Technique of 'Beowulf' and Lawman's 'Brut'* (Abo, 1968).

[12] D. Brewer, 'The Arming of the Warrior in European Literature and Chaucer', in *Tradition and Innovation in Chaucer* (London, 1982), 142–60. Le Saux gives an excellent account and the most convincing reading of *witeȝe* (197–8) as adverbial. The evidence of the manuscript referred to by Le Saux is here virtually conclusive, though the possibility remains of *witeȝe* being a common noun, as for example, applied to Merlin, = 'wise man' ll. 8479, 8692, 8908, 8940.

Although Laȝamon was well enough aware, as were Wace and Geoffrey, of the differences between the *Bruttisc* and English languages (e.g. l. 7473) he was not disturbed by mixing them together, as Le Saux remarks (p. 225), evidenced by the Saxon names he gives to the Bruttisc traitors long before the Saxons appear. He felt he needed names for the smith and the helmet. He gives the smith a characteristically primitive aura (*aluisc*). His name Wygar might have been derived from *wig-heard*, 'battle-hard'. It seems not to have been noticed that it could be another invented compound on the analogue of *wiaxe* 'battle-axe (used a number of times by Laȝamon) and mean 'battle-spear'. The accusative form *gare* is found at line 2533 and other forms appear at lines 877, 925, and 7596. If Laȝamon knew of Weland the smith the chances are that he would have used so suitable a name. Since he did not use it he probably did not know it and so invented another. *Goswhit*, whatever its ultimate origin, is another, less happy invention for a war-helm, given the associations of 'goose', but Laȝamon sometimes nods.[13] At all events, bright and shining armour may well be called 'white'.

The 'arming topos' normally follows a strict order, as I have shown elsewhere, observed in many texts over two millennia, in which the greaves are put on first, for obvious practical reasons, since it would have been impossible, or at least extremely difficult, to fasten them when wearing the body-armour. Then follow corslet, sword, helmet, shield, and spear. Even in Arthur's first formal arming (ll. 10543–58) this order is not quite followed, for Arthur puts his corslet on first, before his *hosen of stele*, which reminds us that Laȝamon, for all his romantic relish for narratives of heroic battle, was a priest and no fighting soldier. This inaccurate variant of the arming derives from Wace, who is more accurate; Wace derived it from Geoffrey, who could have found it in numerous sources, including the *Aeneid* which he obviously knew well.

Arthur's second arming shows even freer invention, beginning with back armour, then *cheisil* and *pallene curtel*, then helmet, sword, and, finally and improbably, greaves and spurs. Arthur leaps on to his horse and is given an ivory shield (rare item indeed) and finally a spear made in Carmarthen by a smith called Griffin, and which had belonged to his father Uther (ll. 11857–

[13] The most obvious example of uncertain literary judgement which can verge on comically crass bathos is illustrated by one use of the colloquial phrase which often concludes a speech *& habbeð alle godne dæie.* The first instance, spoken by the departing Romans, has an appropriately sarcastic ring (6252). Laȝamon uses it again, more or less effectively, at 6331, 6738, 11256, 16068. He varies it as *gode niht*, 9578, when Uther in the form of Gorlois sends all his knights to bed. But when Bedivere, spying out the horrific deeds of the giant of Mont St Michel, having heard the old nurse's tale of death and destruction, must leave as the giant approaches, he grotesquely wishes the distressingly broken old woman, just before her nightly rape, 'Ah hafuen nu swiðe godne dæi, and ich wulle faren minne wæi' (12953).

70). There is nothing from Wace here. The smith Griffin is unknown to fame except in so far as he bears a common Welsh name. Only the sword Caliburne of the weapons is named. Laȝamon is invoking, with variation, his favourite antiquarian theme. He is not quite familiar with the practical details but that is of little importance for the tone. His ignorance of the practical details indicates his modernity.

The exhaustive comparison of the *Brut* with various possible sources, the work of many scholars brought together and sifted by Le Saux, amply demonstrates Tatlock's early emphasis on Laȝamon's inventiveness, but still leaves something to be said about what would appear to be his purposes. Among them must unquestionably have been the traditional story-teller's aim to produce a lively and convincing narrative. This may make for some inconsistencies in a long work, but they are not a major problem in the *Brut*. More important is the shift in the balance of the narrative pointed out by Le Saux, so that 'the central theme is no longer Britain and Rome, but Britain and the outsiders'. Further to this comes 'the "naturalisation" of the Angles to the status of legitimate inhabitants and rulers of what is to become England' (Le Saux, 229). Crucial to the way this is done is Stanley's point about Laȝamon's 'antiquarian sentiments'. He is conscious of the past as past in a rather remarkable and unusual way. And not only is his diction archaistic. He attempts, with varying success, to establish an older order of society, an earlier manner of conduct. The supreme example of this is his struggle to show Arthur both as triumphant and as 'primitive'. In doing this he confronts the problem of 'truth' and 'lies' about Arthur. His task would seem to be to choose, or if necessary to invent, what is the likeliest, the most convincing presentation of the Arthur whose historical existence he traces, but with details in which he cannot always have faith, in Wace.

Although Laȝamon is in many respects behaving like the traditional story-teller, his marked literacy is another source of his ability to 'stand off' from Wace and create a different tone and ethos. Literacy forces separation between teller and recipient, and emphasizes the re-creative element in the recipient. Paradoxically, the modernity of literacy, granting greater freedom to the recipient of the tale, allows Laȝamon to create, or invent, an archaistic ethos, just as Wace's literacy and modernity allowed him, with different tastes, to create a 'modern', contemporary, chivalric ethos for his Arthur. Each writer is conscious of his freedom, and has perhaps an uneasy sense of it, reflected in the comments on the mixture of truth and lies told about Arthur. It is notable that this comment is not made of any other figure in the poem.

Laȝamon, following Wace, remarks on the mixture of truth and lies told about Arthur (*Brut*, ll. 11465–75). With each author the comment arises while relating the creation of the Round Table, which was designed to prevent quarrels amongst the knights over procedure, after one such outburst. In Laȝamon's account, which of the brawl is more elaborate than Wace's, Arthur puts down the riot with more brutality than in Wace: not only are the culprits put to death, but their women-relatives have their noses cut off. Afterwards Arthur orders the feasting to resume in all its jollity, *weoren him leof weoren him læ[ð]* (11416). Minstrels sing and *duȝeðe wes on selen* (11420). This is Laȝamon's own idea of a great primitive king, owing nothing to Wace.

Then Laȝamon remarks,

> Seoððen hit seið in þere tale
> (11422)

This is the only occasion that I have noticed in his 16,095 long lines that Laȝamon uses the common medieval narrative phrase 'the story says', though Tatlock (p. 472) considers it merely a rhyme for 'Cornwale'. Yet it is a frequent expression in the contemporary long thirteenth-century French romances which Laȝamon could have read. The phrase is not in Wace and Laȝamon uses it to give authority to the account of the 'crafty work-man' in Cornwall who offers to make the Round Table. This table is in fact never described by Laȝamon as round, but it will seat 1,600 knights (his own invention), yet be easily transported. Laȝamon increases the aura of magic. When the table is finished a feast is held to celebrate the work, accomplished in four weeks, and all the knights, high and low, eat together amicably, well placed,

> ne mihten þer nan ȝelpen for oðeres cunnes scenchen.
> (11452)

Though Laȝamon must have understood well enough the point of Wace's Round Table he makes no reference to precedence and makes his table sound much more like a table of magic plenty, such as, in later stories, the Grail was able to supply, and as survives in folk-tale. The 'tale' he is following is that in his own creative understanding.

Laȝamon then follows Wace in saying that this is the table that the Britons so boast of, then adds to Wace here that they tell many lies about Arthur the king. Laȝamon's unease may be revealed when he goes on to remark that a man may overpraise his friend. Arthur, the favourite hero, is in the place of the possibly overpraised friend. But Laȝamon comes back to the point that

> ne al soh ne al les þat leod-scopes singeð
> ah þis is þat soððe bi Arthure þan kinge.

Nes næuer ar swulc king swa duhti þurh alle þing.
for þat soðe stod a þan writen, hu hit is iwurðen
ord from þan ænden, of Ar[ð]ure þan kinge,
no more no lasse buten alse his laȝen weoren.
Ah Buttes hine luueden swiðe, & ofte him on liȝeð
and sugged feole þinges, bi Arthure þan kinge
þat næuere nes iwurðen a þisse weorlde richen.
Inoh he mai suggen þe soþ wule uremmen
seolcuðe þinges, bi Arthur kinge.

(11465–75)

The statement that not all is true nor all false that poets sing, that it is certainly true that there never was so brave a king as Arthur, and that what is written is true no more nor less than his laws were, that Britons certainly tell lies about him, but that there are plenty of wonders to tell for one who only wants to tell the truth—all this, if I have understood it correctly, sounds like one genuinely struggling to achieve a certain balance. Morse (op. cit. in n. 2) argues convincingly, though drawing mainly on later and more learned tradition, that 'rhetorical' arguments underpinned many an invention made for the sake of interpretation. The lies are shrugged off on to the Britons.

Laȝamon is telling 'seolcuðe þinges', and the element of wonder is strong. 'Nu þu miht iheren sulku[ð] word' (l. 3803), 'selcuð spelles' (l. 4039). There is nothing of the dry annalist nor of the apparent seriousness of the straight-faced Geoffrey of Monmouth, about his writing. He never admits, as Wace does, that he does not know something. For example, Wace says he does not know whether Cassibelaun had children or not. Laȝamon says he had none (l. 4484). It is true that Laȝamon says that we cannot know all about Arthur's death, and foretells it with references to Avalon and Argante just after the passage quoted above, but that is all part of the romantic mystification which he creates around Arthur, much elaborated from Wace who in turn elaborates on Geoffrey. Laȝamon never refers, like Wace, to what the chronicles say. Despite some rare references to written books (ll. 11468, 14406), and to the mysterious death of Arthur, and the Britons' hope of his return, in this respect he is much closer to the omniscient author of the eighteenth- and nineteenth-century novel, which, it may be recalled, often claims facetiously to be a 'true history'. Yet he does not give the impression, as I have sometimes been tempted to think, of being the thirteenth-century equivalent of a historical novelist.

Laȝamon corrects Wace, as Tatlock long ago pointed out (*Legendary History*, 499), though he makes no show of this. He adds names of minor characters occasionally, as Malory does, as well as omitting much of what seems to him tedious or irrelevant, again like Malory. Malory offers an interesting parallel. They share the same concern for England, *mutatis mutandis*, the same readiness to alter a source, the same romantic interest in history, and of course a comparable obsession with Arthur. But Malory as it were 'modernizes' Arthur. Laȝamon envisages Arthur differently from Malory, as from Wace. Laȝamon's Arthur is the evocation of a primitive ancient king. In a curious way he foreshadows late twentieth-century Arthurian stories, which always attempt to place Arthur in a 'genuine' sixth-century setting, in a kind of late Iron Age, in all its primitive ferocity. Laȝamon has not the resources of modern historical research but he has a developed feeling for the past.

We may return, then, finally to the Prologue, which opens up a wider vista and has further interesting implications. Laȝamon's glorious thought, he tells us, was to write about the English, what they were called and whence they came. This may remind us that despite the glamour of Arthur, he dies at line 14297 and the narrative smoothly continues for 1,798 lines longer, less dramatically perhaps, but by no means without interest. The sorting out of Britons, English, Saxons shows the gradual decline of the Britons, their resentments, the general difficulties, and the gradual assertion of the English hegemony. The English are neither glorified nor vilified. The drama of the land continues, for Laȝamon's point of view is always 'here', 'this lond', a phrase which occurs throughout the poem in various forms some seventy-five times. It is especially frequently used in the sequence of changes between English, British, and Saxons in the last thousand lines or so.[14]

The Prologue also emphasizes both the reading and the writing of Laȝamon. He is writing for a reader or readers, though modern critics often assume an 'audience'. No doubt such a book might well be read aloud in the thirteenth century, but it lacks obvious oral qualities. Despite the famous 'epic epithets', the narrative style is not unduly repetitious but rather sequential. The anecdote of Vortigern's release of Constance from the abbey is told in a brisk direct style. There are no addresses to the audience, real or invented, of the kind that characterize the genre of Middle English romance, or Chaucer.

Laȝamon's references are different: *al swa þe b[o]c tellet* (1860); *ich wullen seggen þe for wan* (2996); *nu ich þe habben iseid* (3014); *al swa þes boc her telleð bi-uore, a þissen spelle* (3531) (referring to an earlier episode in the *Brut*); *Nu þu miht iheren sulke[ð] word* (3803); *Nu þu hafuest soð iherd* (4975); *Herene nu muchel swikedom* (7470); *Hærcne hu heo toc on* (7475); *al-se ich þe wulle telle, a þisse boc-spelle* (8728); *Nu ich þe wulle tellen a þissen boc-spællen* (9691); *Ich mai sugge hu hit iwarð* (11345). The use of 'speak' or 'hear' referring

[14] From l. 14958 I count nineteen occurrences. Without a concordance it is hard to be absolutely certain in such counting, but at least the general impression of a quarter of the instances occurring in the last fifteenth part seems clear.

entirely to the written word is common even today, so counts neither way. The singular pronoun of address is more significant as Laȝamon always strictly observes number. He appears to envisage a solitary reader. The references to *boc-spelle* also suggest the written word. The change from orality to literacy in the Middle Ages is now widely recognized in all its huge complexity and here is no place to enter into its intricacies, and the psychological and social changes it implies. Laȝamon is self-evidently a keen and solitary reader and writer, who illustrates some of these changes. He is, according to his own account, writing about his own idea for his own pleasure and even a possible patron is vague, if indeed he existed. He is re-creating the past history of 'this land' for a small further readership. Such a reader might well share his rather sophisticated, internalized, partially romantic projection of the history of the past of 'this' people and 'this' country. On the other hand it is clear that the Otho scribe had no sympathy with what Laȝamon was about. Paradoxically, his modernizing, his rejection of the archaic, shows him less advanced than Laȝamon. We may hope that Laȝamon was better served by his first reader and will be enjoyed by more in the future. Laȝamon exemplifies a truth splendidly formulated by Burke in his *Reflections on the Revolution in France* (1790), 'People will not look forward to posterity who never look backward to their ancestors.'[15] Laȝamon looks back with an eager sense of participation in the struggle of the 'ancestors'. In so doing he illustrates his modernity.

[15] Ed. C. C. O'Brien (Harmondsworth, 1968), 119.

An Early English Entführung: *A Note on* Floris and Blauncheflur

DOUGLAS GRAY

The attractive Middle English romance of *Floris and Blauncheflur* has always had its admirers, but has usually been considered simply as an early example of an important genre. It can be argued that its interest for the literary historian is greater than has been recognized. This may seem a surprising claim, since it is (*a*) an adaptation of a twelfth-century French original,[1] and (*b*) apparently something of an oddity, or at least unusual, in that it is an 'idyllic' romance, celebrating love and passion in an extreme form. Nor can its date be fixed exactly, although there seems to be general agreement that it comes from about the middle of the thirteenth century—and thus may be taken to represent the chronological endpoint of the present volume.

Floris and Blauncheflur is significant first because of its high literary quality. Studies of Middle English romance have often commented favourably on it, but (with one or two exceptions)[2] briefly and in rather general terms. Its popularity is shown by the chronological spread of the (fragmentary) surviving manuscripts[3]—from the latter part of the thirteenth century to the first half of the fifteenth century. The English redactor had certainly found a very good story, one which was to become known in a variety of languages from Scandinavia to Italy (it is the basis of Boccaccio's *Filocolo*). Whether or not the whole story is of eastern origin remains obscure, but it has oriental themes and motifs—notably the tower of maidens, a harem guarded by eunuchs—and parallels in oriental tales. As Metlitski, its most enthusiastic critic, says, it gives some sense of a 'genuine reflection of life in an Islamic environment'.[4] The bigotry often revealed in the treatment of Saracens in medieval Western literature is notably absent:

[1] *Floire et Blancheflor*, ed. M. Pelan (Paris, 1956). See Jocelyn Price, '*Floire et Blancheflor*: The Magic and Mechanics of Love', *Reading Medieval Studies*, 8 (1982), 12–33.

[2] Notably D. Metlitski, *The Matter of Araby in Medieval England* (New Haven, Conn., 1977).

[3] See *Floris and Blauncheflur*, ed. F. C. de Vries (Groningen, 1966), 1–6. All quotations from the romance are taken from this edition, and normally from the version in MS Egerton 2862; line numbers prefixed by A are from the Auchinleck MS.

[4] Metlitski, *Matter of Araby*, 244.

the marriage of Floris and Blauncheflur 'ennobles and harmonizes two opposite cultures'.[5] At the same time it draws on the mystery and the glamour with which medieval romance invested the east: the story is a heady oriental mixture of love, violence, and tears. The east was a setting in which romantic legend could flourish: witness the tale told of Gilbert Becket, the archbishop's father, whose beloved, the daughter of an emir, came to England to seek him, and found him, though she knew only the words 'London' and 'Becket'.[6] It is, too, a splendid tale of idyllic young love, which has been compared to *Paul et Virginie*. In the 'roman idyllique', although a happy conclusion is expected, joy and sorrow are intertwined: if the ancient story of Daphnis and Chloe gave a foretaste of love's happy resolution, that of the tragic love of Pyramus and Thisbe was a reminder of the disastrous fate which might befall such a pair.

The Middle English romance abbreviates and simplifies its French original, and by so doing contrives to intensify the essential characteristics of the genre. Thus, the youth of the childhood sweethearts is stressed: the words 'child' and 'children' are constantly reiterated. Brought up together, the children are inseparable. When they are seven, and Floris is to be set 'on the book letters to know', he insists 'with wepyng' that they learn together: 'ne shal not Blancheflour lerne with me?' And 'lore' and 'love' are linked: 'wonder it was of hur lore, | And of her loue wel þe more'. They learn writing 'on parchemyne' (33–4) and Latin—though Ovid, whom the French author more knowingly says teaches them the ways of love, is not mentioned. Their love is always childlike and innocent, but of a powerful intensity from the beginning: when he is sent away, Floris cannot learn without Blauncheflur (113).

Young love is rarely without its problems. Here they come from older figures of authority. The king begins to think that their 'graunde amoure' will not lessen when they are older. His reaction has the sudden violence of a ruler in a folk-tale—he is determined that Blauncheflur will die (46), since this is the best way to ensure that Floris will forget her. The folk-tale quality is emphasized by the way the Middle English romance pares down descriptive details: in the French there is a visual indication of his fury—'de sanc ot tout le front vermeil'). The portrayal is deliberately heightened: at a later point his anger is equally violent: 'Let do bryng forþ þat mayde! | Fro þe body þe heued shal goo' (140–1). Fortunately, as is common in such stories, the young lovers are to find a series of generous helpers. The queen (like the other women in the story) shows *pite*, and thinks to save

[5] Ibid, 249–50.

[6] D. J. Hall, *English Medieval Pilgrimage* (London, 1965), 134.

Blauncheflur (53–4). The Middle English romance characteristically avoids any description of a psychological process: where in the French she 's'est porpensee' and speaks 'like a prudent woman', here she simply 'þouȝt with hur reed'. She ('þat good lady' as the English writer approvingly calls her) twice overcomes the king's reluctance (which is marked by the repetition of the word 'unnethes', 63, 153). It is her suggestion that Blauncheflur should be sold to the merchants of 'Babylon' rather than killed. And when she has saved Floris (who thinks Blauncheflur is dead) from killing himself—in the Middle English through a simple action ('she reft him of his lytel knyf, | And saued þere þe childes lyf', 295–6), where her French counterpart makes a learned speech—she pleads successfully with the king to allow Floris to have Blauncheflur as his wife. Again, the reactions of the figures are done in the austere style of popular narrative. The king is suddenly 'converted', and helps Floris with the preparations and equipment for his quest for Blauncheflur, 'þat swete þing' as he now calls her (360). Floris, similarly, reacts in an 'expressive' rather than a 'realistic' way. With no word of recrimination, he simply announces that he will leave to seek her, as if driven in an almost magical way by the overwhelming power of love. This pattern of heightened figures, expressive scenes, and dynamic narrative is characteristic of the whole romance.

Floris and Blauncheflur is an early English example of the 'literature of tears', a 'pitous tale'.[7] It heightens and intensifies the moments of pathos and sentiment. There are constant references to weeping, sighing, and sorrow (emphasized by the repetition of a limited number of simple words: 'woo', 'sorrow', 'wepyng', 'syke', 'morne', etc.). Tears come easily to both the lovers, but Floris in particular seems a prototype of Chaucer's 'feminised hero'[8] Troilus. The lady of the inn compares him to Blauncheflur:

'Þou art ilich here of alle þinge,
Of semblant & of mournyng,
But þou art a man & ȝhe is a maide'
(A53–5)

Intense emotion causes him to swoon, like Troilus: hearing that the Emir yearns for Blauncheflur, whom he has in the harem, he despairs—'thre sithes Flores sownyd anoon | Sore he wept, and sore he syȝt' (643–6). This heightening of the emotional moments serves a variety of purposes: besides increasing the genuine pathos of the story, it may sharply contrast the

[7] Good earlier examples can be found among the *Lais* of Marie de France; later ones in Chaucer. See D. Gray, 'Chaucer and "Pite"', in M. Salu and R. T. Farrell (eds.), *J. R. R. Tolkien, Scholar and Storyteller: Essays in Memoriam* (Ithaca, NY and London, 1979), 172–203.

[8] J. Mann, *Geoffrey Chaucer* (London, 1991), ch. 5: 'The Feminised Hero'.

sensibility of the young lovers with the rigour and severity of the adult world, or suggest the possibility of acts of generosity and 'gentilesse' (with which *pite* is frequently associated). When Floris hears the lady in the inn mention Blauncheflur his sorrow suddenly turns to joy, which he expresses instantly through the giving of gifts (413–24, A58–73; cf. also 475–80, 492). Like a number of the people he meets on his quest, he is genuinely 'hende'. Scenes like this are the 'affective' images of the 'pitous tale'. They are simple and directly fitted to their narrative context. In the French romance, when Floris comes to the house of Daire (or Darys), his uncertainty is expressed through an interior debate between Wisdom (Savoir) and Love. In the English this becomes simply: 'ac euere Florice siȝte ful cold, | And Darys gan him biho[l]d' (A185–6).

Any elaboration is done with the simplest of rhetorical devices. In his lamentation at the supposed tomb of Blauncheflur, Floris echoes the epitaph—'Here lyth swete Blauncheflooure | Þat Florys louyd par amoure' (217–18)—and repeats her name: '"Blaunchefloure!" he seide, "Blauncheflour!" | "So swete a þing was neuere in boure. | Of Blauncheflour is þat y meene."' The repetition of her name, especially in phrases like 'on Blauncheflooure was al his þouȝt' (394, 462), becomes a dominant lyrical motif, whether sorrowfully elegaic or expressing hope. It also has a function in the narrative. The chance mention of her name in the inn (406) is highly dramatic, and sets up a pattern of 'recognition' in the quest: the scene is repeated in the next lodging (461–72).

The narrative technique is simple and straightforward. One of the few exceptions is the elaborate 'prophetic' speech which Darys gives (649–704), instructing Floris how to win the good will of the porter. This stands out and has an interesting effect: it is followed by a piece of very rapid summary narrative—'as he seide, he dide ywys'. The romance's simple formulaic style allows rapid movement: in the almost magic manner of popular narrative Floris and his company seem to arrive almost immediately in the very haven where Blauncheflur had come (426–32). The French romance gives details of his landfall at Bauduc and his journey to 'Babylon', but in the English it is all very general: he thanks God that he has arrived in the land where his beloved is—'him þouȝt he was in Paradyse'. There are deliberate echoes and repetitions, of words and phrases ('seuen sithes of gold', 196, 484), of Floris's story (715 ff.). Against this rather formal background some passages of intense and dramatic dialogue (e.g. 229–41) stand out, as do the occasional rhetorical patterns: 'she wolde haue leuyd, and þow noldest | And fayn wolde y dye, and þow woldest' (285–6).

In general, the descriptive passages are less elaborate than their French originals. The exceptions are exotic scenes or objects which are closely relevant to the plot. Thus there is a detailed account of the wondrous city of 'Babylon' with its many gates and towers, and its great daily 'cheping' or bazaar, and of the tower of maidens, its guardian eunuchs ('as a capon dyȝt'—always a source of fascination for Western writers), with its orchard, its spring (the waters of which come from Paradise, and can reveal an erring maiden by 'yelling') and the magic tree of love with its flowers and blossoms. Less spectacular significant or magical objects are normally described in much less detail than in the French, and stand out with impressive clarity: the marvellous cup (163 ff.) decorated with the story of Paris and Helen; the tomb of Blauncheflur with its inscription; a wonderful horse ('þe oon half white so mylke, | And þat other reed so sylke', 365–6); a magic ring (376 ff.). The repetition of images gives the romance a distinctively lyrical quality. This is most evident in the use of flowers: those of the tree of love, those gathered by the maidens for their baskets which allow Floris access to the tower, etc. The very names of the lovers are associated with flowers (according to the French they were both born on the same day, Palm Sunday—the feast of flowers), and the connection is emphasized through rhyme (e.g. 118–22), or by explicit comment (778–81, 797–8, 809–10).

All of these qualities work together superbly in the final scenes: *Floris* has one of the most impressive climaxes in the whole of Middle English romance. The absolute devotion of the lovers (cf. 785–94) and the intensity of their passion (when they finally meet, 'without speche togeder þey lepe'—and 'hire cussing laste a mile') is balanced by some touches of humour: the girls ('gegges' in two manuscripts) are cross because their basket of flowers is unaccountably heavy; Floris springs out only to find Clarys instead of Blauncheflur, and when she screams jumps back in again. The English author evidently warmed to the quickwittedness of Clarys: she explains that her scream was caused by a butterfly ('þe maydons þerof hadden glee'), and tells the Emir that Blauncheflur has not come out because she is at her prayers. At the same time the narrative is genuinely exciting: the chamberlain discovers the lovers 'nebbe to nebbe, | Nebbe to nebbe, and mouþ to mouþ'; the Emir, armed with his sword, quickly establishes that one is a woman and the other a man. His angry reaction is as violent and heightened as that of the King of Spain earlier: 'he quaked for tene þere he stood', and is on the brink of killing them there and then. The 'children' wake up to see the drawn sword over them (907–8), and we move into a judgement scene of controlled excitement and extreme *pite*. This is intensified by the way their total devotion prevents either of them making use of the magic ring (966 ff.). There is much 'pitous' sorrow and weeping as the 'children' (980, 985) are brought to their death. Their beauty (990–1) begins to move the hearts of the onlookers, but the Emir cannot 'kele his hoot blood', and orders them to be bound and thrown to the flames. But even as with a symbolic gesture he draws his sword to kill them, his 'mod and chere' starts to change ('for aiþer for oþer wolde die', A776), he weeps, and his sword falls to the ground. A second intercession from a 'duke' is successful, but there is a final twist: Floris can have his life if he reveals who brought him in—which he will not do unless there is a promise of forgiveness. The 'pitous' scene becomes one of unrestrained joy, and everything ends in festivities and marriages, demonstrating 'hou after bale hem com bote' (A858).

Metlitski says rightly that 'the emir of Babylon's fairness and moderation contrast with the habitual rashness and temperamental excesses which characterize the stereotyped sultans of the romances composed in the West': he 'deals with a situation which would justify punishment by death under any medieval code, with compassion and humanity'.[9] It is certainly tempting to associate him with the Pasha of a later *Entführung aus dem Serail*[10] who declares, 'Ich schenke dir die Freiheit, Nimm Konstanze', and demonstrates the truth of a later enlightenment:

> Nichts ist so hässlich als die Rache;
> hingegen menschlich gütig sein
> und ohne Eigennutz verzeihn,
> ist nur der grossen Seelen Sache!

—though the Amyral's 'conversion' is rather like that of the truculent King of Spain and demonstrates the power of an innocent and noble love.

The English romance is also of considerable interest in the wider context of medieval English literary history. If we may place it in or near the mid-thirteenth century, in the reign of Henry III (1216–72), our first thought might be that an English audience could well have enjoyed the optimism and general benevolence of a 'roman idyllique': in 1237 Matthew Paris wrote eloquently of the wretched state of the land; the 1260s were to see an internal war between the king and Simon de Montfort and the battles of Lewes and Evesham. This oriental tale is translated in a period much concerned with the splendours and miseries of the last crusades (including the ill-fated attempt of St Louis to capture Cairo or 'Babylon'), and just after the great Mongol incursions which inspired horrific descriptions in the pages of Matthew Paris and other chroniclers, but which were to have an unforeseen effect in the establishment of a Mongol empire in the far east which allowed Western travellers (e.g. Rubruck, 1252–5, Marco Polo, 1271–85) into Cathay. Already in 1249 Matthew Paris records that rumours are circulating that the king of the Tartars has become Christian and been baptized (one such later

[9] Metlitski, *Matter of Araby*, 191.
[10] Mozart's libretto is by Gottlieb Stephanie.

report probably underlies the romance *The King of Tars*). And his recording of the arrival of some Armenians in St Albans in 1252 with stories of the Tartars and the Wandering Jew and the Ark (in Armenia) suggests an interest in the exotic East which the travellers and later 'Mandeville' were to extend. *Floris and Blauncheflur* comes from a period when Western intellectuals like Roger Bacon were beginning to abandon the view that Islam had only a negative role in history: as Southern says, 'he did not know the right things, but he tried to know, and he tried to organize his knowledge'.[11] The story of the romance is from an earlier period, and the English poem certainly belongs to a popular rather than to a learned tradition. Nevertheless, its tolerance is striking. It records but does not dwell on the association of Saracens with sensuality and polygamy which features prominently in the 'life of Mahomet' included in Matthew Paris. 'Babylon' is a wonderland whose inhabitants seem essentially noble.

Finally, the poem is of importance in the context of Early Middle English literature. Our knowledge of the period is woefully inadequate, but there is a good deal of evidence suggesting that it was one marked by variety and creativity. This point, of course, has been confirmed by Eric Stanley's work on *The Owl and the Nightingale*. Just as the earlier lyrics seem to revel in intricate sound-patterns and metrical forms for material of considerable variety, so the early romances show a lively sense of experiment in their adaptation of French, Anglo-Norman, and English matter. If *Floris* had not survived, who would have guessed that an English writer of this period would have been drawn to the genre of the 'roman idyllique' (the treatment of the love of Horn and Rimenhild is perhaps the only surviving hint)? In some ways, the romance looks forward—in the manner in which French romance continued to be adapted to simpler narrative patterns; in a delight in the 'pitous' scene and the 'literature of tears' which culminates in Chaucer; in an interest in themes like that of 'trouthe' in love. It also has an indirect but intriguing link with the literature of the late Old English period—the beginning of the period covered by this book. Writers and audiences then also seem to have enjoyed the sights and scenes of the exotic East: the 'Book of Monsters', 'The Wonders of the East', and pre-eminently the Old English version of the story of Apollonius of Tyre, which Wrenn praises as a 'masterpiece in an exactly appropriate prose style' (remarking that it 'may possess some claim to be called the first English novel', and that it has 'a tone of courtesy and sympathy with romantic love which cannot be paralleled till the days of the Middle English romances').[12] Old English legends (like the

[11] R. W. Southern, *Western Views of Islam in the Middle Ages* (Cambridge, Mass., 1961, repr. 1978), 61.

[12] C. L. Wrenn, *A Study of Old English Literature* (London, 1967), 255–6.

Lives of the Two Offas) and even the Old English language (witness the work of the remarkable 'Tremulous Hand' of Worcester)[13] were not completely forgotten in the thirteenth century. Although the link between the earlier exotic works and *Floris and Blauncheflur* is not a direct one—it is to be traced in the shared and changing Latin and vernacular literatures of Europe—it is of some interest to the literary historian to find that both the eleventh and the thirteenth centuries shared a delight in 'enchanted ground'.

[13] See C. Franzen, *The Tremulous Hand of Worcester: A Study of Old English in the Thirteenth Century* (Oxford, 1991).

A BIBLIOGRAPHY OF THE WRITINGS OF E. G. STANLEY

For books and articles we have aimed at completeness. For reviews, which have always formed an important aspect of EGS's scholarly activity, we have had to be selective in order to keep the list to manageable proportions; all substantial reviews that we could identify are included, but short notices have been omitted. The cut-off date is 1992. The following abbreviations are used: *N&Q* for *Notes and Queries*, and *Archiv* for *Archiv für das Studium der Neueren Sprachen und Literaturen*. (*The Editors*[1])

BOOKS

1956–60 *Evangeliorum Quattuor. Codex Lindisfarnensis. Musei Britannici Codex Cottonianus Nero D.IV.* Permissione Musei Britannici Totius Codicis Similitudo Expressa. Prolegomenis Auxerunt T. D. Kendrick, T. J. Brown, R. L. S. Bruce-Mitford, H. Roosen-Runge, A. S. C. Ross, E. G. Stanley, A. E. A. Werner. 2 vols. (Olten (Switzerland), 1956–60).

1960 (ed.) *The Owl and the Nightingale* (London, 1960; repr. Manchester, 1972).

1966 (ed.) *Continuations and Beginnings: Studies in Old English Literature* (London, 1966).

1969 *The Durham Ritual*, ed. T. J. Brown, with contributions by F. Wormald, A. S. C. Ross, E. G. Stanley (Copenhagen, 1969; Early English Manuscripts in Facsimile 16; 'Glossary to Aldred's Gloss', by A. S. C. Ross and E. G. Stanley, 53–92).

1975 *The Search for Anglo-Saxon Paganism* (Cambridge and Totowa, NJ, 1975).

1983 (ed., with Douglas Gray) *Five Hundred Years of Words and Sounds: A Festschrift for E. J. Dobson* (Cambridge, 1983).

1983 (ed., with Douglas Gray) *Middle English Studies Presented to Norman Davis in Honour of his Seventieth Birthday* (Oxford, 1983).

1987 *A Collection of Papers with Emphasis on Old English Literature* (Toronto, 1987; Publications of the Dictionary of Old English, 3).

1988 (ed., with T. F. Hoad) *Words for Robert Burchfield's Sixty-Fifth Birthday* (Cambridge, 1988).

1990 (ed.) *British Academy Papers on Anglo-Saxon England* (Oxford, 1990).

1991 (ed., with Fred C. Robinson) *Old English Verse Texts from Many Sources* (Copenhagen, 1991; Early English Manuscripts in Facsimile, 23).

[1] The editors gratefully acknowledge the assistance of Rohini Jayatilaka in compiling the bibliography.

ARTICLES

1952–3 'The Chronology of *r*-metathesis in Old English.' *English and Germanic Studies*, 5 (1952–3), 103–15.

1954 'A Note on *Genesis B*, 328.' *Review of English Studies*, 5 (1954), 55–8.

1956 'Die anglonormannischen Verse in dem mittelenglischen Gedicht "Die elf Hollenpeinen".' *Archiv*, 192 (1956), 21–32.

1956 'Old English Poetic Diction and the Interpretation of *The Wanderer, The Seafarer*, and *The Penitent's Prayer*.' *Anglia*, 73 (1956), 413–66; repr. in *A Collection of Papers* (above), 234–80; and in J. B. Bessinger Jr. and S. J. Kahrl (eds.), *Essential Articles for the Study of Old English Poetry* (Hamden, Conn., 1968), 458–514.

1957 'Some Notes on the *Owl and the Nightingale*.' *English and Germanic Studies*, 6 (1957), 30–63.

1959 'An Inedited Scrap of Middle English Verse from the West Midlands.' *Neuphilologische Mitteilungen*, 60 (1959), 287–8.

1959 'The Word *Alfredian*.' *N&Q* 204 (1959), 111–12; repr. in *A Collection of Papers* (above), 409.

1959 'The Use in English of the Word Aufklärung.' *N&Q* 204 (1959), 328–31.

1960 'The Term "Art Gallery": Its Use in Birmingham.' *N&Q* 205 (1960), 3–4.

1961 'An Inedited Nativity Sermon from Worcester.' *English and Germanic Studies*, 7 (1961), 53–79.

1962 'The Use in English of the Word "Schadenfreude".' *N&Q* 207 (1962), 68–9.

1963 'Hæþenra hyht in *Beowulf*.' In Stanley B. Greenfield (ed.), *Studies in Old English Literature in Honor of Arthur G. Brodeur* (Eugene, Oreg., 1963), 136–51; repr. in *A Collection of Papers* (above), 192–208.

1963 '"Weal" in the Old English *Ruin*: A Parallel?' *N&Q* 208 (1963), 405.

1964 'Dr. Johnson's Use of the Word "Also".' *N&Q* 209 (1964), 298–9.

1964 'The Search for Anglo-Saxon Paganism, I–V.' *N&Q* 209 (1964), 204–9; 242–50; 282–7; 324–31; 455–63.

1965 'The Search for Anglo-Saxon Paganism, VI–IX.' *N&Q* 210 (1965), 9–17; 203–7; 285–93; 322–7.

1966 '*Beowulf*.' In *Continuations and Beginnings* (above), 104–41; repr. in *A Collection of Papers* (above), 139–69.

1967 'Ripeness is All.' *N&Q* 212 (1967), 228–9.

1968 'The Date of Laȝamon's "Brut".' *N&Q* 213 (1968), 85–8.

1968 'Stanza and Ictus: Chaucer's Emphasis in "Troilus and Criseyde".' In Arno Esch (ed.), *Chaucer und seine Zeit: Symposion für Walter F. Schirmer* (Tübingen, 1968; Buchreihe der Anglia, 14), 123–48.

1969 'Laȝamon's Antiquarian Sentiments.' *Medium Ævum*, 38 (1969), 23–37.

1969 'Old English "-calla", "ceallian".' In Derek A. Pearsall and Ronald A. Waldron (eds.), *Medieval Literature and Civilization: Studies in Memory of G. N. Garmonsway* (London, 1969), 94–9.

1969 'Spellings of the *Waldend* Group.' In E. Bagby Atwood and A. A. Hill (eds.), *Studies in Language, Literature, and Culture of the Middle Ages and Later: Studies in Honour of Rudolph Willard* (Austin, Tex., 1969), 38–69.

1971 'Studies in the Prosaic Vocabulary of Old English Verse.' *Neuphilologische Mitteilungen*, 72 (1971), 385–418.

1972 'The Use of Bob-Lines in "Sir Thopas".' *Neuphilologische Mitteilungen*, 73 (1972), 417–26.

1974 'Directions for Making Many Kinds of Laces.' In Beryl Rowland (ed.), *Chaucer and Middle English Studies in Honour of Rossell Hope Robbins* (London, 1974), 89–103.

1974 'Some Observations on the A3 lines in *Beowulf*.' In R. B. Burlin and E. B. Irving, Jr. (eds.), *Old English Studies in Honour of John C. Pope* (Toronto and Buffalo, 1974), 139–64.

1974 'The Oldest English Poetry Now Extant.' *Poetica* (Tokyo), 2 (1974), 1–24; repr. in *A Collection of Papers* (above), 115–38.

1975 'Richard Hyrd(?), "rote of resoun ryht" in MS. Harley 2253.' *N&Q* 220 (1975), 155–7.

1975 'Sharon Turner's First Published Reference to "Beowulf".' *N&Q* 220 (1975), 3–4; repr. in *A Collection of Papers* (above), 75.

1975 'Verbal Stress in Old English Verse.' *Anglia*, 93 (1975), 307–34.

1976 'About Troilus.' *Essays and Studies*, 29 (1976), 84–106.

1976 'Did Beowulf Commit *feaxfeng* against Grendel's Mother?' *N&Q* 221 (1976), 339–40; repr. in *A Collection of Papers* (above), 232–3.

1976 '"Of This Cokes Tale Maked Chaucer Na Moore".' *Poetica* (Tokyo), 5 (1976), 36–59.

1977 'How the Elbing Deprives the Vistula of its Name and Converts it to the Elbing's Own Use in "Vistula-Mouth".' *N&Q* 222 (1977), 2–11; repr. in *A Collection of Papers* (above), 336–51.

1978 '"Peytral" and the Like for the OED Supplement.' *N&Q* 223 (1978), 533–6.

1978 '*Sum heard gewrinc* (*Genesis B* 317).' *N&Q* 223 (1978), 104–5.

1979 '*Geoweorþa*: "Once Held in High Esteem".' In Mary Salu and Robert T. Farrell (eds.), *J. R. R. Tolkien, Scholar and Storyteller: Essays in Memoriam* (Ithaca and London, 1979), 99–119; repr. in *A Collection of Papers* (above), 318–35.

1979 'The Narrative Art of *Beowulf*.' In Hans Bekker-Nielsen *et al.* (eds.), *Medieval Narrative: A Symposium* (Odense, 1979), 58–81; repr. in *A Collection of Papers* (above), 170–91.

1979 'Two Old English Poetic Phrases Insufficiently Understood for Literary Criticism: *þing gehegan* and *seonoþ gehegan*.' In Daniel G. Calder (ed.), *Old English Poetry: Essays on Style* (Berkeley, Los Angeles, and London, 1979), 67–90; repr. in *A Collection of Papers* (above), 298–317.

1981 'The Date of *Beowulf*: Some Doubts and No Conclusions.' In Colin Chase (ed.), *The Dating of 'Beowulf'* (Toronto, Buffalo, and London, 1981), 197–211; repr. in *A Collection of Papers* (above), 209–31.

1981 'The Glorification of Alfred King of Wessex (from the Publication of Sir John Spelman's *Life*, 1678 and 1709, to the Publication of Reinhold Pauli's, 1851).' *Poetica* (Tokyo), 12 (1981), 103–33; repr. in *A Collection of Papers* (above), 410–41.

1981 'The Scholarly Recovery of the Significance of Anglo-Saxon Records in Prose and Verse: A New Bibliography.' *Anglo-Saxon England*, 9 (1981), 223–62; repr. in *A Collection of Papers* (above), 3–48.

1982 'The Bibliography of Old English: The Past.' In Stanley B. Greenfield (ed.),

The Bibliography of Old English (1982; Old English Newsletter, Subsidia 8), 3–9; repr. in *A Collection of Papers* (above), 76–82.

1982 'The Prenominal Prefix *ge-* in Late Old English and Early Middle English.' *Transactions of the Philological Society 1982*, 25–66.

1982 'Translation from Old English: "The Garbaging War-Hawk", or, the Literary Materials from which the Reader can Re-create the Poem.' In Mary J. Carruthers and Elizabeth D. Kirk (eds.), *Acts of Interpretation: The Text in its Context 700–1600. Essays on Medieval and Renaissance Literature in Honor of E. Talbot Donaldson* (Norman, Okla., 1982), 67–101; repr. in *A Collection of Papers* (above), 83–114.

1983 'The Continental Contribution to the Study of Anglo-Saxon Writings up to and Including that of the Grimms.' In Thomas Finkenstaedt and Gertrud Scholtes (eds.), *Towards a History of English Studies in Europe: Proceedings of the Wildsteig-Symposium, April 30–May 3, 1982* (Augsburg, 1983), 9–38; repr. in *A Collection of Papers* (above), 49–74.

1983 'Early Middle English "oc" = "but, and".' In *Five Hundred Years* (above), 144–50.

1983 'Richard Bentley's Use of "Persona", 1732.' *N&Q* 228 (1983), 442.

1984 'Alliterative Ornament and Alliterative Rhythmical Discourse in Old High German and Old Frisian compared with Similar Manifestations in Old English.' *Beiträge zur Geschichte der deutschen Sprache und Literatur*, 106 (1984) 184–217.

1984 'Notes on the Text of *Christ and Satan* and on *The Riming Poem* and *The Rune Poem*, chiefly on *wynn, wen* and *wenne*.' *N&Q* 229 (1984), 443–53.

1985 'Ælfric on the Canonicity of the Book of Judith: "Hit stent on leden þus on ðære bibliothecan".' *N&Q* 230 (1985), 439.

1985 'Notes on the Text of *Exodus*.' In Marie Collins, Jocelyn Price, and Andrew Hamer (eds.), *Sources and Relations: Studies in Honour of J. E. Cross*, Leeds Studies in English, NS 16 (1985), 240–5.

1985 'OE *to-gedegled*: A Ghostword.' *N&Q* 230 (1985), 10.

1985 '*The Judgement of the Damned* (from Cambridge, Corpus Christi College 201 and Other Manuscripts), and the Definition of Old English Verse.' In M. Lapidge and H. Gneuss (eds.), *Learning and Literature in Anglo-Saxon England: Studies Presented to Peter Clemoes on the Occasion of his Sixty-Fifth Birthday* (Cambridge, 1985), 363–91; repr. as '*The Judgement of the Damned*, from Corpus Christi College Cambridge 201 and Other Manuscripts, and the Definition of Old English Verse' in *A Collection of Papers* (above), 354–83.

1985 'The Treatment of Late, Badly Transmitted and Spurious Old English in a Dictionary of that Language.' In Alfred Bammesberger (ed.), *Problems of Old English Lexicography: Studies in Memory of Angus Cameron* (Regensburg, 1985; Eichstätter Beiträge 15, Abt. Sprache und Literatur), 331–67.

1985 'Unideal Principles of Editing Old English Verse.' *Proceedings of the British Academy*, 70 (1985 for 1984), 231–73.

1986 'Notes on the Text of the Old English Genesis.' In Phyllis Rugg Brown, Georgia Ronan Crampton, and Fred C. Robinson (eds.), *Modes of Interpretation in Old English Literature: Essays in Honour of Stanley B. Greenfield* (Toronto, Buffalo, and London, 1986), 189–96.

1986 'Rudolf von Raumer: Long Sentences in *Beowulf* and the Influence of Christianity on Germanic Style.' *N&Q* 231 (1986), 434–8.

1987 'The Germanic "Heroic Lay" of Finnesburg.' In *A Collection of Papers* (above), 281–97.

1987 'The Late Saxon Disc-brooch from Sutton (Isle of Ely): its Verse Inscription.' In *A Collection of Papers* (above), 400–8.

1987 'Old English in *The Oxford English Dictionary*.' In Robert Burchfield (ed.), *Studies in Lexicography* (Oxford, 1987), 19–35.

1987 'The Ruthwell Cross Inscription: Some Linguistic and Literary Implications of Paul Meyvaert's Paper "An Apocalypse Panel on the Ruthwell Cross".' In *A Collection of Essays* (above), 384–99.

1987 'Owl and the Nightingale, The.' In J. R. Strayer (ed.), *Dictionary of the Middle Ages*, 9 (New York, 1987), 315–19.

1988 'The Difficulty of Establishing Borrowings between Old English and the Continental West Germanic Languages.' In Graham Nixon and John Honey (eds.), *An Historic Tongue: Studies in English Linguistics in Memory of Barbara Strang* (London and New York, 1988), 3–16.

1988 'Karl Luick's "Man schrieb wie man sprach" and English Historical Philology.' In Dieter Kastovsky and Gero Bauer (eds.), *Luick Revisited: Papers Read at the Luick-Symposium at Schloss Lichtenstein, 15.–18.9.1985* (Tübingen, 1988), 311–34.

1988 'King Alfred's Prefaces.' *Review of English Studies*, NS 39 (1988), 349–64.

1988 'The Meaning of Old English *corþer, corþor*.' *N&Q* 233 (1988), 292–4.

1988 'Parody in Early English Literature.' *Poetica* (Tokyo), 27 (1988), 1–69.

1988 'Rhymes in English Medieval Verse: From Old English to Middle English.' In Edward Donald Kennedy, Ronald Waldron, and Joseph S. Wittig (eds.), *Medieval English Studies Presented to George Kane* (Wolfeboro, NH and Woodbridge, 1988), 19–54.

1988 'Words from *A Supplement to Dr. Harris's Dictionary of Arts and Sciences, 1744*.' In *Words for Robert Burchfield's Sixty-Fifth Birthday* (above), 163–9.

1989 'A *Beowulf* Allusion, 1790.' *N&Q* 234 (1989), 148.

1989 'Chaucer's Metre after Chaucer, I: Chaucer to Hoccleve.' *N&Q* 234 (1989), 11–23.

1989 'Chaucer's Metre after Chaucer, II: Lydgate and Barclay.' *N&Q* 234 (1989), 151–62.

1989 'Notes on Old English Poetry.' *Leeds Studies in English*, NS 20 (1989), 319–44.

1990 ' "Hengestes heap", *Beowulf* 1091.' In Alfred Bammesberger and Alfred Wollmann (eds.), *Britain 400–600: Language and History* (Heidelberg, 1990; Anglistische Forschungen 205), 51–63.

1990 'J. Bosworth's Interest in "Friesic" for his Dictionary of the Anglo-Saxon Language (1838): "The Friesic is far the most important language for my purpose".' In Rolf H. Bremmer Jr., Geart van der Meer, and Oebele Vries (eds.), *Aspects of Old Frisian Philology* (Amsterdam and Atlanta, 1990 (Amsterdamer Beiträge zur älteren Germanistik, 31–2); Groningen and Grins, 1990 (Estrikken 69)), 428–52.

1990 'Old English *belehycge*: A Ghostword.' *N&Q* 235 (1990), 3–5.

1990 'Old English Studies for Japan.' *Mediaeval English Studies Newsletter* (Tokyo), 22 (1990), 1–5.

1990 'The *Oxford English Dictionary* and *Supplement*: The Integrated Edition of 1989.' *Review of English Studies*, NS 41 (1990), 76–88. (Cf. 42 (1991), 81–3).

1990 'Pearl, 358, "And þy lurez of lyȝtly leme": Metanalysed Tmesis for the Sake of Alliteration.' *N&Q* 235 (1990), 158–60.

1990 'The Rune Poem 34: *beornum*.' *N&Q* 235 (1990), 143–4.

1990 'Foreword' to Georgiau R. Tashjian, David R. Tashjian and Brian J. Enright, *Richard Rawlinson: A Tercentenary Memorial* (Kalamazoo, Mi, 1990), vii–x.

1991 'Dance, Dancers and Dancing in Anglo-Saxon England.' *Dance Research*, 9/2 (1991), 18–31.

1991 'The Owl and the Nightingale 1335: "þu liest iwis, þu fule þing!".' *N&Q* 236 (1991), 152.

1991 'Stanley B. Greenfield's Solution of *Riddle* (ASPR) 39: "Dream".' *N&Q* 236 (1991), 148–9.

1992 'Old English ÆR Conjunction: "rather than".' *N&Q* 237 (1992), 11–13.

1992 'Robert Dodsley's Archaizing Chaucer Allusion.' *N&Q* 237 (1992), 278–80.

1992 'Initial Clusters of Unstressed Syllables in Half-Lines of *Beowulf*.' In Michael Korhammer (ed.), *Words, Texts and Manuscripts: Studies in Anglo-Saxon Culture Presented to Helmut Gneuss on the Occasion of his Sixty-Fifth Birthday* (Cambridge, 1992), 263–84.

1992 'Wolf, My Wolf!' In Joan H. Hall, Nick Doane and Dick Ringler (eds.), *Old English and New: Studies in Language and Linguistics in Honor of Frederic G. Cassidy* (New York and London, 1992), 46–62.

REVIEWS

1953 Prins, A. A., *French Influence in English Phrasing* (1952). *English and Germanic Studies*, 5 (1953), 118–19.

1954 Entwistle, W. J., *Aspects of Language* (1953). *Atlante*, 2 (1954), 169–71.

1956 Horn, W., and M. Lehnert, *Laut und Leben: Englische Lautgeschichte der neueren Zeit (1400–1950)* (1954). *Modern Language Review*, 51 (1956), 88–90.

1957 Bliss, A. J. (ed.), *Sir Orfeo* (1954). *English and Germanic Studies*, 6 (1957), 118–20.

1957 Robertson, Stuart, *The Development of Modern English* (1954). *English and Germanic Studies*, 6 (1957), 120–1.

1957 Vleeskruyer, R., *The Life of St. Chad: An Old English Homily* (1953). *English and Germanic Studies*, 6 (1957), 112–18.

1957 (with A. S. C. Ross) Collinder, Björn, *Beowulf översatt i originalets versmått* (1954). *English and Germanic Studies*, 6 (1957), 110–12.

1960 Goolden, Peter, *The Old English Apollonius of Tyre* (1958). *Modern Language Review*, 55 (1960), 428.

1962 Gordon, Ida L., *The Seafarer* (1960). *Medium Ævum*, 31 (1962), 54–60.

1962 Lawrence, William Witherle, *'Beowulf' and Epic Tradition* (repr. 1961). *Modern Language Review*, 57 (1962), 589–91.

1962 Willard, Rudolph, *The Blickling Homilies (The John H. Scheide Library, Titusville, Pennsylvania)*, Early English Manuscripts in Facsimile, 10 (1960). *Anglia*, 80 (1962), 446–8.

1963 Bliss, Alan J., *The Metre of 'Beowulf'* (1958). *English Philological Studies*, 8 (1963), 47–53.

1963 Bonjour, Adrien, *Twelve 'Beowulf' Papers: 1940–1960, with Additional Comments* (1962). *Modern Language Review*, 58 (1963), 550–1.

1963 Ure, James M., *The Benedictine Office: An Old English Text* (1957). *English Philological Studies*, 8 (1963), 66–7.

1964 Blake, Norman F. (ed.), *The Phoenix* (1964). *N&Q* 209 (1964), 434–5.

1964 Davis, Norman, and Charles L. Wrenn (eds.), *English and Medieval Studies: Presented to J. R. R. Tolkien on the Occasion of his 70th Birthday* (1962). *Archiv*, 201 (1964), 130–2.

1964 Raffel, Burton, *Beowulf: A New Translation with an Introduction by Burton Raffel, Afterword by Robert P. Creed* (1963). *Modern Language Review*, 59 (1964), 253.

1965 Masui, Michio, *The Structure of Chaucer's Rime Words: An Exploration into the Poetic Language of Chaucer* (1964). *N&Q* 210 (1965), 389–90.

1966 Bessinger, Jess B., and Robert P. Creed (eds.), *Franciplegius: Medieval and Linguistic Studies in Honor of Francis Peabody Magoun, Jr.* (1965). *N&Q* 211 (1966), 424–6.

1966 Ostheeren, Klaus, *Studien zum Begriff der 'Freude' und seinen Ausdrucksmitteln in altenglischen Texten (Poesie, Alfred, Ælfric)* (1964). *N&Q* 211 (1966), 399–400.

1966 Palmer, D. J., *The Rise of English Studies* (1965). *N&Q* 211 (1966), 238–40.

1967 Endter, Wilhelm, *König Alfreds des Grossen Bearbeitung der Soliloquien des Augustinus* (repr. 1964).
Raith, Josef, *Die altenglische Version des Halitgar'schen Bussbuches (sog. Poenitentiale Pseudo-Egberti)* (repr. 1964).
Schröer, Arnold, *Die angelsächsischen Prosabearbeitungen der Benediktinerregel* (repr. 1964).
Assmann, Bruno, *Angelsächsische Homilien und Heiligenleben* (repr. 1964).
Förster, Max, *Die Vercelli-Homilien: I.–VIII. Homilie* (repr. 1966).
Wildhagen, Karl, *Der Cambridger Psalter* (repr. 1964).
Archiv, 203 (1967), 298–300.

1967 Kuhn, Sherman M., *The Vespasian Psalter*, 1 (1965). *N&Q* 212 (1967), 30–2.

1967 Tucker, S. I., *Protean Shape: A Study in Eighteenth-Century Vocabulary and Usage* (1967). *N&Q* 212 (1967), 436–8.

1968 Schabram, Hans, *Superbia: Studien zum altenglischen Wortschatz, 1* (1965). *Archiv*, 204 (1968), 380–2.

1968 Zupitza, Julius, *Ælfrics Grammatik und Glossar 1: Text und Varianten* (repr. 1966). *Archiv*, 205 (1968), 312–13.

1969 Fehr, Bernhard, *Die Hirtenbriefe Ælfrics in altenglischer und lateinischer Fassung* (repr. 1966).
Hecht, Hans, *Bischof Wærferths von Worcester Übersetzung der Dialoge Gregors des Grossen* (repr. 1956).
Archiv, 205 (1969), 482–3.

1969 Gneuss, Helmut, *Hymnar und Hymnen im englischen Mittelalter: Studien zur Überlieferung, Glossierung und Übersetzung lateinischer Hymnen in England. Mit einer Textausgabe der lateinisch-altenglischen Expositio Hymnorum* (1968). *Archiv*, 206 (1969), 136–8.

1969 Henry, P. L., *The Early English and Celtic Lyric* (1966). *Modern Language Review*, 64 (1969), 128–9.

1969 Irving, Edward B., *A Reading of 'Beowulf'* (1968). *N&Q* 214 (1969), 35–7.

1969 Oliphant, Robert T. (ed.), *The Harley Latin–Old English Glossary*, Janua Linguarum, Series Practica, 20 (1966). *Archiv*, 205 (1969), 481–2.

1969 Westphalen, Tilman, *Beowulf 3150–55: Textkritik und Editionsgeschichte* (1967). *Studia Neophilologica*, 41 (1969), 209–11.

1970 Bessinger, J. B., Jr., *A Concordance to Beowulf* (1969). *Modern Language Review*, 65 (1970), 863–5.

1970 Carnicelli, Thomas A. (ed.), *King Alfred's Version of St Augustine's 'Soliloquies'* (1969). *N&Q* 215 (1970), 109–12.

1970 Kühlwein, Wolfgang, *Die Verwendung der Feindseligkeitsbezeichnungen in der altenglischenDichtersprache* (1967). *Indogermanische Forschungen*, 75 (1970), 352–6.

1970 Pope, John C., *Homilies of Ælfric: A Supplementary Collection*, 2 vols. (1967–8). *N&Q* 215 (1970), 262–6.

1970 Schubel, Friedrich, *Englische Literaturgeschichte I: Die alt- und mittelenglische Periode* (2nd edn., 1967). *Anglia*, 88 (1970), 356–9.

1971 Grünberg, Madeleine, *The West-Saxon Gospels: A Study of the Gospel of St. Matthew with Text of the Four Gospels* (1967). *Archiv*, 208 (1971), 135–6.

1971 Kristensson, Gillis, *Studies in Middle English Topographical Terms* (1970). *N&Q* 216 (1971), 188–9.

1971 Okasha, Elisabeth, *Hand-List of Anglo-Saxon Non-Runic Inscriptions* (1971). *N&Q* 216 (1971), 305–8.

1972 Aitken, A. J., Angus McIntosh, and H. Pálsson (eds.), *Edinburgh Studies in English and Scots* (1971). *N&Q* 217 (1972), 305–7.

1972 Alexander, Michael, *The Earliest English Poems* (1970). *N&Q* 217 (1972), 282–3.

1972 Wilson, R. M., *The Lost Literature of Medieval England* (2nd edn., 1970). *N&Q* 217 (1972), 282.

1973 Breuer, Rolf, and Rainer Schöwerling, *Altenglische Lyrik: Englisch und Deutsch* (1972). *Anglia*, 91 (1973), 514–17.

1973 Göller, Karl Heinz, *Geschichte der altenglischen Literatur* (1971). *Archiv*, 210 (1973), 359–63.

1973 Gradon, Pamela, *Form and Style in Early English Literature* (1971). *Yearbook of English Studies*, 3 (1973), 265–7.

1973 Lindemann, J. W. Richard, *Old English Preverbal 'Ge-': Its Meaning* (1970). *Anglia*, 91 (1973), 493–4.

1973 Schwab, Ute, *Die Sternrune im Wessobrunner Gebet, Beobachtungen zur Lokalisierung des clm 22053, zur HS. BM Arundel 293 und zu Rune Poem V. 86–89* (1972). *N&Q* 218 (1973), 402.

1973 Wienold, Götz, *Formulierungstheorie, Poetik, strukturelle Literaturgeschichte am Beispiel der altenglischen Dichtung* (1971). *Erasmus*, 25 (1973), cols. 673–5.

1974 Clemoes, Peter, *et al.* (eds.), *Anglo-Saxon England*, 1 (1972). *Archiv*, 211 (1974), 418–21.

1974 Gretsch, Mechthild, *Die Regula Sancti Benedicti in England und ihre altenglische Übersetzung* (1973). *N&Q* 219 (1974), 344–7.

1974 Alexander, Michael, *Beowulf: A Verse Translation* (1973). *N&Q* 219 (1974), 402.

1975 Clemoes, Peter, *et al.* (eds.), *Anglo-Saxon England*, 2 (1973). *Archiv*, 212 (1975), 364–5.

1975 Vriend, Hubert Jan de (ed.), *The Old English 'Medicina de Quadrupedibus'* (1972). *Anglia*, 93 (1975), 217–20.

1976 Kane, George, and E. Talbot Donaldson (eds.), *Piers Plowman: The B Version:*

Will's Visions of Piers Plowman, Do-Well, Do-Better and Do-Best (1975). *N&Q* 221 (1976), 435–47.

1977 Bierbaumer, Peter, *Der botanische Wortschatz des Altenglischen*, i–ii (1975–6). *N&Q* 222 (1977), 561–3.

1977 Burrow, John (ed.), *English Verse 1300–1500* (1977). *N&Q* 222 (1977), 563–4.

1977 Clemoes, Peter, *et al.* (eds.), *Anglo-Saxon England*, 3 and 4 (1974–5). *Archiv*, 214 (1977), 134–8.

1977 Darby, H. C., and G. R. Versey, *Domesday Gazetteer* (1975). *N&Q* 222 (1977), 74–5.

1977 Kirschner, Josef, *Die Bezeichnungen für Kranz und Krone im Altenglischen* (1975). *N&Q* 222 (1977), 97–8.

1977 Kristensson, Gillis (ed.), *John Mirk's 'Instructions for Parish Priests'* (1974). *N&Q* 222 (1977), 79–80.

1977 Metcalf, Allan A., *Poetic Diction of the Old English Meters of Boethius* (1973). *N&Q* 222 (1977), 1–2.

1977 Nevanlinna, Saara (ed.), *The Northern Homily Cycle: The Expanded Version in MSS Harley 4196 and Cotton Tiberius E vii*, Parts I–II (1972–3). *N&Q* 222 (1977), 77–9.

1977 Pearsall, Derek, *Old and Middle English Poetry* (1977). *N&Q* 222 (1977), 558–61.

1977 Pheifer, J. D. (ed.), *Old English Glosses in the Épinal-Erfurt Glossary* (1974). *Archiv*, 214 (1977), 131–4.

1977 Seymour, M. C. (ed.), *On the Properties of Things. John Trevisa's Translation of Bartholomæus Anglicus De Proprietatibus Rerum: A Critical Text* (1975). *N&Q* 222 (1977), 463–4.

1977 Swanton, Michael (trans.), *Anglo-Saxon Prose* (1975). *Review of English Studies*, NS 28 (1977), 62–4.

1978 Görlach, M. (ed.), *An East Midland Revision of the South English Legendary*, Middle English Texts, 4 (1976).
Sauer, Walter (ed.), *The Metrical Life of Christ*, Middle English Texts, 5 (1977).
Moe, Phyllis (ed.), *The ME Prose Translation of Roger D'Argenteuil's Bible en françois*, Middle English Texts, 6 (1977).
Bornstein, Diane (ed.), *The Middle English Translation of Christine de Pisan's Livre du corps de policie*, Middle English Texts, 7 (1977).
Beer, Francis (ed.), *Julian of Norwich's Revelations of Divine Love, The Shorter Version*, Middle English Texts, 8 (1978).
N&Q 223 (1978), 543–6.

1978 Korhammer, Michael, *Die monastischen Cantica im Mittelalter und ihre altenglischen Interlinearversionen* (1976). *N&Q* 223 (1978), 246–7.

1978 Reinhard, Mariann, *On the Semantic Relevance of the Alliterative Collocations in 'Beowulf'* (1976). *Anglia*, 96 (1978), 502–3.

1978 *The Thornton Manuscript Lincoln Cathedral MS 91*, with an introduction by D. S. Brewer and A. E. B. Owen (1977).
The Findern Manuscript Cambridge University Library MS Ff.1.6, with an introduction by Richard Beadle and A. E. B. Owen (1977).
N&Q 223 (1978), 165–8.

1979 *The Auchinleck Manuscript National Library of Scotland Advocates' MS. 19.2.1*, [facsimile] with an introduction by Derek Pearsall and I. G. Cunningham (1977). *N&Q* 224 (1979), 157–8.

1979 Bessinger, J. B., Jr., *A Concordance to the Anglo-Saxon Poetic Records* (1978). *Review of English Studies*, NS 30 (1979), 328–31.

1979 Clemoes, Peter, *et al.* (eds.), *Anglo-Saxon England*, 6 (1977). *Archiv*, 216 (1979), 166–8.

1979 Murray, K. M. Elisabeth, *Caught in the Web of Words: James A. H. Murray and the Oxford English Dictionary* (1977; seventh printing with corrections 1978). *N&Q* 224 (1979), 53–5.

1979 Nickel, Gerhard, *et al.* (eds. and trans.), *Beowulf und die kleineren Denkmäler der altenglischen Heldensage Waldere und Finnsburg* (1976). *Anglia*, 97 (1979), 517–25.

1979 Rigg, A. G. (ed.), *Editing Medieval Texts: English, French, and Latin Written in England* (1977). *N&Q* 224 (1979), 98–9.

1979 Rüden, Michael von, *'Wlanc' und Derivate im Alt- und Mittelenglischen: Eine wortgeschichtliche Studie* (1978). *Medium Ævum*, 48 (1979), 271.

1979 Sauer, Hans (ed.), *Theodulfi Capitula in England: Die altenglischen Übersetzungen, zusammen mit dem lateinischen Text* (1978). *N&Q* 224 (1979), 60–1.

1979 Bierbaumer, Peter, *Der botanische Wortschatz des Altenglischen*, iii (1979). *N&Q* 224 (1979), 566.

1979 Clemoes, Peter, *et al.* (eds.), *Anglo-Saxon England*, 7 (1978). *Archiv*, 216 (1979), 404–7.

1979 Mehl, D., *Geoffrey Chaucer: Eine Einführung in seine erzählenden Dichtungen* (1973). *Anglia*, 97 (1979), 238–41.

1980 Shippey, T. A., *Beowulf* (1978). *Review of English Studies*, NS 31 (1980), 67–8.

1981 Andrew, Malcolm, and Ronald Waldron (eds.), *The Poems of the Pearl Manuscript: Pearl, Cleanness, Patience, Sir Gawain and the Green Knight* (1978). *N&Q* 226 (1981), 66–8.

1981 Doane, A. N. (ed.), *'Genesis A': A New Edition* (1978). *Archiv*, 218 (1981), 162–5.

1981 Hamer, Richard (ed.), *Three Lives from the Gilte Legende*, Middle English Texts, 9 (1978).
von Nolcken, Christina (ed.), *The Middle English Translation of the Rosarium Theologie*, Middle English Texts, 10 (1979).
N&Q 226 (1981), 1–2.

1981 Zettersten, Arne (ed.), *Waldere* (1979). *Archiv*, 218 (1981), 165–6.

1982 Bammesberger, Alfred, *Beiträge zu einem etymologischen Wörterbuch des Altenglischen* (1979). *N&Q* 227 (1982), 150–3.

1982 Blake, N. F. (ed.), *The Canterbury Tales by Geoffrey Chaucer*, York Medieval Texts, second series (1980). *N&Q* 227 (1982), 428–9.

1982 Clemoes, Peter, *et al.* (eds.), *Anglo-Saxon England*, 8 and 9 (1979–80). *Archiv*, 219 (1982), 420–3.

1982 Göbel, Helga, *Studien zu den altenglischen Schriftwesenrätseln* (1980). *N&Q* 227 (1982), 97–8.

1982 Hetherington, M. S., *The Beginnings of Old English Lexicography* (1980). *N&Q* 227 (1982), 238–40.

1982 Horrall, Sarah M. (ed.), *The Southern Version of 'Cursor Mundi'*, vol. 1, Ottawa Mediaeval Texts and Studies, 5 (1978). *N&Q* 227 (1982), 158–9.

1982 Ingersoll, Sheila Most, *Intensive and Restrictive Modification in Old English* (1978). *Archiv*, 219 (1982), 419–20.

1982 Ruggiers, Paul G. (ed.), *Geoffrey Chaucer: The Canterbury Tales. A Facsimile and Transcription of the Hengwrt Manuscript, with Variants from the Ellesmere Manuscript* (1979). *N&Q* 227 (1982), 426–8.

1982 Venezky, Richard L., and Antonette diPaolo Healey, *A Michrofiche Concordance to Old English* (1981). *N&Q* 227 (1982), 385–6.

1983 Heyworth, P. L. (ed.), *Medieval Studies for J. A. W. Bennett Aetatis Suae LXX* (1981). *Modern Language Review*, 78 (1983), 894–6.

1983 Perryman, Judith (ed.), *The King of Tars*, Middle English Texts, 12 (1980).
Powell, Susan (ed.), *The Advent and Nativity Sermons from a Fifteenth-Century Revision of John Mirk's Festial*, Middle English Texts, 13 (1981).
Nelson, Venetia (ed.), *A Myrour to Lewde Men and Wymmen*, Middle English Texts, 14 (1981).
N&Q 228 (1983), 97–8.

1983 Scragg, D. G. (ed.), *The Battle of Maldon* (1981). *N&Q* 228 (1983), 161.

1984 'McMaster Old English Texts and Studies' (James E. Cross and Thomas D. Hill (eds.), *The 'Prose Solomon and Saturn' and 'Adrian and Ritheus'* (1982), Maureen Halsall (ed.), *The Old English 'Rune Poem': A Critical Edition* (1981), and Charles R. Sleeth, *Studies in 'Christ and Satan'* (1982)). *N&Q* 229 (1984), 433–6.

1984 Alexander, Michael, *Macmillan History of English Literature: Old English Literature* (1983). *N&Q* 229 (1984), 99–100.

1984 Anderson, Earl R., *Cynewulf: Structure, Style, and Theme in his Poetry* (1983). *N&Q* 229 (1984), 524–6.

1984 Clemoes, Peter, *et al.* (eds.), *Anglo-Saxon England*, 10 (1982). *Archiv*, 221 (1984), 163–5.

1984 Hiltunen, Risto, *The Decline of the Prefixes and the Beginnings of the Phrasal Verb: The Evidence from some Old and Early Middle English Texts* (1983). *N&Q* 229 (1984), 1.

1984 Kiernan, Kevin S., *'Beowulf' and the 'Beowulf' Manuscript* (1981). *Medium Ævum*, 53 (1984), 112–17.

1984 Macrae-Gibson, O. D. (ed.), *The Old English Riming Poem* (1983). *N&Q* 229 (1984), 526–8.

1984 Room, Adrian, *A Concise Dictionary of Modern Place-Names in Great Britain and Ireland* (1983). *N&Q* 230 (1984), 530–1.

1984 Story, G. M., W. J. Kirkwin and J. D. A. Widdowson, *Dictionary of Newfoundland English* (1982). *N&Q* 229 (1984), 103–4.

1984 Torkar, Roland, *Eine altenglische Übersetzung von Alcuins 'De Virtutibus et Vitiis', Kap. 20 (Liebermanns Judex)* (1981). *Anglia*, 102 (1984), 199–200.

1984 Waterhouse, Ruth, *The Triangular Clause Relationship in Ælfric's 'Lives of Saints' and in Other Works* (1983). *N&Q* 229 (1984), 436–7.

1984 Clemoes, Peter, *et al.* (eds.), *Anglo-Saxon England*, 11 (1983). *Archiv*, 221 (1984), 363–5.

1985 Adams, Robert M., *The Land and Literature of England—a Historical Account* (1983). *N&Q* 230 (1985), 89.

1985 Finkenstaedt, Thomas, *Kleine Geschichte der Anglistik in Deutschland: Eine Einführung* (1983). *N&Q* 230 (1985), 98.

1985 Ruggiers, Paul G. (ed.), *Editing Chaucer—The Great Tradition* (1984). *N&Q* 230 (1985), 393.

1985 *St John's College, Cambridge, Manuscript L.1. A Facsimile.* Introduction by Richard Beadle and Jeremy Griffiths (1983). *N&Q* 230 (1985), 391–3.

1985 Taylor, Simon (ed.), *The Anglo-Saxon Chronicle: MS B* (1983). *Review of English Studies*, NS 36 (1985), 546–9.

1985 Urdang, L., and F. Abate, *Idioms and Phrases Index* (1983). *N&Q* 230 (1985), 87.

1985 Yerkes, David, *Syntax and Style in Old English: A Comparison of the Two Versions of Wærferth's Translation of Gregory's Dialogues* (1982). *Medium Ævum*, 54 (1985), 133–4.

1986 Clemoes, Peter, *et al.* (eds.), *Anglo-Saxon England*, 12 (1983). *N&Q* 231 (1986), 201–4.

1986 De Vriend, Hubert Jan (ed.), *The Old English Herbarium and Medicina de Quadrupedibus*, EETS OS 286 (1984). *N&Q* 231 (1986), 403–4.

1986 Edwards, A. S. G. (ed.), with N. F. Blake, L. Braswell and R. Hanna III, *The Index of Middle English Prose. Handlist I. A Handlist of Manuscripts containing Middle English Prose in the Henry E. Huntington Library*. By Ralph Hanna III (1984). *Handlist II. Manuscripts containing Middle English Prose in the John Rylands and Chetham's Libraries, Manchester.* By G. A. Lester (1985). *N&Q* 231 (1986), 97–8.

1986 Ikegami, M. T., *Rhyme and Pronunciation. Some Studies of English Rhymes from 'Kyng Alis[a]under' to Skelton*, Hogaku-Kenkyu-Kai Keio University, Extra Series, 5 (1984). *N&Q* 231 (1986), 532–3.

1986 Mitchell, Bruce, *Old English Syntax*, 2 vols. (1985). *Review of English Studies*, NS 37 (1986), 234–7.

1986 Niles, John D., *'Beowulf': The Poem and its Tradition* (1983). *Review of English Studies*, NS 37 (1986), 70–3.

1986 Pickering, O. S. (ed.), *The South English Ministry and Passion*, Middle English Texts, 16 (1984).
Horrall, Sara H. (ed.), *The Lyf of Oure Lady: The ME Translation of Thomas of Hales' Vita Sancte Marie*, Middle English Texts, 17 (1985).
Mearns, Rodney (ed.), *The Vision of Tundale*, Middle English Texts, 18 (1985). *N&Q* 231 (1986), 289–90.

1986 Roberts, Gildas (trans.), *Beowulf: A New Translation into Modern English Verse* (1985). *N&Q* 231 (1986), 96.

1986 Tite, C. G. C. (ed.), with introductory essays translated by G. E. Turton, *Thomas Smith: Catalogue of the Manuscripts in the Cottonian Library 1696* (1984). *N&Q* 231 (1986), 402.

1987 Anderson, James E., *Two Literary Riddles in the Exeter Book—Riddle I and the Easter Riddle* (1986). *N&Q* 232 (1987), 520.

1987 Boffey, J., *Manuscripts of English Courtly Love Lyrics in the Later Middle Ages*, Manuscript Studies, 1 (1985). *N&Q* 232 (1987), 66–7.

1987 Calder, Daniel G., *et al.* (trans.), *Sources and Analogues of Old English Poetry*, 2 (1983). *Modern Language Review*, 82 (1987), 432–4.

1987 Cardwell, G. (selected with notes and chronology), *Mark Twain: Mississippi Writings—The Adventures of Tom Sawyer, Life on the Mississippi, Adventures of Huckleberry Finn, Pudd'nhead Wilson* (1984). *N&Q* 232 (1987), 279–82.

1987 Clemoes, Peter, *et al.* (eds.), *Anglo-Saxon England*, 14 (1985). *N&Q* 232 (1987), 516–17.

1987 Furrow, M. M. (ed.), *Ten Fifteenth-Century Comic Poems*, Garland Medieval Texts, 13 (1985). *N&Q* 232 (1987), 525–6.

1987 Horner, P. J. (ed.), *The Index of Middle English Prose: Handlist III. A Handlist of Manuscripts containing Middle English Prose in the Digby Collection, Bodleian Library, Oxford* (1986). *N&Q* 232 (1987), 526–7.

1987 Howe, Nicholas, *The Old English Catalogue Poems* (1985). *N&Q* 232 (1987), 519–20.

1987 Ohlgren, T. H. (ed.), *Insular and Anglo-Saxon Illuminated Manuscripts. An Iconographic Catalogue c.A.D. 625 to 1100*, Garland Reference Library of the Humanities, 631 (1986). *N&Q* 232 (1987), 62–3.

1987 Ransom, D. J., *Poets at Play, Irony and Parody in the Harley Lyrics* (1985). *N&Q* 232 (1987), 522.

1987 Smith, Andrea B. (ed.), *The Anonymous Parts of the Old English Hexateuch: A Latin–Old English/Old English–Latin Glossary* (1985). *N&Q* 232 (1987), 248–9.

1988 Bately, Janet M. (ed.), *The Anglo-Saxon Chronicle: MS A* (1986). *Review of English Studies*, NS 39 (1988), 96–7.

1988 Doyle, A. I. (ed.), *The Vernon Manuscript—a Facsimile of Bodleian Library, Oxford MS. Eng. Poet. a.1* (1987). *N&Q* 233 (1988), 209–11.

1988 Fischer, Andreas, *Engagement, Wedding, and Marriage in Old English* (1986).
Obst, Wolfgang, *Der Rhythmus des Beowulf: Eine Akzent- und Takttheorie* (1987).
N&Q 233 (1988), 1.

1988 Frantzen, Allen J., *King Alfred* (1986). *N&Q* 233 (1988), 203–4.

1988 Greenfield, Stanley B., and Daniel G. Calder, *A New Critical History of Old English Literature* (1986). *Comparative Literature*, 40 (1988), 286–9.

1988 [James, Thomas], *The First Printed Catalogue of the Bodleian Library 1605, a Facsimile* (1987). *N&Q* 233 (1988), 348–9.

1988 Lewis, R. E., N. F. Blake, and A. S. G. Edwards, *Index of Printed Middle English Prose*, Garland Reference Library of the Humanities, 537 (1985). *N&Q* 233 (1988), 208–9.

1988 Lutz, Angelika (ed.), *Die Version G der Angelsächsischen Chronik* (1981). *Review of English Studies*, NS 39 (1988), 281–2.

1988 Mehl, Dieter, *Geoffrey Chaucer: An Introduction to his Narrative Poetry* (1986). *Archiv*, 225 (1988), 389–90.

1988 Owen-Crocker, Gale, *Dress in Anglo-Saxon England* (1986). *N&Q* 233 (1988), 204–6.

1988 Pearsall, D. A. (ed.), *Manuscripts and Texts: Editorial Problems in Later Middle English Literature. Essays from the 1985 Conference at the University of York* (1987). *N&Q* 233 (1988), 212–14.

1988 Ruggiers, P. G. (gen. ed.), T. D. Ross (ed.), *The Miller's Tale*, A Variorum Edition of the Works of Geoffrey Chaucer, II, The Canterbury Tales, part 3 (1983).
Pearsall, D. A. (ed.), *The Nun's Priest's Tale*, Variorum Chaucer II. 9 (1984).
Baker, D. C. (ed.), *The Manciple's Tale*, Variorum Chaucer II. 10 (1984).
Corsa, H. S. (ed.), *The Physician's Tale*, Variorum Chaucer II. 17 (1987).
Boyd, B. (ed.), *The Prioress's Tale*, Variorum Chaucer II. 20 (1987).
Pace, G. B., and A. David, *Geoffrey Chaucer: The Minor Poems. Part 1*, Variorum Chaucer V. 1 (1982).
N&Q 233 (1988), 512–16.

1988 Moffat, Douglas (ed.), *The Soul's Address to the Body (The Worcester Fragments)* (1987). *The Yearbook of Langland Studies*, 1 (1988), 150–2.

1989 Brown, P. and E. D. Higgs, *The Index of Middle English Prose: Handlist V. A Handlist of Manuscripts containing Middle English Prose in the Additional Collection (10001–12000), British Library, London*, by P. Brown, and *in the Additional Collection (12001–14000), British Library, London*, by E. D. Higgs (1988). *N&Q* 234 (1989), 489.

1989 Bunt, G. H. V. (ed.), *William of Palerne: An Alliterative Romance*, Mediaevalia Groningana VI (1985). *N&Q* 234 (1989), 220–1.

1989 Busse, Wilhelm, *Altenglische Literatur und ihre Geschichte* (1987). *N&Q* 234 (1989), 216–18.

1989 Cottle, B., *The Language of Literature: English Grammar in Action* (1985). *N&Q* 234 (1989), 84–7.

1989 Hanks, P., and F. Hodges, *A Dictionary of Surnames* (1988). *N&Q* 234 (1989), 373–4.

1989 Heffernan, Carol Falvo, *The Phoenix at the Fountain* (1988). *N&Q* 234 (1989), 218–20.

1989 Hofstetter, Walter, *Winchester und der spätaltenglische Sprachgebrauch* (1987). *N&Q* 234 (1989), 216.

1989 Hülsmann, R. (ed.), *The Erle of Tolous: Eine Paralleledition mit Einleitung und Glossar*, Anglistik in der Blauen Eule, 1 (1987). *N&Q* 234 (1989), 221–2.

1989 Kane, G. (ed.), *Piers Plowman: The A Version—Will's Visions of Piers Plowman and Do-Well, An Edition in the Form of Trinity College Cambridge MS R.3.14 Corrected from Other Manuscripts, with variant readings*, revised edition (1988).

Kane, G., and E. T. Donaldson (eds.), *Piers Plowman: The B Version—Will's Visions of Piers Plowman, Do-Well, Do-Better and Do-Best, An Edition in the Form of Trinity College Cambridge MS B.15.17, Corrected and Restored from the Known Evidence, with variant readings*, revised edition (1988).

N&Q 234 (1989), 363–6.

1989 Kristensson, G., *A Survey of Middle English Dialects 1290–1350: The West Midland Counties*, Skrifter utgivna av Vetenskapssocieteten i Lund—Publications of the New Society of Letters at Lund, 78 (1987). *N&Q* 234 (1989), 363.

1989 Marx, C. William, and Jeanne F. Drennan (eds.), *The Middle English Prose Complaint of Our Lady and Gospel of Nicodemus*, Middle English Texts, 19 (1987).

Mills, Maldwyn, *Horn Childe and Maiden Rimnild*, Middle English Texts, 20 (1988).

N&Q 234 (1989), 145–6.

1989 Masui, Michio, *Studies in Chaucer's Language of Feeling* (1988).

Masui, Michio (ed.), *A New Rime Index to The Canterbury Tales based on Manly and Rickert's Text of The Canterbury Tales* (1988).

N&Q 234 (1989), 369–70.

1989 Mitchell, Bruce, *On Old English: Selected Papers* (1988). *Medium Ævum*, 58 (1989), 317–19.

1989 Myers, J., and M. Simms, *Longman Dictionary and Handbook of Poetry* (1987). *N&Q* 234 (1989), 213–14.

1989 Swanton, Michael, *English Literature before Chaucer* (1987). *Medium Ævum*, 58 (1989), 143–6.

1989 Szarmach, Paul E. (ed.), *Studies in Earlier Old English Prose* (1986). *Modern Language Review*, 84 (1989), 911–12.

1989 Szarmach, Paul E., and Virginia Darrow Oggins (eds.), *Sources of Anglo-Saxon Culture* (1986). *Modern Language Review*, 84 (1989), 913–14.

1990 Barnhart, R. K. (ed.), *The Barnhart Dictionary of Etymology. The Core Vocabulary of Standard English—Produced by American Scholarship* (1988). *N&Q* 235 (1990), 336–7.

1990 Breivik, L. E., A. Hille, and S. Johansson (eds.), *Essays on English Language in Honour of Bertil Sundby*, Studia Anglistica Norvegica, 4 (1989). *N&Q* 235 (1990), 334–5.

1990 Donoghue, Daniel, *Style in Old English Poetry* (1987). *Review of English Studies*, NS 41 (1990), 233–4.

1990 *The Ellesmere Manuscript of Chaucer's Canterbury Tales: A Working Facsimile*, with an introduction by Ralph Hanna III (1989). *N&Q* 235 (1990), 333–4.

1990 Elliott, R. W. V., *Runes: An Introduction* (1989). *N&Q* 235 (1990), 322–3.

1990 Heyworth, P. L. (ed.), *Letters of Humfrey Wanley: Palaeographer, Anglo-Saxonist, Librarian, 1672–1726* (1989). *N&Q* 235 (1990), 70–2.

1990 Kiernan, Kevin S., *The Thorkelin Transcripts of 'Beowulf'* (1986). 235 (1990), 323–4.

1990 McIntosh, A., M. L. Samuels, and M. Laing (ed. M. Laing), *Middle English Dialectology: Essays on some Principles and Problems* (1989). *N&Q* 235 (1990), 328–30.

1990 Mackenzie, J. L. and R. Todd (eds.), *In Other Words: Transcultural Studies in Philology, Translation, and Lexicology presented to Hans Heinrich Meier on the Occasion of his Sixty-Fifth Birthday* (1989). *N&Q* 235 (1990), 324.

1990 Mandel, Jerome, *Alternative Readings in Old English Poetry* (1987). *Review of English Studies*, NS 41 (1990), 379–80.

1990 Minnis, A. J., and A. B. Scott, with the assistance of D. Scott, *Medieval Literary Theory and Criticism c.1100–c.1375: The Commentary-Tradition* (1988). *N&Q* 235 (1990), 330–2.

1990 Pickering, O. S., and S. Powell, *The Index of Middle English Prose: Handlist VI. A Handlist of Manuscripts containing Middle English Prose in Yorkshire Libraries and Archives* (1969).

Simpson, J., *The Index of Middle English Prose: Handlist VII. A Handlist of Manuscripts containing Middle English Prose in Parisian Libraries* (1989). *N&Q*235 (1989), 326–7.

1990 Seymour, M. C., *et al.* (eds.), *On the Properties of Things. John Trevisa's Translation of Bartholomæus Anglicus De Proprietatibus Rerum: A Critical Text*, vol. iii (1988). *N&Q* 235 (1990), 219.

1990 Thomson, R. M., *Catalogue of the Manuscripts of Lincoln Cathedral Chapter Library* (1989). *N&Q* 235 (1990), 324–6.

1991 Alexander, M. J., and F. Riddy (eds.), *Macmillan Anthology of English Literature, i: The Middle Ages (700–1550)* (1989). *N&Q* 236 (1991), 353–5.

1991 Millett, B., and J. Wogan-Browne (eds. and trans.), *Medieval English Prose for Women: Selections from the Katherine Group and Ancrene Wisse* (1990). *N&Q* 236 (1991), 355–7.

1991 O'Keeffe, Katherine O'Brien, *Visible Song: Transitional Literacy in Old English Verse* (1990). *N&Q* 236 (1991), 199–200.

1991 Pelteret, David A. E., *Catalogue Of English Post-Conquest Vernacular Documents* (1990). *N&Q* 236 (1991), 351–2.

1991 Popp, M., *Die englische Aussprache im 18. Jahrhundert im Lichte englisch-französischer Zeugnisse, I, Das 'Dictionnaire de la Prononciation angloise' 1756* (1989). *N&Q* 236 (1991), 365–6.

1991 Scholze-Stubenrecht, W., and J. B. Sykes (eds.), *The Oxford Duden German Dictionary, German–English, English–German.* Edited by the Dudenredaktion and the German Section of the Oxford University Press Dictionary Department (1990). *N&Q* 236 (1991), 206–8.

1992 Baker, D. C. (ed.), *The Squire's Tale*, A Variorum Edition of the Works of Geoffrey Chaucer, II, The Canterbury Tales, part 12 (1990). *N&Q* 237 (1992), 210–11.

1992 Bammesberger, A. (ed.), *Old English Runes and their Continental Background* (1991).
Griffiths, B., *J. M. Kemble: Anglo-Saxon Runes* (1991).
N&Q 237 (1992), 380–2.

1992 Bowden, Betsy (ed.), *Eighteenth-Century Modernizations from the Canterbury Tales*, Chaucer Studies, XVI (1991). *N&Q* 237 (1992), 390–2.

1992 Cable, T., *The English Alliterative Tradition*, Middle Ages Series (1991). *N&Q* 237 (1992), 386–7.

1992 Donatelli, J. M. P. (ed.), *Death and Liffe*, Speculum Anniversary Monographs, 15 (1989). *N&Q* 237 (1992), 216–17.

1992 Edden, Valerie (ed.), *Richard Maidstone's Penitential Psalms, edited from Bodleian MS Rawlinson A 389*, Middle English Texts, 22 (1990).
Whiteford, Peter (ed.), *The Myracles of Oure Lady, edited from Wynkyn de Worde's edition*, Middle English Texts, 23 (1990).
Embree, Dan, and Elizabeth Urquhart (eds.), *The Simonie: A Parallel-Text Edition, edited from MSS Advocates 19.2.1, Bodley 48, and Peterhouse College 104*, Middle English Texts, 24 (1991).
N&Q 237 (1992), 428–30.

1992 Franzen, C., *The Tremulous Hand of Worcester: A Study of Old English in the Thirteenth Century* (1991). *N&Q* 237 (1992), 387–8.

1992 Gimson, A. C. (ed.), and Ramsaran, S. (revised and supplemented by), Daniel Jones, *English Pronouncing Dictionary* (1991). *N&Q* 237 (1992), 396.

1992 Godden, M., and M. Lapidge (eds.), *The Cambridge Companion to Old English Literature* (1991). *N&Q* 237 (1992), 75–9.

1992 Hooke, D. (ed.), *Worcestershire Anglo-Saxon Charter-Bounds*, Studies in Anglo-Saxon History, II (1990). *N&Q* 237 (1992), 382–4.

1992 Moffat, Douglas (ed. and trans.), *The Old English 'Soul and Body'* (1990). *Review of English Studies*, 43 (1992), 401–2.

1992 Ogilvie-Thomson, S. J. (ed.), *A Handlist of Manuscripts containing Middle English Prose in Oxford College Libraries*, The Index of Middle English Prose, Handlist VIII (1991). *N&Q* 237 (1992), 388–9.

1992 Rozakis, Laurie, *The Random House Guide to Grammar, Usage and Punctuation* (1991). *N&Q* 237 (1992), 1–2.

1992 Scragg, D (ed.), *The Battle of Maldon AD 991* (1991). *N&Q* 237 (1992), 79–83.

1992 Starnes, De Witt T., and G. E. Noyes (ed. G. Stein), *The English Dictionary from Cawdrey to Johnson 1604–1755*, Amsterdam Studies in the Theory and History of Linguistic Science, series III, Studies in the History of the Language Sciences (1991). *N&Q* 237 (1992), 218–19.

1992 Tharaud, Barry (trans.), *Beowulf* (1990).
Porter, John (trans.), *Beowulf: Text and Translation* (1991).
Rebsamen, F. (trans.), *Beowulf: A Verse Translation* (1991).
N&Q 237 (1992), 145–7.

1992 Wiesenekker, E., *Word be Worde, Andgit of Andgite. Translation Performance in the Old English Interlinear Glosses of the Vespasian, Regius and Lambeth Psalters* (1991). *N&Q* 237 (1992), 492–3.

INDEX